I0820620

HAMMER of the GODS

Related Potomac Titles

Inside Hitler's Germany: Life Under the Third Reich,
by Matthew Hughes and Chris Mann

Hitler: The Pathology of Evil,
by George Victor

Hitler's Bandit Hunters: The SS and the Nazi Occupation of Europe,
by Philip W. Blood

David Luhrssen

HAMMER of the GODS

the Thule Society and the birth of Nazism

Potomac Books
An imprint of the University of Nebraska Press

Library of Congress Cataloging-in-Publication Data

Luhrssen, David.

Hammer of the gods : the Thule Society and the birth of Nazism / David Luhrssen.

p. cm.

Includes bibliographical references and index.

ISBN 978-1-59797-857-6 (hardcover edition)

ISBN 978-1-59797-858-3 (electronic edition)

1. Thule-Gesellschaft—History. 2. Thule-Gesellschaft—Influence. 3. National socialism and occultism—History. 4. Nationalism—Germany—History—20th century. 5. Anti-semitism—Germany—History—20th century. 6. Mythology, Germanic—Political aspects—History. 7. Sebottendorf, Rudolf, Freiherr von, 1875–1945. 8. Germany—Politics and government—1918–1933. 9. Germany—Social conditions—1918–1933. 10. Germany—Intellectual life—20th century. I. Title.

DD238.L78 2012

320.53'30943—dc23

2011041771

First Edition

To my family

Contents

Acknowledgments ix
Introduction xi

1. The Coming Race 1
2. Shadows on the Danube 19
3. Munchhausen Incarnate 43
4. Hammer of the Gods 71
5. The German Revolution 83
6. The Bavarian Socialist Republic 99
7. The Battle for Munich 121
8. Thule and the Nazi Circle 149
9. Trail of the Crooked Cross 177
10. Thule.org 201

Notes 213
Bibliography 267
Index 281
About the Author 293

Acknowledgments

Hammer of the Gods began as a dissertation in the history department of the University of Wisconsin–Milwaukee. I would like to thank the members of the academic committee that reviewed the original manuscript, Neal Pease, Ronald Ross, and especially Glen Jeansonne, who encouraged me to expand the thesis and find a publisher. I am grateful to Elizabeth Demers, senior editor at Potomac Books, for believing in the project, and to assistant production editor Amanda Irle for shepherding it through the process.

The pioneering work of Nicholas Goodrick-Clarke into the esoteric origins of Nazism provided me with a road map for my research. Barbara Syrrakos of City College, City University of New York, and Christina Maranci, of Tufts University, read the manuscript at various stages on its journey and offered helpful suggestions. Bruce Cole of the Marquette University Memorial Library provided generous assistance with interlibrary loans, and Hartmut and Herwig Luhrssen were invaluable for their aid in researching primary sources. Finally, I wish to thank Mary Manion for her tireless assistance and encouragement.

Introduction

> Why should lust for power, which from the beginning of recorded history has been considered the political and social sin par excellence, suddenly transcend all previously known limitations of self-interest and utility and attempt not simply to dominate men as they are but to change their very nature . . . ?
>
> —Hannah Arendt, *Essays in Understanding, 1930–1954: Formation, Exile, and Totalitarianism*

On the morning of April 30, 1919, the heir to one of Europe's greatest fortunes and a relative of many of the continent's royalty, Gustav Franz Maria, Prince von Thurn und Taxis, was executed by Red Guards along with nine other prisoners in the courtyard of Munich's Luitpold Gymnasium, an elite high school that had once numbered Albert Einstein among its students. The prince, who had grown up in a dozen palaces and enjoyed the comfort of a five-hundred-room castle at Regensburg, endured his final hours as a captive in the cellar of the Munich secondary school, which had been commandeered by the leftist revolutionaries as a barracks and detention center.

The posters that covered the walls of the hallways leading from his cell to the courtyard may have struck the prince as ominous. Posted by the soviet regime that clung tenaciously to power in the Bavarian capital of Munich despite being hard-pressed by Bavaria's legitimate Social

Democratic government (and its right-wing paramilitary supporters), the placards warned that the notorious Guards Cavalry, the unit that had recently transformed agitators Rosa Luxemburg and Karl Liebknecht into martyrs for the left, had put a price of thirty marks on the head of every dead Red soldier. The prince may have also learned that the Red troops had passed a resolution demanding the execution of five hostages for each of their comrades murdered by the advancing "counterrevolutionaries" and that dozens of Red prisoners were already known to have been killed by the Whites.

Two of Thurn und Taxis's fellow captives, who were also being dragged from their cells to the firing squad that had assembled in the courtyard, were cavalry troopers captured outside Munich, part of the advanced guard of paramilitaries and soldiers preparing their assault on the city. Another captive, an elderly Jewish professor named Berger, had been arrested for openly criticizing Munich's soviet regime. The six remaining prisoners were, like the prince, members of a secretive occult lodge called the Thule Society. They were an interesting lot, numbering the Society's secretary, Heila, Countess von Westarp, who had earned the disfavor of her socially prominent family by becoming an art student; the sculptor Walter Nauhaus; Nauhaus's art professor and mentor, Walter Deicke; the teenage nobleman and paramilitary, Franz Carl Freiherr von Teuchert; the railroad official and genealogist, Anton Daumenlang; and the painter and musician, Friedrich Wilhelm Freiherr von Seidlitz, descendant of the famous Prussian general from the reign of Friedrich the Great. It was a representative cross-section of the membership of the Thule Society where aristocrats and officers, bohemians and amateur scholars gathered under the banner of a mystic symbol from the East, the swastika. More than merely espousing a worldview antithetical to the materialism of Munich's Marxist regime, the Thule Society had become the center of counterrevolutionary resistance in Munich, sabotaging and confounding the Reds, and actively recruiting students and war veterans for the paramilitary forces that were descending upon the city.

The prince and his compatriots were gunned down by a hastily gathered execution party, their bullets accompanied by catcalls from spectators cheering the demise of the ruling class. News of the murders, amplified by false reports of mayhem committed against the victims, raced like an electric current across Munich and into the ranks of the counter-revolutionaries. That one of the victims was a woman only heightened the outrage in an age that still remembered chivalry. The papal nuncio in Munich, Cardinal Eugenio Pacelli, who as the controversial Pius XII would occupy the throne of St. Peter through the hard years of World War II, denounced the "bestial hostage murder." Incensed by the execution, anti-Communist troops who seized Munich the day after the incident at Luitpold Gymnasium celebrated May Day by avenging the prince and his party, slaughtering hundreds of real or imagined Reds who fell into their hands. After the Luitpold executions a neologism was added to the German language, *rotmord*, defined as the brutality and terrorism of the far left.

Thus it has been said that the Thule Society was an important player in the Bavarian theater of the civil war and revolutionary upheaval that shook Germany in the months following the Armistice of November 1918 and the collapse of the monarchy. The Thule Society, however, also left a more significant legacy in the crucial role it played in the formation of the Nazi Party and the shaping of several of the party's key members.

Nazism's Tangled Roots

More than half a century following the defeat of Nazi Germany, questions continue to be debated concerning the intellectual formation of Adolf Hitler, the inception of the Nazi movement, and the roots of its ideology. Hitler took great lengths, even before his appointment as Reich chancellor in 1933, to suppress information on his personal life. Also, many of his public statements represented tactical concessions to political reality rather than an expression of his movement's deeply held beliefs. Indeed, there were always divisions within the Nazi Party, adding to the confusion over the meaning of its ideas or whether it even had ideas beyond the will to power. Eyewitness accounts weighed into the historical arguments are no less biased and incomplete than those interpretations of the period according to one historian's preconception or another's. The researcher can choose from the often contradictory words of Hitler or his entourage; from statements by fellow travelers who hitched themselves to the

Nazi cavalcade, only to reverse direction after the Third Reich's defeat; and from the enemies of Hitler and the opponents of Nazism, some of them possessing as many reasons to lie as did the Nazis themselves.

The trail of destruction left by Nazism is easy to follow. So is Hitler's path to power. What remains murky and ill mapped is the road that led Hitler and his confederates to the peculiar worldview that shaped their program. Their view was based on what Hitler called "an ideological glimpse into history in accordance with the basic principle of the blood," which would result in "a new order . . . for a unique spiritual—I would almost say divine—creation."[1] Hitler's "basic principle of blood" would lead to the virtual destruction of Jewry in much of continental Europe and the death of many millions of Slavs and Gypsies. Even before the debate over Daniel Jonah Goldhagen's *Hitler's Willing Executioners,* it was widely acknowledged that the Holocaust, and kindred horrors unleashed by Hitler, could not have occurred without an appeal to widespread and deep-seated prejudices. But the bigotry and chauvinism of ordinary Germans, who may have harbored suspicions and fears about other ethnicities and cultivated feelings of ethnic superiority and even unreflective racism, do not inevitably lead to the ovens of Auschwitz and the killing fields of Eastern Europe.[2] In any event, racism in Germany was no more virulent in the early decades of the twentieth century than it was in the United States, where immigration laws restricted the arrival of unwanted ethnic groups, race riots and lynchings were not uncommon, and distinguished professors warned about the decline of Anglo-Saxon America. "World history is made by minorities," Hitler wrote in *Mein Kampf.*[3] This book is concerned with the intellectual and cultural formation of a minority who seized power in Germany and deliberately took history into their hands. For them, the subjugation of Europe was only a means to the end of re-creating humanity and the world into a new order using the inherited characteristics of the "Aryan" as the basis for their project.

The roots of Nazism and of Adolf Hitler himself are tangled, contradictory, and buried deep. So little is easily explicable about the character of Nazism's leader that Joachim Fest's memorable description of Hitler as an "unperson" continues to haunt historians and biographers alike. Even the most recent research cannot track the whereabouts of Adolf

Hitler for long stretches of time during his impressionable years on the streets of Vienna.[4] Eyewitnesses to this formative time have evidenced faulty and selective memory, giving conflicting reports on their infamous companion.[5] The historian is left to piece together many aspects of the early development of Hitler and Nazism much as the reader of detective novels tries to unravel the riddle of a vexing crime. But unlike that reader, the historian receives no certain revelations in the final chapter. Reconstructing the mind-set of Hitler and his associates has become a matter of ongoing historical and literary detective work. The evidence continues to be sifted, different hands finding different clues, different eyes drawing different conclusions.

Relatively neglected by historians is the part taken in the formation of Nazism by the Thule Society (Thule-Gesellschaft). The neglect is surprising because the Thule Society has been recognized as an important link between the Nazi Party and various *völkisch* associations in Germany and Austria before World War I, often obscure and even furtive organizations that not only sought what they saw as the true essence of the Germanic people in models from premodern epochs but also developed a theory of racism that extolled the Nordic "Aryan" and included a militant imperative toward Aryan dominance of the world. I argue that the Thule Society is the crucial link. A history of Thule, assembled by weighing contemporary accounts and scrutinizing the literature it produced, can only help elucidate existing theories concerning Nazism's *völkisch* roots. My conclusion is that the role of this *völkisch* organization in Bavaria, the setting in which Hitler rose to prominence, has been underestimated in terms of its political importance and ideological impact. I will show that the Thule Society and its confederates worked tirelessly to undermine the leftist and soviet regimes that ruled Bavaria following the downfall of the German Empire and, through the effort to find a popular audience for its arcane beliefs, laid the foundation for the Nazi Party.

Historical accounts of political violence in post–World War I Bavaria, and the radical ideologies attendant to those acts, refer often to the Thule Society. It is shown undertaking covert actions against the leftist regimes in Munich, fielding three of the paramilitary Freikorps (and recruiting personnel for several others), whose actions ultimately ended

Red rule in Germany's southernmost state, and as an occult lodge whose members dabbled in neopagan mysteries and *völkisch* propaganda. More crucially, the Thule Society is credited with founding the German Workers' Party (Deutsche Arbeiterpartei), the nucleus of the National Socialist German Workers' Party, and the German Socialist Party (Deutsche-Sozialistische Partei), which later amalgamated with the Nazis. Thule transformed a dying Munich newspaper into the *Völkischer Beobachter*, which became the principal print organ of the Nazi Party. Thule members were directly responsible for giving the Nazis the swastika as a symbol. Thulists were conspicuous in the Nazi movement during its formative years, and several survived to assume prestigious posts in the government of the Third Reich. Two of its alumni, Alfred Rosenberg and Hans Frank, were condemned to death at Nuremberg after the war; a third, Rudolf Hess, was sentenced by the International Military Tribunal to life imprisonment at Berlin's Spandau Prison. The Thule Society stood at the center of a network of front organizations whose members included such prominent future Nazis as Ernst Röhm, Gauleiter Julius Streicher, and Heinrich Himmler.

Notwithstanding the numerous references made to it by historians, scholars have been wary of writing a history of the Thule Society and its role in the shaping of Nazism. Aside from Nicholas Goodrick-Clarke's *The Occult Roots of Nazism*, which includes an informative chapter on the Thule Society, few factual accounts have been written on the subject. A survey of pertinent political histories and biographies reveals the subject's limited scholarship. In contrast to the clear, strong outlines given many rightist groups whose direct contributions were less pronounced (no other body can claim with such assurance to have fathered the Nazi Party), the historiography of the Thule Society resembles the topography of a sunken continent. It remains a lost realm, its memory altogether submerged except for a few scattered elevations that rise as apparently disconnected yet intriguingly important islands in the chronicles of chaotic, post-Armistice Bavaria.

The Thule Society occupies barely two pages of Joachim Fest's formidable biography, *Hitler*. Yet Fest makes frequent reference to Dietrich Eckart, Hans Frank, Rudolf Hess, and other members of the Society who either helped shape Hitler's Weltanschauung or later rose to prominence in the National Socialist movement. He admits: "Almost all the actors who were to dominate the Bavarian political scene in the following years belonged to the Society, including people who were to be prominent within Hitler's party."[6] Allan Mitchell's *Revolution in Bavaria 1918–1919* never mentions Thule by name, alluding only indirectly to its connection with the assassination of Bavaria's leftist prime minister Kurt Eisner by an aggrieved young aristocrat who had been denied membership in the Society because his mother was Jewish.[7] Yet the execution of Prince von Thurn und Taxis, Countess von Westarp, and five other Thule members in the Luitpold Gymnasium became one of the most recounted events of the 1919 battle for Munich. James Diehl's *Paramilitary Politics in the Weimar Republic* discusses the Oberland Bund, a Freikorps that saw action in Munich (1919), the Ruhr (1920), and during Hitler's Beer Hall Putsch (1923), but this authoritative work neglects Thule's role in the Bund's foundation and direction.

Although a full accounting of the Thule Society's political agitation has been lacking, its importance has been noted. Material scattered through such accounts as Eugene Davidson's *The Making of Adolf Hitler* and Heinrich Hillmayr's *Roter und Weisser Terror in Bayern nach 1918*, when brought together for examination, affords a picture of Thule as the center of rightist conspiracy in Bavaria during the first years of the Weimar Republic. Thule's offices were frequently searched by leftist police and militia, its members arrested for counterrevolutionary activity, but usually released owing to the Society's extensive network of political and military contacts. In Werner Maser's *Hitler: Legend, Myth & Reality* and Charles Bracelen's *Hitler: The Path to Power*, references to the Society form a faint but repeated motif in the narrative of Hitler in the years following World War I.

Even more recent magisterial studies, such as Michael Burleigh's *The Third Reich* and Ian Kershaw's biography *Hitler: 1889–1936: Hubris*, have added nothing to the historiography of the Thule Society, although Kershaw's careful archival research has shed light on many peripheral issues and has helped clarify the context of Thule's activities in post–World War I Munich.

The record of the Thule Society was written not only in deeds. It left behind a paper trail traceable by intellectual historians. The Society and its confederates published several newspapers. Its leader, Rudolf Freiherr von Sebottendorff, authored volumes of memoirs, fiction, astrology, and Theosophy. Its membership included the journalist Karl Harrer, the publisher Julius Friedrich Lehmann, and the playwright and poet Dietrich Eckart. Economic theorist Gottfried Feder worked closely with the Society. Thulists were involved in circulating *The Protocols of the Elders of Zion,* perhaps the most infamous anti-Semitic document ever written, outside of Russia. While it is true that Thule's members produced little of enduring literary merit, their writings were part of the weave of the time and should be examined in the interest of reaching a fuller understanding of the subculture that gave birth to Nazism, whose legacy weighs heavily upon the world even in the twenty-first century. Hannah Arendt wondered whether the crimes of the Holocaust had humanly comprehensible motives. To study the Thule Society and similar organizations is to find motives that are as reprehensible as they are comprehensible.

Despite its legacy of written texts, the Thule Society is ignored as much by intellectual historians as by political historians. Klemens von Klemperer's study of the ideological forebears of Nazism, *Germany's New Conservatism,* entirely disregards Thule and all its members. George L. Mosse's pioneering *The Crisis of Germany Ideology* cites Thule as "the backdrop for the development of the National Socialist drive to power" but provides no clarification.[8]

Klemperer's omissions are understandable. His book is concerned with major intellectual figures, and the Thule Society produced no Oswald Spengler, nor even an Ernst Jünger, only an Alfred Rosenberg. Mosse's attitude is less comprehensible. His work was preoccupied with Thule's milieu, the seamy underside of Germany's pre-Nazi intelligentsia, and his brief acknowledgment of Thule's seminal importance begs for further investigation. The paucity of legitimate scholarship has left a vacuum, which charlatans, fools, and hysterics have gladly tried to fill with fanciful accounts of the Thule Society as the linchpin of a global occult conspiracy. Related ideas of Nazism and its occult roots have found their way into the imaginative literature of fantasy and science fiction.

Shadowy Ideologies

The Thule Society was the Bavarian chapter of the secretive, prewar Germanenorden, a *völkisch* lodge whose anti-Semitic, pan-German nationalism was colored by Theosophical accounts of human prehistory, which assigned prominent roles to proto-Aryans, and by a neo-pagan fascination with the old Nordic gods. The Germanenorden was never more than a minuscule body nationally, but its Bavarian manifestation, under the energetic leadership of Sebottendorff, grew to at least fifteen hundred members by 1919.[9]

Its significance, which was out of proportion to its relatively small size, was felt on two levels. First, on a purely political plane, the Society served as the central clearinghouse for anti-soviet agitation in Bavaria during the state's flirtation with the left and helped raise the military force eventually responsible for stamping out the Bavarian Soviet Republic. According to historian Heinrich Hillmayr:

> Only one group, the Thule Society, had enough will to try to do away with the new government by force. They were seriously preoccupied with the question of how to create political and military conditions in which the Left and Soviet governments could be deposed, and did not hesitate to leave the cover of legality.[10]

One of Thule's front organizations, its Workers' Circle under Karl Harrer, quickly became the German Workers' Party (Deutsche Arbeiterpartei). This was the party Adolf Hitler joined in September 1919. Under his leadership, a political group founded by Thule as a bridge between its esoteric ideology and the working class was transformed into a mass movement that came to dominate Germany and subjugate most of Europe.

Second, on the plane of ideas, Thule acted as a catalyst for virulent anti-Semitism and *völkisch* thought in the cradle of Nazism, early Weimar Munich. Beneath the surface of Thule's propaganda ran a subterranean current linking it to mystical creeds of racism and nationalism expounded by an international, pre–World War I network of occult organizations and personalities. A member of the Germanenorden before reorganizing its Bavarian province into the Thule Society, Sebottendorff was the principal transmitter to National Socialism of the mysticism of Guido von List and its attendant ideology of Ariosophy, an outgrowth of Theosophy preoccupied with visions of Aryan racial superiority.[11] Within the Nazi movement, these themes sounded most loudly in the organization and ideals of the *Schutzstaffel* (SS). The Austrian List was equivalent in many respects to such figures as Ireland's William Butler Yeats and Scotland's William Sharp, literateurs and mystics whose work challenged the materialist assumptions of fin-de-siècle Europe and contributed to a nostalgia for lost national grandeur among their respective peoples. The Thule Society may have been the conduit to Nazism of other shadowy ideologies. During a Turkish sojourn (1901), Sebottendorff became associated with that wing of the Young Turks,[12] whose neopagan racism, foreshadowing many of Nazism's features in its program of an ethnically pure Turkish homeland and its appeal to an idealized Turkish past, resulted in the twentieth century's first concerted, large-scale campaign of genocide outside of colonial Africa: the mass murder of the Ottoman Empire's Armenian subjects beginning in 1915. "Who, after all, speaks today of the annihilation of the Armenians?" Hitler said shortly before the invasion of Poland, which would soon become one of the primary killing fields in the Holocaust against the Jews.[13]

A Twilight Escapade?

Mosse's characterization of one of the Thule Society's leading lights, Dietrich Eckart, as "too marginal, too much of a crank,"[14] exemplifies the prevailing historical view of the Society. Characterized by a weird mélange of occultism, anti-Semitism, and political violence, its membership numbering professional soldiers and morphine-addicted poets, bohemians and aristocrats, idealists and scoundrels, the Thule Society strikes many historians as neither fish nor fowl, a twilight escapade to be passed over in silence. But it would be a mistake to assume that history is not made sometimes in twilight, or that even the strangest programs cannot gain force and currency if they find harmony with the prevailing anxieties of their time. The legacy of the Thule Society has been available to any historian who chooses to look. Like Poe's purloined letter, it remained undiscovered though at arm's distance from investigators. The reputation of the Society fell victim to the bizarre elements of its vision. Thule's preoccupation with astrology and runic lore gave the Society an aura of illegitimacy in the eyes of historians trying to trace the descent of Nazism from Schopenhauer and Nietzsche, or trying to interpret Nazism's rise only by reference to economic factors.

Many scholars have done no better than to travel the road paved for them by the Nazis, who were careful to cover the path that led from their movement to the Thule Society. Sebottendorff was arrested after Hitler's appointment as chancellor for publicizing the Society's influence on Nazism. His memoirs were suppressed. Hitler mocked the German Workers' Party and allied *völkisch* forerunners, disparaging their activities as "club life of the worst manner and sort,"[15] dismissing them as barely worthy of comment. "I shall not even speak of the unworldliness of those folkish Saint Johns of the twentieth century or their ignorance of the popular soul."[16]

Willing to acknowledge only the most illustrious sources of his inspiration, the likes of Richard Wagner and Houston Stewart Chamberlain, Hitler arranged his autobiography to make himself appear as a man who drank directly from the cup of the muses. Historians who take the Führer too much at his word when recounting his political and intellectual development might be cautioned by one of the only historians to seriously examine the Thule Society, Reginald H. Phelps, who discussed "the well-known recipe of Hitler not to tolerate other gods before him."[17]

1

The Coming Race

Anyone who understands National Socialism only as a political movement knows virtually nothing about it. It is even more than religion, it is the will to a new creation of man.

—Adolf Hitler, quoted in Joachim Fest, *Hitler*

By the end of the nineteenth century an existential crisis was felt in the heart of Western civilization. Aptly described as the "flight from reason,"[1] it was caused by the aesthetic ugliness and social dislocations of the Industrial Revolution, the perceived bankruptcy of Western Christianity in the face of scientific advancement, greater contact with non-Western peoples and their spiritual beliefs, and the rapid pace of change—unsettling and unprecedented—resulting from new technology. The embrace of new superrational ideals among educated classes in Europe and North America was part of the ongoing reaction against the spiritual emptiness of post-Enlightenment rationalism and positivism, with its materialistic, mechanistic conception of the universe. The rebellion against rationalism continues into the present day, often drawing from such recent models of discontent as the 1950s Beats, the 1960s counterculture, and the 1980s New Age movement.

For proponents of nineteenth-century materialism, the emancipation of mankind from divine sanctions was felt as bracing. However, many thinkers were troubled by the concept of a cosmos without purpose or design, and many of them were consoled neither by Roman Catholicism nor Protestantism. The dogma of Western Christianity seemed too brittle to hold up against the dogma of scientism, whose acolytes increasingly tried to enact laws for the governance of history, politics, and economics, as well as biology, chemistry, and physics. Many intellectuals and artists were prepared to embrace occult explanations of humanity as an alternative to the faith of their ancestors and the rising tide of rationalism. The "rejected knowledge" of occultism usually sounded a note—and sometimes a symphony—of subversion against the established order.[2]

Visual art mirrored this late-nineteenth-century crisis of consciousness in Art Nouveau, an international style whose curlicues (which would be revisited by psychedelic artists in the 1960s) suggested altered states of perception and the organic structure of nature rather than the machine-tooled geometry of civilization. In literature, the mood was echoed by writers as diverse as Nobel Prize–winning poet William Butler Yeats and French novelist J. K. Huysmans, who shared the common themes of magic and mysticism across their differences of style and intent. Pervasive was the sense that modern life, obsessed with problems of production, consumption, and capital, was unable to satisfy the deepest longings of the human spirit.

Preoccupied as it was with spiritual questions, especially the place of humanity in a world reduced by contemporary science to an engine operating by natural laws, the flight from reason wasn't content with literary or visual depictions of mystical experience. It also took the form of new faiths and theologies. The most prominent was Theosophy, whose first chapter was founded in New York in 1875 by the Russian adventurer Helena Petrovna Blavatsky (1831–1891).

The Theosophical Society rapidly became an international religious movement, appealing to an educated audience troubled by Western Christianity and intrigued by the mysteries of the East, as spiritually discontented Europeans had been since the wane of the Roman Empire. It suffered from inevitable schisms and heresies. A variant strain of the Theosophical movement called Ariosophy, from the obsession of its adherents with the notion of Aryan racial superiority, took root in Austria and eventually found its way to Bavaria, the birthplace of the Nazi movement, where its adherents became known as the Thule Society.

At a time when Western imperialism was at its zenith, "when Christian missionary endeavor was reaching a climax in terms of self-confident belief in its inevitable triumph,"[3] Theosophy embodied a subversive countertendency in Western thought. It opposed the evils of Western materialism with an eclectic synthesis of ideas, many of them adopted from Hindu and Buddhist cosmology.

Even before Theosophy, Western intellectuals had used the example of Asia to criticize Europe, although their Asia was often a blank screen on which they projected their own fantasies. Voltaire, in *The Philosophy of History*, argued for the superiority of China over France with the improbable assertion that Chinese political and religious systems were based on reason rather than heredity and superstition. In *Oriental Enlightenment: The Encounter Between Asian and Western Thought*, John James Clarke notes, "In the Romantic period attention switched to India, where mystical visions of the unity of the Soul with the All, of Atman with Brahman, and the image of an ancient bond between East and West resonated powerfully with the interests and passions of leading European thinkers."[4] A stream of translations of the Bhagavad Gita and other sacred texts had already encouraged interest in faiths born in India.[5] Prominent German thinkers such as Novalis, Karl Wilhelm Friedrich Schlegel, and Arthur Schopenhauer were fascinated by Indian philosophy, as were the New England circles of Ralph Waldo Emerson and Henry David Thoreau.

Hidden Masters

Blavatsky claimed that her teachings were derived directly from immortal "Masters of the Hidden Brotherhood" or "Mahatmas."[6] Secreted in the Tibetan Himalayas, inside a vast network of subterranean halls, the Mahatmas were keepers of many treasures, including the Book of Dyzan, said by Theosophists to be the oldest manuscript in the world and from which Blavatsky claimed inspiration. Reaching Ceylon in 1880, Blavatsky and her closest followers took a step that shocked many Europeans by embracing Buddhism. Suddenly members of "the dominant race" appeared among the Hindus and Buddhists of the British Empire to proclaim their admiration for the ancient wisdom of the East.[7] Annie Besant, who became president of the International Theosophical Society in 1907, was active in the nascent campaign for India's self-governance and was elected president of the Indian National Congress, the party that would lead the country to independence from Great Britain. In his youth, India's first prime minister, Jawaharlal Nehru, had been an enthusiastic Theosophist.[8]

Despite the anti-imperialism of the Theosophical Society, a racial elaboration of Darwinian theories was present in Blavatsky's doctrine, providing the seed of Ariosophy and the Thule Society. According to Blavatsky, a "process of decimation" was occurring among races whose "time is up," races she regarded as "the senile representatives of lost archaic nations."[9]

According to Theosophy, four races occupied the earth prior to the present species of homo sapiens, and the great cultures of our epoch were created by Aryans, one of these four. The idea of an Aryan race had its origins in the search among nineteenth-century German scholars for the common ancestry of languages and peoples stretching from Northern India to Scandinavia. Most European languages were found to be related to one another and to Sanskrit, and were thought to be rooted in an extinct tongue, an Aryan *Ursprache.* Scholars soon inferred that the speakers of this hypothetical language were related by blood, an *Urvolk.* Hegel and the Brothers Grimm were among the early-nineteenth-century philosophers and linguists who contributed to the idea. The word "Aryan" was taken from age-old Hindu legends concerning tall, fair-skinned invaders who subjugated the swarthy natives of India.

Reflecting the scholarship of the day, Theosophists deemed the roots of Indian civilization as Aryan. "The Aryan Race was born and developed in the far North, though after the sinking of the Continent of Atlantis, its tribes emigrated further south into Asia."[10] The source of the original Aryan homeland and the paths of Aryan migration were subjects of avid speculation by cranks and savants alike. The Thule Society's founder, Rudolf von Sebottendorff, adhered to a Theosophical conception of Aryan cultural diffusion, holding that after the Ice Age, "the northern tribes settled as masters in Europe, Asia and America," subduing the natives. According to him, the Aryans migrated along two great pathways, one following the Atlantic coastline, crossing the straits of Gibraltar and traveling east along the Mediterranean shore to Egypt, Troy, and Mycenae; the second cut across Europe and the Caucasus and into the Asian highlands.[11] On the Theosophical Society's seal was the swastika, a primeval religious symbol of nearly universal circulation but associated by the Theosophists with the spirituality of Aryan India.

Theosophy also taught that a new race would soon emerge to supplant the existing human genus. It was on the subject of race that mysticism intersected with the materialistic science of the day. Bigotry based on inherited physical characteristics has a long history. However, not until the height of the Enlightenment, in 1735, when Swedish botanist Carolus Linnaeus devised the modern system for classifying plants and animals, was a hierarchy of races proposed upon a scientific foundation. Even before Charles Darwin, evolutionists wondered whether certain races were better suited and adaptable than others to a wider scope of environments, and whether the world could be seen as populated by many races at different stages of evolution. Perhaps there were different human breeds, even breeds that scarcely deserved to be classed as human, such as the Pygmies of Equatorial Africa, whose humanity was often questioned. Rancorous debate erupted during the early nineteenth century between monogenists, who believed that homo sapiens descended from the same line, and polygenists, whose argument for the separate origin of various races undercut the Judeo-Christian brotherhood of man and its political corollary of universal human rights.

Nowadays phrenology has been discarded as a pseudo-science, but it was rooted in the insistence of materialist, Enlightenment science that psychology is explicable only in terms of physiology. Soon enough phrenologists began measuring human skulls for the breadth of mentality within. In 1842 the Swedish savant Anders Retzius formalized the link between phrenology and race by devising a cephalic index to measure craniological differences between races. A century later the *Schutzstaffel*

(SS) found time for phrenology, collecting specimen skulls from their victims to illustrate inherent racial differences.[12] Ideas of race from the natural sciences came to serve the aims of political and social science. "Particularly since 1850, when industrialization broke traditional bonds and detached man from his native soil without affording him new loyalties, the idea of race has been put forward as a principle of political and emotional union."[13]

In the wake of Darwin's epochal *The Origin of Species by Means of Natural Selection, or the Preservation of Favoured Races in the Struggle for Life* (1859), many reputable anthropologists and biologists in Europe and the United States accepted racial inequality as a function of the natural order and the competition of living organisms in the universal struggle for life. Darwinism was used as a justification by imperialists to explain why some nations were stronger and better fit to rule. British naturalist Francis Galton broke with Darwin, his distant cousin, over natural selection, favoring mutational jumps over slow-going evolutionary change. In *Hereditary Genius* (1869), Galton proposed eugenics, which held that human capacity was a function of heredity, not environment. "It would be quite practicable to produce a highly gifted race of men by judicious marriages during several consecutive generations," he wrote.[14] Science and evolutionary theory "were conferring certainty upon the most diverse fanaticisms."[15] The trend was mirrored in the thinking of some Theosophists.

In many respects Theosophy provided a relatively respectable public face for an occult underground, where contacts were often made by word of mouth and personal introductions. An international web of small, secretive groups, the occult underground should not be confused with a host of other covert political organizations throughout the West, ranging across the ideological spectrum from the Knights of Labor to the Ku Klux Klan. Those latter groups adopted Masonic ritual and hierarchies because of their association with conspiracy against the existing order, but they did not pretend to summon the elemental forces of the universe in pursuit of their aims.

Blavatsky was an admirer of Eliphas Lèvi (1810–1875), a Frenchman whose synthesis of medieval and Renaissance magic, alchemy, tarot, Kabbalism, and other traditions granted many occultists a conceptual framework and gave birth to the modern revival of ceremonial magic. Many Theosophists were active in the newly organized occult lodges, notably Samuel Liddell MacGregor Mathers, author of *The Kabbalah Unveiled* and grandmaster of the Hermetic Order of the Golden Dawn.[16]

The Golden Dawn was a seminal British society with an impressive roster of adherents. Its members included Yeats; Irish nationalist Maude Gonne; the patron of Dublin's Abbey Theatre, Annie Horniman; Florence Farr, actress and mistress to George Bernard Shaw; novelist Arthur Machen; and author Algernon Blackwood, whom Edward Elgar graced by setting one of his stories to music. Aleister Crowley, an alumnus of the Golden Dawn, would become the most notorious occultist of the twentieth century and allegedly made contact with Hitler through occult circles. One of Crowley's followers, Capt. (later Maj. Gen.) John Frederick Charles Fuller, became an associate of British fascist leader Sir Oswald Mosley and would be one of the only Englishmen invited to Hitler's private fiftieth birthday, just months before the outbreak of World War II.[17]

Crowley, in his keynote work *Magick in Theory and Practice* (1929), proposed a Great White Brotherhood whose highest ranks would belong to an order called the S.S. (Silver Star), "composed of those who have crossed the Abyss."[18] Crowley was not the first British occult writer to imagine an organization of that name. M. P. Shiel, in a short story called "The S.S." (1895), prophetically wrote of a society that murdered thousands of people across Europe as part of a conspiracy to purge humanity of tainted blood in order to advance human progress.[19] Perhaps Shiel picked up on the anticipations of an earlier writer of occult-tinged romances, Edward Bulwer-Lytton, whose novel, *The Coming Race* (1871), ostensibly concerned a Utopia tucked into the center of the earth populated by a scientifically advanced "type of man distinct from our known extant races . . . endowed with forces inimical to man." The story's hidden meaning, explained by Bulwer-Lytton in a letter, depended "on the Darwinian proposition that a coming race is destined to supplant our races, that such a race would be very gradually formed and be indeed a new species developing itself out of our old one, and that this process would be invisible to our eyes, and therefore in some region unknown to us."[20] Much as the Leninists hoped to speed the pace of Marx's historical dialectics by making revolution, Shiel imagined that an organization might try forcing evolution forward, a step later advocated by the Ariosophists and finally undertaken by Himmler's SS.

Like Theosophy, with its Masters of the Hidden Brotherhood, the Golden Dawn's grandmaster, Mathers, claimed to be directed by Secret Chiefs. He described them as "human and living on this earth; but possessing terrible super-human powers."[21] The Golden Dawn was riven by much factionalism, but small groups claiming its mantle continue to exist.

Throughout the world a connection was felt between the Theosophical movements and politics. In relatively stable England, initiates of the Golden Dawn were involved in circles that supported the restoration of the Stuarts to the British throne,[22] and even the Spanish Carlists,[23] a movement that was socially conservative but drew support from the frustrated nationalism of the Basques and other minorities. As a member of the Theosophical Society and the Golden Dawn, Yeats fashioned a sense of Irish identity that shaped and gave impetus to the nationalist movement that wrested most of Eire from English rule.[24] In *The Celtic Twilight* (1893), Yeats's mission to construct an Irish national identity from the material of peasant folklore, with its intimations of ancient and hidden wisdom, paralleled the work of contemporary *völkisch* intellectuals in Germany and Austria. Similarly, the Celtic cultural revival spurred a nationalist movement in Scotland. One of its leaders was a colleague of Yeats, the author William Sharp. Sharp published a periodical called the *Pagan Review* (1892) and was a practicing occultist.

Clearly the political interests of this "occult underground" cannot be comfortably contained within the hackneyed definitions of left and right. What united them was opposition to the status quo and the promotion of frustrated nationalisms, in both cases colored by appeals to a glorious, imagined past. Branches of the Theosophical Society established in Germany (1884) and Austria (1887) were planted in fertile, receptive soil. German-speaking Europe numbered many who were unhappy with the political development of their region. For Germans, existential anxiety over the drift of Western civilization, felt throughout Europe, was heightened by the peculiarities of their own history.

Metaphysical Nationalism

At the dawn of the French revolution in 1789, Germany was still an antique patchwork quilt of some eighteen hundred autonomous principalities, bishoprics, free cities, and other jurisdictions. One school of scholarship traces Germany's problems in the nineteenth and twentieth centuries to its arrested development as a nation. As historian Golo Mann observed, "What psychologists teach about the individual also applies to the nation: it can harbor old, unpleasant memories, transform them in strange ways and derive aggressive energies from them."[25] Denied a nation-state of their own during the eighteenth and early nineteenth centuries—the time when nationalism as understood today took root—Germans became accustomed to defining their nationalism in metaphysical terms, and themselves as a nation existing spiritually if not spatially.[26] These attitudes can be traced to the beginnings of modern German culture, especially in the eighteenth-century *Sturm und Drang* (Storm and Stress), an intensely Romantic literary movement that would also shape the development of Gothic literature in the English-speaking world and was emotionally linked to the Romantic privileging of the local over the universal. Like its Gothic counterpart, *Sturm und Drang* often represented a "Counter Enlightenment" by rejecting the eighteenth-century notion that through the exercise of reason, humanity could eradicate error, prejudice, superstition, and fear.[27] Exponents such as Herder and Schiller questioned materialism and denounced the status quo while extolling the cult of nature and Germanic folk culture. Romantic nationalism gained force under the Napoleonic occupation of Germany. As happened elsewhere in Europe, the development of nationalism shifted from an exploration of the unique roots and potential of every given people to the aggressive exultation of one particular culture over all others. An exaggerated sense of national purpose was expressed even by a philosopher as distinguished as Johann Gottlieb Fichte, whose *Addresses to the German Nation* (1807–1808) proclaimed the Germans as the only authentic people—their culture primal and fundamental—in a corrupt world.

Paradoxically, the Germans received much encouragement in this direction from their erstwhile enemies, the French. After the Bourbon restoration of 1815, intellectuals such as the Comte de Montlosier wrote that their nation's aristocratic bloodline descended from the Germanic tribes who conquered the Romanized Gauls at the onset of the Dark Ages.[28] Epitomizing the French vogue for Nordic superiority was Count Joseph Arthur de Gobineau's *Essay on the Inequality of Races* (1853–1855), which warned of the contamination of Aryan blood, sounded the alarm over the yellow peril from Asia, and disparaged the Mediterranean peoples for their Semitic and Negroid features. A *literateur* of the Romantic tradition, Gobineau pictured a remnant of beleaguered Aryans clinging to the European peninsula of Eurasia, assailed by the rising birthrate of lesser races. He had absorbed the new biological ideas of the polygenists, who held that humanity did not descend from common ancestors. Nietzsche, Schopenhauer, and Wagner expressed admiration for Gobineau, and the Theosophical Society circulated his writings.[29]

Racism of one sort or another was, in any event, being propounded by scientists in many Western nations during the nineteenth century. Darwinian racists believed that the modern world, with Northern Europeans and their descendants at the vanguard, resulted from uncounted millennia of progress as the ape ascended to savagery and the savages biologically evolved toward civilization. Many occultists keen to diminish Western civilization nevertheless internalized this fiction, which provided the scientific frame for their own fanciful pictures of social evolution. Interestingly, academic German science was slower to embrace biological Aryanism and racist anthropology, not fully accepting it until the dawn of the First World War.[30]

The goal of German nationalism was to unite the *Volk*, the spiritual community of the German people, into a single entity defined by lineage, language, and culture, not dynastic politics or religious divisions between Protestant north and Roman Catholic south. Proclaimed by Otto von Bismarck in 1871 after a series of political and military campaigns undertaken at the behest of the Prussian monarchy, the German Empire frustrated many nationalists, who were both disappointed by its failure to include the German populations of the Hapsburg Empire and dismayed by its prosaic character. "The unnatural and disconcerting thing was that the German question had been decided by the will of one man who was not an idealist, nor a man of the people, nor a famous liberal," wrote historian Golo Mann of Germany's single-handed, and to many minds, dubious creation by Bismarck.[31] Far from being the hoped-for millennium of the German *Volk*, the Second Reich was a material realm of smoking factory chimneys and bustling bourses.

From the profound disappointment of nationalist idealists emerged the *völkisch* movement, a transcendental political worldview whose goals included putting German society in harmony with the perceived inner spirit of the German *Volk*. As often occurred elsewhere during the nineteenth and twentieth century, extreme nationalism appeared to offer a way around social and economic problems. "Their disappointment with the results of the long-awaited unity, combined with the effects of the Industrial Revolution, produced a longing for a more genuine unity of the *Volk*."[32] These nationalists defined their *volkgeist* as gloomily passionate, arising from the Aryans' formative experience in the murky woods and marshes of northern Europe. Richly endowed with deep melancholy, the Aryans, if not the sole molders of human history, were its foremost, the "genuine shapers of the destinies of mankind" whether as "builders of states or as discoverers of new thoughts and of original art."[33]

Fascinated by German folk culture and seeking in it the mystic heart of the *Volk*, the nationalists who laid the foundation for the *völkisch* movement had already added to the stock of world culture before the German Empire was finally established. Like folklorists from other lands, they believed in the creativity of the *Volk*, conceptualized as a collective author whose primal experiences were manifested in sagas, folk songs, and fairy tales. In 1812 the brothers Wilhelm and Jacob Grimm began to publish their famous fairy tales, gathered from the fast-fading oral tradition of German peasantry. They bequeathed to the world such popular tales as "Hansel and Gretel" and "Rapunzel" and fertilized the nascent field of comparative mythology. The romantic nationalism of the Brothers Grimm had implications beyond the library and the nursery. In 1837 they were dismissed from their professorships and banished from the Kingdom of Hanover for political activity.

Music also drew from this rising interest in Germany's imagined past. In bravura operas such as *The Ring of the Nibelung*, Richard Wagner drew from the timeless power of myth in its Nordic expression. He would become Hitler's favorite composer. While he took many seemingly contradictory stands, the composer's prose writings offered comfort to the emerging *völkisch* movement. Wagner wrote that Aryans "trace back their origins to gods" and that "depravity of blood" threatened Aryan dominance.[34] The Ariosophists would magnify those sentiments. Some authorities all but indict Wagner for the crimes of the Third Reich.[35]

Völkisch thinking criticized bourgeois civilization and conventional Christian dogma for suppressing the inner nature of the Germans. Also under harsh scrutiny was the Jew, whose medieval reputation for money lending and trading was rewritten as a metaphor for materialism. The Jewish association with liberalism, democratization, and Marxism made them a symbol for all the perceived vices of the modern world and threatened the *völkisch* vision of Germany, rooted as it was in romantic nostalgia for a nonexistent past. According to George Mosse,

> The German reaction to positivism (at the end of the 19th century) became intimately bound up with a belief in nature's cosmic life force, a dark force whose mysteries could be understood not by science, but through the occult. An ideology based on such premises was fused with the glories of an Aryan past, and in turn, that past received a thoroughly romantic and mystical interpretation.[36]

Against the Status Quo

Commonalities between the *völkisch* worldview and Blavatsky's doctrine, with its accent on race and its favorable portrayal of the Aryans, are easily discerned. Like *völkisch* ideologues, Theosophists stressed the mystical bond between the individual and the universal.[37] That a confluence of those trends should have occurred is unsurprising. Theosophy came to supply certain *völkisch* circles with an elaborate metaphysical superstructure. Its tendency toward constructing a hierarchy of races darkened to outright racism in a *völkisch* context. With her description of the old pagan gods as useful manifestations of the forces of nature, Blavatsky lent her support to those who would seek after the old gods of northern Europe.

The original membership of Vienna's Theosophical Society, at its foundation in 1887, was drawn from a coterie of intellectuals and bohemians who had been meeting continually since the end of the 1870s. Friedrich Eckstein (1861–1939), the Society's first president and later a "gray eminence of Viennese cultural life,"[38] had been presiding over discussions at a table in a Viennese vegetarian restaurant for a decade before the Society was formally organized in Austria's capital. The circle around Eckstein, who had been composer Anton Bruckner's personal secretary, was diverse in ethnic origin and in politics. It included Polish poet Siegfried Lipiner; Jewish symphonic master Gustav Mahler; Austrian composer of German art songs Hugo Wolf; feminist Rosa Mayreder, who discussed gender roles in terms of the alchemical fusion of opposites; Rudolf Steiner, who later established the Waldorf school movement along with a mystical Christian branch of Theosophy called Anthroposophy; and, occasionally, Victor Adler, founder of the Social Democratic Party of Austria.[39]

Internal contradictions did not seem to separate the early Austrian Theosophists into neat ideological categories. Hugo Wolf, who composed under the spell of the anti-Semite Wagner, was a roommate of Mahler, whose conversion to Roman Catholicism before his appointment as director of the Vienna Court Opera did not placate the anti-Semites. There seemed to be no contradiction between occultism and "progressive" social movements during the late nineteenth century. "Indeed, there was a necessary connection between all idealistic forms of opposition to that which existed," according to historian James Webb.[40]

Within Austrian Theosophy grew the subcult of Ariosophy, a synthesis of occultism and extreme German nationalism, which thrived during the first decade of the twentieth century. It was not by chance that Theosophy's most racist manifestation was born among the German community of the Austro-Hungarian Empire in the years preceding World War I, nor that Ariosophy flourished in the empire's theatrically grand capital. Vienna was "all quite new, barely weathered and not yet, if ever, real,"[41] a city where, as Hitler put it, "dazzling riches and loathsome poverty alternated sharply."[42] Excluded from the German Reich erected by Bismarck, and feeling their position threatened by the growing influence of Emperor Franz Josef's Slavic and Magyar subjects, many Austrian Germans became even more hostile to the existing order than their counterparts within the German Empire. Although Vienna in the early years of the twentieth century is remembered for the art of the Vienna Secession and the artifacts of the Wiener Werkstätte, for glittering balls, café society, and artistic ferment, it was a city of contradictions where crushing poverty coexisted with wealth and atavistic impulses mingled with modernity. Long before Hitler began his Viennese sojourn (1906–1913), the fear and anxiety of Austrian Germans was acute in the imperial capital, where a booming gutter press heated the toxic brew of contentious ethnic politics into a combustible mixture.

Ariosophy was not Theosophy's unwanted bastard child but was firmly connected to the movement's family tree. One of Blavatsky's intimates, Franz Hartmann (1838–1912), was a direct link between the inner councils of the Theosophical Society and its racist Viennese offspring.

Born in Bavaria, the son of a court doctor, Hartmann studied medicine at the University of Munich and came as a ship's doctor to the United States in 1865. By his account he spent the next eighteen years traveling through Mexico and the mining towns of the American West, where he claimed ownership of mining shares. Hartmann encountered occultism through the table-rapping séances that flourished among American Spiritualists. After discovering Blavatsky's writings, he joined the Theosophical Society in Colorado (1883). The Bavarian expatriate (who in some accounts had become a naturalized American citizen) sailed that year, from California via Japan and China, for the Theosophical Society's international headquarters at Adyar near Madras. Hartmann became a close associate of Blavatsky, traveling with her in India, visiting various princely courts, and supporting her in an acrimonious early schism within the movement. He was named to the society's board of control in Adyar, and served for a time as acting president.[43]

Nearly a century later Theosophists still maintained that Hartmann, like Blavatsky, was in direct communication with the Hidden Masters through the medium of letters. One of the replies he is said to have received from a Mahatma is instructive, at least for understanding Hartmann's self-image:

> Were we to employ in our service a man of no intelligence, we would have to point out to him, as you say in the West, chapter and verse, i.e., give him special assignments and definite orders; but a mind like yours, with a background of much experience, can find the way by itself, when given a hint in regard to the direction which leads to the goal.[44]

Between 1884 and 1891, Hartmann published seven books in Britain and the United States on Paracelsus and other Western occultists. After returning to Europe in 1885, he became director of a *Lebensreform* sanitarium for respiratory diseases at Hallein, near Salzburg, which was also the site of a sulfite works owned by Hartmann. *Lebensreform* was a holistic health movement in German-speaking Europe with many affinities to current trends in Western society involving alternative medicine and natural foods. It promoted abstinence from meat, tobacco, and alcohol as a way to ameliorate the deleterious effects of modern life on the human body, as well as encouraged rural communes, nudism, and other alternative lifestyles. It grew alongside and often intersected with *völkisch* ideology, although it also crisscrossed with persons and ideas usually deemed leftist.[45] The often-discussed dietary and medical habits of Hitler and his SS chief, Heinrich Himmler, resulted from the not uncommon convergence of *Lebensreform* and *völkisch* doctrines.[46]

Hartmann also cofounded Fraternitas (1889), a Theosophical lodge with monastic pretensions at Ascona, the lonely Swiss fishing village on Lake Maggiore that became an influential fin-de-siècle magnet for bohemians, vegetarians, artists, and anarchists. "The feminism, pacifism and psychoanalysis we now know took form" in part from the work of those who trekked to Ascona at this time. Perhaps the anarchist leader Mikhail Bakunin, who settled nearby in 1869, opened the door to an international set of well-connected dissenters against Western civilization, but Hartmann was among the first to establish himself at this mecca for discontent. Hartmann's collaborators in Fraternitas included Blavatsky's close friend, the Swedish countess Constance Wachtmeister, and Alfred Pioda, a member of the Swiss parliament. Rudolf Steiner, Vladimir Lenin, Carl Jung, and Hermann Hesse would at one time or other call Ascona home.[47]

Hartmann was tireless and prolific as an activist and writer. The international character of the occult underground can be glimpsed in articles he wrote for a London publication, *Occult Review* (1906–1907), describing "mysterious happenings among the cosmopolitan society of Europe." Among the topics of Hartmann's articles were the teleportation of an Italian prince and healings by the sign of the pentagram.[48]

Hartmann was also in contact with Theodor Reuss (1855–1923),[49] a German secret service agent and grandmaster of the Ordo Templi Orientis (Order of the Templars of the Orient). OTO's upper ranks practiced sex magic in an effort to attain union with the divine through orgasm. The curious career of Reuss, known in occult circles as Frater Merlinus, included work as a journalist in London, acting as a German agent before World War I, and organizing the "Non-National Congress" at Ascona in 1917, ostensibly in protest against the war but likely as a means to mobilize international support for the German perspective.[50] Reuss's operations on behalf of the German government may have included attempts to infiltrate Karl Marx's family circle as a member of William Morris's Socialist League, and a stint with German counterintelligence on the Dutch border at the onset of World War I. By some accounts, Hartmann cofounded OTO as early as 1902 with Reuss and a wealthy Austrian industrialist and yoga adept called Carl Kellner.[51] However, the tangled history of Reuss's activities in irregular Masonry has proven impenetrable, given his penchant for joining, establishing, and networking with an alphabet soup of lodges in Germany, throughout Europe, and as far away as Latin America, often minuscule groups unaffiliated with Freemasonry's governing bodies.[52] In 1912 Reuss visited Crowley in London and authorized him to form a British lodge of OTO called Mysteria Mystica Maxima.[53]

Hartmann is cited by Theosophists as a cofounder of German Theosophy, whose birth (1884) was attended by mysterious letters from the Hidden Masters.[54] Blavatsky, however, entertained certain doubts about her close protégé:

> Poor Hartmann. He is a bad lot, but he would give his life for the Masters and Occultism. . . . He is like the tortoise—one step forward and two back; with me he now seems very friendly. But I cannot trust him.[55]

She kept her thoughts private as Hartmann's reputation continued to expand in all directions. His translation of the Bhagavad Gita was much admired by Hermann Hesse and other fin-de-siècle aesthetes.[56] During the 1880s Hartmann frequented the meetings of the Vienna Theosophical Society presided over by Friedrich Eckstein and, in the 1890s, became president of the German Theosophical Society in Berlin, where Hartmann wrote for Paul Zillman's monthly *Metaphysische Rundschau.* Hartmann was also a key figure in the translation of Blavatsky into German. He published many of her key works between 1892 and 1900 in his magazine, *Lotusblüten* (*Lotus Blossoms*), probably the first German-language periodical to bear the swastika on its cover.[57]

Prior to the swastika's association with Theosophy, the symbol had been largely forgotten in Europe. In the 1888 edition of Meyer's *Konversations-Lexikon,* the standard Germany encyclopedia of the period, the swastika merited only a single sentence. The encyclopedia defined it merely as a prehistoric and Buddhist sign.[58] Interest in the primeval symbol would soon rise in Germany and around the world. Around the time Blavatsky founded the Theosophical Society, the excavations for Troy in Asia Minor by German archaeologist Heinrich Schliemann brought to light hundreds of ancient artifacts decorated with the swastika. Comparing the sign to devices found on ancient Germanic pottery, Schliemann hailed the "suastika" as "religious symbols of the very greatest importance among the early progenitors of the Aryan races in Bactria and in the villages of the Oxus, at a time when Germans, Indians, Pelasgians, Celts, Persians, Slavonians and Iranians still formed one nation and spoke one language." They were "the most sacred symbols of our Aryan forefathers."[59]

Hartmann's association with Guido von List, Ariosophy's founder and leading light, provides additional evidence of Ariosophy's Theosophical paternity. He joined the Guido von List Society (Guido-von-List-Gesellschaft) upon its foundation in 1908 and delighted in discovering parallels between the teachings of Blavatsky and List.[60] Along with his personal relationship with List, several of Hartmann's German associates in the occult underground also attached themselves to List, especially the publishers and editors Hugo Goring, Paul Zillman, Arthur Weber, and Johannes Balzi, who were responsible for a plethora of occult books and periodicals issued under the imprint of the Theosophical Publishing House, established in Leipzig by Hartmann's protégé Hugo Vollrath. Hartmann's diligence as Blavatsky's translator also gives weight to the assumption that Theosophy brought new shape through him to the *völkisch* movement in occult understandings of Aryan racial destiny. It is impossible to read List's mature works without finding Blavatsky between the lines.

2

Shadows on the Danube

Like you I have an indomitable affection for Vienna and Austria, but, unlike you, I know her abyss.

—Sigmund Freud, letter to a friend, 1938

Vienna, capital of the multinational Hapsburg Empire, rivaled Paris as Europe's cultural seat during the reign of Franz Josef (1848–1916). It was a city where Johann Strauss's lilting waltzes mingled with Arnold Schoenberg's atonality, Egon Schiele's erotic nudes with Gustav Klimt's *The Kiss*, and the fiction of Arthur Schnitzler with the psychoanalysis of Sigmund Freud. However, the bright artistic and intellectual ferment was surrounded by dark shadows. "If the Danubian metropolis was a city of dreams, it was likewise a city of contradictions."[1] Poverty rose along with a fivefold increase in population, placing heavy strains on housing, sanitation, and transportation. Public and privately funded welfare agencies provided relief, but many in Vienna made do in cramped dwellings without indoor plumbing, renting bedspace to make ends meet. Politically, Social Democrats clashed with Christian Socialists, the former dreaming of gradually dismantling capitalism and the latter of ameliorating its abuses in accord with Roman Catholic social doctrine. Zionism was born in Vienna, a city where Pan-Germanism flourished; advocates of a Jewish homeland in Palestine found themselves in close quarters with those who sought a Reich for all Germans. Austria's numerous Pan-German organizations provided a forum for anti-Semitism and the disparagement of non-Nordic races.

As with other growing cities in the nineteenth century, Vienna was a magnet for outlying provinces because of its employment and cultural opportunities. Czechs and Sudeten Germans poured into the capital alongside Ukrainians and Poles, Serbs and Croats, Italians and Hungarians. By 1880 Vienna's Jewish population had risen to seventy thousand in a population of two million. Most of the new arrivals were eastern European Jews, distinct in custom and dress, and unwelcomed by the city's Jewish establishment, the Rothschilds and other families assimilated into the financial affairs of Hapsburg Europe. They were welcomed even less by many of the city's Germans. "Once, as I was strolling through the Inner City, I suddenly encountered an apparition in a black caftan and black hair locks. Is this a Jew? was my first thought," Hitler later recalled.[2] In 1885 the army was forced to quell anti-Semitic rioting in the immigrant, eastern-European Jewish district of Leopoldstadt; property was damaged and shouts of "Down with the Jews!" were heard.[3]

Despite opposition to anti-Semitism from Franz Josef and his circle, the cry of age-old resentments and ancient calumnies grew louder as Vienna's Jewish population grew larger. Into this cacophony came a new anti-Semitism. Its ideas were drawn from occult doctrines and the pseudo-science of racism. Its force derived from the siege mentality of those Germans, embracing a conspiratorial theory of history, who were frightened by the growing numbers and influence of the empire's ethnic minorities. Under the Third Reich this new anti-Semitism would prove more dangerous and virulent than old religious and cultural prejudices. For the Nazis there could be no assimilation; the blood of Jewish ancestry was thicker than the water of baptism. It was fundamentally the race, not the religion, that the Nazis tried to destroy. One of the roots for the distinctive Nazi strain of race-based anti-Semitism sprouted in Vienna, during the years of Hitler's sojourn in the imperial city, in the form of Ariosophy.

Pagan Landscapes

Guido von List (1848–1919), born Guido Karl Anton List, founded Ariosophy by cementing *völkisch* Aryan ideology together with Theosophy by way of Wodan and the old gods of northern Europe. The "von" he used consistently after 1907 was of dubious, although not entirely implausible, provenance. His aristocratic affectation speaks more to Romantic historical nostalgia and class insecurity than to genealogy.[4] In German "list" means cunning or guileful, yet beyond the disputed noble origins of his name, there is no evidence that List was less than sincere in the evolution of his beliefs. He was a prolific writer, in the tradition of *völkisch* German Romanticism, of historical fiction, folklore, mythology, and culture. The drift of List's writing grew increasingly and overtly occult. He was prominent in the revival of Wodanism, the conscious reconstruction of beliefs surrounding Wodan (or Odin), the paramount deity of the Nordic pantheon.

Implied in List's youthful writings was a belief in the polygenesis of humanity, but without privileging one race over another.[5] Later he became explicitly racist. The Guido von List Society formed to propagate his ideas became a prominent public nexus in the dense, transnational network of occult organizations espousing countercultural values. It was not a fringe group but numbered the chief of staff of Austria-Hungary's army and two successive mayors of Vienna among its members.

His father, Karl August List, dealt in leather goods; his ancestors were innkeepers. List's upbringing was comfortably bourgeois Viennese with all the trappings, including watercolor portraits of family members.[6] Likely, Karl List's fortunes had risen rapidly along with others of modest means who formed Vienna's growing middle class by the mid-nineteenth century. List nurtured artistic interests as a young man, his talents encouraged but only to a point by his father, who wanted him to inherit the family business. Like the German youth who emerged as a distinct movement in the 1890s, those proto-hippies who called themselves the Wandervögel (Wandering Birds), he spent the leisure hours of his teenage years rambling through the countryside alone or with companions, sketching the scenery and communing with nature.[7]

List claimed that in 1862, at age fourteen, he experienced an ecstatic premonition of his life's mission while touring the bone-filled catacombs beneath Vienna's St. Stephen's Cathedral. Before a ruined altar, he vowed, "When I am grown, I shall build a temple of Wodan!"[8] In June

1875 List and several friends boated down the Danube to the Roman ruins of Carnuntum at Petronell, twenty miles east of Vienna, to commemorate the 1500th anniversary of a victory by the Teutons over the Latin invaders. List and his companions marked the summer solstice at the ancient encampment of the Roman emperor Marcus Aurelius by contemplating the ruined fortress's Heidentor (Heathen's Gate), drinking ritual toasts to the spirit guardian of the place, lighting a solstice fire, and burying eight wine bottles arranged in the shape of a *fyrfos*, a swastika with arms extended at forty-five-degree angles.[9] By the account of one Hitler intimate, the Nazi genealogist Elsa Schmidt-Falk, the German leader spoke of trying to find and unearth this swastika after Austria was added to the Third Reich.[10]

By the time he emerged as a celebrated public figure in the 1890s, List was not alone in his admiration for pre-Christian gods. In fin-de-siècle Britain, the term "pagan" had acquired "an exciting cachet."[11] A subversive countercurrent to Victorian respectability, Puritanism, and a civilization based on the Industrial Revolution, neopaganism was a proposal in mythological garb for returning to the primordial verities of man and nature. List was not alone in his belief that through the Middle Ages a translucent screen of Christianity concealed Europe's pagan heritage. Parallels to his ideas were found in the work of Britain's noted Arthurian scholar, Jessie Winston, who likewise interpreted her materials with occult insight. Among Europe's artists and intellectuals the pagan revival as well as the rise of nationalism was bound up with the academic study of folklore, whose paradigm was set by the emerging field of geology, which constructed the past from consecutive layers of residue. Nineteenth-century folklorists thought that cultural fossils could shed insight into the development of human society. Perhaps the id to society's ego could be found in remnants of primeval culture. With that in mind it becomes less paradoxical that folklore was one of the streams that fed Modernism, lending a primal frisson to Stravinsky, Bartok, and Gauguin. The folklorists' standard work became Sir James Frazer's *The Golden Bough* (1890), a journey into the underworld of belief replete with the sort of pagan survivals and the novel interpretation of rituals and folkways that List found inspiring. The rationalist-materialist Frazer wrote *The Golden*

Bough to discredit religion by excavating its primitive sources, unaware that fascination with all things primeval was on the rise. He must have been sorely disappointed that his material would become useful for those with spiritual or occult interpretations of the cosmos. The study of folklore was also bound up with the Flight from Reason in its turnaround from Enlightenment-era disdain for rustic life, its embrace of a Romantic peasantry, and medievalism sharpened by revulsion for the ugliness of the Industrial Age. "One must flee those places where life throbs and seek out the lonely places untouched by human hands in order to lift the magic veil of nature," List wrote.[12]

For List, understanding the character and destiny of one's race was a pathway both to self-knowledge (gnosis) and harmony with the cosmos. "In the long run no people can be forced to feel, think and to act in ways other than those made possible by the characteristics of their inborn folk-soul," he insisted.[13] With his fierce white beard and sharp, probing expression, List in maturity wore the heavy aura of a prophet with eyes fixed on the unseen.

Among List's earliest writings were accounts of nature hikes and the folklore and folkways of rural Austria published in a periodical for mountain climbers. Mirroring the ethos of his youthful subculture, his articles stressed the sacredness of the landscape and its role in shaping the *völkisch* spirit of those who dwelled there. *Völkisch* organizations grew numerous and noisy among the German intelligentsia and middle-class youth of Austria-Hungary as List came of age in the 1870s and 1880s. As many as 150,000 Hapsburg subjects may have passed through one *völkisch* group or another. "List formed his ideas and political attitudes almost exclusively within this *völkisch*-cultural milieu."[14] One of the organizations he belonged to in his youth was the Österreichischer Alpenverein (Austrian Alpine League), a mountain-climbing association whose Pan-German sympathies attracted members from the German Empire as well as German Austria. Mountains loomed in German consciousness as destiny incarnate, inscrutable places of terror and solace. List nearly lost his life climbing, but his steep tumble was softened by a carpet of snow.[15] In 1871 List became the Alpine League's secretary and edited its yearbook. After the death of his father in 1879, List devoted himself to journalism. In articles for various Pan-German newspapers, he personified the hills, fields, and rivers of the Austrian countryside as figures from Nordic mythology.[16] Those were penurious years for List, who supported himself and his first wife, Hélène Föster-Peters, on freelance fees and dwindling family money.

List became prominent through his connections with influential Pan-Germans, who provided him with an audience and a political agenda while he provided them with a mythology, a vision of a Teutonic past that crystallized as he evolved as a thinker. Within the German Reich, the Pan-Germans were respected in the lobbies of power.[17] In Austria, they were a thorn in the foot of the Hapsburgs, a noisy reminder that virulent nationalism was rendering untenable the old, multiethnic, dynastically based empires, even one whose constitution guaranteed civil rights to all subjects regardless of ethnicity. The Austrian Pan-German leader, Georg Ritter von Schönerer, was a charismatic figure surrounded by a cult of personality and a bevy of spies who reported his movements to the police. His followers addressed him as "führer." That the worst impulses within Pan-Germanism found greater prominence and fervor in Vienna than Berlin, and that Austria, not Germany, should have nurtured a figure like Hitler, is perhaps unsurprising in light of the racial tension within the multiethnic Hapsburg Empire. "The loyal German-Austrians are fifty years ahead of the German Reich on the issue of race policies. . . . We know from everyday experience what an inferior race means as regards moral stance and politics," wrote List's follower Jörg Lanz von Liebenfels in 1908.[18] It was an ironic observation, given that the German dialect of Vienna was laced with words of Italian, Slavic, and Hungarian origin, and that the Pan-German delegation in Austria's parliament, the Reichsrat, numbered the deputies Skaret and Prochazka, names with Slavic resonance. Hitler offered qualified praise for the Pan-Germans but ultimately found them inadequate in vision. "The Pan-German movement could count on success only if it realized from the very first day that what was required was not a new party, but a new philosophy."[19] They fell short of Hitler's fantasy of re-creating the world, but their newspapers, pamphlets, and soapbox orators formed part of his ideological diet during those formative years in Vienna.

With the publication of his historical novel *Carnuntum* (1888), a glorification of the ancient Aryans and their struggle with the Romans, List graduated from obscurity to celebrity among Pan-Germans. *Carnuntum* was not merely historical fiction but a metaphor of contemporary cultural politics. Like the Roman legions of old, the Roman Catholic Church was an alien intrusion to be repelled before a genuinely Teutonic civilization could be restored. In *Carnuntum,* the ancient Germans who dwelled in what became Austria spearheaded the reversal of Roman fortune that culminated in the sack of Rome, a notion that swelled the pride of German Austrians.[20] After the success of *Carnuntum* he became a regular contributor to the weekly *Ostdeutsche Rundschau,* published by Karl Wolf, a Pan-German deputy in the Austrian Reichstag.[21] List's articles for the *Rundschau* and other Pan-German papers were folkloric and *völkisch,* with occasional digressions into folk magic. Anti-Semitic notes could be discerned. Wolf's paper published *Deutsche-Mythologische Landschaftsbilder,* an anthology of List's essays. *Carnuntum's* success brought List to the attention of a patron with even greater influence, the industrialist Friedrich Wannieck, chairman of a pair of important Austrian concerns, Prague Iron and First Brno Engineering. Wannieck's *völkisch* Verein Deutsches Haus published a historical work on the ancient Germans, Heinrich Kirchmayr's *Der altdeutsche Volksstamm der Quaden,* which seemed to validate List's fiction. Wannieck later published three of List's books and gave him financial support. List's growing reputation as a novelist placed him at the center of literary circles dedicated to exploration of the inner self and the overthrow of Realism.[22]

As a popular Pan-German lecturer, List spoke to *völkisch* educational groups on Wodan and the extinct faith of ancient Northern Europe.[23] In his poems and a pair of novels, *Jung Diethers Heimkehr* (1894) and *Pipara* (1895), the protagonists were often German pagans struggling against the encroachment of Rome and Christianity. His increasing celebrity by the end of the century led to List festivals, with lectures on his work, readings from his poetry, and even an arrangement of his poems sung by a choral society, sponsored by the *Ostdeutsche Rundschau* and other *völkisch* organizations.[24]

In his rambles through the countryside and in his library, List found evidence of pre-Christian remnants in the ruins, place names, and the folkways of remote Austrian communities. He found parables of Wodanism in the Germanic fairy tales of the Brothers Grimm and discerned occult significance in the heraldry of old noble families and the shape of Gothic cathedrals. "In these buildings, hieroglyphs were elaborated into extremely high artistic developments, so that those structures speak, when the hieroglyphs are read. And they can convey surprising results," he wrote.[25] When examined through List's spectacles, the cultural landscape of Central Europe was a field of correspondences and interlocking symbols, whose esoteric meaning could be read with reference to runes, Nordic lore, and the cultivation of occult insight. "We must read with our souls the landscape which archeology reconquers with the spade," he declared.[26]

List's exploration of the esoteric dimension of architecture would have been understood by his contemporary, the great British art historian W. R. Lethaby, who devoted his seminal work, *Architecture, Mysticism, and Myth* (1891), to discerning "the thought behind form, embodied and realized for the purpose of its manifestation and transmission" in stone and mortar.[27] List's preoccupation with heraldry was echoed in a swell of books by British amateur scholars; like him, they took comfort in the romance of medieval valor and speculated on the origins of heraldic symbols, but List's systematic interpretation of armorial emblems by reference to their runic, occult significance was probably unprecedented. However, List's fascination with rural, pre-Christian remnants was part of a general movement in European letters and literature, the rustic leg of the Flight from Reason. Intimations similar to List occur in English novelist Thomas Hardy's *The Return of the Native* (1878), which described a remote Dorset village as a place that was "pagan still," where "homage to nature, self-adoration, frantic gaieties, fragments of Teutonic rites to divinities whose names are forgotten, have in some way or other survived." Like neopagans then and now, List believed that the "old religion," persecuted by a medieval Christianity that burned its exponents as witches, had been stamped down but not extinguished. Its bards and priests preserved their beliefs "in strict secrecy," encoded in poems of many meanings, in symbols and in systems of initiation that became the basis for medieval guilds and later for Masonry and Rosicrucianism.[28]

According to List, secret societies preserved elements of ancient Aryan belief, while the stubborn folkways of German peasantry unconsciously maintained the old ways against all encroachments by Christianity. Later, his theory of rural life was extolled by the Third Reich.[29] List did not believe he was founding a new faith but rediscovering an ancient one, soon to regain ascendance as the present cycle of time wound down and a new age took its place. All of this resonated loudly in circles where modernity was suspect and Christianity discredited, among those who projected contemporary anxieties onto the past. For List's audience the anxiety was caused by what they understood as the precarious status of Germans in multicultural Austria-Hungary, threatened by the rising tide of lesser races.

With a typically Viennese enthusiasm for theater, List turned to playwriting. His *Der Wala Erweckung* premiered under the auspices of Karl Wolf's group the Bund der Germanen, or Germanic League (1894). Tickets for the play read "Not Valid for Jews."[30] *Der Wala*'s star during an 1895 performance attended by several thousand patrons, Anna Witteck, became List's second wife. Their marriage ceremony was performed in a Lutheran church (August 1899), reflecting a movement among Pan-Germans called Los von Rom, whose adherents ostentatiously embraced Protestantism to show their affinity for Protestant Prussia and their contempt for the Catholic Hapsburg Empire. The nuptials were the only known gesture toward Protestantism from a man who called upon Wodan to reclaim his power after the millennial twilight of Christianity. List's wife, who in addition to acting gave dramatic recitations of his poetry, was described as "a pretty young woman dressed in a fashion redolent of fin-de-siècle mystery."[31] Immediately following their marriage, List devoted himself primarily to drama, producing *König Vannius* (1899), *Sommer-Sonnwend-Feuerzauber* (1901), and *Das Goldstück* (1903), a trio of Romantic works in historical settings. His 1900 pamphlet *Der Wiederaufbau von Carnuntum* (*The Reconstruction of Carnuntum*) called for a "German-Austrian Bayreuth" in the old city with an amphitheater for plays, bardic contests, and other events to propagate Wodanism.[32] His ideas on theater were not without influence and later became part of the cultural policy of the Third Reich.[33]

Racist Theosophy

After 1902, List's mythological evocations and *völkisch* politics turned distinctly Theosophical. An operation for cataracts during that year left him isolated by blindness from the outer world for eleven months. Not unlike the Nordic myth concerning Wodan's sacrifice of an eye in exchange for foresight, the period of darkness granted List time to contemplate the deeper implications of his folkloric paganism. It bears mention that the final installment of the complete German translation of Blavatsky's *The Secret Doctrine* finally appeared just before 1902. Perhaps he alluded to Blavatsky when he wrote about an epiphany "during the months that my eyes were bandaged," when "previously unperceived Laws of Generation and Evolution belonging to our Aryan people, of its emotion, intellect, speech, and writing, came to me."[34]

List was always willing to acknowledge the subsequent impact of Blavatsky on his own researches. He admitted that *The Secret Doctrine* was the source of his speculations on correspondences between Hindu cosmology and the Edda, the body of Nordic mythology preserved in medieval Iceland.[35] His works were footnoted with references to Blavatsky. In his *Die Rita der Ario-Germanen,* he correlated the imagined ancient Nordic faith in primal fire as the source of cosmic energy with the tenets of Blavatsky. Chapters were headed by Theosophical symbols, notably the swastika.[36] According to List, the Edda validated Blavatsky's conception that the world had been tenanted by other races prior to the present epoch. Blavatsky's Atlanteans, for example, were made to correspond with the clan of the giant Bergelmir, who survived a great flood in Nordic myths.[37] He also maintained that prehistoric megaliths discovered in Austria indicate that the German core of the Hapsburg Empire had been an outpost of Atlantis.[38]

Reading scraps of ancient myth and literature through Theosophical spectacles, List determined that the ancient Aryans of Central Europe had been ruled by a Wodanist priesthood, an elite group of initiates corresponding to the fascination in Great Britain with Druids, whom he called the Armanenschaft. He coined the word "Armanen" as a Teutonization of the Irminons (or Herminones), mentioned in Germania by the Roman historian Tacitus, as one of the three tribes or classes of ancient

Germany.[39] From the masters of this priesthood were drawn the kings and elders of ancient Germany, and from its rank and file came teachers and judges. The Armanenschaft's high places (Halgadome) were centers of all authority and learning.[40] They communicated many of their ideas through runes, which were "more than our letters are today . . . they were 'holy signs' or 'magical characters.'"[41]

Race was crucial to his conception of the world order. "The tribe, the race, is to be purely preserved; it may not be defiled by the roots of a foreign tree. . . . Therefore: your blood, your highest possession."[42]

List's Wodanism centered around a Trinitarian godhead, Walvater (or Allvater, "All Father"), whose persons he called Wodan, Wili, and We. Although Christian parallels are visible, he made his god from the clay of Blavatsky's notion of the three Logoi or manifestations of the deity. For him, the old gods could be read as symbols of cosmic reality, which he conceived as a cycle of death and renewal, of the spirit becoming material and the material becoming spiritual. Wodan "lives in the human body in order to go under, 'he consecrated himself to himself,' and he consecrates himself to 'passing away' in order to rise anew."[43]

Linking the worship of Wodan with the evolutionary doctrine of Theosophy, List held that Wodanism "grew out of the intuitive recognition of evolutionary laws in natural life, out of the 'primal laws of nature.' . . . It set for itself the final goal of bringing into being a noble race, whose destiny it was to be to educate itself and the rest of humanity to the actual task of human beings." He condemned Christianity for inhibiting the progress of evolution by denying reincarnation and for divorcing the spiritual from the material, destroying "the noble race as well as its heroism in the spiritual and physical realms, and in its place breed a population of slaves."[44] Like many spiritual seekers of the modern age, List rejected Christianity but tried to salvage Christ for his pantheon. Comparing him with Wodan, List proclaimed Christ as "one of those rare persons" whose consciousness of God within enabled him to control "the physical and spiritual realms, which he contains comprehensively."[45] List's addition to the history of ideas was to synthesize the largely Hindu cosmology of Theosophy with the mythology of northern Europe, projecting into Wodanism a Gnostic belief in the identity of God with the human spirit.

List worked his speculations on Germanic prehistory into blueprints for a new Reich, which he predicted for the twentieth century. In statements that read like models for the Nazi New Order, specifically its agricultural policy and the Nuremberg Laws (1935), List spoke of a hierarchical society with non-Aryans enslaved as manual laborers. Racial purity would be required of all educators, merchants, professionals, and officials. Strict marriage laws forbidding miscegenation would be promulgated. Only Aryans with proven genealogies could enjoy citizenship. Farms could not be broken up but only inherited by first-born sons.[46] He railed against Jews, Roman Catholics, and Freemasons for conspiring against Aryan culture, and called for a Greater Germany uniting all of Europe's Nordic peoples, including Germans, Danes, Swedes, Norwegians, Dutch, and British.[47] Education would be founded on the "awakening of the spirit of the folk," discarding "foreign and unnationalistic elements."[48] In his hopes of reviving an Armanenschaft to serve as an order of initiates that would rule the new Germany, he anticipated Himmler's conception of the SS as the masters of the millennial Reich. He even prophesied the runic slashes on the collars of the SS uniform in his description of the Vehmgericht, pre-Napoleonic German secret societies (he claimed them as latter day survivals of the Armanenschaft) that executed their notions of justice with secret trials and moonlight lynchings. List wrote that daggers carried by Vehmgericht members were inscribed with the double sig-rune that would be adopted by the SS.[49]

Early in his career as *völkisch* publicist, List expounded on personal and social virtues. In many respects his values were in keeping with the perennial teachings of most religions, albeit he kept obscure the identity of his god, Allvater. List extolled loyalty, fairness, and sacrifice, friendship and freedom, condemned "vain egotism" and those who "try to become conspicuous with empty appearances." In light of the destructive influence of Ariosophy, his thoughts on crime struck an ominous note. He defined it in racial terms as "all those deeds and actions which can lead us, our fellow man, our physical descendants or the future of the general folk to deformity, degeneracy or destruction . . . and thereby can undermine the fortunes of incalculable spans of time . . . of the whole of the folk."[50]

Anti-Semitism motivated by financial envy and anxiety had been pervasive in Austrian society and throughout the West for centuries. Deeply held prejudices were confirmed when the Vienna stock market crashed in 1873 and it was revealed that several Jews were among the culprits. Opposed to big capitalism, big banking and usury, and raging against what he saw as the inordinate influence wielded in those areas by Jews, List the prophet of Ariosophy praised the artisan, craftsman, and small shopkeeper. He postulated a global Jewish conspiracy, whose origins date at least as far back as the suppression of Wodanism by Christianity, and whose contemporary activities were manifest in international finance and all liberal, democratic movements. List's economic views would later be echoed by economist Gottfried Feder (1883–1941), who was active in the Thule Society's circles.

Working from Blavatsky's doctrine of cosmic rounds with its succession of epochs and races, and finding correspondences with the time cycles of Nordic mythology, List speculated in 1911 that the current cycle was running down. It may have been a keen sense for the anxieties of the present rather than the ability to read the future that gave rise to his apocalyptic predictions of great battles when "Ario-German-Austrian battleships shall once more send sparks flying, Donar's battle-lightning shall once more shoot from the colossal cannons of our dreadnoughts," and "once more our Volks armies shall go South and West . . . to battle the enemy . . . and establish order."[51] His vision of mechanized warfare was in keeping with a genre of speculative fiction, popular in Europe since the late-nineteenth century, which in hindsight seemed to predict World War I.[52]

The unexpected appearance in List's orbit of a figure calling himself Tarnhari (Hidden Lord) influenced the old seer. Claiming descent from the ancient Armanenschaft as a chief in the tribe of Siegfried, the Wölsungen (or Völsungar), and ancestral memories of primeval Germany, Tarnhari (originally Ernst Lauterer) asserted that List's reconstructions of the past were correct. List interpreted the arrival of this seer as an omen of good fortune for the Aryans.[53] Tarnhari was not among List's most prolific confederates, but among his projects was a periodical published in Leipzig, *Swastika Letters*, whose chief advertiser was Dietrich

Eckart, later of the Thule Society and Hitler's chief mentor in postwar Munich.[54]

When the lowering storm clouds finally broke in the summer of 1914, List greeted the onset of the world war as proof that his calculations were correct. For him, the conflagration was a Theosophical Armageddon pitting the Aryan Central Powers against the Allied Anti-Wodan. Afterwards a bright future would rise from his vision of a golden past. In the millennium to follow the apocalypse, a superman List called the Starke von Oben (Power from Above) would establish an Ariosophical world order. Germany was being prepared for "a new age, in which nothing pertaining to the old age could survive unless it was Armanist in nature." He was not alone among Theosophists in believing that the Great War was the next link in the chain of evolution. Not unlike socialists and Christians, Theosophists split along national lines during the war, reading the darkest cosmic implications in each move by the opposing side. Based on astrological and Theosophical computations, List determined that the years 1914, 1923, and 1932 would be crucial milestones on the way to the Ariosophical age. The statement was written after World War I began in 1914, but Nazis could later find 1923 prophetic of Hitler's Beer Hall Putsch, which thrust him into the national spotlight. And 1932 was only one year shy of Hitler's assumption of power and his proclamation of the Thousand-Year Reich.[55]

List submitted an essay to the Austrian Imperial Academy of Sciences on *kala,* a runic interpretive system described by him as revealing "the concealed sense" hidden within medieval German poetry, usually opposite to the text's apparent meaning.[56] That the matter of the academy's return without comment of List's manuscript was taken up by a Pan-German deputy in the Reichstat (December 1904) was a marker of List's status as a person of importance in Vienna. The deputy, Rudolf Berger, later joined the List Society. Berger's resolution, signed by fifteen prominent Viennese, moved neither the minister of culture nor the academy, but led in 1905 to a prospectus for a society to propagate Listian ideas rejected by official institutions; this move was parallel to the "Vienna Secession," an influential movement of artists and architects in opposition to the academically sanctioned styles. The prospectus was endorsed by some fifty business leaders, academics, authors, journalists, and political activists in Austria and Germany, many of them Pan-Germans and occultists,[57] but including at least one dignitary who seemed unconnected to either camp, Vienna's demagogic lord mayor, Karl Lüger, an anti-Semite and Christian Socialist whom Hitler admired.[58]

The Guido von List Society (Guido-von-List-Gesellschaft) was established as an exoteric organization to support the esoteric research of its namesake and his associates, meaning it provided a public platform for the views of List and his supporters, yet its aims did not include becoming a mass movement. The Society's members were an influential minority in politics, the media, the arts, and the military throughout Austria and Germany, including leading Pan-Germans, anti-Semites, and *Lebensreform* advocates.[59] After 1908 "the collective membership of the Vienna Theosophical Society" enrolled in the List group.[60] Largely suspicious of anything smacking of democracy, its members hoped instead to shape the thinking of educated elites in German-speaking Europe. The List Society's official founding ceremony occurred in 1908, but the organization likely began to gather after the circulation of its 1905 prospectus. The Wannieck family granted the Society a modest endowment of more than three thousand kronen (nearly 11,000 euros in contemporary money), which along with annual membership dues of ten kronen helped finance seven booklets by List (1908–1914) on runes, folklore, esoteric linguistics, and heraldry.[61]

More covert occult activities were pursued by List with an inner ring of his Society called Hoher Armanen Orden (High Armanen Order). Founded on the summer solstice of 1911, this smaller group was drawn from his most devoted followers in Germany and Austria. HAO left behind few records aside from accounts of pilgrimages to sacred Nordic sites "in the land of Ostara, where the spirit of Hari-Wodan still reigned." HAO traveled to the catacombs beneath St. Stephen's where List experienced his boyhood vision and to other places he connected with Wodan on the Kahlenberg and Leopoldsberg, as well as in Klosterneuberg, Brühl, Burg Kreuzenstein, and Carnuntum.[62]

The intellectual influence of the List Society was wider than its membership, helping shape a fascination with the alleged Nordic roots of world culture, a theme taken up by List's Viennese contemporary, Josef Strzygowski, one of Europe's foremost art historians.[63] A vegetarian-nudist commune based on List's ideas, Breidhablik, was founded near Danzig and lasted from 1919 through 1924.[64] List was lauded by major newspapers in Berlin, Vienna, and Graz, and cited in a French periodical. In February 1911 three academic lectures on List's work were given in Berlin and Vienna, indicators of the growing respectability of his ideas. Several books on topics as various as Hungarian heraldry, domestic architecture, runes, and contemporary literature were dedicated to List. Ernst von Wolzogen dedicated his drama *Die Maibraut* (*The May Bride*) to List and introduced the occultist to the audience at the play's premiere in Wiesbaden (1909).[65]

Wolzogen collaborated in a traveling literary theater company with Hanns Heinz Ewers (1871–1943), the popular German storywriter and screenwriter of horror and the macabre who would pen a novel honoring the Nazi "martyr" Horst Wessel. A fin-de-siècle decadent, Ewers was Germany's greatest author of the uncanny since E. T. A. Hoffman. He was also a pioneering cinema artist with his scenario for *The Student of Prague* (1913), an occultist, and a performance artist long before the phrase was coined. A member of List's circle, though probably not of the List Society, he was also associated with one of List's influences, the Berlin Theosophist and student of sexual magic Max Ferdinand Sebaldt von Werth. While working as a German propagandist in the United States during World War I, Ewers encountered another prominent occultist and German agent, Aleister Crowley. During that time Ewers also met Ernst ("Putzi") Hanfstaengl, later one of Hitler's intimates.

Ewers's fiction often expounded on themes suggested by List and Lanz, but under Sebaldt's influence he also proposed the eccentric idea that both Aryans and Jews were the world's master races. Invited to join the Nazi Party by an avid reader of his stories, Adolf Hitler, Ewers was inducted into the party at a ceremony attended by the former Thule Society member Rudolf Hess (1931). Later he ran afoul of elements within the new regime, especially Goebbels's Propaganda Ministry; most of his works were effectively banned in Germany.[66]

List inspired a network of people who, without necessarily affiliating themselves with the List Society or its central offshoot, the Germanenorden, became proponents of Ariosophical views within the occult underground of German-speaking Europe. Chief among them were members of the Edda Society, founded November 19, 1925, by Thule Society associate Rudolf John Gorsleben (1883–1930). Gorsleben was a writer and German officer who served as adviser to the Turkish army and fought against the Bedouin, whose rebellion was aroused by his Allied counterpart in Orientalism, T. E. Lawrence.[67] There were also several prominent individuals in Germany who took List's lead on the crucial importance of runes. Friedrich Bernhard Marby (1882–1966) developed a yogic application of runes involving gymnastic postures emulating their forms in conjunction with runic incantations. Marby, introduced to runelore by List's writings, was imprisoned by the Nazis in 1936 at Welzheim and later in Flossenburg and Dachau. Freed by the Allies at war's end, he resumed his occult writings and research.[68]

Following List, Marby read medieval heraldry with occult insight to determine the location of the Halgadome, Nordic sacred sites imbued with magnetic force. He was also fascinated by the esoteric meaning of medieval architecture.[69] Similarly, the neopagan practitioner of ceremonial magic, Siegfried Adolf Kummer, employed runic exercises in his practices. In 1927 Kummer founded Runa, a school for runelore, in Dresden.[70]

The impact of List during his lifetime on the wider society outside the precincts of occultists, Pan-Germans, and folkloric scholars is hard to assess in light of the often covert nature of his endeavors. During World War I, soldiers on the front wrote List, describing their discoveries of Europe's Aryan past in far-flung battlefields and drawing inspiration from his writings, yet the extent of his influence over the troops is unclear.[71] Another measure of his scope is the praise he received in the periodical of Germany's largest white-collar union, the Deutschnationale Handelsgehilfen Verband. The union's bookstores also sold *Handbuch der Jugenfrage* by List's German follower, Theodor Fritsch. One of the union's officers, Friedrich Wiegershaus, was an associate of List, another node in a network that conveyed the ideas of the Viennese occultist. Imbued with the spirit of the Wandervögel, the youth league of the Deutschnationale Handelsgehilfen Verband, the Fahrende Gesellen (Wandering Apprentices), conspired in the revolutionary days of 1918–1919 with the Thule Society against Bavaria's leftist regime.[72]

The offices of the List Society were located near Hitler's first lodgings in Vienna, one of many tantalizing missing pieces in the puzzle of Hitler's sojourn in the Austrian capital.[73] According to witnesses, Hitler likely read a copy of List's *Das Geheimnis der Runen* from the Vienna public library. Years later he echoed List in a 1920 speech in Munich, when he declared that Aryans "build all their cults around light and they find the sign, the tool for lighting a fire, the whisk, the cross. . . . It is the swastika of the communities once founded by Aryan culture."[74] There is also testimony from Hitler's associates that he referred to List in conversation and had read his main works.[75] It appears that the List Society was suppressed by the Nazis in the late 1930s or early 1940s as part of a gradual but ongoing crackdown against occult groups, but that it was reformed in 1969, as part of the occult revival that accompanied the era's counterculture. It continues to exist. Especially among German-speaking occultists but also Nordic neopagans and devotees of runelore elsewhere, List's work remains influential.[76]

Electron of the Gods

One other member of the List Society requires special mention in this chapter, both for his purported influence on Hitler during his years in Vienna and for his elaboration on the doctrine of Ariosophy. The bespectacled, balding man of slightly haughty mien who called himself Jörg Lanz von Liebenfels (1874–1954) was born Adolf Josef Lanz. Like List, whom he may have met as early as 1892,[77] he became a spurious aristocrat owing to nostalgia for the grandeur of an age more heroic than his own.[78] Lanz arrived at conclusions similar to List by different routes. He was less interested in Wodanism or Teutonic folklore than his mentor. Even after he turned against the Roman Church, Lanz remained perversely grounded in the Catholic erudition of his youth surrounding the origins of the Judeo-Christian tradition in the Near East, and was also intimate with popularizations of Nietzsche, and the science of his day. The highly idiosyncratic Lanz increasingly accommodated himself to the Theosophical beliefs around him, despite his accent on a heretical

Christianity purged of all Judaic elements and his own odd ideas of Near Eastern history based on fanciful interpretations of archaeology and ancient texts. He extolled Blavatsky for being "nearly a generation ahead of her time and of anthropology." Elaborating on her doctrine of root races, Lanz believed that the fifth root race, the Aryans, had sinned by breeding with the bestial simian branch of the fourth root race, whose origins lay in sunken Atlantis.[79] Like List, Lanz sought to ensure the evolutionary supremacy of Aryans through racial selection and a rigid caste system. Neither man flinched from apocalyptic visions of war. Yet the older seer, who came by steps from the Romantic *völkisch* milieu of his youth to an eccentric account of history and destiny, seems a pillar of emotional stability compared to his protégé. Lanz's fanatical writings and wild claims suggest that he battled demons in a war of words.

It was Lanz who coined the term Ariosophy,[80] but that was never his chief claim on history. Lanz surfaces in most biographies of Hitler; his influence on Hitler during his Vienna sojourn has enjoyed much speculation. He was certainly more than the crank figure usually depicted by Hitler's biographers.[81] Lanz belonged to learned societies, received patents for inventions, and even contributed to a series of scholarly works on the texts of early Judaism.[82] He was, however, bizarre and megalomaniacal to an alarming degree. Many claims made for Lanz by the conspiracy theorists who lurk in the shadows of history, indeed most of the claims by Lanz himself, can be dismissed. Since he maintained that Lenin and Lord Kitchener were his disciples, we are right to look askance when he numbered Hitler as an early follower. It is certainly possible, though, that young Hitler met Lanz, and probable, from Hitler's own admissions of his reading habits and the statements of his associates, that he read Lanz's *Ostara*, a periodical founded in 1905, named for the Nordic goddess of spring and filled with contributions by List's colleagues.[83]

Although he had been a Cistercian monk as a young man, a decision colored by his love of the Middle Ages, Lanz became virulently anti–Roman Catholic.[84] He entered the Heiligenkreuz Abbey near Vienna in 1893 and left the order under cloudy circumstances in 1899.[85] The lively intellectual atmosphere inside the Romanesque monastery was tainted with anti-Semitism. Lanz's earliest published essay and a latter enlargement focused on interpretations of a stone relief found at the abbey depicting a nobleman treading on an unknown creature. Lanz's speculations on the stone can be seen as the beginning of his preoccupation with the noble Aryan beating down the bestial forces of evil, a theme that was not metaphorical to him but represented a literal telling of history.[86] Lanz summarized his Ariosophical doctrines with a pithy phrase: "For the extirpation of the beast-men and the propagation of the higher new man."[87] His ideas continue to find an audience on the fringe right.

List was not alone in his fascination for recent discoveries among the Assyrian ruins of Mesopotamia, the cradle of civilization. The pantheon of deities and rich trove of ancient literature uncovered by Sir Henry Rawlinson and other European archaeologists had only recently helped establish new perspectives on the genesis of the Judeo-Christian tradition. It is in this context that Lanz labored on his eccentric theories of ancient history, working not by careful induction from cuneiform fragments but arranging whatever caught his eye by the light of his own doctrine. For Lanz, the clay tablets and sculptures of Nineveh and Babylon revealed a picture of horror, an ancient world swarming with monsters often descended from man in a reverse evolution caused by miscegenation.[88]

The fundamental expression of Lanz's ideas came in his 1905 book, *Theozoologie oder die Kunde von den Sodoms-Äfflingen und dem Götter-Elektron* (*Theozoolgy or Tidings of the Apelings of Sodom and the Electron of the Gods*). Theozoology was his contribution to the roster of pseudo-sciences that proliferated in the wake of breakthroughs in biology and physics. His fascination with contemporary research into electricity, which included experiments with the cathode ray tubes of television, led him to conceive of extrasensory perception as a function of the ability to receive subtle electrical signals through organs that had atrophied through miscegenation between primeval god-men (Theozoa) and pygmy beast-men descended from Adam (Anthropozoa). God is identified with properties of electricity and radiation. Lanz's interest in the pineal gland as the missing "third eye" of perception echoes Blavatsky. He incorporated Christ into his scheme by asserting that he came to redeem the chosen people, the Aryans, from racial impurity; the author explained his miracles by reference to mysterious properties of electricity. *Theozoologie* is haunted by revolting images of "sex demons" and "lascivious apelings." Even the passion of Christ is interpreted by Lanz as "a struggle with Sodomite monsters." Despite his horrific view of history, Lanz found hope in the future. He predicted that from Germany, "the land of the electron and the Holy Grail," will rise "great sovereigns, strong warriors, God-inspired priests, eloquent bards" who will "put the Sodom-apelings back in chains." As with List, Lanz held that some of the strongest bloodlines resided in the old Germanic nobility, whose lines of descent recede into the Dark Ages.

Like many unorthodox religious thinkers in the century to come, Lanz buttressed his ideas with quotations from apocryphal and Gnostic writings from the early centuries of Christianity whose texts began to excite interest among scholars by the late-nineteenth century. *Theozoologie* was packed with adeptly juggled if idiosyncratically interpreted knowledge gleaned from patristic, Talmudic, and Kabbalistic writings; ancient Egyptian fragments; Greco-Roman mythology, history, and poetry; scholarly works in art history, archaeology, paleontology, and philology; and even American Indian folklore. Like List, Lanz alluded to the secret language of runes. He disparaged Jews and all ethnicities from the Mediterranean and the Near East as "the old brood of Sodom." In the fossil record of the Neanderthal and other early hominids, Lanz read proof that his beast-men had once existed.[89]

Lanz's prolific writings expressed Ariosophy in its most militant terms. His language often emits the same perfervid, obscene scent as *Mein Kampf*:

> Our bodies are scurvy despite all soaps . . . the life of man has never been so miserable as today in spite of all technical achievements. Demonic beast-men oppress us from above, slaughtering without conscience millions of people in murderous wars waged for their own personal gain. Wild beast-men shake the pillars of culture from below. . . . Why do you seek a hell in the next world! Is not the hell in which we live and which burns inside us sufficiently dreadful?[90]

The hell described by Lanz resulted from miscegenation, from the Aryan despoiling his seed in carnal pursuit of lower races. As a solution, he advocated the extermination of those races. Lanz's proposed genocidal methods, all of them adopted at one time or another during the Third Reich, included incineration, castration, sterilization, and death by forced labor. Calling for the creation of a new race from the material of the Aryans, he declared that "the Future Man must become God-like . . . the Future Man will be different from the past. The beast-men will disappear and the remainder diffused as mixed breeds, as the white race exterminates them. The community of men will be improved by the chosen ones."[91] His burning hatred of lower races, whom he called "Tschandala" from a Sanskrit word for the lowest untouchables, echoes in the hate literature of contemporary neo-Nazis.[92]

He suggested deporting some races from Europe to Madagascar, a solution for the Jewish question put forth by the Nazis in 1940. His proposals for breeding farms (Zuchtklöster), where carefully screened Aryans would mate to ensure the continuation of untainted bloodlines, was taken up by Himmler in his program for using the SS as the breeding pool for an Aryan elite. To establish an Aryan-dominated social order, Lanz proposed an apocalyptic world war. "Amid the jubilation of the liberated god-men we would conquer the whole planet," he wrote.[93] Specific suggestions issued under Lanz's auspices were acted upon by the Nazis. In *Ostara* (July 1906), the German Theosophist and List supporter Harald Graevell van Jostenoode advocated returning the Hapsburg crown jewels from Vienna to the medieval imperial city of Nuremberg.[94] This transfer was carried out under Hitler's orders after the 1938 Anschluss of Germany and Austria.

Like many other Theosophists, Lanz unfurled the swastika as a symbol of primeval gnosis. A gold flag with a red bent cross flew over his half-ruined castle, the Burg Werfenstein, overlooking a romantic stretch of the Danube in the Nibelung district near Wachau, Austria.[95] The castle served as "priory" for his more esoteric undertaking, his secret occult lodge, the Ordo Novi Templi (ONT), established in 1907.[96] The ONT's name alludes to the fantasy popular among medievalists of recreating the chivalric Knights Templar. A military brotherhood prominent in the

Crusades, the Templars became one of Western Christendom's wealthiest and most powerful fraternities. Envious of its property, European monarchs suppressed the order on false charges of heresy. Early on, Lanz took seriously the accusations of blasphemy and sodomy leveled against the Templars by their medieval enemies and charged the order with acting as a front for his imagined demonic beast cults.[97] Later he decided that the Templars' exoteric agenda to extend Western Christianity into the Near East concealed the esoteric ambition of Aryan dominance of the Eastern Mediterranean.[98] Not unlike some groups associated with the Golden Dawn, ONT's secretive rites and vestments were steeped in adaptations of Roman Catholic ritual, with rules inspired by monastic discipline, and even a book of hours with daily ceremonies, but with a clause limiting membership to Aryans. The order's brothers wore white cowled robes and carried insignia depending on their rank.[99] In keeping with his heretical Catholic roots, Lanz styled himself Prior of the order rather than grandmaster; ONT maintained the occult-lodge custom (which may have been suggested by monastic practice) of bestowing fraternal names upon its members. List and some of his close associate were "Familiars" in Lanz's lodge.[100] ONT members rose through grades of initiation, starting with Server and continuing through Familiar, Novice, Master, Canon, Presbyter, and Prior.

Following List, Lanz issued predictions of victory for Germany and Austria in World War I, although he relied more on astrology than runic writings as the marker of destiny.[101] After the war ended in defeat, Lanz fled Austria for Hungary. Never short of money, Lanz had his activities financed by the Vienna industrialist and occultist Johann Walthari Wölfl, who rose to the highest rank within ONT. In the malaise of German-speaking Europe following the Allied victory, Lanz's lodge had no difficulty recruiting new, highly placed members such as Friedrich Franz Count von Hochberg, an architect specializing in country homes, and became considerably larger than before the war with a membership list more extensive than most occult lodges ever enjoyed.[102]

In Hungary, Lanz conspired against the short-lived Communist regime as a member of Ebredo Magyarok, an association that brought him favorable attention from Hungarian rightist nationalists. Employed as a press agent by Hungary's foreign ministry, he became a prolific journalist in the newspapers of his adopted country.[103] Purchasing an abandoned thirteenth-century church, he created an ONT priory amid wooded hills on the shore of Lake Balaton. According to eyewitnesses, the priory was "a utopian commune consisting of Lanz, his noble Hungarian lady friend, her exotic cats, and foreign visitors," its walls colorful with gnostic murals. The Ariosophist "cut an eccentric patrician figure" as he stepped out into the neighboring village.[104] At this time Lanz took even greater interest in astrology, reading an Ariosophical world order in the stars.

As with many of Lanz's claims, confirmation is lacking for his assertion of having helped to groom Hitler. No proof exists of direct contact between List and Hitler. Hitler's acquaintance with Lanz's doctrines may have been limited to a few chance perusals of *Ostara,* though it is by no means certain that his knowledge of Lanz was casual. What is clear is that Ariosophy was transmitted to the Nazi movement, regardless of the future führer's Viennese experiences, through the channels of a pair of prewar German anti-Semitic organizations that gave birth to the Thule Society, the Reichshammerbund and the Germanenorden.[105]

3

Munchhausen Incarnate

> Here I observed all the National Assembly marching around a great altar erected to Voltaire; there was his statue in triumph, and the fish women with garlands decking it, and singing "Ca ira!" I could bear the sight no longer, but rushed upon them, and sacrificed them by dozens upon the spot.
>
> —*The Travels and Surprising Adventures of Baron von Munchhausen*

From the eighteenth century onward, generations of Germans delighted in the adventures of Baron von Munchhausen, a comical, dubiously heroic figure who boasted of his exploits in the land of the Turks and elsewhere. The literary legend that grew around the exaggerated accounts of the raconteur and soldier of fortune Karl Friedrich Hieronymus Freiherr von Munchhausen (1720–1797) became pervasive in German culture and familiar elsewhere. The increasingly tall tales spun around Munchhausen were entertaining to be sure but also a defiant affront to the rationalism of Enlightenment Europe.

In many ways the Thule Society's central figure, Rudolf Freiherr von Sebottendorff (1875–1945?), was Munchhausen incarnate. A German adventurer in the East, Sebottendorff left a trail of rumors during his life and became the subject of increasingly bizarre stories after his disappearance (and presumed death) at the end of World War II. By the close of the twentieth century, Sebottendorff and the Thule Society became a preoccupation of conspiracy theorists and the subject of pulp fiction in the most lurid colors. As with Munchhausen, the fanciful tales threaten to occlude the reality of a genuinely interesting, if misguided and irresponsible, life. By the time he emerged from the occult underground of the Near East and Central Europe to play a hand in the turmoil that nearly tore Germany apart after World War I, Sebottendorff possessed an Ariosophical agenda and the will and resources, based in part on his wife's inherited fortune, to shape events on a local level in Bavaria, where he had settled during the war years. His formative influence on the nascent Nazi movement can also be shown, despite exaggerated and unverifiable claims made on his behalf. Sebottendorff was also a prolific author, penning at least a dozen books between 1913 and 1934. Most of them concerned astrology and the occult and were easily found in German secondhand bookshops through the 1960s, but there were also novels and an account of his influence on the Nazi movement. This account resulted in his brief detention by the Gestapo because it displeased Germany's new masters that their roots in the cultural underground of occultism were exposed.

Sebottendorff cultivated mystery throughout his life, and in death the mystery deepened. Confidants and detractors alike suspected he was an agent of mysterious paymasters, perhaps even a double or triple agent.[1] For many years no portrait of him had been located; only a photograph of a stone bust rendered an impression of his countenance. More recently a picture of Sebottendorff was published; taken in Munich, 1933, following his return after a ten-year absence, it shows a radiantly confident figure in a three-piece suit.[2] During his leadership of the Thule Society, Sebottendorff was described as short and corpulent, his eyes protruding slightly. He was a good-humored optimist fond of food and drink, "an artist rather than a pedant, a Sybarite rather than a Platonist, and certainly far more an Epicurean than a Stoic" who "in the light of the conventions of bourgeois society . . . was no doubt a confidence trickster. But then he himself was completely unbourgeois and led his life outside the conventions of bourgeois society."[3]

His enemies reported that he sometimes went about in Germany garbed in the uniform of an Ottoman officer; certainly, Asia Minor became the pole star of his peripatetic life. Sebottendorff's writings reveal an acid-sharp tongue, a broad grasp of occult lore, and a mind sharply critical of the European Enlightenment. As early as 1924 he wrote favorably about experiments to split the atom as an example of how science was passing beyond "the materialistic philosophy and false monism" of the Newtonian Age.[4] For several years he maintained the image of a Byronic aristocrat, forever in motion, traveling by rail from spa to fancy hotel accompanied by a small retinue of faithful servants clutching luggage with the monogram RvS.

Like List and Lanz, Sebottendorff did not enter the world as a nobleman; unlike his pair of intellectual mentors, Sebottendorff never pretended to have an ancient and chivalric lineage but admittedly acquired his title later in life, under circumstances at once curious but tending to bear out the legitimacy of his claims. The future baron was born Adam Alfred Rudolf Glauer on November 9, 1875 in the Saxon market town of Hoyerswerda west of Görlitz, near the cosmopolitan city of Dresden.[5] His father, no aristocrat but a skilled worker, a railroad engineer, left his son enough money at the time of his death (1893) to study engineering.[6]

As recounted in autobiographical reflections, and works of autobiographical fiction that omit key episodes and embroider others while seeming to truthfully reflect the main currents of his life, Glauer apprenticed with the engineering firm of J. E. Christoph in Niesky, a town in Prussian Silesia.[7] A biographical sketch by one of his associates had him studying at the Ilmenau Technical School.[8] Sebottendorff later claimed that he continued at Berlin-Charlottenburg Polytechnic.[9] Rejected by the imperial navy in 1897 for a tendency toward hernia and his small inheritance exhausted, Glauer found employment as a private tutor for two small boys in Hanover through 1898. He forfeited his position following what he described as a romantic flight that took him and the boys' mother, an attractive young widow, to a string of cities on the French and Italian Riviera.[10]

Scandalized, penniless, and lacking the engineering diploma he coveted, Glauer went to sea as a stoker aboard the steamship *H. H. Meier*, sailing from Bremerhaven to New York in April 1898. By September 1899 he was a crewman aboard the steamer *Ems,* and from there became an electrician on the *Prinzregent Luitpold*, which sailed from Naples for Australia on February 15, 1900.[11] Glauer and a crew mate jumped ship at Fremantle (March 13) in scantly populated West Australia and trekked inland for Coolgardie, where they prospected for gold at the rim of the Great Victoria Desert.

An Adventurer's Life

After the death of his prospecting companion in June 1900, Glauer journeyed to Egypt, armed with a letter of introduction to a wealthy, influential pasha given him in Coolgardie by a Parsee, a follower of Zoroaster.[12] Perhaps it was at this crossroads where the young adventurer turned toward a lifelong exploration of hidden doctrines. Glauer disembarked at Alexandria in July 1900 after a sea voyage via Colombo, Aden, and the Suez Canal and traveled straightway to Cairo. There he met the secretary of Hussein Pasha, a Turkish landowner who was summering near Constantinople. By Sebottendorff's account, a telegram from Hussein Pasha summoned him to Turkey. Glauer met the pasha at his mansion on the Bosporus, two hours' journey from the old imperial capital in a narrow-hulled caique.[13] Possibly the Hussein of Sebottendorff's account was actually Abraham Pasha, a landowner near Beikos.[14] A more prosaic version from the pen of a colleague, however, places him in Egypt from 1897 to 1900, working for the Egyptian government as a technician.[15] While it is almost certainly incorrect that Glauer was in Egypt before 1900, those dates may reflect the truth of a slightly longer, less whirlwind stay in Egypt than Sebottendorff allowed in his writings. While in Egypt, Glauer visited the Mevlevi, an ecstatic Sufi order, and Cheops, where an Egyptian companion called Ibrahim informed him of the great pyramid's numerological significance.[16] Sebottendorff would remain fascinated by the mystical Islam of the Sufis, whose practices derived from shamanism and Eastern Christianity as well as Koranic sources, and later claimed initiation into one of their orders.

Glauer enjoyed the friendly concern of the pasha after his arrival in Turkey and was offered a position as surveyor of his estate in the vilayet of Hudawengiar (Khudarinddighair). Glauer apparently learned Turkish at this time, studying Arabic calligraphy under the imam of the mosque at Beikos. By 1901 he was employed on the pasha's Anatolian estates near Bandirma and Bursa, on the slopes of Uluda, known to the ancients as Mount Olympus. He superintended a brickyard and sawmill, which provided housing for Turkish refugees from the crumbling European provinces of the Ottoman Empire. In his capacity as a surveyor, a road was laid from Bursa to a refugee village on Hussein's land, referred to in Sebottendorff's writings with the generic name of Jenikioj (New Village). Mulberry trees were planted under his direction for silk production and hazel trees to service the European market for chocolate. The pasha was a contractor for the Nestlé Company.[17]

That a young German lived in the Ottoman Empire at the service of a Turkish dignitary in the years before World War I was not unlikely, nor was it improbable that he learned the language and immersed himself in the local culture and its esoteric beliefs. A few Germans had already settled at Bursa before Glauer's arrival.[18] The Levant had already become a magnet for disaffected Europeans in the nineteenth century, even before Sir Richard Burton translated *One Thousand and One Nights* and Arthur Rimbaud traded poetry for the soldier of fortune's life. For many Westerners the Near East was at once strange and familiar. From Levantine shores they could find different perspectives on their own civilization and, if not as dramatically as Heinrich Schliemann at Troy or Sir Arthur Evans at Knossos, dig for its roots amid the plentiful ruins. What set Glauer apart from the better-known explorers and expatriates of the period were his obscure and modest origins. He came without academic credentials, cultural cachet, or aristocratic pedigree, but not without ambition. He would return to Europe with a noble title, a changed outlook, and a novel's worth of experience.

Glauer's interest in the occult increased during long conversations on the inner life with the pasha, who was devoted to Sufism. He was also befriended by a Kabbalist and alchemist called Termudi, a descendant of Sephardic Jews who had emigrated in the sixteenth century to Salonica, a crossroads city where Eastern Orthodox Christians and Sunni Muslims mingled with Jews and Sufis. A banker and trader in silk as well as an occultist, Termudi initiated Glauer into a Freemason lodge in Bursa and eventually bequeathed him a library of texts on alchemy, Kabbalism,

Rosicrucianism, and Sufism. Glauer's fascination with Sufism was sharpened by the discovery of a note by the pasha in one of Termudi's books, describing alchemical exercises practiced by the Bektashi, the Sufi order to which Sebottendorff would claim initiation.[19] The Parsee from Coolgardie and the Turk and the Jew from Bursa were links in an occult network stretching across the globe, crossing lines of ethnicity and the outer forms of religion. The image Sebottendorff presented in his autobiographical writings as an adventurer traveling in those circles is at odds with the militant racism and anti-Semitism he expounded in the Thule Society.

In later years Sebottendorff would explain that the magical exercises of "Oriental freemasonry" contain the secrets of the Rosicrucians and the alchemists, and preserved those esoteric teachings that modern Freemasonry had forgotten. According to him, the ancient Freemasons were concerned with ennobling individuals in the hope of eventually reforming society, while modern Freemasonry is concerned with reforming society in the hope of ennobling its members.[20]

Termudi's lodge was probably affiliated with the Rite of Memphis, which had spread into many lands after its foundation in Paris in 1838. Freemasonry was often considered a liberalizing, even subversive force, the engine of political reform. This was true in the Ottoman Empire, where "masonry led a harassed existence." The Rite of Memphis, however, was an anomaly in Freemasonry because supreme power was invested in its grandmaster, giving it an autocratic character. The Memphis order was steeped in Kabbalism and Rosicrucianism, the latter esoteric doctrine providing Sebottendorff with a link to those German Masons who could be termed right wing and would survive the persecution of the Masonry under the Nazis.[21]

The origins of the Rosicrucians (or "Great White Brotherhood," as devotees called it) is obscure, enlightened neither by its own claims of an ancient pedigree in Pharaonic Egypt nor the best efforts of recent scholarship. Secret societies, if they are truly covert and have reason to fear repression, do not always leave paper trails. Occult lodges calling themselves Rosicrucian surfaced in the seventeenth century with the anonymous publication in Germany of manifestos calling for the reformation of the entire world. Cited as the movement's father was the legendary German knight Christian Rosenkreutz, said to be a traveler in the East during the sixteenth century. Tales of Rosenkreutz may well have lit the imagination of Glauer, a traveler in the East during the twentieth century. Organized in Masonic fashion with an initiatory, hierarchical structure around a belief that human potential remained a largely untapped reservoir, the Rosicrucians began to dabble in clandestine politics as early as the seventeenth century, when initiates backed plots to restore the Stuarts to the British throne. Especially in Germany, Rosicruciansim became "right-wing, aristocratic and restorationist." By the 1780s Prussian king Friedrich Wilhelm III was himself a member of a Berlin lodge.[22] Rosicrucians became an influence on the occult underground that emerged in Europe by the close of the nineteenth century, inspiring secretive organizations such as the Order of the Golden Dawn and esteemed cultural figures such as Swedish writer August Strindberg, a correspondent of Ariosophist Jörg Lanz. *Zanoni,* a widely read novel by English author and occultist Edward Bulwer-Lytton, was steeped in Rosicrucianism.

Like the Theosophists who sensed the dawning of another epoch, the Rosicrucians believed that history was giving way to a new age in which the original planetary harmony would be restored. Little wonder that Guido von List was eager to paint Ariosophy in Rosicrucian colors, claiming that their lodges had preserved knowledge of pre-Christian, Germanic Europe. As World War II raged, Heinrich Himmler, with his omnivorous interest in the occult, found time to commission a study of Rosicrucianism, which found an inclination to *völkisch* rebirth in the hidden doctrine. That Rosicrucianism was partly rooted in Kabbalism, a Jewish system of mysticism, was explained away in the SS report with the assertion of Aryan origins for the Kabbalah, a notion that had been embraced by Ariosophists.

By the end of his first Turkish sojourn, Glauer had become acquainted with the seminal teachings of European occultism in Rosicrucianism and alchemy, along with the Eastern practices of the Sufis and dervishes. He was also initiated into his first secretive lodge. All of these influences would be apparent in his occult writings. Like Crowley and List, his esoteric essays were steeped in correlations between planets and elements, letters and numerals, gestures and runes. Referencing Hindu chakras and European alchemy, he called for profound transformation through spiritual exercises.[23]

Glauer's first return to Germany is neither explained in the accounts of his associates nor acknowledged in his writings, probably because of the plebeian nature of those years. In his autobiographical novel *Der Talisman des Rosenkreuzers,* the protagonist enjoyed an unbroken stay with the grateful residents of Jenikioj through 1913, with tellingly few references to the years he actually spent in Germany, 1902 through 1908. In real life Glauer resided for half a year in Munich (September 1902–April 1903), where he registered with the police as an engineering fitter by trade and a freethinker by religion. From there, he moved to the small Thuringian town of Probstzella.[24] Afterward, his trail grows even more obscure.

Married at Dresden in March 1905, to Klara Voss, a farmer's daughter from the Saxon town of Bischofswerda, some sixty kilometers from his hometown, Glauer was divorced two years later in Berlin.[25] In a more enduring accomplishment from the year of his marriage, Glauer, by one report, learned the art of astrology at that time from Dr. Richard Hummel, a dentist, occultist, and occult publisher.[26] According to a hostile article in a Munich Social Democratic newspaper in 1923, Glauer was sentenced by a Berlin court for forgery and swindling in 1909.[27] Since it appears that he returned to Turkey in 1908, 1909 was probably a typographical error, if the report can be granted any credence at all. Sebottendorff was silent about his conviction, though his autobiographical essays corroborate one of the article's other claims: that Rudolf Glauer reappeared in Germany in 1913 as a Turkish subject, calling himself Rudolf Baron von Sebottendorff, having taken the name of an Austrian noble living in Turkey who had adopted him. Perhaps the adventurer alluded to his marital breakup and other legal problems when he later wrote of the cathedral of Freiburg-Breisgau, "a place where I had found comfort in 1908 while severely depressed."[28]

The Young Turks

Sebottendorff implied that his return to Turkey was motivated by the economic opportunities created by the Committee of Union and Progress

(CUP), the loose-knit group that became the leading force in the even more loosely knit revolutionary movement known as the Young Turks. The conspiratorial CUP seized power in a bloodless revolution in 1908 and forced Sultan Abdulhamid II to appoint its members to key positions in government. Ostensibly CUP pursued a policy of Westernization and economic development. Unable, however, to find work with the German-financed Anatolian Railroad Company or the many other construction projects under way in Turkey, Sebottendorff accepted a teaching post in a Jewish community on the slopes of Alemdag near Scutari (Uskuedar), the town on the Asiatic shore of the Bosporus where Florence Nightingale had treated British wounded during the Crimean War.

Interestingly, the lodge he had been admitted to by the Jewish occultist Termudi was, before the Young Turks seized power, the secret Bursa cadre of CUP.[29] Even before the formation of CUP, Turkish Freemasons had been involved in murky conspiracies against the Sublime Porte. That Masons became active with the Young Turks was in step with their centuries-old tradition of dissidence. Jewish Freemasons, especially prominent members of the Salonica community, joined CUP, "making their lodges available for secret meetings and for the storage of secret correspondence and records."[30] Ironically, given Sebottendorff's future associations, Ottoman opponents of CUP and Allied propagandists during World War I maintained that the committee was little more than a front for a cabal of Salonican Jews.

There were several tendencies at work among the Turkish nationalists in whose circles Sebottendorff traveled. The regime founded after World War I and the collapse of the Ottoman Empire by Kemal Atatürk, who had been a relatively pragmatic member of CUP, represented a more moderate vision of Turkish nationalism. Based on his pursuits upon returning to Germany, one can speculate that Sebottendorff may have been infected by the more radical strains that went by the names of Pan-Turkism and Pan-Turanism, the latter referring to a projected nation-state of all Turkic peoples to be called Turan, whose boundaries would stretch north from the Tibetan plateau to the Arctic Ocean and east from Asia Minor to the Pacific Ocean to encompass the Caucasian and Central Asian Turkic domains of the Russian Empire and China.

A comprehensive history of these pre–World War I Turkish ideologies, and their survival today on the far right of Turkish politics, has yet to be written. Much confusion remains because many Young Turks were themselves uncertain about the definition of their own nationalism.[31] As more radical elements of CUP, led by Enver Pasha, gained ascendance, the Young Turks also pursued hidden agendas masked by public statements. According to Turkish historian M. Şükrü Hanioğlu, "Whatever was claimed in the official organs of the movement was contradicted by decisions taken by its executive branches. For instance, while its official organs were promoting an Ottomanist policy, the central committee was shifting to Turkish nationalism."[32] Growing disinterested in building a civil society encompassing many ethnicities, as the Hapsburgs struggled to do within their empire, CUP increasingly pursued the ideal of a monocultural Turkey, often defined in terms easily understood by the Pan-Germans of Austria.

Analogous with the search for pre-Christian values by their *völkisch* counterparts in German-speaking Europe, and contradicting the Western, positivist materialism of many CUP intellectuals, the Pan-Turkists and Pan-Turanians were fascinated with traces of pre-Islamic shamanism found among rural Turks. "The Turkish peasant of Anatolia, previously the object of contempt by the elite, began to be romanticized as the embodiment of national values."[33] As with the *völkisch* movement, Pan-Turkism and Pan-Turanism originated "in the obscure researches of mainly European scholars," notably Mustafa Celaleddin Pasha, a Polish exile whose *Les Turcs Anciens et Modernes* (1869) emphasized the ethnic unity of all Turkic peoples and their contributions to civilization, and French historian David Leon Cahun, whose *Introduction to the History of Asia* (1896) linked the Turks to such pre-Islamic conquerors as Genghis Khan, who became a hero to some radical Turkish nationalists.[34] Such beliefs "spread rapidly among the intellectual classes of the empire, particularly in Istanbul and Salonica,"[35] the milieu inhabited by Sebottendorff during his second Turkish sojourn. Certain factions of the Young Turks showed "a remarkable affinity with 'proto fascist' currents in Europe."[36] Unlike the Westernizers represented by Atatürk's circle, the militant Pan-Turanians often despised Western values; interestingly, their favorite European authors were Nietzsche and Gobineau.[37] The contradictory and incomplete evidence shows that some Pan-Turanians were fascinated by biological, Social Darwinist theories of race and nationality, while others assumed that nationality is culturally constructed and could be imposed or encouraged by assimilation, the strategy favored by Atatürk and his successors in the present struggle between Turkey and its Kurdish rebels.

Historian Arnold Toynbee, in a report written for British naval intelligence in 1917, noted the "anti-Islamic tendencies" in the Pan-Turanian movement, including the employment as a symbol by CUP's youth movement of the Grey Wolf (the mythical beast who led the ancient Turks on their westward migration), and a Turkish army order directing troops to include the Grey Wolf in their prayers. Toynbee quotes from a circular produced by Turkish Hearth, a Pan-Turkist group that exists even today despite periods of suppression by the Turkish Republic. That brochure condemns the "monstrous figment of the imagination which is known as the Community of Islam, and which has for long past stood in the way of present progress generally, and of the realization of the principles of Turanian unity in particular." The language closely parallels Ariosophical attacks on Christianity, which they despised as an alien intrusion, an impediment to the recovery of Aryan culture and values.[38]

The Grey Wolf was appropriated as a symbol under Atatürk, who tolerated and repressed the Pan-Turanian movement according to his own shifting political calculations. The Pan-Turanians and their symbols represented the birth of the fascist tendency in modern Turkish politics. An extreme right-wing terrorist gang, accused of enjoying links with organized crime and factions of the Turkish security forces, continues to call itself the Grey Wolves.[39]

Sebottendorff alludes only casually in his writings to the Young Turks. But his membership in a Young Turk front organization, and his return to the Ottoman Empire once they seized power, opens an intriguing avenue of speculation. Parallels between *völkisch* Pan-Germanism and the most radical Pan-Turanism advocated by elements of CUP are striking. Some authors have gone so far as to suspect links between the Young Turks and Nazism.[40]

In his book *Türkismus und Panturkismus,* published in Germany in 1915 only months after Turkey joined World War I on the side of Germany and Austria-Hungary, the Young Turk ideologue Tekin Alp illuminated a geopolitical point of comparison between his movement and the *völkisch* circles of Central Europe:

> Ten centuries of history have brought about no change in the position of the Germans and Turks toward the Slavs. The two nations have always remained the common foe of Slav power, and both must protect themselves from the menace of the Muscovite empire. As long as the Russian colossus remains, Deutschtum is threatened with isolation, on account of her geographical position and ethnographical formation. In the same way, Pan-Turkism cannot come to its full development and realization until the Muscovite monster is crushed, because the very districts which form the object of Turkish irredenta, such as Siberia, the Crimea, Afghanistan, etc., are still directly or indirectly under Russian rule.[41]

The author of this book was born Moiz Cohen to an Orthodox Jewish family. Tekin Alp (he later called himself Munis Tekinalp) is a fascinating figure who rejected his heritage and embraced militant Pan-Turkism, only to moderate some of his ideas with the ascendance of Atatürk. His long, strange, and seemingly contradictory career is emblematic of the difficulty faced by scholars trying to grapple with the varieties of Turkish nationalism in the early twentieth century.

Like the *völkisch* Germans of Austria-Hungary, anxious over the rising Magyar and Slavic tide, many of the most militant Young Turks came from districts of the Ottoman Empire where Turkish predominance was threatened by the polyethnic realm's other nationalities, and from Turkic areas that had been conquered by foreigners. For example, Ziya Gökalp, of the Central Committee of Union and Progress, was born in the Kurdish city of Diyarbakir.[42] Yusuf Akçura, a Tartar born in the Russian Volga region, wrote several of the foundational essays for the Young Turks in 1903 and 1904. Akçura stressed nationalism based on the Turkish race and called Germany's victory over France in 1870 an example of the superiority of a nation based on race over a nation founded on a civic ideal. The poet Hüseyinzade Ali Bey, whose influential poem "Turan" called for the unification of all Turkic peoples, came to Turkey from Azerbaijan. The Young Turks' embrace of the Grey Wolf, a pre-Islamic symbol,[43] is comparable to the Ariosophists' use of the swastika, signaling their reception of beliefs older than Christianity and their fixation on race. Resulting from the Young Turks' fixation with national supremacy and the creation of a monocultural state were campaigns of genocide and ethnic cleansing against the Greeks, Armenians, and Assyrians of Asia Minor beginning in 1915, under the cover of World War I.

It is interesting to speculate on the degree to which Sebottendorff may have been influenced by aspects of Young Turk ideology, and whether the baron, proud of his Turkish citizenship, carried any intellectual viruses home with him to Germany. As with many other aspects of his life, Sebottendorff remained silent and documentation is lacking. The Young Turks have been called "Westernizers" and *völkisch* ideology "anti-Western," but the milieus in which those ideological positions were born were considerably different, making the blind application of such terminology a misleading exercise. Lacking the infrastructure to compete against the Western powers, the Young Turks sought to increase the efficiency of their society by espousing Western technology. The *völkisch* militants of the industrialized German and Austro-Hungarian empires were inheritors of that technology despite their rejection of Western rationalism. The material needs of Turkey and Central Europe differed markedly, but the spiritual hunger for political transcendentalism and a mystical attachment to race were nearly identical among influential minorities in both regions.

Esoteric Interests

Sebottendorff was in Constantinople on Easter 1909 as the Young Turks crushed an attempted countercoup by Abdulhamid II, which led to his abdication in favor of his more compliant brother, Mohammed V.[44] During this time the German expatriate gave lectures on the occult in his apartment in the capital's Pera district on the Golden Horn, an elegant neighborhood largely inhabited by Europeans, Jews, and Armenians. His autobiographical novel makes sketchy, intriguing references to a "double life"; the protagonist was associated with a Russian pimp who operated out of a billiard cafe in the brothel district but concealed those activities from the audience for his "talks at home" on occultism. Those talks may have led Sebottendorff to found a short-lived lodge by the close of 1910.[45] During this time he closely studied the Bektashi Sufis, whose esoteric teachings were hidden behind a thin screen of Islam. He equated their practices concerning transformational gnosis through ecstasy with alchemy, Rosicrucianism, and esoteric Freemasonry.[46] Sebottendorff would later recount his days with the dervishes in a book published in Leipzig in 1924.

Pan-Turkish and Pan-Turanian scholars were drawn to the Bektashi, considered the most Turkish of all the Sufi orders for perpetuating pre-Islamic and shamanistic elements, and preserving early forms of the Turkish language in their writings. This was analogous to the pre-Christian survivals that fascinated List and other neopagans in Western Europe. The Bektashi were the most covert of Sufis. Having no public worship, their rituals were "guarded with such absolute secrecy," much like the Oriental Freemasons. Engaged in intrigue against the Ottoman regime, the Bektashi had aims that included a political dimension congenial to the Young Turks, such as abolishing the Caliphate and freeing women from the veil. Although Atatürk proscribed all Sufi lodges in 1925, Bektashi literature, considered a reflection of the Turkish soul, continued to be taught in the schools of the Turkish Republic.[47] Despite persecution, the Bektashi secretly continued, feeding a current of resistance to the Atatürk regime, much as they had under the Ottomans.[48]

Turkish records verify Sebottendorff's assertion that he became an Ottoman subject by 1911, contradicting claims made later by the German Social Democratic press that he took foreign citizenship to avoid military service.[49] He was too old for conscription by this time and the world war was three years distant. Although his Turkish nationality proved useful to him during World War I and its aftermath, its benefits derived from circumstances unforeseeable in 1911. From all available evidence, a picture develops of Sebottendorff as a German T. E. Lawrence, a European adventurer who adapted easily to the exotic surroundings of the Near East. Sebottendorff would unfavorably contrast the Germans, who provided an eager audience for Bolshevism, with the Turks, whom he claimed were unreceptive to Communism.[50]

The evidence for Sebottendorff's Turkish citizenship is clear enough, yet his reinvention as a German aristocrat remains foggy. In a deposition made in Munich in 1918, Sebottendorff affirmed that Heinrich Baron von Sebottendorff, an American national, became his stepfather in Constantinople in 1908 according to Turkish law.[51] That a certain Heinrich von Sebottendorff (1825–?), from the Prussian line of the family, lived in Görlitz near Hoyerswerda during Glauer's adolescence lends credence to the story. It is not known whether Heinrich was a naturalized American citizen, but his brother Hugo apparently died in the United States; perhaps Rudolf added a few threads of embroidery to the truth.[52] Under German law, an adoption involving nobility required the kaiser's assent, but the Sebottendorff family appears to have accepted the railroad engineer's son as one of its own. He exchanged his legally dubious baronage for a more tenable baronetcy by being readopted on German soil, at Weisbaden in 1914, by a noble from the Austrian branch of the Sebottendorffs, a retired major, Sigmund Freiherr von Sebottendorff von der Rose. Afterward, the adventurer who would lead the Thule Society was usually known not as Baron but as Freiherr von Sebottendorff, his new title a degree lower than baron in the peerage of Germany and Austria. Evidence of his standing in the Sebottendorff family is provided by the 1915 funeral notice of his foster father, Sigmund, listing him and his second wife among the mourners.[53] The Sebottendorff family had settled before the end of the twelfth century in Silesia, near the young adventurer's birthplace and a place where he had once worked. Otherwise there is no documentable explanation for their willingness to adopt the middle-class engineer.[54] To further complicate matters, it appears that the former Adam Glauer called himself Rudolf Adam Glandeck Baron von Sebottendorff while in Constantinople. It would not be the last time that the name Glandeck turned up in connection with Sebottendorff.[55]

Unlike the fabled Baron von Munchhausen, who fought against the Turks, Sebottendorff claimed a period of service under the sultan. By his account from October to December 1912 he volunteered as a medical orderly at the onset of the First Balkan War, in which Greece, Montenegro, Bulgaria, and Serbia defeated the Turks and expelled them from all but a small corner of Europe. As a result the Young Turk regime, bereft of the empire's Balkan provinces and faced with the growing nationalism of its Armenian, Greek, Assyrian, and Arabic subjects, became more concerned than ever with the project of redefining Turkey in terms of Turkish nationalism, not as a multiethnic empire nor as a component of the Islamic world. Agreeing to command a company of men recruited from Jenikioj, the refugee village he had helped construct, Sebottendorff was injured in combat, struck on the head by a Bulgarian rifle butt.[56]

Return to Germany

Sebottendorff moved to Berlin early in 1913.[57] By now a man of esoteric interests, he sought the company of fellow occultists after his return from Asia Minor, reacquainting himself with astrologer Richard Hummel and meeting Liesbeth Seidler, allegedly a seer and police informant in the circles of Rudolf Steiner.[58] Evidence that he traveled widely in Theosophical circles from 1913 on can be found in references to him by Gustav Meyrink. The Prague author, best known for his Kabbalistic novel *Der Golem*, a fable of an artificially created man later adapted by director Paul Wegener into a classic German Expressionist film (1920), was a well-known figure in Central European occultism. Meyrink was active in the Lodge of the Blue Star, a Prague Theosophical society founded in 1891 under the influence of the Viennese Theosophist Friedrich Eckstein.[59] He reported bad experiences with mystical exercises prepared for him by Sebottendorff, finding they "were somewhat dangerous and were lacking in completeness."[60] Meyrink may have traveled a different political road than Sebottendorff did in Europe's occult underground, as it has been claimed that Meyrink was an outspoken pacifist during World War I. However, he apparently accepted a commission in 1917 from Germany's foreign office to write a novel blaming the war on an international conspiracy of Freemasons. Although never completed, the work was to have been translated into English and Swedish for use as a propaganda tool for the Central Powers.[61] Later, Meyrink's work would be banned in Nazi Germany, a fate he would share with Sebottendorff.

Sebottendorff exhibited no trace of hostility toward Jews earlier in life. Indeed, his relationship with the Jewish occultist Termudi was by his own telling a formative experience. His writings preserve no turning point on the road to anti-Semitism. It is likely that his anti-Semitism dates from his immersion, after returning to Germany, in the deepening racism of many Central European Theosophists. For Sebottendorff, the racism of the Young Turks may have found focus in the Jews after he encountered Ariosophy through his journeys in Theosophical circles.

Sebottendorff's rising anti-Semitism could only have been sharpened after a clash with a Jewish lawyer, Max Alsberg, over the substantial trust fund of his second wife. Alsberg possessed power of attorney over the trust belonging to the divorcée, Berta Anna Iffland, who after her marriage to Sebottendorff in Vienna in 1915 was known as Anna Freifrau von Sebottendorff. Described by one of the freiherr's associates as "well to do and very stout," she apparently took no active role in her husband's occult and political activities.[62] When he dismissed Alsberg, his wife's Berlin solicitor and executor of her estate, the outraged lawyer incited a Dresden police official called Heindl to defame him as a fortune hunter. At one point his accounts were placed under court supervision and he was forbidden to withdraw funds without its permission.[63] He later added that Alsberg, a Jewish convert to Christianity and a "relative by marriage," tried to sabotage his home life.[64] It would not be Sebottendorff's final encounter with the wrathful in-law; Alsberg emerged after the 1919 siege of Munich, in which Sebottendorff played a leading role in the toppling of Bavaria's leftist regime, as legal adviser to some of the freiherr's enemies.[65] Sebottendorff's retort was literary. In one of his autobiographical novels he portrayed Alsberg and Heindl as transvestites.[66]

Evidence exists that Sebottendorff may have entertained regrets about his anti-Semitism and *völkisch* political activism. In *Der Talisman des Rosenkreuzers*, he complained on behalf of his alter ego that "he who did not wish to become involved in politics was now editing a political newspaper. He who had always stood up for the equality of human rights was getting more and more involved in anti-Semitism. He was now becoming more and more entangled in the mess." Sebottendorff's protagonist, Torre, also stated, "I am not anti-Semitic in the present sense of the expression. And even less am I pro-Jew. But I am not indifferent to the question." Torre goes on to describe the Jew as a necessary ferment in society, to praise the Sephardim and especially the Jews of Salonica as "useful members of society," while casting doubt upon the utility of the Ashkenazim from Eastern Europe.[67] That Sebottendorff later returned to Germany and tried to take a measure of credit for the birth of Nazism speaks to a current of opportunism than ran alongside his genuine devotion to the occult and opposition to Bolshevism and materialism. Perhaps he, who was more cosmopolitan in his experiences than List or Lanz and their parochial German followers, flew the flag of Ariosophy from convenience as much as conviction?

Sebottendorff was reticent about naming and dating his initial encounter with Ariosophy. "I am a student of Theosophy without adhering to any of today's modern interpretations," he stated.[68] His early works, though evincing a thorough knowledge of German anti-Semitic writings, were composed in parlance peculiar to List and Lanz. Ariosophy permeates page after page of Sebottendorff's voluminous prose during his tenure with the Thule Society, regardless of his occasional posturing as a thinker of unprecedented ideas. To his credit, however, he was usually generous in citing the ideologues he admired: high on his list were Fritsch, List, Lanz, and List Society member Philipp Stauff (who headed the Germanenorden faction opposed to Sebottendorff's wing!).[69] He ascribed to Aryans, "the wise white homosapiens of the North," a race "the Ice Age created,"[70] the inception of every world-shaping concept, even the belief in a monotheistic God "as world creator and sustainer."[71]

Sebottendorff's choice for the name of his secret group, the Thule Society, smacks of List. Thule is sometimes identified with Iceland, a nation admired by List as the last medieval stronghold of the old Norse gods. In Iceland, the Nordic myths, the Edda, were compiled. Like List, Sebottendorff was fond of fanciful interpretations of the prehistory of humanity. He claimed that runes were visible in Palestine, tokens of the world dominion enjoyed by Aryans of an earlier age.[72] In the initiation rite of Sebottendorff's Bavarian Province of the Germanenorden, "the candidate had to swear absolute faithfulness to the master [Sebottendorff]. Symbolically, this signified the return of the errant Aryan to the German Halgadome."[73]

That Sebottendorff strove to recreate List's mythical Armanenschaft is demonstrated by his terminology. Halgadome was the Viennese Ariosophist's word for ancient centers of Armanenschaft power. Although they disagreed on specifics, List and Sebottendorff both ascribed the Kabbalah to Aryan rather than Jewish sources.[74]

At an emergency meeting of the Thule Society after the fall of Bavaria's Wittelsbach Dynasty (November 9, 1918), which followed Germany's collapse before the final Allied advance of World War I and marked the beginning of a leftist wave of revolution that engulfed Germany, Sebottendorff issued a call to arms studded with Ariosophical premises:

> I assure you and swear by this holy sign [the swastika], with the victorious sun as my witness, that I will remain loyal. Trust me as you have trusted me thus far. Our difficult struggle will be on two fronts: the inner, requiring us to be diligent and hard; the outer, requiring us to fight everything unGerman.
>
> Our order is a Germanic order. Germanic means loyalty. Our God is Walvater, his rune is the Aar-rune, and the trinity is Wodan, Wili and We, the unity in three. Never will the mind of a lower race understand the unity in trinity. Wili is as we are, the polarity of Walvater, and Wodan is the divine inherent law.
>
> The Aar-rune means Aryan, primal fire, sun and eagle. And the eagle is the symbol of the Aryan. To depict the eagle's capacity for self-immolation, he was colored red.[75]

In using occult, runic terminology borrowed from the writings of List and invoking his conception of divine unity in trinity to rally resistance in a moment of crisis, Sebottendorff spoke volumes about himself and his audience. Ariosophy was the argot of the Thule Society.

In contrast to Lanz's painful misogyny, Sebottendorff declared himself a feminist. "It is impossible for the Bedouin to worship a female god since he sees in a female only a workhorse and a sex object. This can only be achieved in an Aryan society where the woman is an equal," he wrote.[76] Women were initiated into Thule's lowest degree of membership, and Heila, Countess von Westarp, a victim of the Luitpold executions, became the Society's secretary.

Sebottendorff certainly cast his ideological net beyond the Ariosophy of Central Europe. "During the rise of Islam we see persecution of

Jews," he mentioned approvingly, though not with complete accuracy.[77] Despite Koranic injunctions of tolerance for Christians and Jews, those minorities in the Middle East came under increasing pressure with the decline of the Ottoman Empire. Thus, Sebottendorff's view of Islam was consonant with his Turkish experience. Though residing in Germany from 1913 through the early 1920s, he never loosened ties with his adopted nation. According to an associate, Sebottendorff published a book on mysticism in Turkey as World War I raged.[78]

Aside from immersing himself in Ariosophy during his first years after returning to Germany, Sebottendorff financed a prototype for a military tank, which was displayed at Breslau for the Century Exhibition in 1913 but rejected by the army.[79] He may have traveled widely, stopping at Freiburg and wintering at Wiesbaden in 1914, perhaps in the company of Sigmund von Sebottendorff, before returning to Berlin early in 1915.[80] He also constructed an expensive villa in the Kleinzschachwitz neighborhood on the Elbe River in Dresden, where he settled with his wife in the fall of 1915. According to gossip, they left suddenly as the result of "unfavorable rumors."[81] From there the couple moved in rapid succession from Frankfurt to Berlin, often staying in the elegant Bavarian spa of Bad Aibling beginning in 1916. It was in that year that Sebottendorff joined the Germanenorden, the parent organization of the Thule Society.

Anti-Semitic Catechism

The Reichshammerbund and the Germanenorden were established by "one of the most important early racist and violently anti-Semitic publicists," Theodor Fritsch (1852–1933).[82] A milling engineer by trade, Fritsch came to anti-Semitism by way of the *Lebensreform* movement in the 1870s.[83] Echoing widespread anxiety in the Western world over the decline of artisans and the inability of small business to compete against larger concerns, Fritsch's first political foray was an attempt to organize German millers into a guild to combat the influence of corporations. The cry for artisanship against mass production and smallholders against big capital had already found its most influential exponent in England's John Ruskin, who like many of his *völkisch* counterparts idealized medieval life. The sentiment was widespread. As far afield as the

American Midwest, the Grange, a fraternal farmers' guild organized on Masonic lines, fought the railroads over unfair freight charges. Neither was Fritsch unique in his view that corporate interests were pawns of the Jews.[84] However, he soon took unreflective, resentful anti-Semitism into the emergent realm of quasi-Darwinian biology. In his 1881 book *Leuchtkugeln* (*Flares*), Fritsch anticipated Lanz's line of thought with the supposition that Jews were transitional beings between apes and humans. He followed *Leuchtkugeln* with a succession of pamphlets called *Brennende Fragen* (*Burning Questions*) before producing his *Antisemiten-Katechismus* (later retitled *Handbuch der Jugenfrage*).[85]

The catechism, whose impact on German anti-Semitism can be measured by its print run, numbering forty editions by 1936, condemned capitalism as a Jewish conspiracy and denied that Jews could create anything of culture and beauty. Hitler himself testified to the importance of Fritsch's catechism. "I have thoroughly studied the *Handbuch der Jugenfrage* since my youth in Vienna. I am convinced that it helped prepare the ground in a very special way for the national socialistic anti-Semitic movement."[86] Fritsch's familiar public persona as an anti-Semitic agitator may be the reason why he was accorded greater honor in the Third Reich than most figures associated with Ariosophy. To the Nazis, he was the Altmeister, the Old Master.[87] Drawing from similar *völkisch* influences, Fritsch had developed his own perspective on Aryan racism and neopaganism independent of List, but he seems to have been drawn gradually into List's orbit through association with the Vienna Ariosophist's network of initiates and followers. His Utopian tendencies were expressed in his 1896 book, *Stadt der Zukunft* (*City of the Future*), which envisioned garden cities whose dwellers could live in harmony with nature.

The extreme *völkisch* aspect of Fritsch's thought was clearly stated in his *Zur Bekaempfung Zweitausenjaehriger Irrthuemer* (*Struggle Against Two Thousand Years of Error*) (1886), which emphasized the pagan context of Aryan traditions and demanded a complete restructuring of German society to the exclusion of the Jews. A prolific author, Fritsch subsequently published at least three of his own anti-Semitic books plus the ranting of other anti-Semites through his publishing house, Hammer Verlag (established in 1887).[88] His complaints about capitalist "interest monopoly" came years before Thule Society confederate Gottfried Feder took up the theme and incorporated into the Nazi economic platform.

In 1889 an explicitly anti-Semitic German political party was co-founded by Fritsch and Max Liebermann von Sonnenberg, the Deutsche-Sozialistische Partei, which later merged into the Deutsch-Soziale Reformpartei. The mechanics of Germany's parliamentary system ensured that the anti-Semitic party grew more moderate, alarmingly so to Fritsch, after its deputies took their seats in the Reichstag. Angered by sectarian infighting between Protestant and Catholic members, Fritsch abandoned the party in 1894. Organized anti-Semitism was, at any rate, not a potent factor in prewar German politics. The Deutsch-Soziale Reformpartei held only sixteen seats at its high watermark in 1895, and its numbers dwindled precipitously by 1914.[89]

Fritsch was in all events determined to work outside the system. Like List, he was more concerned with changing the cultural paradigm than with changing the government. Fritsch wrote that "Anti-Semitism is a matter of Weltanschauung, which can be accepted by anyone, no matter what party he belongs to. . . . Our aim is to permeate all parties with the anti-Semitic idea."[90] In 1902 in Leipzig he founded the *Hammer*, a monthly and later fortnightly publication subtitled "Blätter für Deutschen Sinn" ("Bulletin for German Thought"). He railed in those periodicals against all symptoms of modernism: big department stores, motion pictures, women's fashions, mass media. He perceived the Jews behind every despised aspect of modern life. *Lebensreform* permeated the *Hammer*, including vegetarianism, a bias for agrarian over industrial life, and the call for a practical and nationalistic socialism. After the war, *Hammer*'s circulation increased to some eight thousand subscribers.[91] Contributors to the *Hammer* included Lanz, Ernst Wachler, and other List Society members.

Fritsch's greatest publishing coup was his German translation of industrialist Henry Ford's *The International Jew*, an anthology of a series of anti-Semitic articles originally published in the *Dearborn Independent*, a Michigan newspaper owned by Ford.

Fritsch's edition went through twenty-one printings in 1921 and 1922. Later, copies of *The International Jew* would always be on display in the waiting room of Hitler's office in the Brown House, the Nazi Party central headquarters in Munich. Although Fritsch engaged in obscure disputes with the Nazi Party after Hitler took control, even criticizing the führer as "some tongue artist [who] emerges and grabs the leadership," he was given a state funeral by the Nazi regime upon his death in 1933.[92]

Whatever Fritsch's influence as a publisher on shaping the intellectual landscape, his activities soon took concrete form in a new organization. In 1905 *Hammer* subscribers began organizing themselves into Hammer Gemeinden (Hammer groups), local circles that studied Fritsch's ideology and even discussed establishing a utopian community according to the master's principles.[93]

Growing from this modest soil were organizations that would enjoy greater influence. Stung by anti-Semitism's failure in parliament, especially after the January 1912 elections, which left the Social Democrats as the largest party in the Reichstag, Fritsch called in March 1912 for a new anti-Jewish association, one that would remain "above the parties."[94] Out of a meeting in his Leipzig home on May 24–25, 1912, with some twenty prominent Pan-Germans and List Society members came the Reichshammerbund. Headed by Karl August Hellwig, a retired colonel living in Kassel and a List Society member, the Bund consisted of activists from the Hammer groups. A fortnight earlier, on March 12, 1912, Fritsch approved the transformation of the Wodan Lodge, a secret society within the Magdeburg Hammer group, into the nucleus of the Germanenorden under the leadership of Herman Pohl, a sealer of weights and measures.[95] The Germanenorden became the Reichshammerbund's secret parallel organization.

Along with Hellwig and Fritsch, authority over the Reichshammerbund was vested in a twelve-member Armanen Rat, a council whose name derived from List's imaginary ancient Aryan priesthood. Members had to prove that they and their spouses were of unimpeachable Aryan stock.[96] The Reichshammerbund canvassed actively for members. Fritsch and Hellwig were interested in making common cause with Roman Catholics and reaching out to farmers and workers, teachers and civil servants, the military and the universities. However, the atmosphere of Wilhelmine Germany was not conducive for a mass *völkisch* movement with occult undertones. The Hammerbund recruited no more than a few hundred members scattered among nineteen chapters.[97] Its most active branch, in Nuremberg, numbered only twenty-three members by the end of 1912.[98] In spring of 1914 a Reichshammerbund chapter was established in the Thule Society's future home, Munich. It was founded by Wilhelm Rohmeder, who later joined Thule.[99]

Organized in lodge fashion, whose robed initiates were grouped into hierarchies and gathered for solemn, candlelit rites, the Germanenorden embodied the ceremonial of List and Lanz more fully than its public counterpart. The identity of the small circle that governed the Germanenorden was hidden even from Orden members, just as members hid their affiliation from the public. A 1912 photograph of a daylight gathering of the Orden's Leipzig lodge shows a collection of distinguished-looking men and women, wearing formal frock coats and long dresses. A confidential summons has survived for a 1913 initiation ceremony at the Berlin lodge held under the guise of a Hammerbund meeting at a reserve army officers' club. It was a white-tie, white-glove affair for the men. Women were advised to wear light-colored dresses.[100]

The Germanenorden cooperated closely with the Reichshammerbund in distributing anti-Semitic flyers and in other activities, but it was seldom mentioned directly in the *Hammer.* The Orden's lodges kept their existence secret, hiding their activities under the banner of the Hammerbund or registering with the authorities under innocuous names with charters that masked their true purpose. The Berlin lodge called itself the League for Nordic Art and Science. Sebottendorff would gather his group under the name of the Thule Society. After war's end Germanenorden members attempted to influence their country's financial direction through the establishment in Berlin of the Germanen Bank, but the venture was not successful.[101] Publications authorized by the Orden were to be distributed with the greatest discretion, with the organization's true purpose kept veiled. Paper trails were to be minimized, with most recruitment accomplished verbally.[102] As a secret society, its lodges were positioned to quietly keep watch on the Jews.[103] In an internal manifesto of January 12, 1912, Pohl, the Orden's chancellor, wrote of a rebirth of Aryan Germany, which necessitated the deportation of Jews and Gypsies. By 1912 the Orden numbered over three hundred "brothers and sisters," with lodges in Breslau, Dresden, Königsberg, Hamburg, Berlin, Nuremberg, Munich, and Duisburg. Their numbers may have increased by many hundreds by the start of World War I.[104]

Applicants for membership were required to "prove the purity of their blood through the third generation. This was to prevent the offspring of Jews, the Judtizen [child of a Jewish father and an Aryan mother] and Judlinger [of an Aryan father and a Jewish mother] from entering the Orden."[105] The genealogy of a candidate's spouse was also demanded.[106] A recruiting guide stated that acceptance was based on guidelines set forth in Lanz's *Ostara.*[107] According to an internal newsletter, the rites and articles of the Orden were drawn up in consultation with Karl August Hellwig of the Reichshammerbund leadership.[108] In keeping with the Ariosophical nature of the Orden, its central newsletter, the *Allgemeine Ordens-Nachrichten,* bore a swastika on its cover after mid-1916. Advertising appeared in the publication for swastika and rune tie pins, rings and jewelry, "worked from designs submitted by members of the List Society."[109]

With the outbreak of World War I, many Orden brothers volunteered for service and lost their lives at the front. Lodge activity became relatively dormant.[110] Toward the end of 1916, the remnant of the Orden underwent a schism after a power struggle between Pohl and the Berlin lodge. Chief among the anti-Pohl faction was Philipp Stauff, an anti-Semitic journalist who had risen to high station in the List Society before the war, in part on his claims of having spoken in séances to members of the long-dead priesthood of pagan Germany. Stauff embellished List's ideas on the esoteric significance of runes in his book *Runenhauser* (1913), which discovered the secret runic language of the wooden beams of medieval buildings.

Stauff had already gained prominence beyond occult circles for compiling *Das Deutsche Wehrbuch* (1912), a directory of anti-Semitic groups. He also published *Semi-Gotha, Semi-Alliancen,* and *Semi-Kuerschner* (1912–1914), registers of Jews (and some individuals falsely identified as Jews) prominent in Germany's aristocracy and professions. These rosters were compiled and published to demonstrate what was for anti-Semites the alarming degree of influence exercised by Jews in German society. After the death of List in 1919, allegedly in Berlin while en route to the estate of his follower Eberhard von Brockhusen, Stauff took charge of the List Society and ran it from his home in Berlin-Lichterfelde. Stauff held court with such followers of the Viennese master as Tarnhari and Gunther Kirchoff, a pioneering student of what occultists would later call ley lines. Stauff was also responsible for reprinting many prewar publications of the List Society. When he committed suicide (July 17, 1923), his wife, Berta, continued his publishing operations, while the Society's presidency fell to Brockhusen, by then the Germanenorden's grandmaster. Brockhusen held the office until his death in 1939.[111]

A Brandenburg landowner and retired army captain, Brockhusen had been prominent in the anti-Pohl Orden, along with Johann Albrecht Grand Duke von Mecklenburg and Maj. Gen. Erwin von Heimerdinger.[112] The group became affiliated in the early Weimar years with the Deutschvölkischer Schutz-und-Trutzbund, an umbrella organization for ultrarightist organizations. The Schutz-und-Trutzbund employed the swastika as its symbol. Operating under the name of Organisation Consul, a cell of its members engaged in the assassination of Republican notables, including former finance minister Matthias Erzberger, and tried to murder the pro-Republic author Maximilian Harden.[113] The Germanenorden was only following the instruction set out in List's writings, where the Vehmgericht was praised as an instrument of Aryan justice.

While the anti-Pohl Orden became a numerically small but murderous cell on the widening lunatic fringe of Weimar Germany, we must turn to Pohl's group, called the Germanen-Orden-Walvater after the schism, to follow the trail of Ariosophy to Nazism. Rudolf Freiherr von Sebottendorff, who joined Pohl's faction in late 1916, revived the Orden's Bavarian Province at Munich on the Winter Solstice of 1917. The Pohl Orden's Bavarian lodge would soon disguise its activities under the name of the Thule Society.

Sebottendorfff as Anti-Semitic Activist

Sebottendorff claimed to have discovered the Germanenorden through a cryptic newspaper advertisement, placed by Pohl, seeking "fair-haired and blue-eyed German men and women." He came upon the ad, partially composed in runes, while consulting with his Munich lawyer, Dr. Georg Gaubatz (later of the Thule Society), regarding a legal action relating to his Turkish citizenship, a dispute that would later provide his enemies with grounds for falsely accusing him of posing as Turkish for nefarious ends.[114]

At their first meeting, Sebottendorff and Pohl conversed about the esoteric significance of runes, a subject the latter came to through List. The chancellor held that miscegenation with Jews had clouded the ability of Aryans to read the ancient script's magical meaning. He alluded also to confusion within his secret society. Following the Orden's schism into contending factions (shortly after Christmas 1916), Pohl met with Sebottendorff to discuss his Germanen-Orden-Walvater.[115] Sebottendorff became more than a member; Pohl entrusted him with an address list of some one hundred *völkisch* radicals in Bavaria and the task of contacting each of them in hopes of reviving the Orden's dormant Bavarian Province. He may also have furnished Sebottendorff with one thousand marks, and additional sums later, to establish a newsletter and to circulate propaganda by whatever means.

Sebottendorff worked tirelessly through 1917 from his home at Bad Aibling, corresponding with and meeting many of the people on the list. Eventually he gave lectures to small groups of prospective Orden members. By October, Sebottendorff moved to Munich and took a secretary, Anni Molz, who would become a member of the Thule Society. During ceremonies at the winter solstice, December 21, 1917, the Bavarian Province was officially rededicated. Sebottendorff was made master of the province, the nucleus of what soon became the Thule Society.[116]

Less than a year later the German Empire would disintegrate, and the postwar chaos would give the Thule Society opportunity to rise from the margins and into the heart of the fray. The shock of defeat, and the political and economic collapse that followed, ensured an audience for even the most fantastic explanations of what was, for most Germans, an inexplicable chain of events.

4

Hammer of the Gods

We don't want to be the anvil anymore, but only the hammer.
—Rudolph Freiherr von Sebottendorff, *Bevor Hitler kam*

Sebottendorff's energetic campaign of correspondence and personal contact with *völkisch* militants netted results in the early months of 1918, as he noted in his 1934 memoir:

> The two Southern German tribes, the Bavarians and the Swabians, are more easily moved, more hospitable than the Northern Germans. They are not so critical, not so intent on going it alone. The men [of the Orden] working in Central and Northern Germany had a difficult job. While in the South the movement increased mightily, the growth in the North for our Orden was slow.[1]

Sebottendorff became editor of the Germanenorden publication *Runen* (*Runes*) in January 1918. Sebottendorff also recruited members for the Germanenorden's Bavarian Province by placing newspaper advertisements for a "*völkisch* lodge," a strategy that apparently departed from the Orden's previous strictures of absolute secrecy.[2] Respondents received a circular from Sebottendorff's address in Bad Aibling that described the Germanenorden's agenda in general terms and included an application form in which "the understated states that to the best of his knowledge no Jewish or colored blood flows in his or his wife's veins and that none of his ancestors were of the colored race."

After signing the pamphlet's declaration of interest, or "blood confession" as Sebottendorff called it, applicants received a follow-up brochure. On its title page a variant swastika in the form of a Greek cross with a set of hooked arms accompanied a picture of Walvater, a manifestation of the chief Nordic deity Odin, dressed in the garb of a Viking warrior and escorted by a pair of black ravens, Hugin (Thought) and Munin (Memory). The birds, an almost universal symbol of dark prophecy, were Odin's companions in Nordic mythology. The pamphlet spoke of the struggle against materialism and democracy but carped at length about the financial obligations of Orden members. Applicants, who were required to supply a photograph to be examined for racial characteristics, received a rune-inscribed pamphlet warning of a powerful conspiracy to destroy the German race by miscegenation. The pamphlet reassured its readers that the "Germanenorden exists to steer us away from such negativism" and to solve the question of racial mixing by advocating stringent racial purity laws. "By strict adherence to the laws, there should be honorable blond, blue-eyed Germans living in the German lands." There was a twenty-mark initiation fee, plus quarterly dues of ten marks. Accepted applicants spent a year in the Orden's lowest grade, the Freundschaftgrad, where "permanent admission to the Orden will be tested." The flyer ended on a note that would resound across Germany within a few years: "With the old Teutonic greeting, Heil and Sieg," a phrase borrowed from Guido von List.[3]

Network of Conspiracy

Precedents for *völkisch* militancy were present in Bavaria well before Sebottendorff began his membership drive. In 1892, the Pan-German League established a branch in Munich. Among its leaders was Julius Lehmann (1864–1935), the proprietor of a prominent medical textbook publishing house called J. F. Lehmanns Verlag. He was "perhaps the most significant personality of the *völkisch* movement in Munich" and official publisher of the league's pamphlets and printed material.[4] In the years before World War I, Lehmanns Verlag became "one of the leading producers of books on racial hygiene in Germany." Lehmann would become a prominent associate of the Thule Society, and from there would attach himself to the Nazi Party, which viewed him as a distinguished member.[5] During Hitler's unsuccessful Beer Hall Putsch of November 1923, it was to Lehmann's villa that another Thule alumnus, Rudolf Hess, brought members of the captive Bavarian cabinet.[6]

Munich also possessed a chapter of the Orden's public sister organization, the Reichshammerbund, under Franz Dannehl.[7] Dannehl would later join one of Thule's paramilitary groups, the Thule Combat League (Kampfbund), and became master of the Society in the early 1930s.[8] The attorney Dr. Hans Dahn led the local branch of the National Liberal Party (German People's Party),[9] which received nine seats in the Bavarian Diet (Landtag) in the election of January 12, 1919.[10] Dahn became "a leader of Thule."[11]

One of Sebottendorff's closest associates, the young sculptor Walter Nauhaus (1892–1919), already belonged to the Orden at the time of their meeting. Nauhaus was the son of a German missionary, born in the Boer republic of Transvaal in South Africa. Following his father's death, he returned to Germany in 1906 and settled in Berlin. As a teenager, Nauhaus took up woodcarving and rambled through the countryside of Prussia and Thuringia with a *völkisch* youth group. He was discharged from the army for serious wounds in hand-to-hand combat on the western front during the early months of the war,[12] and became a student of Guido von List's writings.[13] In April 1917 Nauhaus accompanied his art teacher, Dr. Wackerle, from Berlin to Munich, where he soon opened his own studio.[14]

Sebottendorff became aware of Nauhaus through the list of *völkisch* activists handed him by Orden chancellor Pohl. Before long the freiherr and the artist collaborated on the Orden's recruiting campaign; Nauhaus sought members of his own generation, while Sebottendorff concentrated on older prospects. Among the earliest recruits who joined the Thule Society by the end of January 1918 were Dr. Georg Gaubatz, attorney for the Bavarian equivalent of the Audubon Society; Schulrat Wilhelm Rohmeder, chairman of the German School Association; and Johannes Hering of the Reichshammerbund.[15] In the spring of 1918 the

Society numbered only two hundred members; by fall the number had swelled to 1,500.

By the time he met Sebottendorff, Nauhaus had already organized a group called the Thule Society, whose members met to discuss the Edda and Nordic mythology.[16] The group was an informal affair, unregistered with the authorities and numbering among its participants Nauhaus's friend, the graphic designer Walter Deicke, who would be executed along with fellow Thulists at the Luitpold Gymnasium. Sebottendorff only offered, "A cover name for the Society was proposed by Mr. Nauhaus, which was Thule." Pleased by its Listian connotations, Sebottendorff accepted the suggestion, "for not only was the name somewhat esoteric sounding, but an informed person knew immediately what it referred to."[17]

Thule became a prominent word in the era's popular culture through the exploits of Danish polar explorer Knud Rasmussen, who launched several "Thule Expeditions" before and during World War I from base camp Thule at the rim of Greenland. As an adventurer from a neutral nation engaged in one of the age's great heroic exploits, arctic exploration, Rasmussen earned great acclaim across Europe and the world. Opponents of the Thule Society not immersed in esoteric Nordic lore may have been lulled into a false security by associating the Society's name with the Thule Expeditions.

The Thule Society did not register with the municipal authorities until March 21, 1919. In keeping with its covert structure as a branch of the Germanenorden, Sebottendorff was not included in the municipal registry as an officer. The railroad official Friedrich Knauff was listed as chairman and Heinrich Meyer, a legal officer with the city of Munich, as deputy chairman.[18] Thule registered a second time that year, after the liberation of Munich, on June 20. Despite the Thule's leading role in the recent counterrevolution against the Reds, the papers filed in June maintained the cover story that it had existed since January 1, 1918 as an "order for research into German history and the development of the German sensibility."[19] What is true is that during 1918 and 1919 the Thule Society posed as a harmless literary and scholarly circle, while "in reality it served as camouflage for the Germanenorden."[20] The disguise was necessary originally because political meetings fell under Germany's wartime state-of-siege regulations. Secrecy was redoubled after war's end for fear of arousing the ire of successive Bavarian leftist regimes. The maintenance of the cover story after a center-right regime took control of Munich with Thule's aid indicates that the Society took seriously its identity as a secret society.

The Sebottendorffs and their house servants were established by early 1918 in an apartment on Munich's Zweigstrasse, in the city center near the Deutsches Theater and the government district. The apartment became a gathering place for the growing Society. "As a stone thrown into water causes ripples, so came additions in membership."[21] Sebottendorff presented himself as a man of mystery, speaking little of his past but able to peer into the future. "Because he was a first-class psychologist he often succeeded in making predictions which were actually fulfilled."[22] By the coming of summer, when Thule had outgrown Sebottendorff's home, the freiherr rented a suite of five rooms for the Society in the former quarters of an athletic club. The suite had two separate exits (which would provide escape routes during police raids) and a capacity for three hundred guests. It was located on an upper floor of one of Europe's grand hotels, the posh Hotel Vier Jahreszeiten (Four Seasons) on Maximilianstrasse. Its owners, the brothers Walterspeil, were Germanenorden sympathizers. For reasons of secrecy, members of the Thule Society entered the Four Seasons through a servants' door off Marstallstrasse.[23]

Thule's quarters were dedicated on August 17, 1918. Orden grandmaster Pohl, along with his associates G. W. Freese and a certain Mr. Hommel, attended the ceremony. Pohl invested Sebottendorff as Logenkopf (lodge head). On August 18, thirty men and women "were accepted ceremoniously" into the Society's first grade.[24] Sebottendorff also reported the dedication of a "Nauhaus Lodge" (August 30), which presumably was the sculptor's study group on Nordic history within the Thule Society. Pohl remained on hand to address initiates on the esoteric significance of the "sun castles" of the Bavarian town of Bad Aibling, and Johannes Hering spoke on German poetry.[25]

Each of the Society's rooms in the Four Seasons was decorated with swastikas by the Thule member Arthur Griehl. At ceremonies held every third Saturday, a choir performed under the direction of the Society's voice teacher Gertrude Riemann-Bucherer. Her husband was Studienrat Hans Riemann, an education official who did not join Thule until October 1919 and later became a prominent Nazi agitator in the Saxon city of Mittweida. Accompaniment on harmonium was provided by Hering or Friedrich-Wilhelm Freiherr von Seidlitz. Politics frequently took a back seat to occultism at the meetings.[26] On one occasion, Sebottendorff lectured the Society on the psychic properties of pendulums.[27] During the autumn of 1918, Thulists went on excursions to the "sun castles" near Bad Aibling and other rustic locations said to have mystical significance and held at least one joint meeting with Julius Lehmann's Pan-German League.[28] Male members of the Thule Society, called "brothers," sported a bronze pin of a swastika on a shield crossed by two spears. "Sisters" wore a plain swastika of gold.[29] All members received copies of *Runen* and the *Beobachter*.

Publishing Propaganda

In July 1918 Sebottendorff acquired control of a minor Munich weekly whose named he changed to the *Münchener Beobachter und Sportblatt* (*Munich Observer and Sports Sheet*), the newspaper that would serve as Thule's mouthpiece; later, as the *Völkischer Beobachter* (*People's Observer*), it became the flagship periodical of the Nazi Party. Published under various names since 1887, and owned since 1900 by Franz Eher, the *Beobachter* had possessed "a middle class, somewhat anticlerical and antisemetic bias."[30] When Eher died in June 1918, his paper had no subscribers and was hawked on street corners. Eher's attorney, the Justizrat Dr. Georg Gaubatz, who happened to be a member of the Thule Society, arranged the sale of the paper for five thousand marks on behalf of Eher's widow. It may be that Sebottendorff acquired the *Beobachter* in response to complaints by some Thule members that the Society needed to engage in more "practical work" on behalf of the *völkisch* cause.[31]

The publishing concern called Franz Eher Verlag, which would survive under that name as the central publishing house of the Nazi Party and the German publisher of *Mein Kampf*, was not purchased outright by Sebottendorff but by a certain Thule sister, Kathe Bierbaumer (born 1889), who grew up in Burgenland in Austria-Hungary. According to Sebottendorff, her farm family had emigrated to Turkey in the years before World War I, but nowhere did he indicate if he had known her during his Turkish sojourn or under what circumstances they met. Bierbaumer hired him as the *Beobachter*'s editor.[32] Bierbaumer has been pronounced as Sebottendorff's mistress by at least one authority.[33] The assertion is supported circumstantially by Sebottendorff's apparent control of her shares of Eher Verlag stock. If so, the unconventional character of the Sebottendorff entourage can be surmised from references in his work to dinner parties consisting of himself, his wife, and his putative mistress, and the possibility that she had lived at the Sebottendorff residence in Bad Aibling.[34]

By calling his publication the *Münchener Beobachter und Sportblatt*, Sebottendorff hoped to camouflage his *völkisch* propaganda sheet as a sports paper "so that young people would read it," and also because "a Jew is only interested in a sport if it is profitable for him; so they would neither buy nor read the *Beobachter* for they had no vested interest in any sport."[35]

Sebottendorff wrote many of the paper's articles. His journalism reflected Lanz's vision of Aryan and Jew struggling for control of the planet in such declarations as this:

> Two agents of contrasting world views are locked in battle-contrary races. On one side is the Germanic creative race and on the other, the parasitic capitalist race.[36]

He complained bitterly of Walvater's dethronement and replacement by Christianity, a faith "which did not conform to our Germanic religious being."[37] Sebottendorff claimed that five thousand copies were printed of the first issue under his editorship and that circulation increased afterward.[38]

When Germany's old regime collapsed with the Allied victory, the *Beobachter* declared,

> We must continue to work on Germany's renewal. To combine our strength, to walk down the well-worn steps until we reach the rich depths of Germanic spiritual wisdom. None of you fathoms how

> lofty is the knowledge of the German, how high his culture, which permeated everything and everywhere.
>
> Six thousand years ago, when it was night in India, Egypt and the Fertile Crescent, our forebears measured the stars by the stone circles at Stonehenge and Udry, pinpointing the year and its festivals. They cut runes, which were the basis of all alphabets.[39]

From July 1918 through May 1919, the *Beobachter* was published in Thule's offices in the Four Seasons. Following the defeat of Bavaria's soviet regime in the battle for Munich, Sebottendorff moved its editorial office to the headquarters of the German Socialist Party. The party's chairman, Hans Georg Grassinger, a factory manager and veteran of the Thule Combat League, became the paper's production manager. In the aftermath of the battle of Munich the *Beobachter* began to publish twice weekly. Apparently in the interest of sorting out disputes over management, Sebottendorff incorporated Franz Eher Verlag in the summer of 1919 with two shareholders, Bierbaumer (as majority owner) and Sebottendorff's sister Dora Kunze (minority owner). By March 1920 Bierbaumer had sold the bulk of her shares to the Thulists Gottfried Feder, Franz Freilitzsch, Theodor Heuss, and Dr. Wilhelm Gutberlet, and to two unidentified parties, Franz Xaver Eder and Karl Alfred Braun. Around this time Sebottendorff passed the editorship of the paper to Hans Georg Mueller, a member of the Thule Society. In December 1920 the German military under its Bavarian commander, Franz Ritter von Epp, using Thule Society member Dietrich Eckart as intermediary, covertly provided the rising National Socialist German Workers' Party with funds to purchase the *Beobachter* in the name of the party's founding member, the Thulist Anton Drexler. Eckart became editor. Another Thule alumnus and rising Nazi, Alfred Rosenberg, was hired as his assistant. In November 1921 ownership of Eher Verlag's stock passed into the hands of Adolf Hitler.[40]

When a wave of revolution shook Germany to its foundation in the waning hours of World War I, Sebottendorff wasted no time in using his newspaper as a megaphone for shrill recriminations at those he deemed guilty for the situation. On November 9, 1918, the *Beobachter* chastised those who had allowed the events of the preceding days to occur. "One speaks of German loyalty, but this is from the long ago. Loyalty and oaths do not mean anything anymore in everyday life." The same article blamed the war on "International Jewry, International Masonry and International Capitalism." It berated the Independent Socialist orator Kurt Eisner, who had proclaimed himself prime minister of Bavaria in the wake of the upheaval, and Social Democratic politician Erhard Auer, soon to become a Thule collaborator, for precipitating the flight of Bavaria's King Ludwig III.[41]

On the same day, Sebottendorff, though suffering from flu and high fever, called for a counterrevolution before a Thule Society gathering. His address was written in Ariosophical language. "As long as I am holding the iron hammer, I am willing to involve the Thule Society in this struggle," he stated, referring to the symbol of his office as master of the Thule Society, the mythic hammer of the Nordic god Thor. "Now my brothers and sisters, is no longer the time for beautiful speeches and festivities. Now is the time to fight, and I shall fight until the swastika rises victoriously at the end of this winter."[42]

His words proved to be prophetic. By the following May Day, the Bavarian left had been smashed, and many of the hammer blows had been wielded by the Thule Society. At a Thule meeting the following day, the ailing Sebottendorff outlined his organization's role in the counterrevolution. Thule was to operate on an inner and outer plane: its inner campaign leading to Germany's spiritual growth, and its outer actions promoting the overthrow of Eisner.[43]

The Rings of Thule

The inner campaign revolved around a number of study circles, "the rings of Thule" as Sebottendorff called them.[44] Inspired by lectures delivered at the Society by the economic theorist Gottfried Feder, who scorned international capitalism and the role played in it by the Jews, Sebottendorff "wanted to win over the workers" and chose Karl Harrer to organize the Political Workers' Circle.[45] From the onset, Feder offered to edify the circle with his talks. Although his ideas were later embedded in the Nazi Party's economic platform, Feder served the Third Reich only in a secondary capacity as undersecretary of state. The sometimes pragmatic Hitler, who sought to use the resources of German industry to wage a war of conquest, was loath to dismantle Germany's capitalist economy.

Walter Nauhaus led a discussion group concerned with Nordic culture. Anton Daumenlang's circle examined the esoteric implications of heraldry and the racial significance of genealogy. Johannes Hering's ring studied proposals to replace Germany's Roman-derived civil code with the imagined laws of ancient Northern Europe. One of the law ring's members was a young student, Hans Frank. Frank later shaped Nazi jurisprudence in his capacity as president of the Association of German National Socialist Jurists. After 1933, he was Bavarian minister of justice and, in an example of the Nazi penchant for creating long-winded titles for unprecedented public offices, Reich Commissioner for the Standardisation of Justice in the States and for the Renewal of the Legal Order. During World War II, Frank served as governor-general of Nazi-occupied Poland, where his role in the Holocaust and in terrorizing the Polish nation led to the gallows at Nuremberg.

In its outer campaign, Thule became the eye of the gathering White storm. Its offices in the Four Seasons "provided asylum for all who worked in any way against the revolution."[46]

Thule's disguise, as a club of amateur scholars who chatted over cake and coffee about history and mythology, succeeded for some time in concealing its activities from Eisner's regime and from the workers' and soldiers' soviets that formed spontaneously in Munich and throughout Germany, in emulation of similar groups in Russia, during the chaotic days of the kaiser's abdication and its aftermath. Under its cover story as a study group, Thule's headquarters became Bavaria's counterrevolution central. "Within a short time, all important *völkisch* meetings took place at the Vierjahrezeiten."[47] On any given day, two or three conspiratorial meetings were in session simultaneously in Thule's bustling rooms. Despite the traffic through the Thule Society's suite, Munich's leftist-led police, under Interior Minister Auer, were slow in becoming suspicious about the apparent increased public fascination with German history and mythology. The blind spot may have had less to do with inattention than with deliberate policy. The left was bitterly divided against itself, and the center-left Social Democratic Party formed alliances with the far right in the struggle for power with the far left. Usually the Social Democrats conspired with paramilitary groups that emerged from Germany's collapsing military. As far as can be ascertained, Munich was the site of the only alliance between Social Democrats and an occult society.

5

The German Revolution

A truce to words, mere empty sound,
Let deeds at length appear, my friends!
While idle compliments you round,
You might achieve some useful ends.
—Johann Wolfgang von Goethe, *Faust*

The world changed irrevocably during the war years of 1914–1918, and aside from Russia, no nation changed more profoundly than Germany. Romantic *völkisch* ideas had permeated the dream world of many educated middle- and upper-class Germans before World War I, but the political influence of *völkisch* ideology was slight. After the war ended in defeat and revolution, it became possible for even the most extreme *völkisch* organizations, including the Thule Society, to leverage chaos into influence. Although the empire founded by Bismarck in 1871 did not represent the fulfillment of national ambitions for many prewar Germans, their dissatisfaction was a subject for conversation, not confrontation. Few Germans felt any urgency in overturning the existing order. "The German people had experienced over a quarter century of peace and increasing prosperity" as mortality declined and life expectancy rose.[1]

The pressing political questions revolved around the persistence of poverty; class strife aggravated by rapid industrialization; sectarian conflict, often manifested in regional rivalries between the Protestant north and Roman Catholic south; the tension between autocratic and democratic elements in Germany's 1871 constitution; and the role on the world stage for Germany, a late starter in the race for colonial empires. Contemporaries noted "the marked inertia which characterized German political life."[2] The elected parliament, the Reichstag, functioned largely as a debating society despite its authority over the country's budget. For many Germans, national life was most vigorous and characteristic on the cultural plane, in the world of ideas.

Wandering Youth

Völkisch ideas became especially prevalent among the Wandervögel (Wandering Birds), a loose-knit youth movement that swept middle-class Germany from the fin-de-siècle through the onset of World War I. Framed by an appreciation for hiking and nature, the Wandervögel represented a revolt against the rigidities of German education, a popular theme in prewar novels by Hermann Hesse and others. The movement was yet another flowering of romantic idealism in its search for the spiritual essence of the German *Volk*. The Wandervögel were guided by a rosy utopian light, glowing on the horizon beyond the industrialization and stultifying conformity of bourgeois life. In a spirit similar to the Ariosophists, the Wandervögel celebrated the summer solstice by lighting bonfires and held other rites of Teutonic origin. Some groups employed the swastika as a symbol. Philipp Stauff of the List Society and Theodor Fritsch, organizer of the Thule Society's parent organization, the Germanenorden, were in contact with the Wandervögel's leadership and helped inseminate a darkening anti-Semitism in the movement's ranks. List Society member Dankwart Gerlach even edited a youth movement publication with the prophetic title of *Wandervögel Fuhrerzeitung*. Holding to Ariosophy's racist view, he editorialized that "a Jew is not suitable for us even if he is baptized ten times over."[3]

With guitars slung around their necks, members of the Wandervögel embodied not only the eternal restlessness of youth but also a half-coherent ideology, which would ring a responsive chord during the 1960s counterculture. The youth movement extolled liberation from adult authorities and the sad world of the present, but not necessarily from the past, when understood as a source for meaningful roots in the land and primordial folk culture. It may have numbered no more than sixty thousand active members, but the Wandervögel had wider influence. Among its spiritual beneficiaries was the Brücke, an art movement that sought freedom from the adult establishment and whose fascination with woodcuts and Germany's Gothic past laid the foundations for German Expressionism, one of the twentieth-century modernisms that looked backward as well as forward for inspiration.[4]

Although the movement largely disdained the Philistine saber rattling of the older generation, its members enthusiastically responded to the drumbeat of war in 1914, eager to serve that mystical union of blood and soil known as the Fatherland. They were divided in their attitudes toward Jews. Like most prewar *völkisch* activists and thinkers, many were not as radical in their anti-Semitism as the Ariosophists. Some among the youth movement held Jews to be racial pariahs, others were willing to accept culturally assimilated Jews into their ranks, and still others regarded the Jews as a distinct race, honored but kept apart from the Nordics.

Party Politics

Although it was unable to constitute a parliamentary majority under an electoral system that did not reflect the growth of Germany's urban industrial districts, the Social Democratic Party was the largest single party in the Reichstag at the outbreak of the war. Indeed, it was the largest socialist party in the world; its support rested on the most extensive, best-organized trade union movement on earth. Although influenced by Marxism in its call for class struggle and its denunciation of capitalism, most Social Democrats adhered to a legal evolutionary process of socialization rather than the revolutionary approach advocated by more radical groups. The specter of socialism had already prompted Bismarck to institute the world's first social security system, in 1889. Social Democrats hoped to build on that foundation by supporting voting rights for women and the gradual democratization of government at all levels. Since the kaiser declined to appoint them to his government, the Social Democrats had little hands-on experience beyond administering their own trade unions when history called them to govern. Likewise, the Social

Democrats were little represented in two crucial centers of Germany's political structure: the civil service and the military. "No other country in the world employed so large a proportion of its total population in the administration of government," nor were civil servants elsewhere accorded such high social rank.[5] The respect shown to Germany's bureaucrats paled before the deference paid to the military, especially the army's aristocratic officer corps. A story was told of a prewar trolley conductor who was fined for driving his streetcar in between two military hay wagons. His offense was in showing disrespect to the army.[6] The exclusion of socialists from those circles would leave the party ill prepared to govern after the empire's collapse, especially in the face of armed revolution by radical leftists. As a result the Social Democrats were forced to enter into some strange partnerships, including alliances with their old enemies in the civil service and officer corps and, odder still, with the Thule Society.

Germany's civil service and officer corps had been largely conservative, supporting throne and altar, law and order, monarchy and the established churches. After November 1918 with the country's various monarchies dissolved, laws openly flouted, and the threat of Bolshevism emerging from the chaos of revolution, many of these men became more open to unorthodox visions of hierarchy, including those expounded by *völkisch* mystics.

The Beleaguered Fortress

In June 1914 the assassination of the heir to the throne of Austria-Hungary by a militant Serb nationalist triggered war. Like nationalist extremists in other countries uncertain of their borders, the assassin may have been inspired by the example of Bismarck, who used violence to achieve the unification of Germany. Germany's bellicose support of Austria's claims against Serbia made war almost inevitable.

World War I violated widely held assumptions of social progress along with the notion that the new century would usher in an era of peace and understanding. Millions of citizens in all belligerent nations cheered the declaration of war in 1914. Many volunteered to fight, anticipating a short paid holiday from the tedium of their constricted lives. They expected to experience the dash and daring of warfare as depicted in the era's popular literature and to return covered in ribbons of glory. Even the politicians who promised quick victory were not deceitful; the military plans of the leading belligerents counted on a swift war of movement.

Reality did not conform to the dreams of those who were drunk on war in the summer of 1914. What happened instead, especially on the western front, was a static war of attrition. A threshold of repugnance was crossed during the four years of sustained violence, spurred by the willingness of political and military leaders to sacrifice the progeny of their nations on the altar of victory. The psychological toll paid by front-line soldiers and even noncombatants to a war that mobilized the labor of virtually every citizen is measurable not only in the damage done to individuals but also in the wreckage of civilizations. "The totalitarian regimes of the twentieth century, including Nazism's, were but an aftershock of the first upheaval," wrote French historian Stéphane Audoin-Rouzeau.[7]

When the kaiser proclaimed the Burgfrieden (civil truce) in August 1914, Germany's Social Democrats, like all major socialist parties in Europe's belligerent nations, broke with the international perspective of class struggle to support their nation's war. Berlin's police president was pleased to report that even in his city's working-class districts, "which were formerly hardly responsive to patriotic emotion," tenements were festooned with the imperial colors of black, white, and red.[8] The Burgfrieden also muzzled the Ariosophists of Germany. Theodor Fritsch's *Hammer* was obliged to tone down its anti-Semitism.

After quick victory failed to materialize, Germany transformed itself into a beleaguered fortress, its field army suffering grave losses but paying the enemy in kind, its foreign trade largely severed by the British naval blockade. State-of-siege regulations gave regional military commanders authority over the civil administration. From 1916 effective power was in the hands of the country's top military leaders, Field Marshal Paul von Hindenberg and Gen. Erich Ludendorff.

Following Germany's defeat, Ludendorff crossed into the occult underground and Nazism. After the Thule Society's Rudolf Hess brought Hitler to his attention in May 1921, the old general became eager to lend his prestige to the Nazi movement.[9] Ludendorff's wife, Dr. Mathilde von Kemnitz, was introduced to the general by the Thule confederate

Gottfried Feder. She has been depicted by historians as the malevolent influence on her husband's postwar life and blamed for encouraging his alliance with Hitler. A student of psychiatry and one-time scientific debunker of astrology, Kemnitz was a charter member of the Edda Society, which was steeped in List and founded by an associate of the Thule Society. "My acquaintance with the earliest work of Dr. Mathilde Kemnitz was of decisive influence on the course of my inner struggles," Ludendorff wrote, especially concerning "secret supranational forces" such as Jews, the Roman Catholic Church, Freemasonry, and "occult and satanistic structures" bent on diminishing the Aryans.[10]

During the war Germany experienced social disruptions similar to other warring nations, including women filling jobs ordinarily held by men and levels of delinquency rising among unsupervised youth.[11] Despite its industrialization and the intelligent cultivation of its farm lands, Germany could neither feed nor clothe itself but depended on imports of food and raw materials that could no longer be delivered. By the autumn of 1916 conditions had already grown desperate.[12] In the terrible Turnip Winter (Kohlrubenwinter) of 1916–1917, coarse turnips normally used for animal fodder were substituted for scarce potatoes. A stingy, monotonous diet became the rule for the majority. Warm clothing was in short supply. Even the quality of beer suffered from lack of cereals. The burden fell less heavily on the rich and those with access to the black market, an illicit zone found in the shadow of every controlled economy anywhere in the world. Strikes during the winter of 1917–1918 were fanned by leftist agitators, who found eager listeners in an environment of hunger and cold.

Hope of victory was kept alive against mounting war weariness by German successes on the eastern front. The Bolsheviks under Lenin, whom Germany's military leaders dispatched to Russia from his exile in Switzerland, overthrew Russia's provisional government in October 1917 and took the battered nation out of the war. As was often true of the strategy of Germany's wartime leaders, their goal of neutralizing Russia was realized as a Pyrrhic victory. Already in his famous address to the crowd at Finland Station upon arrival in Petrograd, Lenin sounded a note that would haunt Germany's rulers, even mentioning one of the most intransigent German dissidents by name. "The hour is not far off when, at the summons of our comrade Karl Liebknecht, the people will turn their weapons against the capitalist exploiters."[13]

A Bolshevik delegation under Trotsky turned Russia's peace negotiations with Germany into an opportunity to spread the contagion of Communist revolution. Trotsky "demonstratively abandoned the traditional practices of diplomacy, appealed to the belligerent peoples over the heads of their governments," and "openly carried on anti-war propaganda among the German troops." The German high command was not amused and on March 3, 1918, pressed the harsh Treaty of Brest-Litovsk on the Bolsheviks, forcing Russia to abandon the Ukraine and huge swaths of productive territory.[14]

Germany did not have time to economically exploit its conquests. Brest-Litovsk boosted German morale but did little to alleviate shortages of food and other essentials. By the time Ludendorff launched his final offensive on the western front on March, 21, 1918, even front-line soldiers were going hungry, resorting to making pancakes from the barley intended for their packhorses.[15] The German attack achieved success in its opening rounds, inflicting terrible casualties on the enemy, but Ludendorff was unable to press forward. In July and August, Allied counterattacks, stiffened by the arrival of American troops and spearheaded by tanks, began the drive toward German defeat. Sebottendorff later recalled how the mood on Germany's home front turned darker during those months:

> All kinds of rumors went around within the population during the summer of 1918. Milk was to be sent clandestinely from Bavaria to Prussia. The king was called the milk farmer, and it was said that he was the main black marketeer. On the other side, it was said in northern Germany that flour and vegetables were being shipped to Bavaria. Whoever experienced the misery of those times will understand the important role these necessary exchanges of products did to create hatred among the [German] tribes.[16]

Mobilizing Discontent

As the war dragged on inconclusively, with mounting casualties on the battlefield and increased privation at home, Marxist critics of German society saw an opportunity to mobilize discontent. In 1917 a new political party, the Independent Social Democrats, split from the majority Social Democrats when their most radical delegates to the Reichstag refused to vote in favor of the war budget. Protected by parliamentary immunity, Independent Socialist delegates began to speak out against the war and their own government. Many members of the new party, notably Karl Liebknecht and Reichstag member Rosa Luxemburg, supported the militant Spartacist League. The courage and intellectual acuteness of Liebknecht and Luxemburg, the outstanding personalities of the German left, were undermined by lack of realism and prudence.[17]

Strikes by dock workers in Kiel during the summer of 1917 and by munitions workers in Berlin in January 1918 were motivated by complaints over wages and food rations, but the Independent Socialists and Spartacists were determined to use worker discontent as the wedge to drive home their program. As early as October 1917 the Reich navy minister admitted to the Reichstag that radicals were circulating "incitatory literature among the fleet."[18] Many of the January 1918 strikers were drafted and sent to the front lines, a punishment that only spread the bacillus of revolution. The far right reacted with uncomprehending horror. Sebottendorff called the strikes "the stab in the back" that allowed the Allies to "breath freely, for they knew that, as so often in history, a German stabbed another German in the back."[19]

Like the epidemic of Spanish influenza that gripped the world in 1918 and seemed to symbolize the weakened immunity of the old order, revolution was a contagion in the air. The warning signs were already lit before the war entered its final year. Although the German Empire was locked in deadly struggle with Russia, the abdication of the tsar in March 1917 must have been cold comfort to German monarchists. The fall of the tsarist regime "was a factor whose influence and consequences in Germany can hardly be exaggerated."[20] The Independent Socialist press glorified both the First Russian Revolution, which installed a provisional government representing democratic and socialist parties, and the Second Russian Revolution, which installed the Bolsheviks, in a sly manner calculated to inspire imitation without alarming Germany's censors.

After Brest-Litovsk, the revolutionary Russians lent direct assistance to their German comrades through the offices of their ambassador to Germany, Adolph Joffe. Ensconced in the former tsarist embassy on Unter den Linden, Joffe and his staff conducted a vigorous campaign of covert Bolshevik propaganda, smuggling pamphlets, money, and arms into Berlin under diplomatic seal, and meeting secretly with Independent Socialists to discuss tactics. Even if the Independent Socialists never unanimously adopted the Leninist party line, Germany's proto-Communists fervently embraced the example of Lenin's revolution, which they hoped to adapt to their own circumstances. Joffe was finally expelled from Germany on November 6 just as the revolution began.[21]

By the fall of 1918 the world war had entered its final phase. Germany's ally the Ottoman government signed an armistice with the Allies on October 30, followed by Austria-Hungary on November 3. As Allied armies turned the tide on the western front, the German high command finally began to lose its nerve. The kaiser's liberal cousin, Prince Max von Baden, was appointed chancellor. His appeal for peace on October 3 was an open concession of defeat. Germany's government began to democratize itself to become a better negotiating partner in the eyes of Woodrow Wilson, the idealistic American president who imagined a world without autocracy emerging from the ruins of war. The Social Democrat Philipp Scheidemann became a minister in Prince Max's cabinet, the first socialist so honored; similarly in Bavaria, King Ludwig III added Social Democrats to the cabinet. An October 20 general amnesty freed Liebknecht, who immediately called for a worldwide revolution of the proletariat, and Kurt Eisner, who would soon lead the revolution in Bavaria. On October 23, Wilson responded to Prince Max with a note that virtually required Germany's unconditional surrender. Germany's military leaders, however, were willing to gamble that one last victory, or at least a successful rearguard action, could force better terms from the Allies.

The Forgotten Revolution

The German high command was shocked when the nation's soldiers and sailors proved unwilling to be spent as bargaining chips. Their refusal sparked the German Revolution, which brought the Independent Socialist Eisner to power in Bavaria and prompted the Thule Society to begin its campaign of counterrevolutionary agitation and violence. The German Revolution, largely consigned by historians to the endnotes of World War I, warrants closer attention as the first seizure of power by Marxists in a highly organized industrial society (which, unlike Russia, was the setting for revolution predicted by Marx). The effort to put down the revolution also laid much groundwork for the rise of Nazism.

That the revolution failed to take hold (in most places its reign was measured in weeks, but in Bavaria its quarreling proponents managed to govern for six months) is one reason for its obscurity. Also, the turmoil of late 1918 and early 1919 might better be called the German Revolutions. They were a series of localized uprisings, owing to the federal constitution of Germany and the mixed causes of the upheavals. It was not a centrally directed effort of the sort mythologized by the Russian Bolsheviks with their seizure of the Winter Palace, despite the best efforts of German Communists and Spartacists to run the movement. In its earliest phase the German Revolution was a "spontaneous, popular upheaval in which exasperation, war-weariness and genuine revolutionary enthusiasm all played a part."[22]

Although workers carrying red flags massed outside the Reichstag as early as October 26, 1918, the German Revolution began with the mutiny at Kiel of the High Seas Fleet on October 28 and ended with the crushing of the Bavarian Soviet Socialist Republic on May Day 1919 by paramilitaries, including units raised by the Thule Society.

The German Revolution shared several common characteristics across its many local manifestations. It began when mutinous sailors, soldiers, and workers informally and hastily elected their own soviets or councils in imitation of the Russian model. At first these soviets were generally Independent Socialist in orientation, although they may have included individuals who could be termed "nonpartisan." In many areas the soviets enjoyed the reluctant but active participation of the majority Social Democrats, "who were not prepared to abandon their traditional belief in parliamentary democracy," and although they regarded the revolution as a deviation, "sought to contain it and control it."[23] In the revolution's latter stages, including Bavaria by April 1919, the soviets were often dominated by Communist hard-liners. Some soviets actually ran cities and districts for short periods; more often they coexisted uncomfortably alongside Germany's traditional governing institutions as they tried to find their compass after the empire played out its abrupt final act. The government ministries were usually dominated by Social Democrats, whose Reichstag delegate Philipp Scheidemann reluctantly proclaimed on November 9, with as much informality and haste as a mutinous sailor, the German Republic. He did so only to forestall Liebknecht from gaining the advantage should a power vacuum open with the kaiser's abdication and flight to the neutral Netherlands (which finally occurred November 10). Like the Labour Party in Great Britain, the Social Democrats would have been pleased to pursue a gradual program of democratization and socialization under the orderly auspices of a constitutional monarchy.

From the day the largely unwanted republic was born, the Social Democrats found themselves keeping odd company to prevent it from being smothered by the far left, bent on erecting a dictatorship of the proletariat. Germany's first Reich president, the Social Democrat Friedrich Ebert, received a surprise phone call from imperial headquarters at Spa on November 9. It was Gen. Wilhelm Groener, offering a deal on behalf of the army to support the Social Democrats in their fight against Bolshevism in exchange for the new government's promise to preserve the integrity of the officer corps.[24]

However, this was not the end of the Social Democrats' need for military muscle. Most of the army's rank and file had little stomach for further service after the November 11 Armistice with the Allies. Many units simply evaporated upon reaching their home depots. Filling the vacuum left by the old imperial army in the troubled months to come were paramilitary units called Freikorps, often led by recently discharged officers and filled in part with soldiers who continued to savor combat or who feared the triumph of Bolshevism. Novelist Ernst Jünger articulated their experience, celebrating the community of the trenches, an adrenalized camaraderie born in battle. Many combatants never recovered from the heady sensation of war. The Thule Society would soon organize several of these Freikorps in Bavaria.

The Mutiny Begins

On October 28, the German Admiralty ordered the High Seas Fleet at Kiel to put to sea. The crews were dismayed, knowing that armistice negotiations were already under way and that the war would probably end within days. The fleet's battleships, more precious than diamonds in the kaiser's sight, had been idle since their inconclusive joust with the British at Jutland in 1916. Sailors with derring-do had long since volunteered for destroyer or submarine duty, leaving the dreadnoughts to conscripts bored with an endless routine of maintenance. Moreover, the Independent Socialists had planted secretive cells among their ranks. Numerous sailors had sewn an inconspicuous red thread on the collar of their jumpers as a sign of their affiliation, yet many were sympathetic to the Reds less from ideology but "only because the Independent Socialists stood for ending the war."[25]

The admiralty counted on either a victory at sea to improve Germany's negotiating position or a glorious last stand in defeat. The sailors would have neither, putting out the fires in the boiler rooms and refusing to raise anchor. By November 3, shore patrols fired on the mutineers, killing eight sailors, the first casualties of the German Revolution. On November 4, troops sent to restore order went over to the rebels. The red flag was raised over Kiel and a sailors' soviet was elected.

Later that day the man who would play a crucial role in crushing the German Revolution arrived in Kiel. Gustav Noske, a rough-spoken, mustachioed Social Democratic Reichstag delegate, had been dispatched to the port by Berlin. Carried aloft on the shoulders of the mutineers, Noske was quickly elected cochairman of the Kiel soviet. He restored order in the city but could not prevent the spread of revolution as delegations of Kiel sailors set forth for Hamburg, Bremen, and more than a half-dozen other cities, raising the red flag and electing soviets who proclaimed solidarity with the world revolution. Noske soon became the German Republic's first Reich minister of war. His responsibility was to make war inside his own nation, a civil war against the Marxists whom he despised as intellectual charlatans. Willing to deploy whatever forces were at hand, even those of the far right, Noske would have overall responsibility for sending troops from all over Germany to fight alongside the Thulists and other Bavarians in the battle for Munich.

Meanwhile, all of Germany seemed in danger of falling into the hands of the soviets. Although officers were frequently abused, the first phase of the German Revolution was often carried out politely, even courteously. In Saxony the soviets deposed the king and declared capitalism abolished, but as happened in many other places, the Social Democrats gained the majority of seats in the Saxon soviets, and prepared not only to put the breaks to the revolution but also to backpedal.

The revolution's outcome was at first far from certain. The Social Democrats had problems enough maintaining a tenuous hold over Berlin. Only hours after Scheidemann proclaimed the German Republic from the Reichstag, his nemesis, Liebknecht, hoisted the red flag over the royal palace, declared Germany a socialist republic, and pronounced capitalism dead. But despite the proliferation of red armbands and occasional, confused firefights, the majority of workers' soviets backed the Social Democrats on major votes, especially the election of a Constituent Assembly, which would convene in February 1919 at Weimar, the cultured city of Goethe and Schiller. Shielded by Freikorps against the Reds, the assembly would write a democratic constitution for the Weimar Republic, as the new German regime would be called.

Everywhere in Germany during the early phase of its revolution violence and danger mingled with comic-opera farce. In Berlin a rebel sailor came with an armed party to occupy the war ministry. He was asked by the undersecretary to show his credentials. When the sailor showed him a paper stating that the Social Democratic government had been deposed, the undersecretary politely pointed out that it was unsigned and asked him to obtain the proper signature. In this case the German proclivity for orderly process trumped the revolutionary spirit.[26]

The humor of revolution wore thin in the new year. By January 1919 the situation deteriorated. The Social Democratic leadership was in hiding and armed Spartacist bands roamed the streets of Berlin. Noske, who established headquarters in a girls' school in suburban Berlin, was undeterred. "Someone's got to be the bloodhound. I won't shirk responsibility," he said.[27] He was counting on the Freikorps to honor Groener's pledge, and they did, albeit in a fashion that could have made even a bloodhound blanche. The first atrocities of the revolution occurred in

January when the Freikorps, after recapturing the offices of the Social Democratic newspaper *Vorwarts*, executed or brutally mishandled all survivors.[28]

On January 13, Freikorps troops, alerted by an informer, captured Luxemburg and Liebknecht. They were brought to the Eden Hotel, headquarters of the Guards Cavalry Division, the soon-to-be-notorious Freikorps unit whose involvement in the battle for Munich in April 1919 would be among the factors that precipitated the execution of the Thule hostages at Luitpold Gymnasium by Red Guards. When Liebknecht arrived at the hotel he was struck over the head with a rifle butt, questioned, struck again, and given a short, final car ride. The Guards Cavalry claimed he was shot trying to escape. Luxemburg, brought to the Eden within minutes after her coconspirator, suffered a similar fate. Her body was found months later when it surfaced in a Berlin canal. As A. J. Ryder wrote in his analysis of the German revolution, "The pair became martyrs of the revolution, the heart of a myth which gave Liebknecht a more potent influence after death than he had in life."[29] At a trial held in May 1919, four of the Guards Cavalry officers were acquitted on charges of murdering Luxemburg and Liebknecht; one trooper was given a short sentence for attempted manslaughter for striking them with his rifle.

Victims of War and Peace

Over nine million men on both sides had died on the battlefield before the armistice, and uncounted thousands perished at home from the privations of hunger and sickness imposed by the war. Along with the death of individuals came the destruction of entire societies, ways of life, and certainties. Spiritualism ran rampant through Europe, among victors and vanquished, as survivors tried to contact the spirits of the departed.[30] Astrology gained popularity as Europeans pondered the hidden forces that moved world events and individual fate. In Germany the war's end would topple apparently stable dynasties and political systems, and with them assurances about the social order symbolized by those crowned heads and their institutions. Although the German Empire had originated within living memory of many of the war's survivors, its components were often venerable. The Wittelsbach dynasty, for example, had ruled in Bavaria for eight centuries before Bismarck created the German state.

In Germany the psychological desire to find scapegoats was grotesquely magnified by the seemingly unaccountable chain of events that had overtaken the nation. In spring 1918, Germany had knocked Russia out of the war and, at least on paper, secured much of that vast empire's resources. That by fall Germany should suddenly be defeated by Britain, France, and their new American ally came as a deep shock for many of the kaiser's subjects. Censorship had partially isolated the German home front from the reality of the war's progress, although there were many with their ears to the ground who discerned rumblings of the coming catastrophe. In the end what may have surprised many Germans more than defeat was the harshness of the peace imposed on their country, which not only lost its overseas empire and border lands inhabited by Germans but was also forced to accept responsibility for starting the war. Although prepared to impose draconian terms on their enemies, Germans felt themselves to be victims of both war and peace.

The new republic, its Social Democratic leaders, its opponents on the left, and in some minds the Jews, all became synonymous with defeat, turmoil, and loss of confidence in the values that had sustained German society. The future became uncertain and frightening. From its inception as a modern nation-state, a disaffected minority had been unhappy with the Reich's prosaic character, yet only in the humiliation of defeat, and the more grievous humiliations of the peace that followed, did *völkisch* malcontents swell in number. In the aftermath of the war a sizable audience assembled for agitators who had labored for years on the lonely marches of the far right. Because of their history as a persecuted and often envied minority within Europe—the eternal Other in otherwise often homogenous societies—Jews received unfavorable attention from those gripped by a conspiratorial theory of history and who believed in an inevitable struggle for dominance between races.

This dovetailed nicely with a widespread superstition, the ironclad laws of heredity. "If somebody has the makings of a thief or murderer, it just can't be helped, he'll be a criminal and that's that. It's horrible. You believe it, don't you? It's absolutely scientific," says Albert, a pretentious young man in Hermann Hesse's prewar novel *Rosshalde.* It was only a short step from there to accept that alleged racial characteristics, including the negative ones ascribed by anti-Semites to the Jews, were as determined by heredity as complexion and hair color. Throughout the world the scientific and popular mind-set was prepared to entertain the most pernicious racist doctrines. For the Alberts who returned from war to a shattered society, it was plausible that a Jewish race with definable and immutable traits should wage an inexorable, almost predestined struggle against the dominant Aryans, as the Ariosophists maintained.

Whether they appear rational or irrational, ideas can only gain popularity in the context of favorable political, cultural, and economic events. When security gives way to doubt and anxiety, the ideas proposed to explain political, cultural, or economic upheaval may take strange paths. Myths providing an interpretive framework for past, present, and future events can grow popular. Ariosophy's racial explanation of humanity's past and future succored Germany's damaged national pride by providing comfort to a people wounded in defeat. It promised an Aryan millennium, a cycle of Nordic dominance to follow the present tribulations. Days after the fall of the German Empire, the Thule Society already steeled itself to take Ariosophy to the barricades, transforming an esoteric, bookish creed into a battle plan. Most Germans had never heard of Ariosophy, nor would they ever encounter the term, but every German would soon become familiar with many of its tenets through Ariosophy's child, the Nazi Party.

Political myths can be galvanized by the appearance of mythic figures, leaders whose magnetism can convert ideas into action. On October 2, 1918, the sportswriter Karl Harrer, a Thulist, witnessed a machinist, Anton Drexler, address a public meeting at Munich's Wagner Hall.[31] Within the month, Harrer, at the behest of the Thule Society, cofounded with Drexler the Political Workers' Circle, the organizational nucleus of the Nazi Party. Neither Harrer nor Drexler possessed the charisma of leadership, but their efforts created the vehicle for a magnetic leader's ascent to power.

6

The Bavarian Socialist Republic

Outside the grand laws of nature, man's plans are mere calamities.
—Karl Marx, *On History and People*

The kaiser was not the first German monarch to abandon his throne. Faced with mounting popular discontent, Bavaria's aged King Ludwig III, his wife, Queen Therese, and their daughters quietly slipped out the back way of the royal Residenz in Munich on November 7, 1918, four days before the kaiser's abdication. Ludwig would never see the city again. His departure marked the beginning of a leftist revolutionary phase in Bavaria, which would not abate until the following May, months after most other regions in Germany adjusted themselves, however uncomfortably, to the Weimar Republic. Afterward Bavarian revolutionary activity continued on the right, led by the Nazis, working initially through a network tied to the Thule Society, in an environment toughened by Thule's tireless agitation during Bavaria's leftist period.

Ludwig's flight was only one example of the loss of confidence experienced by Germany's ruling class in response to imminent defeat on the western front and the prospect of revolution. Bavaria's army was paralyzed in the face of the revolution, which for many participants represented a protest against the old order that had allowed the situation in Germany to fall to such a low condition. Overnight, Munich shops removed the royal warrant, the Hoflieferant (Supplier to the Court), from their storefronts. Like their king, many Bavarians felt themselves carried along on an irresistible tide of history.

While few regions of Germany were untouched by the civil unrest that overtook the country in the days before and the months following the armistice, Bavaria provided extremists on the left and the right with a unique forum for promoting their visions of the future. Bavarians had long contrasted their easygoing nature with the militarism of the Prussians, their Roman Catholicism with the Protestantism of Germany's north, their ancient Wittelsbach dynasty with the nouveau royalty of the Hohenzollern Reich, the cultivation of Munich with the dreariness of Berlin. Of all the states that made up the German Empire, the spirit of particularism was strongest in Bavaria, where it was embedded in law as well as in custom. Under the reserved rights clause of Germany's imperial constitution, Bavaria continued to possess its own army and general staff as well as its own post office and foreign service.

As the armistice and abdication of German monarchs brought politics to the boiling point of crisis, it was already possible for militants of all stripes, including natives and émigrés from elsewhere in Germany, to imagine Bavaria as a discrete entity. Bavaria could be a social laboratory in its own right and, perhaps, a stepping-stone toward control over the entire Reich. Aside from the short-lived Hungarian Soviet Republic, Bavaria was the only post–World War I revolutionary regime beyond the boundary of the former Russian Empire to engage in foreign policy and to measure its authority in a span longer than days or weeks. Had one of the several leftist experiments in Bavaria succeeded, Germany's southernmost state would have become a beacon for revolutionaries across the country and the continent.

The new leaders of the Bavarian Socialist Republic soon belied their belief in the inevitability of a Marxist utopia through their own incompetence and inability to persuade the people in whose name they claimed to speak. The spirit of resistance to the new regime grew stronger, fanned by the Thule Society and encouraged by the failure of far-left revolutions across Germany. Once the heady enthusiasm of the earliest days had passed, the revolutionaries were often left with thin support among the working class but dogged opposition by coalitions of conservatives and

Social Democrats. The counterrevolution was spearheaded by the Freikorps. Like the freebooters of fourteenth-century Europe, these veteran fighters often acknowledged no higher authority than their own commanders. Unlike their medieval forebears, who fought for plunder, the Freikorps were motivated by an inchoate ideology that rapidly assumed shape around Pan-German militarism and *völkisch* doctrines. They were not above plunder, but they had a cause. It would prove easy for the Thule Society to raise Freikorps from such men.

Ludwig III fled Munich in the face of a formidable demonstration for peace and democracy. Unopposed by Bavaria's dispirited military, the protests were transformed into revolution. While it appeared to be a spontaneous uprising, the genius of revolution was present in the form of Munich's rising Independent Socialist leader, Kurt Eisner, who worked to capitalize on public discontent. Runaway events enabled Eisner—a fifty-one-year-old Jewish theater critic from Berlin, a man excluded by normal circumstances from Bavarian politics—to thrust himself onto center stage.

After writing for *Vorwarts*, the Social Democratic party organ in Berlin, Eisner, like many Europeans drawn to the arts, moved to Munich. At the time of his arrival in 1910, Munich was a glorious mélange of medieval and Renaissance architecture, a city of 600,000 residents astride the gravel banks of the Isar River. It was staunchly Roman Catholic, honoring the first Protestant with citizenship only in 1800. In the following century Munich was transformed by its culture-loving Wittelsbach rulers into a cultural mecca rivaling Vienna and Paris but without entirely losing its conservative Catholic character.

Wagner had lived in Munich, patronized by the "mad" King Ludwig II, who spent lavishly on music and architecture. At the start of the twentieth century Munich was a center for Jugendstil, Germany's version of Art Nouveau. It boasted galleries where the newest work from abroad was exhibited and an art institute that drew students from across Europe. In the years before World War I the city attracted the Russian painter Wassily Kandinsky, a Theosophist who applied Blavatsky's theories to canvas in pathfinding abstractions, and the Viennese watercolorist Adolf Hitler, who would leave his mark on culture through the avenue of politics. Munich was home to celebrated authors Heinrich and Thomas Mann, who described the city in rapturous words; the great poet Rainer Maria Rilke; and the unknown Oswald Spengler, who began to publish his influential critique, *The Decline of the West* (1918), just as the German Empire showed signs of cracking. The city's thriving theaters attracted Bertolt Brecht, who enrolled at the University of Munich in 1917 only a few years before he began to change the direction of twentieth-century theater with his playwriting. It was a city where students could sometimes pay their rent with sketches or paintings. Lenin's long exile included a brief sojourn in the bohemian neighborhood of Schwabing, Munich's Greenwich Village, where he launched his underground paper *Iskra* (*The Spark*) from the Schwabinger Cafe in December 1900. Trotsky also spent a few months in Schwabing.

It was to that same neighborhood that Hitler repaired upon his arrival in Munich in 1913. His artist's imagination was drawn to this city of dreams. He later wrote that Munich was already "as familiar to me as if I had lived for years within its walls."[1] Hitler's feelings were no different from those of the young artist Paulo in Thomas Mann's pre-war short story "The Will for Happiness," who proclaimed, "I like the city, I like it a lot! The entire ambience—you know? The people! Why—and this is not unimportant—my social status as a painter, even a totally unknown one, is exquisite; it couldn't be better anywhere else."

Another side of Munich consisted of smoking factory chimneys and pinched Dickensian housing for the workers, conditions worsened through the rapid industrial expansion of the war years. A Krupp artillery plant was established in Munich and the local Bayerische Motoren Werke (BMW) factory made armaments. Thousands of workers, imported from industrial districts in the Ruhr and Saxony, provided an eager audience for radical leftist views. The Schwabing intelligentsia would provide much of the leadership for the coming Bavarian revolution. Factory workers would fill the rank and file.

Eisner was determined to incorporate the working class into the bohemian-Utopian dreamworld of Schwabing, where he pieced together a slender living as critic, essayist, and poet. He was a moderate Social Democrat until the course of the war drove him leftward and into the

Independent Social Democrats, from whose rostrum he galvanized audiences with attacks on Prussian militarism and the cruelty of war. Although he was described by a sympathetic historian as "a picture-book intellectual with beard and spectacles,"[2] the unraveling of established authority within Germany as the war entered its final act swept this unlikely political leader into the foreground. Arrested for helping organize one of the munitions workers' strikes of January 1918, he was held for nine months without a hearing until Prince Max's October 20 amnesty. Abruptly released from Stadelheim, the same prison where Ernst Röhm and his Brown Shirts would be summarily executed by the SS after the Night of the Long Knives (June 30, 1934), Eisner prepared to stand for a seat in the Reichstag as an Independent Socialist candidate.

Munich was in an unsettled mood when Eisner was clamped into prison and spirits had sunk still lower by the time he was freed. The prices of milk, butter, and beer were rising. Although Bavaria was one of Germany's breadbaskets, the British blockade and the exigencies of war had charged a heavy toll. As early as 1916 Munich saw street protests over a cut in the bread ration. Vile ersatz eggs and coffee were substituted for the real articles, and even beer, the staple of Bavarian life, was watered down to conserve grain. By fall of 1918, complaints were heard in the long lines outside the bakeries and groceries of Munich, rumors of commissars from Berlin requisitioning Bavarian cattle and grain for a war instigated by the hated Prussians.

Wild rumors circulated, fanned by hunger and ominous signs such as the conversion of classrooms into hospital wards for new waves of casualties anticipated by the military authorities. Nerves were rattled when a few bombs were dropped on the city by Italian aviators. Influenza, probably related to the epidemic of "Spanish flu" that ravaged Europe and North America in 1918, had begun to claim victims in Munich. The men who congregated nightly in the city's many cafes and beer halls murmured more loudly about their leaders. Growing numbers of Bavarians held Ludwig III responsible for their deepening misfortune. Along with Germany's other princes, he "had weakly followed the mood of their peoples, the mood of the nation" in 1914. Now that the mood of war hysteria had cooled, Ludwig was blamed for committing Bavaria to the conflict.[3]

Eisner wasted no time in turning the situation to his advantage. Wearing an untidy gray beard and a black floppy hat, trademarks of the bohemian intelligentsia, Eisner ventured from the coffee houses of Schwabing to speak in the Schwabinger Brauerei and other beer halls frequented by the city's workers and middle class. Smelling of tobacco and hops, the beer halls were places where men in leather shorts quaffed liters of beer from stone mugs. Speakers who held forth there in a tradition similar to the soapbox orators of London's Hyde Park were often interrupted with catcalls and cries of encouragement. Public opinion was molded in such places in an age innocent of radio, television, and the Internet. It was in Munich's beer halls where Hitler would soon make his debut as a political orator.

A witty and caustic speaker (even Sebottendorff grudgingly conceded his talent), Eisner found a receptive audience of workers and soldiers for his message of peace and the abolition of the monarchy. Shortly after his release from Stadelheim, Eisner organized a protest outside the gates of his former prison, causing its governor, stricken with the loss of nerve that suddenly afflicted Germany's leadership, to release all remaining political prisoners.

Red Flags over Munich

It would not be Eisner's final act of persuasion backed by mobs of supporters. A legally sanctioned demonstration, sponsored by the Social Democrats and Independent Socialists, was scheduled for the afternoon of November 7 on the Theresienwiese, the grassy commons near the city center where Munich's famed Oktoberfest is held each year. An unseasonably warm day helped swell attendance. Many of the more than 100,000 participants were trade unionists, but the crowd also included soldiers who had defied orders to stay in barracks. The Social Democratic leader Erhard Auer, recently named to Bavaria's cabinet, marched at the head of one of the city's many brass bands, leading thousands of supporters on a peaceful ramble through the city. Eisner, however, had other plans. "Scatter throughout the city, occupy the barracks, seize weapons and ammunitions, win over the rest of the troops, and make yourselves masters of the government," he urged the crowd.[4]

His oratory had its intended effect. Carrying the red flag of rebellion, Eisner and his supporters marched west from Theresienwiese to the munitions depot at Guldein School, where they pushed aside the officers and distributed rifles. Afterward they headed north to Maximilian Barracks, whose garrison offered no resistance. Within a few hours and with only a few shots fired, the red flag flew over every military post in Munich.

The old regime evaporated. The royal family fled to their estate in the mountains at Wildenwarth in rented cars after their chauffeur had gone over to the rebels. Under Eisner's encouragement, workers and soldiers' soviets were rapidly instituted. Eisner was made chairman of the Central Soviet at a rally in the Mathaeser Brauhaus, Munich's largest beer hall. Marching with Eisner were elements of a thousand-man contingent of rebellious sailors formerly stationed at the Austro-Hungarian naval base at Pola on the Adriatic. The sailors had stopped in Munich during their transit home in the aftermath of the Austrian armistice when the German naval mutiny began. This large party marched to the massive building housing Bavaria's state assembly, the Landtag, where Eisner was acclaimed prime minister. Auer, choking back his rage at events he was unable to control, had to content himself with the portfolio of interior minister.

By the morning of November 8, red flags flew from the domed twin steeples of Munich's landmark cathedral, the Frauenkirche. The new regime, supported by Social Democrats and Independent Socialists, called for peace, democracy, law and order, and a new constitution. Echoing the Pan-Germanists, Eisner at first called for a Greater Germany, which would include the German-speaking subjects of the rapidly disintegrating Hapsburg Empire.[5]

Favoring the erection of a democratic socialist state on the basis of freely elected soviets, Eisner was "an idealist in the tradition of Shelley rather than Marx" with no taste for purges and repression.[6] "It seems to us impossible, at a time when the productive power of the land is nearly exhausted, to transfer industry immediately to the possession of society. There can be no socialization when there is scarcely anything to be socialized," he said.[7] Although he spoke with moderation, his association with the tide of revolution forever painted him Red in the eyes of many Germans.

The Bavarian army began to melt away, although it dwindled more slowly than the military in other parts of Germany because the soldiers' soviets insisted that Eisner's government feed all troops who remained in barracks. It was a tempting offer at a time of rising unemployment and hunger. BMW laid off thirty-four hundred workers on a single day in December 1918; with the Allied blockade in place despite the armistice, shortages remained acute.

Carried along on the gray tide that washed back into Bavaria was Cpl. Adolf Hitler, who returned to Munich at the end of November from a military hospital in Pasewalk, where, when the war ended, he had been recovering from wounds suffered in a mustard-gas attack. Apparently he had no place to call home, and no meaningful occupation. By his own account, Hitler tried to resume military life in the Turkenstrasse home barracks of his regiment, the 16th Bavarian Reserve Infantry (often called the List Regiment after its first commanding officer). Finding the garrison in the hands of a "repellent" soldiers' soviet, he left "as soon as possible." Unwilling or unable to return to civilian life, he served as a guard at a camp for French and Russian prisoners of war at Traunstein near the Austrian border and did not return to Munich until March 1919.[8]

While Eisner was willing to take such pragmatic steps as keeping returning soldiers on the state payroll, his regime was idealistic, more concerned with molding the intellect and character of Bavarians than in redistributing wealth. His intellectual workers' soviet issued proposals "to encourage man's moral improvement as a means to prepare him for a fuller political life" and "to imbibe everyone with a sense of personal responsibility."[9]

Although he was no Bolshevik, Eisner emulated one of their actions on November 24 when he published secret documents from Bavaria's Foreign Ministry concerning the origins of the war. Trotsky had already published the tsar's foreign policy documents to expose the machinations of imperialism that led the world into war in 1914. Eisner's purpose was to show Bavarian innocence and German war guilt. The move infuriated the already hard-pressed head of Germany's fledgling republic. Reich president Friedrich Ebert berated Eisner for weakening the German bargaining position out of personal vanity, a desire to be a big player at the table in Versailles seated at the right hand of Woodrow Wilson. Responding to Ebert's rebuke, Eisner broke off diplomatic relations with Berlin. Germany's national government, whose writ in November 1918 barely extended into the streets of Berlin, was in no position to tighten the reins on the country's southernmost state. Bavaria would go it alone for the next few months. Some members of the local soviets even advocated a confederation of Bavaria, Austria, and Hungary, leaving Germany to its own destiny.[10]

While Eisner was anathema to the right on account of his ethnicity, his foreignness (as a Berliner), and his liberal politics, he managed to antagonize the center through his quixotic policies. He also drew fire from the left, which demanded the immediate creation of a Soviet Republic on the Bolshevik model. Rosa Luxemburg despised him. "May you drown in the moral absolutes of your beloved *Critique of Pure Reason*," she wrote Eisner in a scornful letter.[11] Although surrounded by a circle of admirers, Eisner often appeared to be a politician without a constituency. Dissatisfied by his moderation, Munich Spartacists and rebel sailors attempted a putsch on December 7. They succeeded only in obtaining Auer's resignation as interior minister, which he retracted as soon as he was out of pistol range.

It struck most everyone at the time that no one prominent in Eisner's clique was Bavarian by birth but were "conspicuous types of the antibourgeois and often Jewish intellectual."[12] Before long, officers and civil servants who had been oath bound to Ludwig III, as well as many common citizens, began to experience profound guilt for abandoning the Wittelsbachs in their hour of necessity. The leaders of the revolution had no indigenous roots, while the counterrevolutionaries expressed the response of citizens against an upheaval they had not desired.[13]

Surely it was an odd twist of fate that elevated another outsider, the Saxon-born Turkish national Sebottendorff, to the center of Bavaria's counterrevolution. The "focus for the gathering of civilian resistance forces in Munich became the offices of the Thule Society in the Hotel Vier Jahreszeiten."[14]

Thule Responds

The Thule Society may well have the distinction of founding Germany's first Freikorps, the Thule Combat League (Thule Kampfbund), on November 10.[15] The weapons provided by Thule associate Julius Lehmann, a leading publisher of eugenic and Pan-German literature,[16] transformed Thule's rooms in the Four Seasons into an armory. The Society became a deadly lending library for all *völkisch* radicals, even nonmembers. Sebottendorff wrote of providing pistols and ammunition to Hans Stiegler, a *völkisch* author who opened a Munich printing shop and headed an obscure club called Urda.[17]

Thule's activities aroused some suspicion, its cover story of being an innocent study group notwithstanding. By Sebottendorff's account, Thule's offices were searched for weapons in December 1918 by the Schutzwehr, an ostensibly pro-Republican Freikorps commanded by Alfred Seiffertitz. Later, Seiffertitz's force conspired with the Thule Combat League in the unlucky Palm Sunday Putsch of April 13, 1919. Sebottendorff's favorable references to Seiffertitz indicate early linkage between Thule and Schutzwehr. One authority maintains that the state railroad official Friedrich Knauff, who later headed the Thule Society after Sebottendorff's departure, was a go-between for the two groups.[18] In his memoirs Sebottendorff claims to have returned on intuition to the Four Seasons in time for the Schutzwehr's arrival. The incident was described in slapstick terms, with guns concealed under the eyes of the security force. It is not unlikely that Seiffertitz scheduled the search with Sebottendorff ahead of time. Despite the Schutzwehr's inability to discover weapons, Sebottendorff was taken into custody. Playing the card of his Turkish citizenship, Sebottendorff secured a speedy release.[19]

The Combat League tried to arrest Eisner on December 4, 1918, as he spoke at a public hall in the resort community of Bad Aibling, where Sebottendorff maintained a residence. Sebottendorff suggested that two Social Democrats in Eisner's cabinet, Interior Minister Erhard Auer and Justice Johannes Timm, sympathized with the plot.[20] It is possible that Thule intended to proclaim Auer prime minister after seizing Eisner.[21] Sebottendorff held out hope from the first days of the Bavarian revolution that an understanding could be reached with Auer. On November

9, 1918, the *Beobachter* pointed to a speech Auer had recently made to his Bavarian party congress, proving "that there is a strong current within the Social Democrats into the *völkisch* mainstream. It is up to us to use this current."[22]

Corroboration for Auer's foreknowledge of the coup has not surfaced, but it is likely that he would have welcomed the move. Auer and Timm represented the most conservative wing of the German Social Democracy. "Auer was perpetuating an old Social Democratic habit of talking Left and turning Right."[23]

Though present at the events leading up to the toppling of Bavaria's monarchy, Auer did not anticipate the outcome. He was a gradualist, committed to a slow, legal evolution toward a socialist *Volkstaat,* or people's state. Auer's pragmatism clashed sharply with Eisner's dreamy utopianism; they were bitter opponents in a Reichstag election shortly before the November Revolution,[24] a race in which the Independent Social Democratic Party was harshly denounced by the *Beobachter* for nominating a "Russian Jew who has been convicted of treason."[25] As a minister in Bavaria's last royal cabinet, Auer dismissed Eisner's importance only days before the one-time theater critic took power. "Eisner is taken care of. You can be sure of that," he assured Prime Minister Otto Ritter von Dandl.[26]

After the revolution, Auer accepted Eisner's offer to remain in the cabinet. Auer later testified before the Munich People's Court that his decision resulted from a concern for social order, "since otherwise the anarchy would have become unmanageable for him [Eisner]."[27] Auer fought Eisner to limit the role of the workers' and soldiers' soviets. Auer criticized Eisner for attempting to conduct a foreign policy independent of Germany and castigated his anti-parliamentarianism. Cabinet meetings were punctuated with harsh recriminations.[28]

Eisner was unshaken by Sebottendorff's intended coup; indeed, it was little more than a scuffle. The Bad Aibling adventure was led by Sebottendorff and one of his Thule initiates, Lt. Hermann Sedlmeier, a young Bavarian officer who had served in the same regiment as Hitler and would found the Freikorps Schaefer in 1919 before settling down as the owner of a Munich cafe. A fifteen-man Combat League detachment accompanied them to carry out Eisner's arrest.

A counterrevolutionary manifesto was hastily printed for the occasion at the shop of Klaus Eck's anti-Semitic newspaper, the *Miesbacher Anzeiger*. Although published in the small Upper Bavarian town of Miesbach, the paper would soon gain notoriety throughout Germany for its "violence and vulgarity."[29] A getaway car waited outside the hall in Bad Aibling to spirit the captive Eisner to the mountains, where he would be kept "until the new government was formed." Thulists circulated through the neighborhood on bicycles, encouraging the peasants to attend Eisner's speech, for Sebottendorff anticipated support from the rural population. He did not anticipate the presence of a strong contingent of radical leftist workers from nearby towns. The Combat League lost heart, and the coup fumbled in its opening moments.[30]

Auer's encouragement of non-soviet paramilitary forces led to additional contact with Thule before year's end. As early as the beginning of December 1918, he authorized and gave arms to civil guard units (Bürgerwehr) in several small Bavarian communities.[31] Without permission from the full cabinet, Auer and Timm issued a decree on December 27 creating a Munich Bürgerwehr. Dr. Rudolf Buttman, librarian of the Bavarian Landtag and a former army officer, was named commander. Sebottendorff gave permission to Buttman and the commander's close friend Lt. Heinz Kurz, a Thule initiate, to use the Society's offices for the Bürgerwehr's first meeting. Sebottendorff hinted that Buttman possessed different plans for the Bürgerwehr than Auer and Timm did.[32] The Social Democrats viewed the civil guard as a centrist counterweight to the soldiers' soviets, who increasingly assumed security responsibilities in Munich. For Buttman and other *völkisch* militants, the Bürgerwehr was a rightist Freikorps wearing Republican colors.

The Bürgerwehr met on the night of December 27 at the Four Seasons. A Lieutenant Colonel Haack told the gathering that the civil guard intended to defend Munich "against a revolt from within." With the aid of a large city map, he showed defensive positions to be manned by the Bürgerwehr. Sebottendorff offered to operate the civil guard's recruiting office on Salvatorstrasse, which had already been rented by Buttman. A spy from the Bavarian war ministry reported every detail to his superiors.[33] The remarkable speed of the Bürgerwehr's formation indicates collusion and forethought among the parties involved.

According to Sebottendorff, three hundred volunteers arrived the following morning at his recruiting station, pledging "to fight any revolt, whether from the right or the left." At noon, he closed the station and returned to the Four Seasons. The doorman informed him that the Munich Military Police, Eisner's praetorian guard, had raided Thule offices and arrested thirty-five Bürgerwehr members, including Haack and Julius Lehmann. Buttman had narrowly escaped through a rear exit. Sebottendorff claimed he met Eisner that afternoon and obtained speedy hearings for the suspects. Thirty-three civil guards were released that night; Haack and Lehmann spent several weeks at Stadelheim prison for counterrevolutionary activities. It was the end of the Bürgerwehr, but all thirty-three detainees joined the Thule Combat League.[34] Several names that would become famous in Germany were on the Bürgerwehr's application list, including Rudolf Hess, Alfred Rosenberg, and Hermann Esser (who under the Nazis became editor of the scurrilous anti-Semitic paper *Die juedische Weltpest*).[35]

Attention was drawn to Thule in the local press because of the Bürgerwehr incident. One newspaper identified the Four Seasons as "the rooms of the Germanen Orden,"[36] indicating that the Society's cover had been exposed by the end of 1918. That Thule continued its work at that location relatively unmolested by leftists until the siege of Munich in April 1919 indicates cooperation between the Society and officials of the Bavarian Socialist Republic.

The Bürgerwehr affair generated great controversy, with cries rising from the left for the resignation of Auer and Timm. Suspicion that they were conspiring to overthrow Eisner was widespread,[37] a supposition lending credence to the idea that they cooperated with the aborted Thule coup earlier that month.

Demonstrations by Munich's unemployed turned violent in the early weeks of January 1919, and the new year was greeted by other politically motivated exchanges of gunfire. One of the most curious episodes of leftist Bavaria was the so-called Sailors' Putsch on February 19. Marching at the head of six hundred seamen who had recently arrived from Wilhelmshaven, Sailor 1st Class Conrad Lotter, a member of the soldiers' soviet, led the coup. His forces seized the Landtag, the railroad station, and the telegraph office, arresting Munich's army commandant and police president. A brief shoot-out between Lotter's men and Eisner loyalists on the Bahnhofplatz took the life of a streetcar passenger. Suddenly, at the insistence of the Social Democratic ministers, his force retired, declaring that their action had been "an error." There was talk of Krupp financing for the aborted coup.[38] Lotter was arrested and spent a few months in Stadelheim prison.

Auer had brought Lotter and his sailors to Munich on the pretext of using them to maintain order. The minister was widely accused of stage-managing the affair; though his role in the putsch was never proven, the password of the rebellious sailors was "Auer." A member of the Thule Combat League, Lt. Edgar Kraus, helped Lotter engineer the coup attempt.[39] Oddly, Sebottendorff never mentioned the incident in his memoirs.

In the confused weeks that followed, Thule offices were raided again and again. One search for anti-Semitic pamphlets was led by police president Pallabene. Tipped off by an informant in the Schutzwehr, Sebottendorff claimed he struck up an understanding with the police official by the end of the encounter. The two men agreed to share information. On another occasion, a Thulist hawking a satirical paper called *Rote Hand* (*Red Hand*) was pursued by leftists to the Four Seasons, where the assailants were beaten off by Combat Leaguers wearing the red armbands of the soviets.[40] The Thule Society had not only infiltrated the ostensibly centrist Schutzwehr, but it had also made inroads into the Red Guards as well.

Long-standing radical groups stood beneath Sebottendorff's wide umbrella, taking advantage of his cover story and his financial generosity. The charismatic Sebottendorff augmented his own resources with a successful fund-raising effort among Bavaria's industrialists, nobility, landowners, and right-wing intellectuals.[41] Among the organizations meeting at Thule's offices to conspire against Eisner, and whose personnel often merged into the Society, were Julius Lehmann's Munich branch of the Pan-German League, Hans Dahn's National Liberal Party, Franz Dannehl's chapter of the Reichshammerbund, Wilhelm Rohmeder's German School Association, and the Fahrenden Gesellen (Wandering Journeymen), a youth league dedicated to long hikes and communion with nature as part of its repudiation of bourgeois society.[42] Gottfried Feder was a regular hanger-on at the Four Seasons. In Thule's offices, the poet and playwright Dietrich Eckart, to whom Hitler dedicated *Mein Kampf*, produced his mimeographed newspaper *Auf gut deutsch* (*In Plain German*) beginning in December 1918. Regular contributors to Eckart's paper included Feder and the young Baltic émigré Alfred Rosenberg, whose role as official philosopher for the Nazi Party resulted in a death sentence from the Nuremberg tribunal. Although angry at Sebottendorff for not paying for the printing of *Auf gut deutsch* (Sebottendorff claimed his resources were already spread thin by the Thule Society), Eckart also wrote for the *Münchener Beobachter* and by some accounts lavished high praise on Sebottendorff.[43] Operating from the Four Seasons in its guise as a sports paper, the *Beobachter* was the bulletin board for the activities of diverse rightist groups. The "Thule Society was a state within a state, a collection point for all reactionaries."[44] Virtually all organized anti-left civilian resistance in Munich was traceable to Thule, which provided "a sort of common leadership."[45]

The Killing of Eisner

The influence of the Thule Society's militantly anti-left agitation in the *Beobachter* and elsewhere, its campaign of "inner growth" and its role as the junction for Bavaria's *völkisch* network can be seen in the sad story of Anton Count von Arco auf Valley. After Sebottendorff rejected his application for membership in Thule on the grounds that his mother was Jewish, the despondent twenty-two-year-old—Austrian by birth but a decorated officer in the Bavarian cavalry during the war—took a drastic step to secure Thule's esteem. He decided to assassinate Eisner.[46]

Sebottendorff recalled that "there were bad rumors circulating around Munich regarding what would happen when parliament opened on 21 February: the Communists were to blow up parliament house, Eisner would not leave office, etc."[47] Eisner had failed to secure a parliamentary majority for his government in the general election of January 12, and his plans remain the subject of historical speculation.[48]

The election represented a serious defeat for Eisner's program and registered widespread discontent within Bavaria. Unemployment was high, commerce was hampered because of locomotives turned over to the Allies under the armistice agreement, and thousands of soldiers continued to collect demobilization pay from the new regime because they could find no jobs or housing. Students gathered in the Max-Joseph-Platz outside the Residenz to revile Eisner with anti-Semitic taunts based on rumors, spread by the Thule Society, that he was really a "Russian Jew" and an agent of Lenin. Faced with gathering discontent before the January election, Eisner's Independent Socialists received only 86,000 votes (2.5 percent of the ballots) and secured a mere three seats in the 180-member Landtag. Following the first Bavarian election in which women could vote, and with the voting age lowered from twenty-six to twenty-one, the assembly was dominated by the Social Democrats and the conservative Bavarian People's Party (which remains a dominant force in contemporary Bavarian politics under its post–World War II name, the Christian Social Union). More than half of those who went to the poll on Election Day had never cast a ballot before. The Communist party boycotted the race, fearing that "a bad election result would show the weak support of the party by the populace in undesirable clarity."[49]

Unable to form a coalition, Eisner wrote a farewell speech in preparation for resigning as prime minister. Regardless of parliamentary politics, Eisner was determined to remain a leading figure in the soldiers' and workers' soviets. Some believe he would have led a revolution against the parliament, albeit as bloodless as possible, in support of his socialist utopia. Eisner's dreams of transforming Bavaria would end sooner than he could imagine. He never knew that an assassin was stalking him.

Arco followed the prime minister from early morning on February 21 but could not get a clean shot at Eisner before he made for his office in the foreign ministry. Waiting in a nearby doorway with a revolver in his pocket, Arco bided his time until Eisner emerged from the ministry in his trademark black floppy hat, flanked by two secretaries and preceded by a pair of guards. The party walked briskly down the Promenadenstrasse toward the Landtag. Emerging from the shadows, Arco discharged two bullets into Eisner at point-blank range; the prime minister collapsed and died instantly. His guards returned fire, shooting Arco in the neck, mouth, and chest, in a way saving him from an angry mob that gathered instantly around the fallen leader.

News of the assassination spread rapidly. Within hours an unemployed butcher named Alois Lindner strode into the Landtag with a rifle under his coat as Auer delivered an impromptu eulogy for his political rival. Making his way quietly to the front of the chamber, Lindner shot the Social Democratic leader, seriously wounding him in the chest. In the confusion that followed more shots were fired. A People's Party delegate and a Landtag porter fell dead to the floor. The assembly dispersed in panic.

Meanwhile police brought the seriously wounded Arco to a famous Munich surgeon who saved his life. Arco was sentenced to die in 1920 for killing Eisner but Bavaria's cabinet commuted his sentence to life in prison at the fortress of Landsberg, thirty-five miles west of Munich. In 1924 he was forced to surrender the comfortable Cell No. 7 to a more infamous celebrity prisoner, Adolf Hitler, who had been sentenced to Landsberg for leading the failed Beer Hall Putsch against Bavaria's conservative government. Arco was transferred to another prison, pardoned a year later by the Bavarian government but rearrested by the Nazis in 1933. He survived the Third Reich, only to die in American-occupied Austria, struck by a passing Jeep in 1945.

Even before the revolution of November 1918, the *Beobachter* had attacked Eisner as a traitor to his fatherland.[50] After Eisner's ascent to power, Thule circulated threatening pamphlets about Bavaria's Independent Socialist leader, turning up the heat of hatred. According to Sebottendorff, Arco "wanted to show that even a half-Jew could do this deed."[51] Despite his role in inspiring Eisner's murder, Sebottendorff regarded Arco as foolish for making a martyr of a man whose political career was in sharp decline. Arco's act only galvanized the left and brought more radical elements to the fore.[52]

Sebottendorff's analysis was correct. Arco's blow against the left seemed to have backfired; in the wake of Eisner's assassination, pressure mounted for the promulgation of a Bavarian Soviet Republic. The call to arms echoed events elsewhere. Scarcely one month before Eisner's assassination, the Bolsheviks broadcast an invitation to all revolutionary parties of the world to attend the March inaugural meeting in Moscow of the Third Socialist International (Comintern), which became the global front for Soviet Communism. Meanwhile, the German Revolution continued elsewhere in the country. In January Communists seized control of Bremen, Hamburg, and other port cities, but were quickly crushed by Noske and his Freikorps. In the Ruhr, where antigovernment movements had broad support among miners and factory workers, strikes and gunfights ended only at the end of April when Social Democrats granted miners a seven-hour shift and better rations. In February and March, strikes and street fighting led by Communists and Independent Socialists broke out in Saxony and Berlin. At the time of Eisner's death and in the months that followed, it was not altogether clear that Marxist-Leninist predictions of a worldwide dictatorship of the proletariat might not soon be realized.

In Bavaria, Eisner was acclaimed more warmly in death than he had ever been in life. "Overnight Eisner became a martyr to many people who had called for his ouster, or even for his death, just a few days before."[53] During his state funeral on February 26, which used ceremony previously reserved for the Wittelsbach monarchs, the city's church bells tolled incessantly, although by some reports the priests were forced to ring them at gunpoint.[54] What was most surprising was the appearance of thousands of peasants who marched in native dress and doffed their plumed hats in honor of the slain prime minister.

The Thule Society did not mourn its late adversary. At the spot on the Promenadenstrasse where the assassination took place, Eisner's supporters had placed his portrait, garlanded with flowers. Thule activists despoiled the shrine by sprinkling it with a mixture of flour and the urine of two bitches in heat, which attracted the attention of male dogs from the surrounding neighborhood. The animals descended upon and ruined the Eisner shrine, despite valiant efforts by Red Guards to save it.[55]

The many questions that remain about the daily activities of the Thule Society and its confederates under the Eisner regime cannot be answered unless new sources surface, including diaries and letters of rightists who met at the Four Seasons, and, more important, until a thorough search is made of German archives for references to associations meeting at the hotel from late 1918 through early 1919. Without this work, we are left with a broad sketch containing many uncolored spaces.

What the sketch does show is that the Thule Society assumed the leadership role among assorted disgruntled political groups by virtue of Sebottendorff's energy and financial resources, as well as his access to a suite of offices under the convincing ruse that Thule was an antiquarian society. No longer was the group concerned exclusively with theories of racism and violence; the breakdown of social stability made possible, necessary from Thule's standpoint, the transformation of idea into action. Thule not only transmitted Ariosophy to its Nazi offspring, it also fortified the esoteric doctrine with a paramilitary spirit. During the Eisner regime and the Soviet Republic, the Society managed to publish a weekly newspaper denouncing the revolution and its leaders in the harshest language.

The First Soviet Republic

In the confused days that followed Eisner's death, the soldiers' and workers' soviets that sprang into existence with the November Revolution called a three-day general strike to mourn his murder. The cry of "Avenge Eisner!" was on the lips of street corner agitators. Even so, the vengeance of Bavaria's Independent Socialists proved to be mild. An attorney named Eller and a party of twenty-five Red Guards rousted from bed one of the leaders of December's abortive Bad Aibling coup, Lieutenant Sedlmeier. Rather than shoot him, they forced the Thulist, at gunpoint, to read aloud an apology that had been written for him. "I am asking for forgiveness for insulting the Prime Minister, and I regret that it was a member of the officers corps who murdered him," he recited.[56]

For several weeks after the assassination Bavaria functioned without an executive authority. The democratically elected Landtag was unimpressed by the ability of the soldiers' and workers' soviets to govern and alarmed by their far left agenda. The Landtag attempted to preempt the birth of a Soviet Republic by empowering a Social Democrat, the schoolteacher Johannes Hoffmann, to form a cabinet on March 17, 1919. Prime Minister Hoffmann may have been a source of discomfort to Bavaria's conservative Roman Catholic leadership but was in any case preferable to the more radical alternative offered by the soviets, whose supporters were electrified at the news of the proclamation of a Hungarian Soviet Republic on March 21 under the Bolshevik Bela Kun. Once again, it appeared that history was racing toward the communist order envisioned by Marx and propagated by Lenin.

The left radicals of Munich decided to speed the course of history. Despite an abnormal cold wave and twenty inches of snow on the ground, a meeting took place on the night of April 6 that pushed events to their next stage. Under the chairmanship of Ernst Niekisch (head of Munich's Central Workers' Soviet), a group of cafe intellectuals, soviet delegates, trade unionists, Independent Socialists, and Social Democrats convened in the queen's bedchamber of the Wittelsbach palace. The meeting declared itself a constituent assembly with the authority to devise a new constitution for Bavaria on the soviet model.

Hoffmann and his ministers slipped out of Munich, but arranged for the following leaflet to be airdropped over the city as a declaration of their intent to hold onto power:

> The regime of the Bavarian Free State has not resigned—it has transferred its seat from Munich. The regime is and will remain the single possessor of power in Bavaria and is alone qualified to release legal regulations and to issue orders.
>
> —Signed by Hoffmann in Nuremberg 7 April 1919[57]

A few days later Hoffmann was safely ensconced in the city hall of Bamberg in northern Bavaria. After easily putting down pro-soviet demonstrations in Würzburg, Furth, Ingolstadt, Regensburg, and Schweinfurt, most of Bavaria outside the capital city and a triangle bounded by Augsburg, Garmisch, and Rosenheim was securely in his hands.

Politics followed a different line inside Munich. By morning of April 7, the more bohemian and utopian elements at the Wittelsbach palace meeting had organized themselves as the government of the first Bavarian Soviet Republic. In a deliberate affront to the Roman Catholic Church, the traditional guiding light for Bavaria's schools, the Jewish Shakespeare scholar and literary translator Gustav Landauer was elected people's deputy for education. Landauer promptly declared Munich University, whose students openly embraced Arco as a hero, open to any eighteen-year-old regardless of previous schooling. He also proclaimed the work of American poet Walt Whitman as the cornerstone of his educational program.

The new regime vested authority over economic affairs in an unlikely duo, the free enterprise advocate Silvio Gesell and the Marxist Otto Neurath. The transportation ministry went to an auto mechanic, Georg Paulukun, and the war ministry to a waiter. The new housing commissar would soon decree that living rooms and bedrooms be located above the kitchen in all residences. The eccentric Dr. Franz Lipp became people's deputy for foreign affairs, apparently because "he owned a gray frock coat and sported a well-tended beard of aristocratic cut."[58] Within days, Lipp declared war on Switzerland for ignoring his request for foreign aid. Lenin was undoubtedly dismayed by Lipp's cable accusing Hoffmann of stealing the key to the washroom in the foreign ministry before departing to Bamberg.

The comic-opera regime of the first Bavarian Soviet Republic was headed for a short time by Niekisch. After becoming convinced that the project was doomed, he resigned and handed over authority to a figure considered by some as an exemplar of the period's German literature. His successor was the romantic twenty-six-year-old poet Ernst Toller, an idealist described as having "an unfeigned passion for social justice" but "an actor's flair for dramatizing himself, a consciousness of the effect he was able to produce with his melodious voice and his writer's gift for the telling phrase."[59] Even more so than Eisner's, Toller's regime "reflected the Bohemian and intellectual life of Schwabing, the artists' quarter in Munich, rather than the working people of Bavaria."[60] Toller's program was at least as concerned with encouraging the development of new art forms as it was in restructuring the social order:

> Thus one step after another was taken to make the new government offensive to thousands of Bavarians. Having decisively rejected the Eisner regime as foreign and extreme, Bavaria was now to be confronted with a new one even more radical and just as dominated by outsiders and upstarts.[61]

The German Communist Party wanted no truck with Toller's regime, which it rejected as the work of childish dilettantes. The Communist rebuff of Toller mirrored the bitter split across the world between socialists of the Second International, who were more inclined to democratic reform, and those of the nascent Third International (Comintern), who obeyed the party line as established in Moscow. Bavaria's Communists were led by the Russian-born Eugen Levine, a dashing figure who had earlier been sent to Moscow by Rosa Luxemburg as a delegate to the first Comintern congress. Unable to complete the difficult journey, Levine was dispatched in March by the party's Berlin headquarters to take charge of the situation in Munich. Levine purged five of the seven members of the Bavarian Communist central committee and regrouped the local party into a tightly organized three-thousand-member body.[62] He decried the first Bavarian Soviet Republic as a "sham soviet" in his newspaper, the *Red Banner*, despite the regime's insistence that it was a dictatorship of the proletariat and its call for the establishment of a Red Army and a Revolutionary Court. Social Democrats involved in the Soviet Republic intrigued against it, even as their party comrades in Bamberg continued to insist that they constituted Bavaria's only legitimate government. Bamberg became the rallying point for all anti-soviet activists, including the Thule Society.

At this time an organization founded by Sebottendorff at Thule's crossroads meeting on November 10, 1918, became prominent.[63] The Society's paramilitary arm, the Thule Combat League (Kampfbund), may have failed in its attempts on Eisner but would play an active role in undermining the Soviet government. At Hoffman's commission, Sebottendorff founded a second paramilitary group, the Freikorps Oberland, a force that later would put down workers' insurrections, fend off Polish incursions into German territory, and march with Hitler in his unsuccessful bid for power on the streets of Munich in 1923.

7

The Battle for Munich

I know of a savage family who hold nothing sacred that others honor. Everyone hates them, as I do. I was called to vengeance to make amends for family blood. I came too late and, now returning home, the tracks of the villain who fled I discover in my own house.

—Richard Wagner, *Die Walküre*

Although it had been forced from Munich to humbler offices in Bamberg city hall, the Hoffmann administration governed all the cities of northern Bavaria and most of the state's countryside. Sporadically, his forces closed rail links to Munich with the goal of starving out the Reds, but these measures only increased the hardship of Munich's residents. Wiring his Social Democratic party comrades in Bamberg, Reich president Friedrich Ebert demanded that Hoffmann and his military affairs minister, Ernst Schneppenhorst, mount a military expedition to restore order in Munich:

> I consider it necessary that the restoration of the former condition in Bavaria be accomplished as soon as possible. . . . If the economic measures which you have in prospect do not succeed in short order, a military procedure seems to be the only possible solution. Experience in other places has taught that the quicker and more thoroughly this is accomplished, the less resistance and bloodshed are to be expected.[1]

Ebert was reacting to the French threat of sending its occupation troops deeper into the Reich, and cutting off much-needed food supplies, if lawlessness was not quickly curbed. However, intervention by the Reich was a prospect Hoffmann hoped to avoid or at least minimize. By this time Berlin could muster forces sufficient to crush the Soviet Republic, but Bavarians had to be prominent in any march on Munich. Bavaria's particularist sentiments allowed for nothing less. To accomplish this, Hoffmann was forced to solicit assistance from groups inimical to his Social Democratic program. It seemed that the only battle-hardened Bavarians not aligned with the far left were encamped on the far right. Hoffmann's dilemma, of being forced by Berlin to act against the Munich soviets but without Berlin playing too prominent a role, enhanced the existing situation in which Ariosophist and Social Democrat could work in common cause against the Marxist foe. Although Schneppenhorst had recently issued a decree banning the recruitment of paramilitary "volunteer groups" on penalty of a year in prison and a five-hundred-mark fine,[2] the Hoffmann regime discovered that it needed every volunteer it could muster. On April 19 Hoffmann's subordinates declared from Bamberg:

> The legitimate Government has called for the establishment of Freikorps. We are asking the clergy to promote this cause not only from the pulpit but also in their house calls, so that as many as possible among the populace might follow the call to arms. It is of urgency that we stand together, for danger looms. Within the shortest timeframe we must achieve the liberation of the capital city, so that a real democratic government can be established.[3]

The *Beobachter* stepped up its lurid tabloid attacks on the left, calling Bavarian Communist leader Max Levien a syphilitic and accusing Kurt Eisner's widow of having an affair with Gustav Landauer, a minister of the first Bavarian Soviet Republic.[4] An advertisement in the paper for the Schutz-und-Trutzbund, a national coalition of *völkisch* groups numbering Thule as one of its members, exemplifies the *Beobachter*'s linkage of Jews with Bolshevism and social decline:

> Arrest the Jews, then there will be peace in the land! Jews incite Spartacism! Jews incite people! Jews push to the top everywhere! Jews prevent Germans from understanding each other! Therefore, let's get rid of the Jewish troublemakers and instigators![5]

The Thule Society added more than fighting words to the fray. One of its members, Friedrich Knauf, an official of the Bavarian state railway, arrived at Bamberg on April 10 with a message for Hoffmann from Sebottendorff and a certain Werner von Heimburg:

> The citizenry of Munich is willing to take part in the struggle for freedom. Despite the dangers looming over every individual at this time, thousands of people have agreed, in conjunction with clubs and associations, to join the Citizens Council of the City of Munich, and shall go on to strike as soon as loyal troops have reached the gates of the city, in order to hinder the Red Army's defense.
>
> In addition, armed youth groups from Munich will assemble at Eching to form a Munich Battalion. We request that rifles and machine guns, hand grenades and other supplies be brought to the house of farmer Angermeier in care of Lieutenant Bauer. We ask that the bearer of this letter be given explicit information of any of your pertinent plans, so that cooperation can be achieved. We regard you, Prime Minister, with utmost respect and confidence.[6]

Heimburg belonged to the "Citizens Council of the City of Munich," which claimed to speak for a broad segment of the capital's population,[7] and was an initiate of the Thule Society.[8] Thus, "in the struggle against the Soviet Republic, the Hoffmann government joined forces with the Thule Society, a forerunner of fascism."[9] A Combat League contingent under Captain Römer was already stationed at Eching, in alliance with local peasants, as a civil guard.[10] Eching was only one of the league's "agitation centers" in outlying communities not far from Munich. Others were located in Treuchtlingen and Eichstaett.[11]

At the time the Soviet Republic was proclaimed, the Combat League was divided in two detachments, operating separately and unaware of the other. The first detachment, including Eching and the other agitation centers, was commanded by 1st Lt. Heinz Kurz, who went on to earn a doctorate in philosophy before joining the SS as an officer. It was primarily a recruiting depot for Freikorps Epp,[12] whose commander, Col. Franz Ritter von Epp (1868–1946), was a grim-visaged, steel-helmeted figure who had formerly served with the Bavarian Life Guards. Epp led the most prominent of the Bavarian Freikorps, whose main depot was the former army training grounds at Ohrdruf in neighboring Thuringia. Freikorps Epp was founded in January 1919 at the behest of Ebert's war minister, Gustav Noske. Initially numbering seven hundred men, Freikorps Epp became the spearhead of Hoffmann's military forces. Epp recruited several members of Thule, including Hans Frank and Rudolf Hess, both destined for prominence in the Nazi movement. Epp later joined with the Nazis (1928) and was appointed governor of Bavaria after 1933.[13]

The Combat League's second detachment acted as Thule's self-styled "intelligence service." It was commanded by Lt. Edgar Kraus, the seventeen-year-old son of Augsburg's state prosecutor and a resourceful leader despite his youth. According to Sebottendorff, the commander of the Bavarian Red cavalry was an agent of this service, and virtually every Soviet unit and committee was infiltrated by Kraus's men. Thule operatives usually acted as stenographers and clerks. Every evening the spies brought their reports to the Four Seasons, where the information was correlated and dispatched to Bamberg via Augsburg on the night train. Urgent information was telephoned to Bamberg. It would not occur to the Reds to sever or monitor phone lines until after the failed Palm Sunday Putsch. Kraus's detachment also waged a campaign of sabotage against the Reds by disabling automobiles and planes at the Schleissheim airfield.[14] Sebottendorff admitted that some of his own agents were susceptible to the lure of leftist ideology, explaining that his "whole power of persuasion was often necessary" to keep them from straying.[15] It was an acknowledgment that many Germans, disoriented by recent events and the collapse of political and economic stability, were willing to lend one ear to the far left and the other to the far right if either provided compelling explanations for the bitter present and the promise of a better future. Sebottendorff also claimed that his intelligence service helped spirit out of Munich the gold reserves at the Reichsbank and the Prussian legation, but the assertion cannot be confirmed.[16]

The Palm Sunday Putsch

On April 13, the Schutzwehr, an ostensibly pro-Republic Freikorps commanded by Alfred Seiffertitz, a supporter of the Thule Society, staged the Palm Sunday Putsch in a bid to overthrow the Soviet regime from within Munich. The Schutzwehr broke into the former royal Residenz before dawn and arrested several members of the Central Soviet. Among those rounded up were the eccentric Foreign Commissar Lipp and Erich Mühsam, a cabaret writer and essayist who had been part of the first Bavarian Soviet Republic's leadership and would later die in a Nazi concentration camp. The coup was supported by Hoffmann and his comrade-in-arms, Schneppenhorst.

As boss of the Nuremberg lumbermen's union, Schneppenhorst had become the Social Democrats' political commissar to the 3rd Bavarian Army Corps, headquartered at Nuremberg, following the collapse of Imperial Germany. During the week after Eisner's assassination, Schneppenhorst arranged for thousands of leaflets to be scattered over Munich from airplanes, promising that the 3rd Corps would "reject the domination of Dr. Levien and his armed supporters." He was rewarded for his enterprise by being named military affairs minister in Hoffmann's cabinet on March 18. Exemplifying the murkiness of postwar Bavaria, Schneppenhorst supported the proclamation of the Bavarian Soviet Republic on April 6. Was he an agent provocateur? One authority believes that "Schneppenhorst himself did not have a clear idea of what he was doing."[17]

The Palm Sunday plan called for Schneppenhorst and his men to liberate Munich once Seiffertitz's Schutzwehr occupied key positions. Schneppenhorst gathered six hundred infantry, cavalry, and artillery for the operation at Ingolstadt, a city on the Danube thirty miles north of Munich.[18] The propaganda aspect of the putsch was well planned. In the days before Palm Sunday, airplanes from Bamberg showered Munich with the following leaflet, which Sebottendorff claimed the Thule Society reprinted and distributed throughout the city:

> People of Munich!
>
> The whole state [of Bavaria] is disgusted over the tyranny in Munich. Foreigners and fantasts rule there. You are confused and discouraged. Come to your senses and take courage!
>
> The whole state is rising up. The whole of northern Bavaria is behind the Hoffmann-Segitz government. From hour to hour the situation is improving. Last Wednesday a Communist putsch in Wurzburg was completely beaten down, hostages were freed and the Spartacist ringleaders from Munich, Sauber and Hagemeister, were arrested with their whole entourage.
>
> The workers, except for those who are crazy, will enthusiastically support us in the fight against Bolshevism. The peasants throughout the countryside are standing up to protect their socialist government. Our soldiers are forcefully clearing out the nests of anarchists.
>
> In southern Bavaria the movement is stirring. The Swabian and old Bavarian peasants are mobilizing against the pigsty in Munich. The claim that Freikorps Epp is on its way to Bamberg to help topple the [Munich soviet] government is a great lie. Bavaria does not need help from outside.
>
> People of Munich, how long will you stand by and watch? Rise up! Down with the tyrants! Long live the Free State of Bavaria! Long live the government of Hoffmann-Segitz!
>
> Bamberg, 10 April 1919
> The Social Democratic Party[19]

The flyer was truthful except for the reference to Freikorps Epp, which would soon march south to help the Bamberg regime topple the Bavarian Soviet Republic. Despite its Bavarian commander, the unit was a convenient symbol of a Freikorps organized under the auspices of Berlin. For Hoffmann, it was politically necessary at every turn to emphasize the Bavarian character of his bid to regain control of Munich.

By the time Munich's citizens rose from bed on Palm Sunday, posters had been plastered across the city, grossly overstating the strength of Seiffertitz's position:

> Workers and Soldiers!
>
> The entire garrison in conjunction with comrades who are concerned for the welfare of the proletariat has deposed the Zentralrat [Central Soviet] during the night.
>
> Ambitious alien agitators who only pursue selfish aims have misled us. Our fate has been entrusted to men like Lipp. . . . Today Munich stands alone cut off from the region. We need to be saved. Therefore support the legitimate government which will procure peace, work and bread. Food trains are standing by, some distance from the capital. Safeguard yourselves against the reaction by supporting the Socialist regime.
>
> Munich, 13 April 1919
> The entire garrison of Munich[20]

Seiffertitz's claim to represent the Munich garrison was spurious. He could count only on support of Thule Combat League units within the city. An alleged eyewitness account, an anonymous letter supposedly written by Seiffertitz himself, was critical of Thule's contributions to the coup. It claimed that only a dozen Thulists arrived at the barricades. One of them was a captain "in gala uniform! Patent leather riding boots, riding whip, monocle!" [21] Sebottendorff claimed that his forces returned to headquarters after seeing the hopelessness of the situation, realizing that the loyalty of the Munich garrison to the Reds (or at least their indifference to the Whites) and the failure of Schneppenhorst's force to advance doomed the adventure. Schneppenhorst claimed his trucks were stuck in the April mud. Others murmured that his plans had been sabotaged.[22]

Many soviet officials escaped arrest, warned by frantic phone calls from the wife of Erich Mühsam. After a five-hour gun battle, which began in the Marienplatz where the Schutzwehr was opposed by a crowd of armed workers, revolutionary sailors, and the pro-Red 1st Infantry Regiment, the Schutzwehr retreated to the railroad station. Enduring shelling by Red mortars, the counterrevolutionaries fled by train before the end of the night to Bamberg, taking with them some twenty officials arrested that morning. The Palm Sunday Putsch claimed more than twenty deaths and a hundred injuries.[23]

Although the 1st Infantry fought with the Reds, other units of the Munich garrison, commanded by soldiers' soviets since Eisner's revolution in November, sat out the fight. By one account a loud debate over whether to join the fray at the barracks of the 2nd Infantry Regiment ended when Corporal Hitler mounted a chair and shouted, "Those who say we should remain neutral are right! After all, we're no pack of Revolutionary Guards for a bunch of Jews from who knows where!"[24] Hitler himself never mentioned the incident, possibly because he addressed his unit as an elected member of the soldiers' soviet, and wrote nothing about this period of his life beyond the following two sentences: "In the course of the new revolution of the Councils [Soviets] I for the first time acted in such a way as to arouse the disapproval of the Central Council. Early in the morning of April 27, 1919, I was to be arrested, but, faced with my leveled carbine, the three scoundrels [Red Guards] lacked the necessary courage and marched off as they had come." [25] If true, Hitler was to have been taken in the wave of arrests following the April 26 raid by Reds on the Four Seasons, which netted the Thule Society's membership list and the arrest of the seven initiates executed at Luitpold Gymnasium on April 30.[26]

Hitler's account does capture the irresolution of many Red Guards in the final days before the fall of Munich. The machinist Anton Drexler, who under the auspices of the Thule Society organized the Political Workers' Circle, the nucleus of the Nazi Party, was also on a list of suspects to be arrested. Drexler was spared when a Communist coworker at his railroad workshop told Red Guards that the frail, nearsighted man "can't shoot and he is a bit touched in the head as well."[27] Both the cofounder of the Nazi Party and its future leader may have narrowly escaped arrest and execution in the waning hours of Red rule in Munich.

Raising Arms and Men

Some authorities maintain that Sebottendorff arrived in Bamberg on April 16 begging permission to found a new Freikorps from elements of the Combat League and fresh volunteers.[28] Sebottendorff asserted that the Hoffmann regime, acting "through a well-known attorney in Augsburg," requested him to expand the Combat League into a force capable of helping retake Munich. Sebottendorff claimed that he went to Augsburg to negotiate with the legitimate government through the attorney, and narrowly escaped arrest by Red sailors at his lodgings at the Golden Lamb Inn.[29] If the Red sailors were colorful embroidery, the essentials of his story ring true.

Sebottendorff received authorization on April 19 to found a new paramilitary group:

> By order of the Cabinet and the State Soldiers Soviet, Rudolf von Sebottendorff receives permission to establish, at Treuchtlingen, Freikorps Oberland.
> State Soldiers Soviet Minister for Military Affairs
>
> Signed—Simon
> Signed—Schneppenhorst[30]

Hoffmann needed manpower. The authorization was given to Sebottendorff one day after White Guards were defeated at Dachau by Reds on April 16. Money for the endeavor was raised from Munich citizens by Sebottendorff's protégé Werner von Heimburg and a non-Thulist, Johann-Erasmus Freiherr von Malsen-Ponickau. Weapons were purchased in the city from black-marketeering Red Guards. Rudolf Hess, a much-wounded and decorated infantryman who had ended the war as a second lieutenant with a fighter squadron on the western front, was introduced to the Combat League through the Thulist Max Hofweber. Hess met Hofweber in flight school and worked for him after the war as a salesman for Münchener Wohnkunst, a firm manufacturing rustic furniture. Hess was "one of the most successful procurers of weapons for Thule," storing them at the Four Seasons and in the Wohnkunst offices. The ambitious future deputy führer of the Third Reich also recruited students and ex-officers for the Freikorps Oberland and would be wounded in the leg during the assault on Munich in May 1919.[31] Combat League members Karl Witzgall and Karl Stecher, both university students, smuggled rifles, pistols, grenades, and ammunition from Munich to agitation centers in outlying Bavaria.[32]

To facilitate their departure from Munich, Thule gave its Freikorps volunteers free train tickets (issued by the transportation minister in Bamberg) and soviet travel passes legitimized by rubber stamps purchased from dishonest Red Guards by Thule's intelligence service. "Equally sloppy was the way in which the Communist cells handled membership cards." Sebottendorff claimed that every Combat Leaguer was also a card-carrying member of the Spartacist League.[33] Dubious loyalty as much as cowardice may explain the virtual disappearance of many Red Guard units when the Whites finally marched into Munich on May Day.[34] Meanwhile, Sebottendorff escaped from Munich just ahead of orders for his arrest by the soviet regime by impersonating a railroad official called Kallenbach. He fled with his putative mistress, Kathe Bierbaumer (who told the Red Guards that she was a Hungarian Communist), and Adelheid Baroness von Mikusch, an initiate of the Thule Society.[35]

On April 20, the ink barely dry on his day-old authorization from Bamberg, Sebottendorff presented his orders at the headquarters of 3rd Army Corps in Nuremberg, and received arms and equipment for Freikorps Oberland.[36] During the days before his arrival in Nuremberg, several members of the Combat League departed from Munich to Oberland's encampment at Eichstaett, a small town forty miles northwest of Munich. Thulists continued to slip out of the capital by presenting false papers identifying them as railroad employees.[37]

The leader of the Combat League's Eching detachment, Lieutenant Kurz, suggested Maj. Ritter von Bekh, a Bavarian army veteran, as Oberland's field commander. By agreement with 3rd Corps Command on April 22, Bekh took charge of the Freikorps' military affairs and arrived at Eichstaett on April 25. At its peak strength Freikorps Oberland numbered 120 officers, 180 noncommissioned officers, and 1,350 men, organized into five infantry companies, two machine-gun companies, one artillery battery, one "pioneer" (combat engineer) company, one supply company, and one recruiting depot.[38] On April 29, Oberland was ordered by Maj. Gen. Arnold Ritter von Möhl, Hoffmann's adjutant, to proceed by train to Freising, an assembly point for the march on Munich. Only the supply depot and recruiting office remained at Eichstaett.[39] From Sebottendorff's suite at Nuremberg's Hotel Fürstenhof, Oberland

Central organized logistics, supplies, and even publicity for the advancing Freikorps Oberland as well as a smaller group, Freikorps Chiemgau.[40]

The Palm Sunday Putsch was Hoffmann's last chance to overthrow the soviets internally without help from Berlin. The destruction of the Soviet Republic was left to the expeditionary force gathering in northern Bavaria. Reich war minister Noske promised 20,000 troops but finally dispatched only 7,500–12,000 men from northern Germany,[41] including the notorious Guards Cavalry and the dreaded 2nd Marine Brigade under Lt. Cdr. Hermann Ehrhardt.[42] The Ehrhardt Brigade would be prominent in the farcical Kapp Putsch (March 1920), marching into Berlin with swastikas painted on its steel helmets. In his chronicle of the Freikorps movement, British historian Nigel H. Jones wrote, "Indeed, it was the Ehrhardt Brigade that first brought the evil symbol of the crooked cross, adopted by Hitler as his emblem, to the notice of the world."[43] One wonders if Ehrhardt's men embraced the swastika while marching in Bavaria alongside Thulist contingents.

The Bavarian Freikorps and Volkswehr totaled 22,000 men and were supported by the 3,750-member Wurttemberg Freikorps. Bavarians provided the most numerous and visually prominent contingents, both for their position at the front of the assault and their distinctive dress, which was mixed with government-issue gray uniforms. Ritter von Möhl's troops, Freikorps Epp, Freikorps Oberland, and other, smaller formations would eventually enclose Munich in a ring of plumed hats, leather britches, knee stockings, and double-breasted jerkins.[44] Their archaic costumes contrasted colorfully to the drab modernism of their proletarian enemies. Despite the predominance of Bavarians in the expedition, Hoffmann was forced to invest supreme command in the hands of Noske's delegate, a seasoned Prussian officer, Maj. Gen. Burghard von Oven.

The Second Soviet Republic

The Palm Sunday Putsch spelled the end of the first Bavarian Soviet Republic, but not according to Hoffmann's plan. As with Arco's assassination of Eisner, this action from the right only pushed the situation further to the left. The sound of gunfire from the putsch had barely ceased on April 13 when a gang of "tough young Communists, mostly of

Russian-Jewish origin, took advantage of the situation to set themselves up as a second Soviet dictatorship."[45] They were able to do this because it was their men who took the lead in defeating Hoffmann's forces on Palm Sunday. Already impatient with the shenanigans of the first Soviet Republic, they were determined to establish a dictatorship of the proletariat by Lenin's rulebook.

Led by Bavaria's Communist Party chairman Eugen Levine, "a young man of startling and tempestuous energy,"[46] the second Bavarian Soviet Socialist Republic cast itself as a cold, diamond-hard facet of the worldwide Communist revolution. Impatient to fulfill the program of Marx and Lenin, it declared war against the bourgeoisie and took immediate steps to reduce middle-class life to misery. Decrees were issued for the confiscation of private and business bank accounts. An indefinite general strike, decreed on April 13 to cow the bourgeoisie, also succeeded in deepening Munich's economic quagmire. Armed patrols fanned out through the city, searching homes and businesses for guns, money, and food, and carting off whatever took their fancy. Stadelheim, where Eisner had once been confined for his political activities, was now filled with aristocratic and middle-class prisoners. The Red Guards gave citizens twelve hours to turn in their guns with death as the penalty for delay.[47] The streets of Munich were increasingly empty by day, except for knots of grim, armed workmen wearing red armbands, and trucks bristling with Red soldiers speeding from one raid to the next. Between sundown and sunrise, a curfew was enforced by summary shootings.

Although it was said that Levine was the most intelligent member of the Bavarian Communist Party's ruling cadre, "his closest lieutenants were, in their own way, almost as improbably cast for the roles assigned to them as their predecessors" under Eisner and Toller.[48] Levine's adjutants included Towia Axelrod, a Russian Jew who had accompanied Lenin in Petrograd before being dispatched to Germany as part of Joffe's revolutionary embassy, and Max Levien, a Russian-born Jew and naturalized German citizen who had assisted Lenin in his Zurich exile. Levien lent the Munich enterprise a dash of Bolshevik élan by going about in riding boots, spurs, and tunics of Russian cut. The fanatical Levien repeatedly called on the proletariat to die for the revolution and threatened death to any member of the bourgeoisie who stood in the way of his Communist utopia. One of his plans was to kidnap the former King Ludwig III and drag him back to Munich as a hostage. History would deny him the time to achieve that project, yet his eagerness to use hostages as a tool of state terror provides part of the context for the detention and execution of the seven Thule members at Luitpold Gymnasium. So widespread was the seizure or threatened seizure of middle-class citizens that in the final weeks of April the city's children began to play "Reds and Whites," a game of hostage-taking.[49] Because Bavaria's Communist leaders had touched the hand of Lenin, or at least had been born in his country, some leftists viewed them with awe and deference. Through them they could bask in the reflection of the Bolshevik Revolution's lurid glow.

Munich's municipal police was disbanded and replaced by a workers' Red Guard. Named as its commander was Rudolf Egelhofer, a twenty-three-year-old sailor who had taken part in the Kiel mutiny and had distinguished himself by leading the April 13 assault on the Munich railroad station, which broke the Palm Sunday Putsch. Egelhofer was one of the only native Germans among the Soviet Republic's leadership. Installed in the War Ministry, he "surrounded himself with a numerous and swaggering bodyguard, and was soon notorious for his lordly style of living in public and private."[50]

The Red Guard was thought to number as many as twenty thousand men, though it is likely that more than half of its volunteers joined for the generous allotments of food and money and never raised a gun in defense of the revolution. By the time the battle for Munich began in earnest, a great many Red Guards had disappeared. They were in any event an undisciplined mob, whose units often elected their own commanders. Most of the Red Guards were recruited from workers at the Krupp and Maffei plants, which had largely stood idle since the end of the war. By April forty-five thousand men were listed as unemployed in Munich. Many Russian prisoners of war, men with a destitute present and no certain future, also enlisted in the Red Guards.[51]

One of the new regime's first acts was to arrest Ernst Toller, but he was quickly released because of his genuine popularity among the workers, whose support Levine needed and in whose name he claimed to govern.

Because of Toller's wartime service and despite his pacifist ideals, the poet-politician was named a Red Guard commander after his pardon. Riding to the front on a borrowed horse, the quixotic Toller met the Thule Combat League on April 16 at Dachau, then an obscure market town eleven miles north-by-northwest of Munich. Faced down more by an irascible mob of local women than by the advancing Red Guards, the Thule forces retreated after an exchange of gunfire. One of their number was captured and imprisoned in the Dachau firehouse, but he managed to escape his captors and flee on a stolen bicycle.[52] Toller took Dachau and Freising, ten miles northeast of Dachau, with casualties numbering only a few wounded. On principle Toller ignored orders from the bloodthirsty Egelhofer to shell Dachau and shoot all captured White officers. After a victory parade through the streets of Munich, complete with a short procession of prisoners from the recent engagements, Levine promptly rearrested the "liberator of Dachau" for disobedience. In any event Dachau and Freising would soon slip from Red hands into the grasp of the advancing Freikorps.

The new regime was broke financially as well as administratively. The new finance commissar, a twenty-five-year-old former bank clerk called Emil Männer, tried to cope with a cash shortage caused in part when the Munich branch of the Reichsbank removed all stocks of cash and printing plates for bank notes. In order to pay the swelling ranks of Red Guards, he ordered the confiscation of all bank accounts and safety deposit boxes. After netting only fifty thousand marks from these actions, the regime ordered a paper firm in Dachau to print several million marks on behalf of the Bavarian State Bank in order to maintain the illusion of solvency.[53]

Food became scarce in Munich and coal stocks were nearly exhausted at a time of abnormally cold weather. Red Guards continued to enter homes and plunder middle-class pantries for food. In many cases official confiscation turned into blatant theft, and what was confiscated was used to provision the Red Guards. The benefits of socialist expropriation seldom trickled down to the masses. Posters exhorted farmers: "Everyone knows that historical development necessarily leads to the Soviet system—every reasonable man will accommodate himself to it." But appeals to Marx's law of historical inevitability were greeted coldly by peasants, who aided Hoffmann's economic blockade of Munich. By the end of April, with coal stocks dwindling, bakeries and breweries would be forced to close within days if relief did not arrive. Eugen Levine was defiant in the face of starvation:

> What does it matter if for a few weeks less milk reaches Munich. Most of it goes to the children of the bourgeoisie anyway. We are not interested in keeping them alive. No harm if they die—they'd only grow into enemies of the proletariat.[54]

Fascinated by the potential of airborne propaganda, Hoffmann and Schneppenhorst dropped yet another payload of leaflets over the city. The broadside advised residents to "avoid streets and squares. The government will break all resistance pitilessly."[55]

In this hostile environment, the Thule Society continued to recruit officers and students for the Freikorps and acted as a fifth column for the Bamberg administration. During the period of April 18–26, the day of the Red raid on Thule's offices at the Four Seasons, five hundred free railroad tickets were distributed by Thule to Freikorps volunteers.[56]

Raiding the Thule Society

Although the Thule Society's offices had been the subject of police raids and newspaper publicity since December, Soviet authorities seemed unaware of the extent of the counterrevolutionary hubbub at the Four Seasons until tipped off by a hotel clerk. The owners of the hotel, the brothers Walterspiel, were interrogated at the war ministry by Levien, who forced them to divulge Sebottendorff's name. The brothers were released the same day they were taken captive, at the request of the Four Seasons' workers' soviet. Armed with a floor plan of Thule's rooms, three plainclothesmen from the Munich Military Police searched the Thule offices on April 26, discovering large quantities of incriminating material, including Germanenorden and Thule Society membership rosters, notes on Red Guards positions around Munich, rubber stamps bearing the signature of their commander Egelhofer and his adjutant Karpf, the seal of Munich's military commandant, anti-Semitic material, and weapons.[57] A detachment of Red sailors sent to guard the offices was ordered to arrest anyone suspicious.[58]

Learning of the raid almost immediately, Thule's spy network warned members of the Society to lie low.[59] Seven Thulists were soon arrested, however, on suspicion of counterrevolutionary activity. At least two of the aristocratic captives, Heila, Countess von Westarp and Gustav Franz Maria, Prince von Thurn und Taxis relied on past experience that had taught them that nothing could hurt them.

The military police conducted its investigation into the Thule Society with remarkable professionalism. Information was gathered from hotel employees, neighbors, and friends of the suspects before arrests were made. Westarp, Thule's secretary, was seized at the Four Seasons, briefly questioned, and released on April 26. She was arrested again at six o'clock that evening in her apartment on Nymphenburger Strasse, released, and rearrested two hours later.[60]

Thurn und Taxis, a member of Bavaria's wealthiest family and relative of several royal houses, had been dispatched to Munich by Sebottendorff after conferring with him at Oberland Central. Revolutionary upheaval disrupted train service, nearly sparing the prince death, but he proceeded against all difficulty and arrived in Munich by rail on April 26.[61] Thurn und Taxis was entrusted with safeguarding Sebottendorff's secret papers, deposited in a pair of wooden chests with the RvS monogram. He was arrested at the Park Hotel before he could begin his mission but was released,[62] probably through the good offices of Franz Cronauer. Chairman of the Revolutionary Tribunal and possibly a Thule agent, Cronauer granted him a safe conduct pass. Early the next morning Cronauer begged Thurn und Taxis to change his address immediately, for in the deteriorating environment he could no longer guarantee the prince's safety. When Thurn und Taxis was arrested later that morning, Cronauer tried to bring the prince before his tribunal, but other officials, suspecting collusion, denied the request.[63]

On the evening of April 27, Ernst Toller, who by then had been released from captivity a second time by the Communist regime, also tried but failed to gain the prince's freedom. Among other charges, Thurn und Taxis was accused of possessing a counterfeit travel pass and, by one account, trying to buy his release from the Red Guards with twenty thousand marks.[64]

Of the five other arrested Thulists, two were caught haphazardly, and three as a result of investigations based on material discovered at the Four Seasons. Franz Carl Freiherr von Teuchert (1900–1919), captured by Spartacists on April 28 near Neufahrn, was on a reconnaissance mission in his own car for Freikorps Regensburg, a battalion-sized unit advancing on Munich.[65] Because his name was on Thule's membership list, he was taken to Luitpold Gymnasium and confined with the other Thulists. The art instructor Walter Deicke (1892–1919) was arrested by Red sailors as he tried to enter Thule's offices on the evening of April 26. Remarkably, he was released. By one account he was rearrested outside his house a few hours later, but according to Sebottendorff, he was captured in Walter Nauhaus's apartment.[66] The railroad official Anton Daumenlang (1870–1919), head of Thule's genealogy and heraldry circle, was arrested in his apartment on the same date. Also taken that night in their homes were Sebottendorff's close associate, the sculptor Nauhaus (1892–1919), and the painter and musician Friedrich Wilhelm Freiherr von Seidlitz (1892–1919).

The efficiency of the Thule Society, and the rapidly unraveling morale of its adversaries, can be measured by the relatively small number of members caught in the Red dragnet. Thulists Arthur Griehl and Capt. Friedrich Utsch were also arrested and released on April 26 but evaded recapture. Others slipped away through good fortune. Dietrich Eckart and Friedrich Knauff arrived by car at the Four Seasons that same day but immediately sped away, being warned "by a sixth sense." A young woman of the Thule Society who walked into the aftermath of the raid persuaded Red Guards that she had landed on the wrong floor and was looking for the laundry room.[67]

The arrest of the seven members of the Thule Society was trumpeted on posters throughout the city on April 27:

> REACTIONARY THIEVES AND PLUNDERERS ARRESTED!
>
> On Saturday afternoon, 26 April, a dangerous gang of criminals, male and female, were arrested at the plush Hotel Four Seasons by authorities of the Soviet Republic. Those arrested were for

> the most part ladies and gentlemen of high society; among them a 1st Lieutenant and a countess.
>
> These people copied and falsified military rubber stamps and used them for purposes of widespread theft and plundering. Enormous quantities of goods of all kinds were confiscated by them for their own use: numerous motor cars, and money apparently in the millions. Out in the country, these people "requisitioned" livestock from farmers.[68]

Aside from possessing rubber stamps, the charges were false. By denying them the status of political activists and branding them merely as plunderers, the Reds hoped to discredit the Thulists, even if the truth suffered as a consequence. Likewise, their deaths in the Luitpold Gymnasium, the Blood Gymnasium as it came to be called, were used indiscriminately by the right to paint the left as monsters. Adherence to the facts was not a consideration in *völkisch* circles either.

Massacre at Luitpold Gymnasium

Given the chaos accompanying the fall of the Soviet Republic, it is likely that the treatment of the Thule prisoners varied with their handlers. They were interned at first in various places. Egelhofer interrogated all of them except for Thurn und Taxis at the War Ministry, where they denied the charges brought against them. The six prisoners stuck to a more developed version of Thule's cover story and maintained that the Society had two branches: a political group headed by Sebottendorff, and a cultural study group to which they belonged. From the War Ministry, Deicke and Nauhaus were taken to a cell at police headquarters before being transferred to Luitpold Gymnasium on April 28. It appears that Thurn und Taxis was brought to Luitpold after the other Thulists.

Commandeered by Red Guards as a bivouac and prison after the Palm Sunday Putsch, Luitpold had been an elite high school whose classical curriculum, emphasizing Latin and Greek, prepared its students for admission to university. With its "reputation as an enlightened, liberal institution," it numbered such distinguished alumni as mathematician Abraham Fränkel, musicologist Alfred Einstein, and physicist Albert

Einstein.[69] Neither Latin nor Greek were heard at the school after Palm Sunday. Luitpold's cellar was turned into a holding pen for prisoners, its hallways covered in posters declaring that the notorious Guards Cavalry had put a price of thirty marks on the head of every Red Guard.

Fritz Seidel, commandant at the Luitpold Gymnasium, received orders to transfer the six Thulists at the War Ministry and police headquarters to his custody. He brought them to Luitpold through a snow squall, guarded by a detail of soldiers and an armored car. Seidel later testified that he could not recall who issued the instructions to move the Thulists to his custody. On April 29, Thurn und Taxis joined his colleagues at Luitpold. Because discipline was weak to start with and deteriorating rapidly among Seidel's men, the prisoners were certainly abused physically and verbally by some guards, and treated with consideration by others. While Daumenlang was threatened with a pistol by Seidel and severely beaten after an escape attempt on his way from the War Ministry to Luitpold, Thurn und Taxis was allowed to receive female visitors.[70]

The mood at Luitpold darkened as reports circulated of summary executions by Whites of captured Reds. The 1st Infantry Regiment, the only component of the Munich army garrison to support the second Soviet Republic with enthusiasm, passed a resolution demanding the execution of five bourgeois hostages for every Red prisoner murdered. "The enemy is at the gates! Every man to arms! Everything is at stake!" screamed a proclamation from Egelhofer.[71] Red posters claimed that advancing troops ("White Guard dogs") intended to plunge Munich into a blood bath. The assumption was not unreasonable, given the record of some Freikorps units, but the deadly Red response to those reports, the murder of the Luitpold prisoners, only ensured that bloodier recriminations would follow.

Rifles were loaded at the gymnasium on the morning of April 30, after the arrival of a courier with orders from Egelhofer to execute two cavalrymen captured outside Munich. Both were suspected of belonging to the Guards Cavalry, responsible for the death of Spartacist leaders Rosa Luxemburg and Karl Liebknecht during the suppression of the Berlin revolt in January. As Red morale crumbled, it became difficult to muster volunteers for a proper firing squad, and the two soldiers may have been simply gunned down after enduring a bloody beating rather than executed in the customary manner. A number of Munich citizens were being held at the gymnasium, as hostages or on trumped-up charges, but Seidel was determined to kill the Thulists, whom he viewed as his most dangerous prisoners.[72]

Thurn und Taxis nearly avoided his fate. Egelhofer's adjutant Seyler, who was probably an agent of the Thule Society, tried to intervene on the prince's behalf, but Seidel insisted that his death warrant was issued by "the supreme command," presumably Egelhofer, and that all aristocrats deserved death regardless.[73] The two hussars were the first to face the firing squad. Afterward, the seven Thule prisoners, plus an elderly Jewish professor called Berger who had been caught tearing down a Red poster, were taken from their cells in pairs to be executed in the school's courtyard. They were permitted to write their farewells and final requests on scraps of paper. Seidlitz and Nauhaus insisted on facing their executioners. The others were shot while facing the wall of the courtyard. Thurn und Taxis's loud protests of innocence apparently delayed his execution, but only for a short time. Witnesses reported that the executions did not proceed with dignity but were accompanied by catcalls and recriminations from the crowd of some two hundred Red Guards and their girlfriends. Apparently the last pair to be killed were Thurn und Taxis and the fulminating Professor Berger.[74] Following the execution the victims' bodies were removed to a woodshed. Wages were paid to the Red Guards, who began to slip away from the gymnasium and disappear, as did many of their comrades stationed elsewhere in the city.

The unstable regime responsible for arresting the prisoners at Luitpold had already disintegrated before the White Guards reached Munich, indeed, before even the Luitpold executions began. On April 27 a congress of workers' and soldiers' soviets meeting at the Hofbräuhaus addressed the rising pitch of complaints against the measures taken by the second Soviet Republic. The congress passed a vote of no confidence against Levine's regime and forced his resignation. Toller reproached Levine for violence and berated his entourage for caring only if their course "conforms to the teachings of Russian Bolshevism, whether Lenin or Trotsky in a similar circumstance would react thus or thus."[75] Toller hoped to negotiate with Hoffmann, but the most hardened elements of the Red Guard (inspired by the fantasy of last-minute assistance from Bela Kun's Hungarian Communist regime and a childlike faith in Marx's laws of history) were determined to continue the revolution under Egelhofer. "In the final days of April the decisive voice was that of Rudolf Egelhofer," who issued a proclamation, supported by the Communist Party, insisting that his "General Command" would "defend the revolutionary proletariat" against "the counterrevolution of the White Guard" and denounced the "betrayal" by the workers' soviets.[76] His Red Guards blockaded streets, barricaded public buildings, and waited for the White assault.

The Whites in their fervent hatred of the Reds may have chosen to ignore Hoffmann, even if he had called for a truce. Acting on instructions from Berlin, however, Hoffmann demanded nothing less than "unconditional surrender." In any case the turn of events at Luitpold Gymnasium precluded any peaceful settlement. On April 29, Dachau was retaken by Freikorps units, and by the time of Luitpold execution on April 30, Munich was entirely surrounded.[77]

The killings proved the most foolish action of a regime characterized by foolishness. In his history of the Bavarian revolution, Allan Mitchell declared, "This was not only a wicked and futile act—it turned the civil war into a virtual slaughter."[78] The Luitpold executions served no military purpose (it could not have deterred the White assault on Munich) and was calculated to outrage the average German. The murder of aristocrats (especially a woman), artists, and civil servants was viewed as an atrocity in a country that respected the highborn and members of the professions. That it took place in a schoolyard only deepened the infamy.

While the executions were certainly a logical outcome of the doctrine of class warfare preached by the soviet regime, they can also be understood in the context of the worsening violence of the German Revolution's second phase, which began with the murder of Liebknecht and Luxemburg by the Guards Cavalry Division, one of the formations pushing toward Munich. The soviet regime posted placards warning that the killers of the famous Spartacist leaders were on their way, hoping to redouble the will to resist among the working class.

In fact, some of the advancing Freikorps units were not acting in accord with the rules of war. At Pucheim, fifty-two Russian prisoners of war who had been freed by the Reds, probably to serve with the Red Guards, were herded into a stone quarry and executed. Twenty medical orderlies on their way to assist Reds wounded in an engagement near Munich were killed. At Perlach, near Munich, twelve workers were executed out of hand. Eight Red Guards were massacred near Dachau.[79] These killings were dismissed by most Germans as battlefield incidents during a civil war.

Rightist students sneaked through the front to alert Epp of the massacre and spur the Freikorps to greater speed.[80] The response was spontaneous. Major General von Oven, Noske's commander of the march on Munich, lost control of the Bavarian Freikorps leading the assault. Instead of Oven's methodical, Prussian-style advance, Freikorps Epp and smaller formations broke ranks and stormed the city on May Day, against Oven's injunction (and the wishes of Social Democrats in Bamberg and Berlin) that the capital be given a short reprieve on the international workers' holiday.

A concern to prevent additional executions motivated some Freikorps units. A member of Freikorps Regensburg later recalled in a deposition:

> During the morning of 1 May, while encamped, we learned the facts of the hostage murders. At the same time further rumors began circulating about further executions and bloodbaths by the Reds toward the population of Munich. To thwart these developments our company commander, Dr. Sengmueller, decided to march on Munich. This march was begun without any further orders from anyone else.[81]

Other commanders had vengeance in mind. In light of the news from Luitpold, Ritter von Epp's aide-de-camp, Ernst Röhm, vowed to give Munich "a thorough cleansing."[82]

After the fighting subsided, the Luitpold executions became a major news story around the world, an emblematic event at a time when the United States and Europe alike experienced anxiety over the prospect of Bolshevik-style revolution.[83] More significant was the long-term impact on Germany. The Luitpold murders gave the right its first martyrs, although the Jewish origin of one victim presented problems for *völkisch* radicals. The specter of the Blood Gymnasium was raised again and again during the Weimar Republic; the deaths of the "hostages," as they were termed, was a bloody flag waved by the right as its rallying banner. It was proof that Communists were Jacobins, that Rudolf Egelhofer and Eugen Levine were the Danton and Robespierre of the German revolution. Thurn und Taxis's social prominence and Westarp's gender lent a tabloid quality to the Luitpold murders. The seven Thulists were viewed as the central victims of the Red terror in Munich even during the Third Reich, when references to the Thule Society were muted if not altogether suppressed.

Their bodies had barely gone cold before debate began over the reasons for their execution and their treatment inside the gymnasium.[84] Decades later, German historians continued to divide along the political spectrum. Leftists still branded them "looters and troublemakers" and termed allegations of torture and mutilation as the impetus for "a pogromatic mood against the proletariat, in order to justify from the onset any cruel deeds conducted by the White Guards."[85] Rightists painted the killings in language taken from Edmund Burke's *Reflections on the Revolution in France*:

> When the executions were performed, there was dancing in the school by soldiers, together with civilians who had been called in off the streets by the sounds of an accordion. The hostages were paired together and rushed into the yard; they were not only shot, but had to endure tortures before their death.[86]

From the evidence introduced at the hostage murder trial convened in September 1919, which resulted in death sentences for Seidel and seven of his men and long prison terms for other accused participants, it seemed that neither the worst horror stories of the right nor the whitewashing of the left were accurate. Westarp was not raped and the prisoners were not mutilated while alive, though dumdum bullets and rifles discharged at close range mutilated them at the point of death.

The Fall of Munich

Backed by aircraft and an armored train bristling with artillery, Hoffmann's forces marched on Munich from all sides. The Guards Cavalry and Erhardt's Marine Brigade advanced through Freising and Dachau. Wurttemberger and Bavarian Freikorps drove to Munich from the west while Freikorps Epp circled around to cut off the city from the south. A smaller force swung in from the east through Mühldorf. Moving by trucks whose radiator grills were painted with white skull and crossbones and moving by rail, marching on foot, and riding on horseback, the Whites met little resistance in most places, helping themselves to guns and munitions abandoned by the Reds. Heavy fighting commenced only when the Whites reached the outer suburbs of Munich. "We watched the approach of the northern German groups and were much impressed by their military conduct and discipline. Within our ranks we adhered to a more free conduct," recalled a Bavarian veteran of Freikorps Regensburg.[87]

Rumors of the murders spread like fire through a dry woods on the evening of April 30. Gruesome details compounded as the tale circulated, including reports that the victims' genitals had been hacked off and tossed into dustbins.[88] Sebottendorff's assessment of the Luitpold executions was sober. "The bodies were not mutilated and the soldiers did not rob them," he later wrote.[89]

In the immediate aftermath of the executions, however, Thulists inside the city were incensed and emboldened. The municipal police, disbanded by the Soviets, as well as an association of former noncommissioned officers, had continued to meet as social "clubs" under the leadership of Thule Combat League commanders.[90] The old police and the former subalterns of Bavaria's royal army resurfaced with the approach of the White troops and sprang into action. The Combat League opened a second front behind the lines.[91] "Right wing vigilantes," presumably Combat Leaguers, as no other organized resistance group is known to have operated inside Soviet Munich, seized the royal Residenz, the War Ministry, and the Prussian legation by the afternoon of May 1. Red flags fell to the ground in the city center before the arrival of troops; Bavaria's blue and white colors greeted White Guards from several key buildings.[92]

As Lenin addressed a huge May Day crowd in Moscow with the words, "Today the liberated working class is celebrating its anniversary freely and openly—not only in Soviet Russia, but also in Soviet Hungary and Soviet Bavaria," the end of Communist rule in southern Germany was already in sight. Even before the final assault on Munich began, many Red Guards had begun to shed their red armbands and toss their arms into the River Isar.[93]

Max Levien snuck out of Munich and crossed the border into Austria. Red positions inside the city were shelled from the Freikorps' armored train. Spartacists inside the Palace of Justice waved a white flag from a window after a few rounds from the Freikorps Regensburg field artillery.[94] Red Guards made a stand at the railroad station and the Malthäser Brauhaus, where Eisner's rousing speeches had led to the formation of the Bavarian Socialist Republic only five months earlier. The beer hall was the site of one of Munich's roughest engagements and was gutted by Freikorps' flamethrowers, grenades, and artillery. By May 3 the combat had ended, but not the reprisals by angry White troops.

Some seventy White soldiers were killed in the fighting for Munich. Red casualties may have amounted to six hundred or even a thousand, although many of them were people merely suspected of association with the left. In the clampdown that followed the city's capture, real and imagined Spartacists were hauled out of their homes and shot. Some Freikorps units meted out summary executions of suspects; others preferred the more orderly routine of courts-martial. Gustav Landauer, education commissar for the first Soviet Republic, remonstrated with his captors about the path of nonviolence on the way to Stadelheim, where he was beaten to death with rifle butts.[95] Innocent bystanders were murdered on unfounded suspicions. The most notorious incident concerned twenty-one Roman Catholic workers, members of the Society of St. Joseph meeting in a hall to discuss putting on a play, who were beaten to death, shot, and bayoneted by the Guards Cavalry on suspicion of being Communists (May 6). Many such arbitrary killings were committed by Freikorps from northern Germany, who treated Munich as an occupied enemy city and had difficulty understanding the local dialect.[96] The "Prussian" units from northern Germany exited the city before Hoffmann returned to Munich on May 13.[97]

Although Thule members fighting in Freikorps Epp and other units helped lead the charge into Munich, and the Thule Combat League fought the Reds from within the city, the two Freikorps advancing from outside under Sebottendorff's authority played only a secondary role in the battle for Munich.

The small Freikorps Chiemgau occupied the strategic railroad station at Haar, five miles southeast of Munich, on April 27, a move that helped complete the encirclement of the besieged city.[98] Early on the morning of May 3, with sections of Munich already occupied by Epp and other commanders, Freikorps Oberland streamed without resistance into the city's east end. The unit's advance had been delayed by transportation problems and a skirmish with the Reds at Kolbermoor forty miles southeast of Munich.[99] The Thulist troops streamed down Wienerstrasse and Maximilianstrasse, unscathed by Red snipers and machine gunners, and rooted out resisters house by house. A security company under Julius Lehmann took the Hofbräuhauskeller. By nightfall, with Oberland machine guns guarding the Hoftheater, the Freikorps had suffered only a few wounded.

The following day, Oberland secured key bridges on the Isar, and Major Bekh established headquarters at Franziskanerkeller. Oberland also captured Spartacist leader and "notorious free thinker" Sontheimer. As Bekh interrogated him, Sontheimer cried, "Major, you can have me shot! I do not fear death! I fear life!" Along with many other real or suspected Reds, Sontheimer's cause of death was listed as "shot while trying to escape." Lehmann's men seized several Russians, prisoners-of-war-turned-Red Guards, present at the Luitpold executions. The Russians were lined up in a gravel pit and used for target practice.[100] On May 4, Bekh's men netted additional prisoners and caches of arms. During the next few days, Oberland reinforcements continued to pour into Munich from the country.

As Red resistance collapsed, Egelhofer tried to escape the city in an automobile, but he was pulled from the car and killed on the spot by Freikorps troops.[101] Eager Lieutenant Kraus and his Thule intelligence agents pursued suspects in the Luitpold killings following the capture of Munich. On May 16 they apprehended Axelrod, who was turned over to the police for trial. Later they tracked down Levine, who was hiding in the studio of a painter in Heidelberg. He was convicted of treason and executed.[102] Kraus's detective work led to a career; by the mid-1930s as a captain with the Bavarian State Police, he assisted the new Nazi regime in its investigation against Sebottendorff. Ernst Toller, hiding in a Schwabing studio after the fall of Munich, was betrayed by a woman friend and sentenced to five years of fortress imprisonment, where he wrote several Expressionist plays that were successfully produced in Germany. Fleeing Germany when the Nazis came to power, Toller ended his own life in a New York hotel room in 1939.

A week after the shooting in Munich had subsided and the forces aligned with the Thule Society had triumphed came news of the death of Ariosophy's founder, Guido von List. It was announced that he had passed away in Berlin from a lung inflammation and exhaustion on May 17, but, in common with many crucial events in the lives and deaths of Ariosophy's leading figures, there are discrepancies in the accounts. Philipp Stauff, who had worked tirelessly through the Germanenorden to spread List's theories in the Reich, honored his memory with an obituary in the *Münchener Beobachter.*[103]

Meanwhile Sebottendorff and Oberland Central returned to the Thule Society's suite in the Hotel Four Seasons on May 3. It was probably no coincidence that the hotel also became headquarters for Ritter von Epp,[104] promoted to general after the Munich siege. Epp was given command of the new Reichswehr District IV, consisting of remnants of the former Bavarian army and units of local Freikorps to be incorporated into the reconstituted German military, including portions of Freikorps Oberland.[105] At this time Ernst Röhm and the Thulist Rudolf Hess were officers on Epp's staff. Six months before, the Four Seasons had sheltered the ceremonies of an obscure occult society. In the turmoil of postwar Germany, it became the right's Bavarian command center. The changes at the hotel mirrored the transformation of Ariosophy from a fringe creed to a battle cry.

8

Thule and the Nazi Circle

> A sharing of the same world view and the readiness to seize certain possibilities are the pre-determinates that from the beginning guide fate.
>
> —Martin Heidegger

In *Bevor Hitler kam*, an account of the Thule Society published several months after the Nazis took power in Germany, Sebottendorff claimed the Society as a primary root of the National Socialist movement: "Thule people were to whom Hitler first came, and it was Thule people who joined him in the beginning."[1]

Sebottendorff's assertion has considerable merit. Several Thulists became prominent in the emerging Nazi Party, and his claim for Hitler's involvement in the Society does not break the bounds of plausibility. Sebottendorff neither crowned himself Hitler's personal mentor nor claimed to be a Nazi himself; he wrote only that the future führer "entered the halls of Thule" a few weeks after Sebottendorff resigned as the Society's master in the summer of 1919.[2] He described Hitler as a "guest" rather than a full Thule member.[3] This too speaks for the plausibility of his assertions. Because regulations restricted soldiers from pledging an oath to any organization but the army, many rightist groups admitted active military personnel as "guests." This device, circumventing army rules, applied to any lodge or secret society that Hitler, who was in no hurry to be demobilized, cared to join before his discharge on April 1, 1920.

Although Hitler's participation in the Society as its guest cannot be verified, and there is no record of him referring directly to Thule, Hitler did try to establish a relationship with one of Thule's front organizations, the *Münchener Beobachter*, by offering to become a correspondent in the summer of 1919.[4] There is no dispute about his eventual role in another group that began as a Thule front, the German Workers' Party (Deutsche Arbeiterpartei), which under his leadership became the National Socialist German Workers' Party.

On September 12, 1919, Hitler, wearing a dark blue suit and donning a mustache recently clipped in the Charlie Chaplin–style that would become his trademark, attended his first meeting of the German Workers' Party. In spite of his civilian clothes, he made no attempt to hide his identity as a military operative, signing his name in the party guest book as a lance corporal.[5] He gave the following version of his encounter with the party at their meeting in the smoke-filled Sternecker Beer Hall:

> One day I received orders from my headquarters to find out what was behind an apparently political organization which was planning to hold a meeting in the next few days under the name of "German Workers' Party." Gottfried Feder was one of the speakers. I was told to go and look at the organization and then make a report.[6]

Working since the summer of 1919 as a "V-Mann" or "liaison man" for the Reichswehr's District IV Command in Munich, Hitler had duties that included conducting political discussions to edify the troops and, ostensibly, surveillance of many of the political organizations that proliferated in Bavaria after the fall of the soviet republic, especially on the far right. He served in an army whose Bavarian units continued to behave with alarming autonomy in relation to the national government in Berlin.[7] As it was during the time of the Bavarian Socialist Republic, Germany's southern state remained not only a distinct political entity but also a supportive environment for extremists who hoped to use the state as a stepping-stone to Berlin. In his capacity as a V-Mann, Hitler wrote his first recorded statement on the Jewish question, terming the

Jews "a non-German alien race," which produced "a racial tuberculosis" to be combated by "the deliberate removal of the Jews," all statements in accord with radical *völkisch* ideas.[8] If, as Hitler maintained in *Mein Kampf*, he had no previous knowledge of the German Workers' Party before receiving orders to report on its activities, how does this square with Sebottendorff's assertion that Hitler joined the party's parent organization, the Thule Society, during the summer of 1919?

Inconsistencies riddle Hitler's story. Although the German Workers' Party and its predecessor sometimes gathered in the backrooms of small taverns, it also met regularly at Thule's offices at Four Seasons, the hotel where the Reichswehr's district commander, Ritter von Epp, had his quarters. The idea of District Command spying on its commander's neighbor down the hall is the stuff of comedy. Another difficulty is presented by Hitler's admission that Feder was the meeting's speaker. Hitler and his superiors were already quite familiar with the man. Feder was an associate of Thule, and since the November Revolution, he had frequently expounded his ideas on economics at the Society's offices.[9] A Munich engineer and building contractor–turned–economic theorist, Feder founded the German Combat League for the Breaking of Interest Slavery (Deutscher Kampfbund zur Brechnung der Zinskneckschaft) in 1917 but did not become a prominent voice in *völkisch* circles until Thule gave him a forum.[10] Feder was then employed by District Command to lecture the army's liaison men on the evils of international capitalism, behind which he discerned a Jewish conspiracy. Hitler was admittedly an avid pupil, stating that Feder's conclusions "caused me to delve into the fundamentals of this field [economics] with which I had previously not been very familiar" and that "right after listening to Feder's first lecture, the thought ran through my head that I had now found the way to one of the most essential premises for the foundation of a new party."[11] One may wonder why District Command would order Hitler to spy on a group being addressed by one of its own minions. On the night of Hitler's first meeting of the Workers' Party, Feder spoke on "How and by What Means Is Capitalism to Be Eliminated?" He had been substituted by the party for the originally scheduled speaker, the Thulist poet Dietrich Eckart.[12] The disingenuousness of the *Mein Kampf* account is demonstrated by a letter on September 1, 1919, from Capt. Karl Mayr, the officer who sent Hitler to report on the meeting, to Eckart, ordering subscriptions for his men to Eckart's newspaper, *Auf gut deutsch.* By enrolling his men as Eckart's subscribers, Mayr demonstrated the collusion prevailing between Thulists and Bavaria's military commanders.[13] Evidence exists of an ongoing line of contact between Mayr and the Workers' Party. In December 1919, after Hitler had joined the party, Mayr arranged for the disbursement of army funds to provide the growing organization with its own office in the Sternecker Beer Hall, and for the June 1920 publication of a party brochure, which attacked the Versailles Treaty, by the Thule confederate Julius Lehmann. He would later claim that his office underwrote the party's earliest mass meetings.[14] Even if Sebottendorff lied by naming Hitler as a Thule guest, Hitler already traveled in circles defined by the Society before he attended his first meeting of the German Workers' Party.

Hitler would later laugh at the tiny Workers' Party, with its ludicrous reading of minutes and its treasury of seven marks, five pfennings. "Terrible, terrible," he chided in *Mein Kampf.* "This was club life of the worst manner and sort. Was I to join this organization? . . . There was nothing, no program, no leaflet, no printed matter at all, no membership cards, not even a miserable rubber stamp, only obvious good faith and good intentions."[15]

Here too, Hitler's narrative is inconsistent. Only a few pages before his criticism of the party's lack of program and literature, he recalled that as he left the September 12 meeting, party chairman Anton Drexler pressed into his hand a pink-jacketed, forty-page booklet, *My Political Awakening.* Tossing and turning on his army cot early next morning, Hitler absentmindedly perused Drexler's autobiographical manifesto, which mingled its opposition to Marxism with anti-Semitism (the Jews "have almost made themselves masters of the world") and anti-capitalism ("the systematic strangulation of the manual worker"). *My Political Awakening* argued instead for a distinctly German socialism. "In the course of the day, I reflected a few times on the matter," he wrote, evidently impressed by the program it contained.[16]

By minimizing the party in its early days, Hitler maximized his role as the shaper of the National Socialist movement. The German Workers' Party was certainly not a powerful group when Hitler entered it, but neither was it the pathetic conclave portrayed in *Mein Kampf.* At the September meeting were forty-four men and one woman, among them a physician, a chemist, businessmen, bank employees, skilled workers, soldiers, students, and the daughter of a judge, "a small gathering, but representing far more of a cross section of society than could usually be found at the meetings of the larger partisan gatherings in Munich."[17] During 1919 the German Workers' Party was growing. By September it possessed an executive committee with two secretaries responsible for handwritten, hand-delivered invitations to increasingly large gatherings, and two treasurers. The party was planning ways to continue its expansion at the time Hitler joined.[18] In summary, Hitler cannot be fully trusted as a source for his own history. The scope of his egotism did not leave room for many predecessors. His self-mythologizing account would have made for better reading if he had created the Nazi Party out of nothing; since the existence of the German Workers' Party was well known, he had no recourse but to denigrate the party as an organization of little account until he transformed it into an instrument of destiny.

The cofounder of the German Workers' Party whose pamphlet so impressed Hitler, Anton Drexler (1884–1942), is usually depicted as a naive and unworldly character who gladly became the tool of more ambitious figures. Drexler was a man of proletarian background. His father had been a Social Democrat; his anti-Marxism resulted from negative encounters with trade unions, and his anti-Semitism came from a period of employment under a brutal Jewish cattle dealer. Barred for a time from his trade, he earned a living by playing a zither in cafes.[19] After causing a minor stir for writing a pro-war article in the *Münchener Zeitung* in January 1918, the Munich railroad repairman formed the Free Workers' Committee for a Just Peace. "We were all poor, powerless, unknown," Drexler later recalled.[20] The organization he founded was small as well as unknown. At its inception in March 1918, the committee numbered only twenty-seven men, most of them Drexler's coworkers. After Drexler penned a few more articles for the *Münchener Zeitung,* membership climbed to around forty by October.[21] "After that, I brought the Freien Arbeiter-Ausschuss into touch with another little group called the Politischer Arbeiter-Zirkel, run by a journalist by the name of Harrer," Drexler said.[22]

The Political Workers' Circle was one of several "rings of Thule" founded after the November Revolution in answer to Sebottendorff's call for "inner struggle" against the new regime. Sebottendorff cited Feder's ringing denunciations of capitalism at Thule Society meetings as inspiration for founding the Workers' Circle under Thule Society member Karl Harrer (1890–1926). A sportswriter for the *Münchener-Augsburger Abendzeitung,* Harrer is usually described as a shabbily dressed, club-footed man. Feder immediately offered to edify the group with his lectures.[23]

Harrer was already acquainted with Drexler before the ring was established. At a rightist rally in Munich's Wagner Hall on October 2, 1918, Harrer was favorably impressed by the railroad worker's call for a national "Bürgerbund" representing politically unattached officials, bourgeois, and proletarians.[24] "Citizens, workers, unite!" Drexler cried.[25]

Drexler, who became a guest of Thule in December 1918 but never a full member,[26] agreed to unite his group under Harrer as the German Workers' Party. Drexler's poor, powerless, unknown group was taken under wing by relatively sophisticated benefactors who systematized its inchoate nationalism and anti-Semitism:

> He [Harrer] got together all sorts of books and facts about the War, the Russian Revolution—and our own Revolution—which we all set out to study hard, by way of trying to find some way out of the debacle. We discussed a new name for our combination, and decided on a new departure. United, we numbered perhaps thirty-five members. We agreed to meet on January 5th in a little eating-house in Munich called "Fuerstenfelder Hof" to found the Deutsche Arbeiter-Partei.[27]

The goals Drexler expounded at that first meeting show the presence of what would become the familiar social rhetoric of Nazi Germany from the Nazi Party's inception. The German Workers' Party would work for ending divisive Marxist class war, for making the upper class aware of its responsibility to the workers, for elevating skilled workers into the middle class and expanding the middle class at the expense of "big capitalism."

Drexler suggested "German National Socialist Party" as the group's name, "but there was an objection that the word 'socialist' might be misinterpreted." The party's anti-Semitism was couched in cautious terms: "Religious teachings contrary to the moral and ethical laws of Germany should not be supported by the state."[28]

The party's second meeting, on January 18, 1919, was held in Thule's offices at Four Seasons. Harrer was elected first chairman and Drexler second chairman.[29] "Since initially Harrer was the more dominant partner, the earliest political activity of the two men was organized along lines suggested by him."[30]

Thule's Workers' Circle was not subsumed by the party, but continued to function as the organization's ideological motor and leadership cadre. The Circle met once or twice a week, and was limited, at Harrer's insistence, to seven members.[31] Given Thule's occult foundation, the membership restriction was significant. Seven is a number loaded with mystical implications.[32] Although Drexler freely expressed his thoughts at meetings of the larger, more proletarian German Workers' Party, Harrer dominated Circle discussions held at Thule's office, Cafe Gasteig, or private apartments. Among Harrer's topics were anti-Semitism, the use of newspapers for political propaganda, and the implications of the lost war. "Harrer and not Drexler was the spiritual leader of this small group."[33]

During the turbulent winter and spring of 1919, the Workers' Party also met regularly at Thule's offices or the Sternecker Beer Hall. Harrer retained the top office as Reich chairman. Drexler became chairman of the party's chapter in Munich. Apparently, there were no other local chapters during that period. Records of a party meeting on May 3, held as White Guards mopped up Red stragglers in Munich, show the increasing stridence of Drexler's anti-Semitism in his address on "Jewish World-Bolshevism."[34] At other meetings during that period, Drexler derided the rich and demanded laws limiting annual profits to ten thousand marks.[35]

Hitler's Mentor

Several other Thulists were decisive in the German Workers' Party. For his early impact on the young group and his later importance in the Nazi movement, few figures loom larger than Dietrich Eckart (1868–1923).

Although Eckart never lived to see the Third Reich, he was acknowledged by the Nazis as John the Baptist to Hitler's Messiah. The title of one of Eckart's poems, "Deutschland Erwache" ("Germany Awake"), became the motto of the Nazi movement. Hitler was himself, for a change, generous in his acknowledgment. *Mein Kampf* ended with the following tribute: "And among them I want also to count that man, one of the best, who devoted his life to the awakening of his, our people, in his writings and his thoughts and finally in his deeds: Dietrich Eckart."[36]

Johann Dietrich Eckart has been called the founder of Hitler,[37] whose "tutelage proved to be indispensable in devising the tactics which the Fuehrer later employed."[38] He was born in Neumarket, Bavaria, the son of a successful and prominent attorney. Eckart never completed his medical education at the University of Erlangen, but as a student, he developed a morphine addiction that haunted him through life. The addiction was so central to his personality that even his Nazi hagiographers made no attempt to conceal it. "Without the sweet poison he could not live, and he applied the whole cunning of a man possessed by this craving to get himself dose after dose," Alfred Rosenberg wrote.[39]

Like Guido List, Eckart rejected the conventional career his father pressed on him to become a writer. He worked as a music critic, poet, newspaper editor, satirist, playwright, and contributor to Theodor Fritsch's publication, *Der Hammer*. Although he earned enough money in the first decade of the century to found the publishing house Herold Verlag, later renamed Hoheneichen Verlag, publisher in future years of Rosenberg's *Mythus des 20. Jahrhunderts* and other prominent Nazi works, he was often reduced to a penurious bohemian existence, even sleeping on park benches. It was an up-and-down career in drama; Eckart's *Familienvater* was popular in the 1905–1906 season. He was acclaimed for an idiosyncratic translation of Henrik Ibsen's play *Peer Gynt* (1914), which under the kaiser's own patronage became a great success on the Berlin stage. It brought him a taste of financial success. Eckart blamed the hostility of Berlin's Jewish theater critics for his lack of greater acclaim.

Eckart was the *völkisch* equivalent to Eisner and the bohemian utopians who seized power in Bavaria in November 1918. Well-read and eloquent, if sometimes pointedly crude, Eckart was at home in the cafes of Munich, where he held court and imbibed wine with unbridled gusto, bursting into conversation at any opening. Shaven headed, wearing a close-cropped mustache, and clad comfortably in country-house tweeds, he was described as an "intellectual buccaneer" who played "Falstaff to Hitler's Prince Hal in Munich's ribald night-world."[40] As put by one Nazi biographer, Eckart "was never a politician in the usual sense. As a politician he remained—as he did as a poet—a seer of essentials, and from this standpoint he passed judgment on mean and events."[41]

While the war continued, Eckart became involved in November 1916 in launching an abortive right-wing periodical, *Unser Vaterland*, published by Julius Lehmann. The publication was short lived and apparently suppressed by government censors.[42] He would enjoy greater success in newspaper publishing in the revolutionary upheaval of postwar Bavaria, where he launched a periodical called *Auf gut deutsch.* Its early editions (December 1918), produced at Thule's office,[43] were written almost entirely by Eckart in his characteristically earthy, mocking style. Soon enough he attracted other writers from his circle, including Feder. For Eckart, Germany's cultural, political, and international problems stemmed from a common source, the Jews. Like the Ariosophists, Eckart proclaimed a German-Jewish polarity representing opposing values of idealism and materialism. Along with letters from readers and opinion pieces on current events, *Auf gut deutsch* published Eckart's poems and scenes from his plays. Of this book Ralph Engelman writes, "In its pages Eckart outlined a comprehensive anti-Semitic *Weltanschauung* which had previously been expressed in an incomplete and symbolic form in his plays."[44]

Using his family's social connections, Eckart became a go-between for Bavaria's *völkisch* far right and its more pragmatic conservatives. After the Landtag elections of January 1919, Eckart negotiated on behalf of Hans Georg Grassinger with Gustav Ritter von Kahr, a conservative politician who assumed control of Bavaria in 1920 and would be coerced into joining Hitler's unsuccessful 1923 putsch only to repudiate his support as soon as he had the freedom to do so.[45] Grassinger, a Thulist and an editor of the *Beobachter* (March 1919), formed the German Socialist Party (Deutsche-Sozialistische Partei) in collaboration with his two coeditors, the Thulists Max Sesselman and Dr. Fritz Wieser. The German Socialists were yet another organization by which Thule hoped to reach the working class,[46] although its Gottfried Feder–based economic theory was indistinguishable from the ideology of the German Workers' Party. The German Socialists numbered in its rank the future Nazi Gauleiter Julius Streicher, the regional party boss whose pornographic anti-Semitic periodical, *Der Stürmer,* contributed so much to the obscene atmosphere of the Third Reich that the Nuremberg Tribunal dispatched him to the gallows. The German Socialist Party voluntarily dissolved in December 1922 and advised its members to join the Nazis.[47] Sesselman later marched with Hitler in the Beer Hall Putsch.

Eckart's *Auf gut deutsch* soon attracted the interest of a newcomer to Munich, a recent initiate of the Thule Society named Alfred Rosenberg. The young Baltic architect, culturally German regardless of his uncertain ancestry, had fled the Russian Empire after the Bolshevik Revolution. From his earliest articles in *Auf gut deutsch,* Rosenberg set himself up as an expert on Russia and the Bolshevik Revolution.[48]

On April 5, 1919, Eckart and Rosenberg outraged the Munich soviets when they showered city streets with thousands of pamphlets hurled from fast cars. The Eckart-penned broadcast, "An alle Werktaetingen!" ("To All Workingmen!"), was rooted in Feder's critique of capitalism.[49] The leftist regime responded with the following poster, whose outrage seemed as directed toward the mode of delivery as the message:

> Since the proclamation of the Red Republic, public safety has been threatened on the most part by anti-Semitic agitators, cowardly types who throw flyers from speeding automobiles, who without any doubt will be, in the shortest period of time, brought by the government to the Revolutionary Tribunal, as will all persons who disturb the peace.[50]

The influence of this pamphlet and other materials influenced by Feder's critique of capitalism, which fed an anxiety over Jewish influence in banking and commerce, was registered in reports by Munich police president Ernst Poehner, who noted the connection between Feder's ideas and the spread of anti-Semitism in his jurisdiction.[51]

As Hoffmann gathered his forces for the march on Munich, Eckart worked inside the capital with the Thule Combat League to "prepare" the city for its liberation from the soviets. Sought by leftists, Eckart, his wife, and their children fled to Wolfratshausen, south of Munich, the Bavarian town where lived the partners in his publishing firm Hoheneichen Verlag. On April 7, Eckart traveled from there by train for Bamberg. He never reached Hoffmann's headquarters but harangued soldiers along the way on the necessity of overthrowing the soviet regime in Munich before he returned to Wolfratshausen for a few days.[52] His desire to be at the center of the coming storm led him back to Munich after April 13. During the April 26 raids on the Four Seasons, Eckart, alerted to the impending Red Guard action, rushed to the hotel to warn his colleagues. He was arrested, but convinced his captors of his socialist sympathies after showing them selected passages from "An alle Werktaetigen!" and *Auf gut deutsch.* He was quickly freed. After learning that a Red tribunal had issued a warrant for his arrest, and fearing his luck was about to expire, Eckart once again fled with his family to Wolfratshausen, where he waited until Munich had been secured by Hoffmann's forces in the early days of May.[53]

In issues of *Auf gut deutsch* published after the end of the leftist regime, when a common front against the far left was no longer necessary, Eckart attacked the Roman Catholic Church and conservative, monarchist Bavarian separatists as well as Jews with increasing bitterness.[54] All of these were to become favorite targets of the coming Nazi movement. In *Mein Kampf,* Hitler claimed to have shouted down a monarchist separatist, a spectator like himself, during his first visit to the German Workers' Party.[55]

In May 1919 Eckart founded the Citizens' Union (Bürgervereinigung), an anti-Semitic league that aspired to bridge class differences between the proletariat and the bourgeoisie. In the group's manifesto, Eckart stressed that a German renewal could not occur unless Jews were stripped of economic and political power.[56] The short-lived Citizens' Union met at Thule's office until it faded from existence in August 1919.[57] Some of its members, including Fritz von Treutzschler, were veterans of the Thule Combat League and had helped Eckart circulate anti-leftist propaganda under the Soviet Republic.[58] The group never achieved its goal of reaching a broad constituency and was viewed by its founder as a failure.[59] But the Citizens' Union had barely expired before Eckart pinned his hopes on another association, one that would prove more enduring. On August 15, the *völkisch* polemicist spoke for the first time before a meeting of the German Workers' Party. His topic was "Bolshevism and the Jewish Question."[60]

Eckart was familiar with the party long before August, having been a friend of Drexler since at least May.[61] Eckart was not present at Hitler's first Workers' Party meeting on September 12 and missed all of the party's October sessions because of illness. Although the two men swam the same waters, it is not possible to positively link Hitler and Eckart until late November, during the drafting of the party's program.[62]

Alfred Rosenberg and the Elders of Zion

One of history's most malicious forgeries was *The Protocols of the Elders of Zion.* The spurious document, which purported to record a Jewish conspiracy for world dominion, originated in France and was apparently conveyed by the Theosophist Yuliana Glinka to Russia, where it was first published in reactionary newspapers and finally in book form by 1905.[63] Despite its fantastic tone and content, the *Protocols* became a powerful weapon in the arsenal of anti-Semites throughout the world after it reached Germany in the baggage of White Russian émigrés. It was cited approvingly by Hitler in *Mein Kampf,* distributed in millions of copies by American industrialist Henry Ford, and translated into every major European language. After the establishment of the State of Israel, the *Protocols* continued to circulate widely in the Muslim Middle East.

From Konrad Heiden, an early chronicler of Nazism, comes the legend that Alfred Rosenberg carried the bacillus from Russia to Munich, where it found an eager host in the Thule Society and from there infected the globe. The full truth is difficult to recover, although it is clear that members of the Thule Society and their confederates were instrumental in circulating the *Protocols.* According to Heiden, Rosenberg was reading in his room during the summer of 1917, when "a stranger entered, laid a book on the table and silently vanished." The book, by the Russian Orthodox monk Sergei Nilus, included the *Protocols* as an appendix.[64]

Heiden explained that Rosenberg often spoke of this mysterious annunciation. Nowhere in his writings did Rosenberg mention where he first encountered the *Protocols*, though he later edited a popular annotated edition, *Die Protokolle der Weisen von Zion und die juedische Weltpolitik* (1923).

According to Norman Cohn, whose account remains definitive, a variant of the *Protocols* was published in Germany as early as January 1918 in the rightist newspaper *Deutschlands Erneuerung*.[65] The paper was published by Julius Lehmann, an associate of the Thule Society, and would later number Rosenberg as a contributor. The Ariosophist and founder of the Germanenorden, Theodor Fritsch, alluded knowingly to the *Protocols* in his magazine *Hammer* (April 1919). The first complete German edition, *Die Geheimnisse der Weisen von Zion*, was published in mid-January 1920 by the Association Against Jewish Presumption (Verband gegen Überhebung des Judentums). This organization was headed by a Ludendorff protégé, Ludwig Mueller, who received a Russian copy of the *Protocols* as early as November 1918 from a pair of refugee czarist officers, Piotr Shabelsky-Bork and Fyodor Vinberg.

After its publication by Mueller, the *Protocols* was quickly serialized in a number of rightist newspapers.[66] The *Beobachter* published the entire text on February 25, 1920, the day after a speech in which Hitler dwelled on the document's themes of worldwide Jewish conspiracy.[67] Fritsch's Leipzig-based publishing house, Hammer Verlag, issued a best-selling version in the early months of 1920.

Along with his role in publishing the *Protocols*, Julius Lehmann assisted in the development of Nazi ideology by vouching for Rosenberg with the authorities. His kind words prevented Rosenberg's deportation after the fall of the Bavarian Soviet Republic, a time when Russian refugees were eyed with suspicion.[68]

In other respects Rosenberg's association with Thule, dating from December 1918, with Eckart as his probable mentor, "must have been a godsend" to the penniless refugee, a young man inclined to art, architecture, and Indian mysticism.[69] One historian noted that "the impressions received in the Thule Society marked the direction and style of his [Rosenberg's] secondary philosophical undertakings."[70] Although he admitted that his exposure to the concept of Aryan racial superiority occurred only after he came to Germany,[71] Rosenberg passed quickly over Thule in autobiographical accounts. Perhaps taking Hitler's lead, he singled out Eckart as the only Thule member worthy of gratitude.[72]

At the end of his life, Rosenberg stated that the encounter anchored him to Munich and determined his fate.[73] It was, in the words of one historian, "the beginning of a relationship that would affect the career of Adolf Hitler."[74] Rosenberg's first article for Eckart, "Die russische-juedische Revolution" (February 21, 1919), sounded a note that would be heard in Germany until the collapse of Nazism. To Rosenberg, the Bolshevik Revolution was a Jewish conspiracy. It was a theme he repeated in issue after issue of Eckart's paper, and in books and policy papers written after he became a Nazi.[75]

While no one disputes that Hitler was, to a large degree, Eckart's apprentice at the beginning of their friendship, Rosenberg's influence has been more controversial. Although it is now generally acknowledged that Hitler's preoccupation with combating Bolshevism was "influenced above all by Alfred Rosenberg,"[76] many historians have followed the path of those unable to take the Nazi Party's chief philosopher seriously because of the strangeness of his ideas. From this perspective it is easy to pretend that Rosenberg was the butt of Hitler's scorn in the inner sanctuary of Nazism. Support for this view rests uncomfortably on Hitler's supposed statement that he read no more than a few pages of Rosenberg's major philosophical tome, *Der Mythus des 20. Jahrhunderts,* because it was too difficult to understand. [77] This statement comes from transcripts of Hitler's private conversations, edited with an eye toward inclusion in some future Nazi archive, by one of Rosenberg's opponents, party boss Martin Bormann.

While it is likely that Hitler would eventually grow impatient with Rosenberg's mediocre aptitude for leadership, eyewitness accounts contradict the notion that Hitler tolerated Rosenberg as a harmless eccentric. Hitler's friend Ernst "Putzi" Hanfstaengl abhorred Rosenberg but admitted, "I soon found that he [Hitler] was deeply under the spell of Rosenberg" and esteemed him highly as a writer and philosopher.[78] Careful scrutiny of Hitler's earliest recorded speeches shows the influence of Rosenberg's ideas.[79] In commenting on the *Mythus,* Hitler said, "That book contains much that is true, but it is not timely. It is not intended for the masses; it is rather ideological education for the intelligentsia."[80] When Rosenberg issued a veiled attack on Goebbels's tolerance of modern art in the *Völkischer Beobachter,* his remarks "were incorporated almost verbatim" in Hitler's speech on culture at the 1933 Nazi Party rally.[81] Kurt Luedecke, a well-connected adventurer who joined the Nazi Party in the summer 1922 and became one of its major early financial donors, would later recount that Hitler told him to get to know Rosenberg: "Get on good terms with him. He's the only man I always listen to. He is a thinker."[82]

Many of Rosenberg's thoughts were quite strange, embodying the bizarre interpretation of human prehistory offered by Theosophy and the Ariosophists whom he must have encountered in the Thule Society. H. P. Blavatsky wrote, "The Aryan race was born and developed in the far North, though after sinking of the continent of Atlantis, its tribes emigrated further south into Asia."[83] The *Mythus* also accepts Atlantis as the original home of the Aryans:

> And these waves of Atlantean people traveled by water on their swan and dragon ships into the Mediterranean, to Africa; by land over Central Asia to Kutschka, indeed, perhaps to China, across North America to the south of the continent.[84]

Although Rosenberg cited as his inspiration Houston Stewart Chamberlain's philo-Germanic *The Foundations of the Nineteenth Century,* he was much more certain than Chamberlain that races formed distinct and discernable bloodlines. Chamberlain's genealogy of the Germans would have been heresy to the Nazis:

> There is no clear distinction between the Germans of Tacitus, the Celtic predecessor in history, or the successor—the Slav. They are varieties of a common stock.[85]

Rosenberg's ideas more closely echo those of Ariosophy:

> Today, a new faith is awakening—the myth of the blood, the belief that the divine being of all mankind is to be defended with the blood. The faith is embodied by the fullest realization that the Nordic blood constitutes that mystery which has supplanted and surmounted the old sacraments.[86]

Chamberlain was ambivalent about the Jews and gently mocked the Manichean conspiracy theories of contemporary anti-Semites, writing, "the Jew is alien to us, and consequently we to him, and no one will deny that this is to the detriment of our culture, yet I think that we are inclined to underestimate our own powers in this respect and, on the other hand to exaggerate the importance of the Jewish danger."[87]

In company with the Ariosophists, Rosenberg finds "pure Nordic types" in ancient Egyptian and Indian artifacts, proving that "the meaning of world history, shining out from the North, has passed over the whole earth, borne by a blue-eyed blond race."[88] Aryan stock will provide the material for the next leap in human evolution. "This is the mission of our century: out of a new life to create a new human type."[89]

Like Sebottendorff, Rosenberg attacked Christianity as alien to the Aryan character. He wrote of the "almost two-thousand-year-old conflict between church and race," contrasting the value placed by Christians on love with the primacy given by Aryans to honor. His description of Aryan religion is unmistakably Ariosophical:

> The Nordic gods were figures of light who bore spears, the cross and the swastika, and were crowned with haloes, symbols of the sun, of ascending life.[90]

Rosenberg spoke in grand and general terms about a "German church," shorn of Judaic elements and somehow rooted in an imagined Aryan past, in "Nordic sagas and fairytales." He interpreted such mythic figures as "symbols" of a "dream of honor and freedom which must be understood through the Nordic Germanic tales, beginning with Odin."[91]

Although Hitler never publicly echoed the anti-Christianity of the *Mythus*, his personal hostility to Christian teaching was reflected in the book's content and in private conversations recorded for posterity.[92] Hitler's silence on questions raised by the controversial book was a tactical maneuver to reassure German church leaders and the faithful. As the party's ideological spokesman, Rosenberg would never have been permitted to publish the book had Hitler opposed its message. The *Mythus* would not have been imposed on the curriculum of German schools if Hitler had found it objectionable.

Rosenberg's voluminous output of articles, essays, and books has been subjected to few close readings and little analysis. For one his work is difficult to read, couched in academic verbiage bordering at times on impenetrable. Little wonder that a book was published during the Nazi period whose purpose was to define the hundreds of neologisms in *Mythus.*[93] That the *Mythus* alarmed the Roman Catholic Church, which placed it on the Index of Forbidden Books, did nothing to dampen sales in Germany, where more than a million copies were sold. Like twentieth-century intellectuals of many persuasions, Rosenberg sometimes claimed that activism was more important than book learning. "The myth has to be experienced, not merely understood," he told a Nazi scholar.[94]

In the *Mythus* and later writings, Rosenberg refined a conception of the evolution of Aryan spirituality, transcending without entirely rejecting the pagan past. He perceived a "certain unity in Aryan concepts of religion, whether they manifested themselves in Wodan, Varuna, Zeus or Ahura Mazda,"[95] and that a new German religion would arise from the soul of the Aryan character, perhaps always in the process of becoming rather than ossified in any dogma.[96]

Careless historians have often repeated the charge that Hitler, before his imprisonment at Landsberg, cynically placed the Nazi Party in Rosenberg's hands, wagering that his failure of leadership would leave the power seat open. Ian Kershaw rejects this, believing instead that Hitler acted "to entrust the party's affairs to a member of his Munich coterie whose loyalty was beyond question." Rosenberg had a difficult time as acting head of the banned and brawling party but performed capably enough, concealing its activities in the form of hiking clubs and other innocuous organizations, much as Thule had operated clandestinely.[97]

The extent of Rosenberg's power in the Nazi state never matched that of Goebbels, Goering, or Himmler, yet he was entrusted with offices of some influence. Rosenberg introduced the infamous Norwegian National Socialist leader, Vidkun Quisling, to German officials in his capacity as chief of the party's foreign section. As Delegate of the Führer for the Supervision of the Total Education of the Spiritual and World View of the National Socialist Movement, Rosenberg was held accountable by the Nuremberg tribunal held for preparing Germany psychologically for war and genocide.

With its wide mandate the Rosenberg Office was always at odds with more powerful institutions in the Nazi state. It crossed into the domain of the SS in its preoccupation with prehistory and runes. List's ideas were one strain among Rosenberg approaches.[98] The Rosenberg Office became a cultural jurisdiction outside the control of Goebbels's Propaganda Ministry, maintaining a Reich Center for the Advancement of German Literature, which employed thousands of editors, and supporting organizations such as the National Socialist Cultural Community and the Halle Society of Knowledge, which awarded the annual Rosenberg Prize. Among the many problems confronting occupied France in the war's darkest days was Strike Force Reichsleiter Rosenberg, which confiscated books and other cultural property from Jews in occupied France, much of it earmarked for a system of academies Rosenberg planned for after war.

With Germany's invasion of the Soviet Union, Rosenberg was named Minister of Occupied Eastern Territories (1941). Rosenberg advocated abolishing collective farms and establishing limited autonomy for conquered peoples, but his authority was continually undermined by the SS and other Nazi organizations. Like Hans Frank, Rosenberg sometimes argued against Himmler's brutal outrages on grounds that it made the occupied territories unviable.

Along with fellow alumni of the Thule Society, Hess and Frank, Rosenberg can be viewed apart from the Philistines and vipers of the Nazi Party. Clinging precariously to a destructive set of ideals amid much jostling for position with his rivals, when power came into Rosenberg's hands, "he used it with a certain restraint."[99] Rosenberg was not a corrupt man but lacked great reserves of courage, and his moral vision was clouded by the hazy concepts of Ariosophy. It is oddly suggestive that there is little evidence for his German ancestry; he never applied for an honorary rank in the SS, for which he would have been required to prove unimpeachable Aryan descent.

In keeping with the fervor of his arcane philosophy, which he imagined as the heart of Nazi ideology, he condemned Goebbels and Borman as men with no "real understanding of the great idea of National Socialism."[100] During his trial at Nuremberg, Rosenberg endeavored to minimize the authority he wielded under the Third Reich, yet it is also significant that, rejecting the counsel of his attorney, he never recanted his core beliefs. "But the more I search my heart, the less reason I can find for retracting anything," he wrote from his prison cell.[101] In his closing address to the Nuremberg Tribunal, U.S. Supreme Court justice Robert H. Jackson called Rosenberg the "intellectual high priest" of Nazism, "who provided the doctrine of hatred which gave the impetus for the annihilation of Jewry."[102] Rosenberg was executed on October 16, 1946.

The Flight of Rudolf Hess

Rudolf Hess exerted only slight influence on the course of events in Nazi Germany, yet it was Hess to whom Hitler dictated *Mein Kampf*, and Hess who was rewarded for his tireless service as adjutant by being installed as deputy führer, the party's number two position. The motivations behind Hess's bizarre peace mission to Great Britain in 1941 remain one of the great mysteries of World War II. Unlike Rosenberg, Hess was not intellectually prolific, penning only a few political articles and leaving no writings of substance. He remained taciturn to the end, yet was the alumnus of Thule in the upper ranks of the Nazis who most openly, in today's language, enjoyed an occult lifestyle. His habits continued amid the restrictions of Spandau prison, where his reading material included works on astrology and he refused to attend Christian services.[103]

As noted earlier, Hess was introduced to the Thule Society early in 1919 by Max Hofweber. Apparently he was not anti-Semitic before joining the Society but was impressed by Sebottendorff's arguments that the Jews were behind the revolutionary chaos gripping Germany. During the struggle against Bavaria's leftist regimes, Hess gathered an arsenal in the Four Seasons, often purchasing rifles and grenades from Red Guards with money from middle-class Munich donors. Hess also recruited hundreds of students and former officers for the Thule-led Freikorps massing outside Munich, and he led a campaign of sabotage against the Reds inside the capital. During the capture of Munich, Hess was slightly wounded while storming a Red position.

Afterward, he continued to move in Thule circles and became a companion of Dietrich Eckart at the Brennessel wine bar in Schwabing.[104] He joined the Nazi Party in July 1920, just as Hitler began to draw attention for his impassioned oratory. Hess identified him as the strong leader, the savior figure promised by Sebottendorff and Eckart. As Hess later recalled, he was "as though overcome by a vision" upon meeting Hitler.[105]

Before long Hess became Hitler's constant companion at coffeehouses, bars, and cinemas, assisting Eckart in grooming the provincial upstart for presentation in high society, where the Nazis sought financial support. The relationship between Hitler and Hess has been described as strangely close, "well-nigh magical" in the words of Hess's wife.[106] The accepted picture, so eloquently expressed by historian Joachim Fest in his depiction of Hess as Hitler's worshipful assistant, a servant with dog-like devotion to his master, may have been overdrawn.[107] Hess was ardent about Hitler, but Hitler may nonetheless have been his pupil in the early years. Hitler's military intelligence handler, Karl Mayr, was convinced of Hess's profound influence. "Before every important speech Hitler was, sometimes for days, closeted with Hess who in some unknown way got Hitler into that frenetic state in which he came forth to address the public."[108]

Hitler's embrace of Lebensraum, the doctrine that Germany required additional living space for its growing population through the conquest of Russia, likely came through Hess from Karl Haushofer, professor of geopolitics at Munich University and mentor to Hess. Shortly before committing suicide, Haushofer testified at Nuremberg, asserting unconvincingly that Hitler was not influenced by his concept of Lebensraum.[109] "I did not have a positive impression of him," Haushofer claimed of Hitler.[110] In careless accounts of Thule, Haushofer has been called a member of the Society, but there is no evidence that he intersected with Thule circles except in his friendship with Hess, which extended to hiding his former student in the days after the Beer Hall Putsch and visiting him at Landsberg.

Like Hans Frank and Alfred Rosenberg, Hess clung tenaciously to what he saw as a set of ideals, even amid the deadly scramble for power in Nazi Germany. It was through his prompting that Julius Streicher, the odious and corrupt Nazi pornographer, was brought to trial before a party tribunal. On May 10, 1941, Hess flew to Scotland with a Tibetan amulet in his pocket, a gift from Swedish explorer Sven Hedin.[111] It was an idealistic and Quixotic peace mission, an unauthorized attempt to broker a deal between Nazi Germany and Great Britain. Hess hoped to secure a treaty through the good offices of the Duke of Hamilton, a well-known aviator and the first man to fly over Mount Everest. In his capacity as wing commander, the duke happened to be the RAF officer responsible for the zone where Hess landed. It was altogether the most bizarre episode of the war, giving rise to all manner of interpretations. Among them is the idea that the Duke of Hamilton was associated with Hess through the international occult underground.[112]

The most likely explanation lies with Hess's mentor, Karl Haushofer, and his son, Albrecht, a senior official in the foreign ministry. Along with the amulet, Hess carried greeting cards from the Haushofers on his person. As the architect of Lebensraum, one of the building blocks of Hitler's worldview, Karl worried that Germany could never overtake the Soviet Union while simultaneously engaged in war with Great Britain. Albrecht was also known for supporting the German-British alliance advocated by Hitler in *Mein Kampf*, an idea whose seeds had probably been sown by the elder Haushofer. Albrecht, a friend of the Duke of Hamilton, had hoped to arrange a covert meeting between Hess and the British aristocrat in neutral Portugal after the war began, using a Lisbon post office to write the duke in September 1940. The envelope was addressed to Mrs. Violet Roberts, another family friend of the Haushofers. Her nephew, Walter Roberts, was a member of Special Operations 1 (SO1), Britain's black propaganda unit. It is possible that SO1 was running a disinformation campaign to dissuade Hitler from invading Britain and "quite accidentally caught Hess in its net," luring him with promises of a negotiated peace. Hess seems to have understood his mission differently. In a letter from British captivity to his four-year-old son, he explained, "There are higher . . . let us call them divine powers . . . which intervene at least when it is time for great events. I *had* to come to England to discuss an agreement and peace."[113]

The official German explanation for Hess's flight, expounded in the *Völkischer Beobachter*, implied that he had become unstable. "Hess had been in poor health for some years," the editorial claimed, adding that he had "sought relief to an increasing extent from mesmerists and astrologers," who became responsible for Hess's "mental confusion."[114] Privately, Goebbels blamed the Haushofers, complaining that they filled Hess with "mystic rubbish."[115]

At the onset of the Third Reich, no objection was raised to the practice of astrology. Professional astrologers and palm readers were allowed to join the independent professionals section of the Nazi trade union, the German Labor Front. Astrological literature continued to circulate under the watchful gaze of the Reich Writers' Chamber, an organ of the Propaganda Ministry. International astrology conferences were held in Germany with the permission of the authorities. However, 1937 saw the first wave of suppression against occultists. In that year the German Theosophical Society, the Theosophical Publishing House, the German Astrological Society, and several astrological publications were proscribed. At least two astrology journals continued to publish until the spring of 1941, when Hess's flight triggered a second crackdown on the occult.

In the aftermath of Hess's peace mission, the Propaganda Ministry banned June 24, 1941, "public performances" by astrologers, clairvoyants, telepaths, spiritualists, and occultists. The Gestapo had already been at work in the days following Hess's flight, arresting hundreds of astrologers in an operation called "Aktion Hess." Many were released within days. Others suspected of having some link with Hess died in custody or languished until the Allied victory. Ernst Schultz-Strathaus, a literary historian, occultist, and astrologer on Hess's staff at Munich's Brown House, was accused of having advised the deputy führer that May 10 was an auspicious date for his flight to Scotland. He was released from prison in 1943. On October 3, 1941, a confidential circular from the

Propaganda Ministry banned all articles on astrology, divination, and the Ariosophical teachings of Jörg Lanz. Despite the clamp down, the Rosenberg Office continued to patronize and shelter astrologers, even commissioning horoscopes of Allied generals.[116]

Hitler was at first outraged by Hess's actions but his anger was later tempered by reflection. He complained to Elsa Bruckmann, the wife of German publisher Hugo Bruckmann, that he was "deprived of the only two human beings among all those around me to whom I have been truly and inwardly attached: Dr. Todt [the architect of the Autobahn] is dead and Hess had flown away from me."

"That is what you say now and to me," Bruckmann snapped back, "but what does your official press say? . . . When our unhappy age at last produces a man who, like a Valkyrie, fulfills the deeper meaning of Wotan's command—seeks to carry out *your* most sacred wish with heroism and self-sacrifice—then he is described as insane!" Hitler was almost pensive in his reply: "Is it not enough, what I have said to you—and to you alone—about my real feeling? Is that not enough for you?"[117]

Hitler Takes Control

It is not necessary to trace Hitler's remarkable and rapid ascent to leadership of the German Workers' Party, spurred as it was by the increasingly persuasive power of his public speaking, except to note that his rise was accompanied by conflict between him and the party's cofounder, Karl Harrer. The standard explanation for their dispute, that Harrer "was wedded to the secret-society notions inherited from the Thule Society and would have liked to continue running the DAP as a little discussion circle," is facile.[118] The Workers' Party was already expanding before Hitler's arrival, sending invitations by the hundreds to talks given by such *völkisch* notables as Eckart and Feder. It had ceased to be a little discussion circle before Hitler became a member in September and, in fact, was always intended as a means to popularize the Thule Society's anti-Semitic and *völkisch* political views. A likelier explanation is that Hitler saw the small party as the vehicle for conveying his will to power and recognized Reich chairman Harrer as a more formidable obstacle to the achievement of his ends than the more vacillating Drexler. Hitler stated only that Harrer disagreed on the timing of the party's first mass meeting in early 1920, and "being an honest, upright man, he withdrew from the leadership of the party." [119] Harrer resigned in January 1920 and was replaced by Drexler. After July 1921, Drexler was merely "honorary chairman," having surrendered all authority to the party's Führer.[120]

Hitler did not undermine Thule's leadership of the party before being influenced by members of the Society. The damp clay of prejudices and anxieties that constituted Hitler's internal life when he returned to Munich after war's end, much of it already molded by his encounter with Ariosophical publications and *völkisch* militants in Vienna, was given final shape by Thulists. Regardless of whether Hitler actually joined the Society as Sebottendorff stated, or if he merely came to the September 12 German Workers' Party meeting with more knowledge than he later admitted, Hitler was by the fall of 1919 under the influence of Thulists and their confederates in the party's membership, notably Eckart, Rosenberg, and Feder.

Eckart's impact on Hitler is undisputed. However, Eckart's ties through Thule to Rosenberg, Feder, Drexler, and Harrer are overlooked by historians who concur with Hitler that only one or two individuals influenced him in postwar Munich, not a network of individuals linked to the Thule Society. All standard accounts of Hitler's life in the early days of Nazism agree that Eckart provided the young man with his reading material, corrected his grammar, introduced him to Munich society, and spoke to him for hours about art, literature, music, and politics. It has even been noted that the more vigorous turns of phrase in *Mein Kampf*, the "shameless enemies" and "national criminals," actions taken as "swift as lightning," and even the welling up of substantives, echoes Eckart's writing style.[121] In 1921 Eckart moved to Thierschstrasse, a few doors from Hitler's residence in Munich; the two men vacationed together at Berchtesgaden in the Bavarian Alps, where Hitler would later construct the Berghof, his hilltop retreat. Through Eckart's contacts money began to flow into the Nazi Party's coffers. Thule Society associate Lehmann became an important early donor.[122] Eckart may have seen in Hitler the leader he had spoken of in the summer of 1919. Germany needed, he said,

> A guy who can stand the rattle of a machine gun, who won't fill his pants in fear. I can't use an officer; the people don't respect them any longer. Best of all would be a worker who's got his mouth in the right place.[123]

The phrase "I can't use an officer" indicates that Eckart actively sought such a leader; the verb "use" implies a master-apprentice relationship, with Eckart in the top position. "Best of all would be a worker" correlates with Sebottendorff's motive of building a bridge between esoteric *völkisch* ideology and the working class, the purpose behind the Workers' Circle.

Eckart's search for the coming leader gave contemporary expression to the messianic strain of German social and political thought, nurtured by German nationalists during the long prelude to Germany's unification in the nineteenth century, maintained by the *völkisch* discontents of Bismarck's Reich. This element was amplified before World War I in the ruminations of Ariosophists, especially Guido von List in his call from a "Strong One from Above" to redeem the Germanic peoples and establish an Aryan-dominated world order. The trauma of German defeat and the upheavals that followed provided a larger contingent of the disaffected eager to follow a messiah to the German Promised Land.[124] In appearance Hitler was hardly the knight in white armor, the Teutonic thunder god, that *völkisch* activists had sought. Yet his worldview "and the conviction with which he expressed it transformed him into a personality of quite extraordinary dynamism," and his frothing rage found an echo in a society where fear and anger had been fed by Germany's unexpected defeat and the economic and political uncertainty that followed the Versailles peace.[125]

Eckart apparently felt estranged from Hitler at the time of his death from heart failure in December 1923. It was ironic that this tireless promoter of Hitler as the German messiah came to feel that his protégé had developed delusions of grandeur. "The way Adolf is carrying on now goes beyond me. The man is plain crazy," he said, complaining of the total identification of Hitler with the movement, whose existence beyond Hitler became increasingly incomprehensible. Whatever reservations Eckart may have entertained toward Hitler in the end did nothing to lessen Hitler's public estimation of his mentor. Eckart was buried near Hitler's home in Berchtesgaden, statues and busts were carved in his honor, and a Dietrich Eckart Prize was awarded by the Nazi regime to German writers.[126]

Nazi Party Program

The Twenty-Five Points was the official program of the Nazi Party, adopted on February 24, 1920, and never abrogated. Konrad Heiden, an anti-Nazi journalist and witness to many events who became one of the most important early chroniclers of Nazism, claimed it was written by Hitler, Drexler, Feder, and Eckart.[127] Another account has Hitler working with Drexler, rewriting the latter's rough draft of the party program until past midnight in a workers' canteen.[128] In yet another telling, Hitler took the trolley to Drexler's home in Nymphenburg, where Drexler's daughter climbed onto the future führer's knee, and Drexler's wife interrupted the two men by imploring them to eat the supper she had prepared.[129]

The program contained condemnations of the Versailles Treaty, an issue that cut across party lines in Weimar Germany. Among its eight anti-Semitic planks were provisions to strip Jews of citizenship, public office, and editorial positions, all measures later taken during the Third Reich. The point declaring that "we demand legal prosecution of all tendencies in art and literature of a kind likely to cause the deterioration of our life as a people" became the basis for Nazi cultural policy. Points 11 through 18 concisely enumerated Feder's economics by calling for the "abolition of the thralldom of interest," "the nationalization of industrial trusts," "the creation and maintenance of a healthy middle class," and "ruthless war upon all those whose activities are injurious to the common interest," including usurers and profiteers. Point 19 restated the premise of the Thule Society's law ring: "We demand that the Roman Law, which serves the materialistic world order, shall be replaced by a German common law." The Twenty-Five Points showed many similarities to programs previously floated in the circles of the Thule Society, especially the manifesto of the German Socialist Party and a twelve-point program published in the May 31, 1919, edition of the *Münchener Beobachter.*

The Twenty-Five Points were unveiled at the German Workers' Party's first mass meeting on February 24, 1920, before an audience of two thousand at the Hofbräuhaus-Festsaal, a large, noisy beer hall filled with rows of wooden tables. The room was often hired out for political meetings, which tended to be interrupted by drunken catcalls and beer-spilling brawls.[130] Drexler sought to shore up attendance for the still little-known Hitler, who presented the Twenty-Five Points to the crowd, by inviting a well-known Munich homeopathic physician and Thule Society member, Johannes Dingfelder, to deliver the main address. The doctor complained that "we have lost touch with the powers of nature . . . the God-given Sun-order . . . and have chased after the good life." Hitler's role at the meeting may have been to reiterate ideas circulating in Thule circles in more table-pounding language, just as his role in editing earlier drafts of the Twenty-Five Points may have been to add such forceful assertions as "Wir forden" ("We demand").

In Nazi Party legend Hitler's proclamation of the Twenty-Five Points would be compared to the bold strokes of Martin Luther as he nailed his Ninety-Five Theses to the church door in Wittenberg. Hitler would recall "violent clashes" with Communist hecklers even as his speech "was accepted with steadily mounting joy" by most spectators, suddenly "united by a new conviction, a new faith, a new will." However, in the February 28, 1920, issue of the *Beobachter*, which reported on the mass meeting, it was Dingfelder's speech that received the most coverage. The paper confined its remarks on Hitler to a single sentence: "Herr Hitler (DAP) presented some striking political points which evoked spirited applause, but also roused the numerous already prejudiced opponents present to contradiction; and he gave a survey of the party's program, which in its basic features comes close to that of the German Socialist Party."[131] The reporter had heard nothing new or unusual in Hitler's address.

Hitler maintained that his ideology was more or less complete before he left Munich for the front in 1914: "Since that time I have never been forced to undertake a shift in my own inner view on this question [Marxism]."[132] Hitler's megalomania permitted few admissions of personal growth after he reached adulthood. Still a relatively young man when catapulted from the anonymity of his previous existence to the forefront of a growing political movement in the early 1920s, Hitler underwent a period of rapid transformation in the unforeseeable circumstances of postwar Bavaria. It was for him a time of unprecedented learning.

9

Trail of the Crooked Cross

> I mean: our stage is that of civilization—a very praiseworthy state no doubt, but also neither was there any doubt that we should have to become very much more barbaric to be capable of culture again.
>
> —Thomas Mann, *Doctor Faustus*

It is now generally accepted that Hitler was more than a phrasemonger, a politician whose rhetoric was nothing but a rationalization of his will to power. Before the publication of *Mein Kampf* (1925), Hitler had developed or acquired a coherent ideology that remained unchanged in essentials, through the Holocaust and the destruction of much of Eastern Europe, down to his death in 1945.[1] The most obvious fixed points of Hitler's ideology included a belief in history as the struggle between races—especially a Manichean view of conflict between Aryan and Jew—and the conviction that Germany, the vanguard of the Aryan race, could only secure its future by obtaining Lebensraum (living space) in eastern Europe at the expense of racially inferior Slavs. Hitler's other obsessions included his hatred of Marxism, nourished by his conviction that Jews, engaged in a covert campaign to dominate the world, were willing to use such apparently contradictory means as capitalism and communism to achieve their ends.

The emotional source of Hitler's hatred of the Jews may be unknowable.[2] The intellectual sources of his ideas, however, can be discerned easily enough in the *völkisch* subculture of pre-1914 Germany and Austria, including the Ariosophical variant that flourished during his Vienna sojourn, and from the Ariosophists among his circle in postwar Munich. The radical disconnect between National Socialism and earlier forms of German nationalism can be explained in part by Hitler's *völkisch* ideology, colored in part by Ariosophy. Hitler "had added a new theme that went beyond the naive, imperialistic greed" of his predecessors, "a racial utopia that promised to lead to a new age . . . sustained by several hundred million genetically conscious people resolutely following their historic mission, conquering land and exterminating all 'inferior races,' or holding them in subjugation."[3]

Recent scholarship has demolished the idea that Hitler came from a family of rabid anti-Semites. His father, Alois, was at worst a moderate Pan-German. Staunchly loyal to the Hapsburg dynasty, Alois was affiliated with the German People's Party, which admitted Jews as members.[4] It is entirely plausible that Hitler was honest when he told Albert Speer that the "danger of Jewry" was revealed to him only in Vienna,[5] and when he asserted in *Mein Kampf* that he became anti-Semitic within two years of arriving in the Austrian capital.[6] Some eyewitnesses recall that Hitler enjoyed cordial relations with Jewish residents at the Vienna Men's Home where he lived from 1910–1913, but his supposed friendship with Jews could have been a matter of convenience. Moreover, his dependence on Jewish peddlers to sell his watercolors may have wounded his sense of artistic genius. Another alleged witness recalls Hitler casting aspersions on the Jews as a "different race" than the Germans.[7] Historian Ian Kershaw believes that Hitler was an avid and well-read anti-Semite by the time he set out for Munich in 1913, but that his views "had not yet coagulated into a fully-fledged ideology." Yet, as he readily admits, "the argument from silence is . . . not conclusive."[8] Who would have noticed the deepening racism of Hitler, a marginal figure in Vienna, or paid much attention to the ruminations of their fellow front-line soldier when survival was a more important concern?

It will never be possible to establish with complete certainty the date or the reason for Hitler's hatred of the Jews, but there is the strong probability that Ariosophy helped shape his beliefs in Vienna and that Ariosophical writers sustained his grievances during the war. "As early as 1914, after volunteering for service, I read in Philipp Stauff's book of the brazen incitements published in the German press at behest of Jewish tyranny," Hitler admitted.[9] There can be no doubt that he was influenced by contact with Ariosophists from the Thule Society following World War I, although the length and breadth of that influence will always be measured by speculation. His first documented statement on the Jewish question, in response to a letter sent to the Reichswehr's Munich command in 1919, already reflects the aims of militant Ariosophy. In it, Hitler insisted that the Jews were a race not a religion, that pogroms were ineffective, and that "the final aim" of anti-Semitism "must unshakably be the removal of the Jews altogether."[10] Many years later, in a 1942 conversation, Hitler spoke knowingly of "Herr von Sebottendorff" in connection with the transfer of the Franz Eher Verlag, Sebottendorff's publishing house, into his hands.[11]

"Hitler is one of our pupils," the Ariosophist Jörg Lanz stated in 1932.[12] Respectable scholars have increasingly accepted that Hitler learned of Ariosophy in its birthplace, turn-of-the-century Vienna.[13] When Nazism was on the rise in Weimar Germany, Lanz proudly claimed Hitler had been his acolyte. The assertion cannot be substantiated. When Nazism lay broken after World War II, Lanz grew more cautious. He was understandably reticent with Vienna under Allied occupation and the de-Nazification commissions hard at work to establish levels of guilt among Nazis and fellow travelers, and to punish the worst offenders. During the 1950s, Lanz told an investigator, the psychologist Wilfried Daim, that Hitler came to him once in 1909 to buy back issues of his magazine, *Ostara.* Pitying the shabby vagabond, Lanz gave him the issues for free and cab fare besides. Lanz recalled that Hitler lived on Felberstrasse, where he regularly purchased *Ostara* from a tobacco kiosk. By checking public records, Daim confirmed that Hitler lived on Felberstrasse in 1909, and that a licensed tobacco kiosk was in the neighborhood. Daim also interviewed Josef Greiner, supposedly Hitler's friend for a portion of his Vienna sojourn. Greiner had already authored a Hitler biography wanting in factual details and verifiable evidence. Greiner told Daim that Hitler kept a large *Ostara* collection in his room and that he animatedly discussed Lanz's ideas with other boarders.[14] Kershaw points out that there are no reliable witnesses to Hitler during his nine months at Felberstrasse. He adds, "It has often been presumed, nevertheless, that it was in precisely these months that he became an obsessive racial anti-semite."[15]

Hitler never spoke of *Ostara* after becoming a public figure but admitted in *Mein Kampf* to reading publications on that order in Vienna:

> For the first time in my life, I bought some anti-Semitic pamphlets for a few pennies. They all started with the supposition that the reader already knew the Jewish question in principle or understood it to a certain degree. Finally, the tone was such that I again had doubts because the assertions were supported by such extremely unscientific arguments. . . . The matter seemed so monstrous, the accusations so unbounded that the fear of committing an injustice tortured me and made me anxious and uncertain again.[16]

Eventually, Hitler's notion of justice was won over by the kind of unscientific, monstrous, and unbounded accusations trumpeted by *Ostara.* In Hitler's worldview, and Lanz's exegesis of Ariosophy, history was a Manichean clash between light and darkness, Aryan and Jew. Any struggle between good and evil, order and chaos, is an outgrowth of primordial racial conflict. Aryans are the source of all civilization, of everything noble and constructive. Jews are the agents of decomposition, of everything corrupt and negative. To ensure Aryan supremacy, miscegenation must be strictly banned, and breeding of purebred Aryans encouraged. Echoing *Ostara,* Hitler declared, "The Jew is the anti-man, the creature of another god. He must have come from another root of the human race.[17]

However, no record exists of Hitler describing himself as an Ariosophist, and there is evidence that he ultimately rejected some ideas associated with Ariosophy. Echoing Alfred Rosenberg, he confided to intimates, "It seems to me that nothing would be more foolish than to reestablish the worship of Wotan. Our old mythology ceased to be viable when Christianity implanted itself. Nothing dies unless it is moribund."[18]

Conversely, Hitler spoke to a similar gathering of Nazi elite in the language of the occult, regardless of whether his listeners understood him. "I imagine to myself that one day science will discover in the waves set in motion by the Rheingold, secret mutual relations connected with the order of the world," he said in words reminiscent of the Golden Dawn magicians. On another occasion he told his listeners, "A new age of magic interpretation of the world is coming, of interpretation in terms of the will and not of intelligence."[19]

Hitler's belief in the intangible realms of being described by Ariosophy can be felt in such queer, enigmatic statements as "having achieved possession of this earth, [the Aryan] will have a free path for activity in domains which will lie partly above it and partly outside it."[20] Blavatsky, whose Theosophy was the mother of Ariosophy, spoke of the "Cyclopean eye" enabling humans to see into the spiritual world, the future, and the minds of other men.[21] Hermann Rauschning, the Nazi president of the Danzig senate, recorded Hitler speaking privately in a distinctly Theosophical-Ariosophical tone:

> To have "magic insight" was apparently Hitler's idea of the goal of human progress. He himself felt that he already had the rudiments of this gift. He attributed to it his success and his future eminence. A savant of Munich . . . had also written some curious stuff about the prehistoric world, about myths.
>
> And visions of early man, about forms of perception and supernatural powers. There was the eye of Cyclops, or median eye, the organ of magic perception of the Infinite, now reduced to a rudimentary pineal gland. Speculations of this sort fascinated Hitler, and he would sometimes be entirely wrapped upon in them. He saw his own remarkable career as a confirmation of hidden powers. He saw himself as chosen for superhuman tasks, as the prophet of the rebirth of man in a new form.[22]

Blavatsky and her Ariosophical successors taught that a new race was destined to take possession of the earth. Hitler said, "Creation is not yet at an end. . . . Man has clearly arrived at a turning point. . . . A new variety of man is beginning to separate out."[23] According to Blavatsky, "Mankind is obviously divided into God-informed men and lower creatures."[24] Hitler took up the same theme: "The two types [of humans] will rapidly diverse from one another. One will sink to a sub-human race and the other rise far above the man of today. I might call the two varieties the god-man and the mass-animal."[25]

Hitler's writings on miscegenation closely follow Lanz's perfervid descriptions of the hell caused by race mixing. For Hitler, the danger of degrading Aryan blood through miscegenation with Jews provided one reason for the total elimination of the Jews:

> The Aryan gave up the purity of his blood and, therefore, lost his sojourn in the paradise which he had made for himself. He became submerged in the racial mixture, and gradually, more and more, lost his cultural capacity, until at last, not only mentally but also physically, he began to resemble the subjected aborigines more than his own ancestors.[26]

Hitler stressed the racial dualism of Aryan against Jew, an idea espoused constantly by Sebottendorff. "The mightiest counterpart to the Aryan," said Hitler, "is represented by the Jew."[27] For Hitler political power was an instrument for the realization of his worldview. The state "was only a means to an end, and as its end it [Nazism] considers the preservation of the racial existence of men."[28] He warned in Listian terms of what would happen should the racial struggle be lost:

> Human culture and civilization . . . are inseparably bound up with the presence of the Aryan. If he dies out or declines, the dark veils of an age without culture will again descend on this globe.[29]

Hitler advocated something on the lines of Lanz's Ordo Novi Templi (ONT) when he said, "How can we arrest racial decay? Shall we form a select company of the really initiated? An Order, the brotherhood of Templars round the holy grail of pure blood?"[30] Heinrich Himmler's SS was to become that brotherhood.

The product of a small-town, Bavarian Catholic setting, Himmler became one of the most vocal foes of Christianity among the Nazis, an advocate for recovering the ethos of Germany's pagan past and a virulent racist entrusted with engineering the Holocaust. During the struggle against the Bavarian Soviet Republic, Himmler took his first step into the militarized politics of Nazism as aide to the commander of a reserve company of Freikorps Oberland, a paramilitary force raised by the Thule Society. He never saw action in the battle for Munich. Afterward, Himmler gravitated toward the nucleus of the Nazi party as reconstituted under the leadership of Hitler.[31]

A direct line between the ONT and the SS can be drawn through Karl Maria Wiligut, a much-decorated colonel in the Austro-Hungarian army who became associated with the ONT before World War I. As early as 1903 his book of poetry, *Seyfrieds Runen,* echoed List in its references to the Aryan roots of the Austrian landscape. According to witnesses years later, Wiligut had already begun to claim, not unlike List's associate Tarnhari, possession of ancestral memories covering many eons, back to an age when three suns rose in the sky and dwarves and giants inhabited the earth. He also maintained that he was the last in a primordial line of Aryan sages and noblemen who traced their descent from gods.

Ariosophy's fascination with ancestral memory parallels the exploration by Carl Jung into the tribal, racial, and universal unconscious. For Jungian analysts, the unconscious is a trove of archaic memories, a record of the mythic past in the background of each individual psyche. Even before the close of World War I, Jung worried that this archaic underworld might break through the consciousness of Western civilization, whose boundaries had become brittle veneer as Christianity receded and state-sanctioned slaughter raged on. He warned that "relics of antiquity in the collective unconscious" of the Germans would engender "a peculiar and increasing activation of the collective unconscious" until "the pacing to and fro of the blond beasts in their subterranean dungeon" would grow louder, "threatening us with an outburst which is bound to have devastating consequences." Later, Jung warned that Germany had become a medium through which the archetype of Wodan had reentered the world.[32]

Wiligut's occult circle from 1908 through the outbreak of war included Theodor Czepl and other members of ONT, the actress Marie Thaler, and, according to the unsupported assertion of one informant, Hitler. After the war the ONT renewed contact with Wiligut upon Lanz's direction. In 1924 his wife arranged for his commitment to a Salzburg mental hospital, where physicians diagnosed him as schizophrenic and paranoid, noting that he traced "his descent back to Wodan." The latter reference may have been a misunderstanding by alienists confused by Wiligut's cosmology. He apparently preached that his ancestors were prophets of the god Krist, the Aryan prototype of Christ, whose teachings were corrupted into Christianity as they filtered into Asia.[33] Frieda Dorenberg, Nazi Party Member No. 6 and an initiate of the Edda Society, an offshoot of Thule, arranged for Wiligut's passage to Munich in 1932 where he was extolled as a seer by local occultists. Before long he published rune rhymes and numerological essays in Edda's magazine, *Hagal*, under the name Jarl Widar. The year after Wiligut arrived in Germany, an ONT brother and Edda member already enrolled as an SS officer, Richard Anders, introduced him to Himmler.

It was a fruitful encounter. Later in 1933 Wiligut joined the SS as a hauptsturmführer (captain) under the name Karl Maria Wiligut-Weisthor, and was appointed chief of the division for prehistoric research within the SS Office for Race and Settlement. He was promoted, eventually reaching the rank of brigadeführer (brigadier general).

By 1935 Wiligut joined Himmler's Persönlicher Stab (personal staff), which "became the focus of influence in the SS" because of its accessibility to the Reichsführer. The staff controlled a number of SS enterprises, including Nordland Verlag, a publishing company devoted to Himmler's arcane interests. The Persönlicher Stab also governed such SS organizations as the Ahnenerbe, a foundation that searched for the Aryan past, mounting archaeological expeditions as far afield as South America and Tibet.[34] Wiligut designed the *Totenkopfring* worn by SS members with its death's head and runes; composed rituals and designed ritual objects used in SS ceremonies for marriage, the naming of children, and other rites of passage; and prepared reports on esoteric subjects for Himmler, many of them records of his ancestral memories of Europe's prehistoric past, along with studies for the preservation of Germanic monuments and the reestablishment of the old religion to be financed in part by seizing church properties. He also worked on the reconfiguration of Wewelsburg, a seventeenth-century castle near Buren in Wesphalia, into the chivalric lodge of the SS. Wewelsburg was remodeled as the ritual space for ceremonies peculiar to Himmler and the SS. Wiligut presided over SS wedding rites at Wewelsburg, wielding an ivory-handled staff carved with runes, and over solstice and equinox ceremonies.

It was through Wiligut that a member of the Guido von List Society, Gunther Kirchoff, came within Himmler's orbit as a writer of private reports on esoteric topics for the Reichsführer-SS, including a collaboration with Wiligut on artifacts in the Black Forest, studying inscriptions and half-timbered houses from a Listian perspective and concluding that the region had once been a center of cultic activity. Wiligut retired from the SS in 1939, only weeks before the outbreak of World War II, ostensibly for health reasons but possibly owing to internal intrigue within Himmler's camp.[35] The scholars employed by the Ahnenerbe, trying to apply more rigorous academic standards to its researches, were often in conflict with Wiligut and Kirchhoff's intuitive pursuit of spiritual knowledge.

In 1942, four years after Austria was absorbed into the Reich, the ONT was banned by the Gestapo.[36] The silencing of Lanz may have been nothing more than an episode in the Third Reich's periodic crackdowns on occultists without official patronage. The thought persists, though, that Hitler was uncomfortable acknowledging his spiritual parents. The Thule Society's Johannes Hering, who became the Nazi Party's expert on occultism and appeared to be engaged in a campaign to obscure the party's ties to the occult, wrote that "from a National Socialist, that is from a sober scientific perspective, many elements of his [Lanz's] teachings have to be rejected."[37] Nevertheless one of Lanz's works, the Ariosophical liturgy book *Das Buch der Psalmen Teutsch* (published in 1926), was discovered among the two thousand surviving volumes of Hitler's personal library. Also uncovered in the collection was a book presented to Hitler in 1921 by Dr. Babette Steininger, an early member of the Nazi Party. She inscribed it "To Adolf Hitler, my dear Armanen Brother." "Armanen Brother" was a reference to the priesthood envisioned by Lanz's master,

Guido von List.[38] Several other surviving occult works from Hitler's library are signed with earnest dedications from his followers.[39] There are also the unsupported recollections of Hitler's Munich bookseller, the List disciple and genealogist Elsa Schmidt-Falk, who claimed Hitler owned List's *Deutsch-Mythologische Landschaftsbilder* and had read his main works with great interest.[40] Hitler also told her that Viennese List Society members gave him a letter of introduction to the Munich occultist Friedrich Oskar Wannieck, who died shortly before Hitler's arrival in Bavaria.[41]

Other circumstantial or unsubstantiated suggestions of Hitler's affinity for List can be inferred. According to Hitler's Vienna friend August Kubizek, Hitler composed a play (1908) concerning conflict between Christian missionaries and the ancient Wodanist priesthood, a theme that had already been articulated in List's fiction.[42] During his Vienna sojourn, Hitler wrote the following poem in a spirit echoing List:

I often go on bitter nights
To Wodan's oak in the quiet glade
With dark powers to weave a union
The runic letters the moon makes with its magic spell.[43]

Schmidt-Falk's statement about Hitler's letter of introduction from the List Society, the record of his wartime reading habits, and his known involvement with Thulists after the war suggest an Ariosophical continuity stretching from Vienna through his takeover of the Nazi Party. Hitler's last preserved words, the conclusion of his final testament dictated as Soviet shells rained on his Berlin bunker, could have been written decades before by Lanz:

> Above all I charge the leaders of the nation and those under them to scrupulous observance of the laws of race, to merciless opposition to the universal poisoner of all peoples, international Jewry.[44]

Another known point of exposure for Hitler to Ariosophy were the lectures Hitler attended in the company of Rudolf Hess in 1922 at the Munich home of Hugo Bruckmann, the publisher of Houston Stewart Chamberlain, and his wife, Elsa, née Princess Cantacuccene of Romania. The speaker, Alfred Schuler, was a follower of List and a notorious denizen of the bohemian precincts of Schwabing. Schuler longed for a pagan unity of Volk and landscape, and believed that *völkisch* instincts were biological, grounded in bloodlines.[45]

At the turn of the century Schuler had been part of the loose-knit Munich circle called the Cosmics, whose most prominent members were philosopher Ludwig Klages and poet Stefan George. Klages became a learned denouncer of modernity and extoller of the *völkisch* soul. George was ranked alongside Rilke as Germany's greatest poet of the early twentieth century. Photographs from the 1890s of this German Yeats, whose poetry reflected neopagan and Theosophical influences, reveal a brooding, slouchy fin-de-siècle figure. George used the swastika in his publications and spoke of creating a spiritual aristocracy. He eventually broke with Schuler and Klages over their extreme racism and anti-Semitism. George's relationship with the Third Reich was curious. Some of his followers joined the Nazi Party, while others, notably Count von Stauffenberg who tried to assassinate Hitler in 1944, conspired to overthrow the Nazis. George's poetry was read aloud at Party Day in Nuremberg, but he refused the offer to head the official organization for poets in Nazi Germany, opting for exile in Switzerland. Some have suggested that George "invested the title of 'Fuhrer' with the specific qualities that Hitler, in his use of it, arrogated to himself."[46]

Along with the intellectual nourishment he may have received at the Bruckmann salon, Hitler benefited financially through the intervention of his hosts. Elsa arranged a meeting between Hitler and industrialist Emil Kirdorf, who paid off the Nazi Party's debts.[47] Hitler received money from Hugo enabling him to live in higher style. The Bruckmanns remained in touch with Hitler through the early years of World War II.

Origins of the Swastika

Swastika is a word of Sanskrit origin meaning "so be it" or "amen." The swastika is an archetypal symbol whose wide dispersal around the globe was taken by Nordic racists as evidence of Aryan colonization and influence in ancient times. In Nazi hands it became a grotesque symbol for evil and remains a defiant emblem of racism in the West.

The swastika was almost forgotten by Western civilization until the excavations of Heinrich Schliemann and the theorizing of the Theosophists brought it to public attention in the 1880s. By the 1910s and '20s the swastika had become a good luck symbol through much of Europe and North America but meanwhile had also been embraced by champions of Aryan superiority. The Polish savant Michael Zmigrodski, from Paris exile, defined it as the "armorial shield" of the Aryan race.[48] The German Social Darwinist Ernst Krause, in his book *Twiskoland* (1891), called the swastika a uniquely Aryan symbol.

The swastika in its variant forms was a symbol sacred to Theosophists, Austrian and German Ariosophists, the Germanenorden, and the Thule Society. It was transmitted to the emerging Nazis by the dentist Friedrich Krohn, a Thulist who became an early member of the German Workers' Party. Krohn's influence on the movement was felt through his collection of twenty-five hundred books, which became a lending library for the new party. Hitler often perused Krohn's shelves in 1920 and 1921.[49] Krohn wrote a memorandum on May 2, 1919, titled "Is the swastika suitable as the symbol of the National Socialist Party?" He answered his own question by designing the prototype of the Nazi flag, a black swastika in a white circle on a red field. In modified form, Krohn's banner appeared publicly for the first time on May 20, 1920, from the podium of a party meeting in Starnberg, and was adopted the following day by the Munich party leaders with Hitler's approval.[50] Hitler backhandedly acknowledged Krohn when recounting the origin of the Nazi flag, writing in *Mein Kampf*, "Actually, a dentist from Starnberg did deliver a design that was not bad at all, and, incidentally, was quite close to my own, having only one fault that a swastika with curved legs was composed into a white disk."[51] The swastika with curved legs referred to the Thule Society's version of the symbol. Krohn later claimed that Hitler made an additional change to his design, shifting the swastika from left to right. As Krohn explained, in Buddhism a left-facing swastika signifies good fortune and salvation, while a right-facing swastika signifies annihilation.[52] Krohn left the Nazi Party in 1921.[53]

Sebottendorff claimed the Nazi flag was based on a banner displayed at Thule offices after the fall of the Bavarian Soviet Republic, consisting of a captured red flag with the Ariosophist swastika on a white circle sewn over the proletarian hammer and sickle.[54] The particular, curved-arm form of the swastika favored by the Thule Society would reappear on the belt buckles of the SA, in the emblem of the SS Nordland Division and on the World War II Anti-Partisan Service Medal for the Eastern Front.

The Fate of Sebottendorff

Hard after the fall of Munich, the Thule Society gathered on May 10, 1918, to mourn the seven members who had been executed at Luitpold. In following weeks the Society kept busy, holding joint meetings with the Hammerbund and the Germanenorden, in which Prince Lippe was initiated into the Orden, and enjoying a reading by Eckart of his play *Lorenzaccio.* Even as he busily worked on behalf of the counterrevolution during the spring of 1919, Sebottendorff found time to shift the allegiance of the Thule Society from the schismatic Germanenorden Walvater to the original Orden, merging Thule with the Orden's small Munich lodge headed by a man called Ulsson. The Germanenorden's secretive newsletter gratefully acknowledged the turnaround: "Our thanks are due to Freiherr von Sebottendorff . . . for this happy event."[55] No record of Walvater's reaction to the defection has been recovered, but one can imagine the displeasure of its leadership, and perhaps even some Thule members.

Sebottendorff was given little time to enjoy either his enlargement of Thule or the fruits of the rightist victory in Bavaria for which he had worked so assiduously. He found himself under attack from all corners. Along with internal squabbling in the *Beobachter* office during the summer of 1919, a libel suit was brought against Sebottendorff by a Jewish business concern that had been a target of the paper's scurrilous articles. Reichswehr general Arnold Ritter von Möhl relieved Sebottendorff of his responsibilities at Freikorps Oberland, charging him with using it as a breeding pool of anti-Semitism.[56] The Social Democratic Party's *Münchener Post* accused Sebottendorff of impersonating an aristocrat, accepting Turkish citizenship to avoid conscription into the German army, "cowardly deserting Thule" during Munich's soviet period, and financial improprieties.[57] The first three charges were false, and the merits of the fourth cannot be judged for lack of evidence.

Within Thule, Sebottendorff was accused of negligence in the death of the seven members at Luitpold Gymnasium. At a Thule meeting on June 22, 1919, Friedrich Knauff, the Society's titular chairman, charged that Sebottendorff left Munich in such haste to organize Freikorps Oberland that he gave no thought to Thule's membership lists, whose discovery by Red Guards led to the Luitpold murders.[58] Sebottendorff's rejoinder that the membership lists were Knauff's responsibility did not satisfy a contentious faction of Thule's membership demanding his departure.[59] Not surprisingly, Sebottendorff blamed his problems on a Jewish conspiracy.[60] Sebottendorff kept no accounts of his funds as he collected and disbursed a great deal of money in the struggle against the leftist regimes in Munich. His penchant for secrecy left him open to accusations that he profited personally, especially from those members of Thule who envied his position.[61]

Sebottendorff resigned as Thule's master in June and appointed as his successor the lawyer Hans Dahn. Despite Dahn's confirmation by the Germanenorden's national leadership, he was quickly sacked by the membership in favor of Johannes Hering.[62] Knauff briefly took the master's position himself but bowed down in favor of Hermann Bauer (February 1920).[63] Despite its membership in the Vereinigten Vaterlaendischen Verbaende (United Fatherland Association), an umbrella group for the German far right in the early 1920s,[64] the Thule Society was never the same without Sebottendorff's energetic stewardship. The squabbling over his succession must have fractured the organization, and the focus of many members shifted to the rising Nazi Party, a creature of Thule that quickly assumed an independent character under Hitler's leadership.

In the early years following Sebottendorff's departure, the Thule Society hosted numerous concerts, poetry readings, and theater performances, but underwent a rapid decline, indicated by its move from the spacious quarters it had occupied in the Four Seasons.[65] In June 1919 a petition under Thule Society letterhead was delivered to the Munich city council, urging the municipality to continue to pay for upkeep of the graves of two Thule members who died at Luitpold, Walter Nauhaus and Walter Deicke.[66] Eventually Thule members seldom gathered except to lay wreaths on the graves of the Luitpold Gymnasium victims. In the wake of Hitler's failed putsch of November 1923, and the prohibition of the Nazi Party, "most members of the NSDAP, under the leadership of the present [1934] lord mayor of Munich, Fiehler, joined the Thule Society," according to Sebottendorff. His claim is probable, because Nazis gravitated to a variety of legal *völkisch* organizations during this period to provide cover for their ongoing campaign of agitation. The upsurge in membership did not last. By 1925, Sebottendorff claimed, Thule shrank to twenty-five active members. He may have had his own reasons to exaggerate the Society's demise without his leadership. Sebottendorff added that after its fortunes dwindled further, Thule was finally stricken from Munich's list of registered societies by local authorities in 1930 when the Society's chairman, Max Sesselman, claimed he no longer had a membership. The brief power struggle between Sesselman and Sebottendorff upon the latter's return could cast doubt on the veracity of the account. Sebottendorff maintained that his return to Munich in 1933, after Hitler's assumption of power, resulted in Thule's reregistration with Munich authorities.[67]

Despite the apparent evaporation of membership, Thule's continuing importance in *völkisch* circles is shown by the upward movement of Bauer, who used his office as the Society's master as the springboard to the chairmanship of the powerful rightist league, Vereinigten Vaterlaendischen Bayerns (1923). Max Sesselman succeeded Bauer as chairman.

Because of Sebottendorff's resignation as master of the Thule Society in the summer of 1919, the *Münchener Beobachter* moved its offices at Four Seasons to a storefront leased by Grassinger, chief of one of Thule's creatures, the German Socialist Party. Thulists retained all key positions: Sesselman and Hans Georg Mueller became editors; Johann Ott, business manager; and Wilhelm LaForce, advertising manager. On August 19, the paper was renamed the *Völkischer Beobachter.*

The operation did not run smoothly that summer. Sebottendorff, speaking through the paper's publisher, his mistress, Kathe Bierbaumer, criticized Sesselman and Mueller for sloppy journalism. They responded by spreading rumors in *völkisch* circles that Bierbaumer was Jewish as well as Sebottendorff's bed partner.

Sebottendorff reorganized the paper at a meeting in Konstanz on September 30, 1919, with Bierbaumer and his sister, Dora Kunze. They decided to reconstitute the *Beobachter*'s publishing house, Franz Eher Verlag. Afterward, Bierbaumer owned capital in the paper worth 110,000 marks and Kunze, 10,000 marks. By March 20, 1920, Bierbaumer sold most of her interest, retaining only 46,500 shares. Gottfried Feder had purchased ten thousand; Thule members Freiherr von Feilitzsch and Wilhelm Franz Xaver Eder twenty thousand and ten thousand respectively; and the unidentified Karl Alfred Braun, thirty-five hundred. Sebottendorff's sister retained her ten thousand marks of capital.[68]

In December 1920, Drexler, acting as proxy for the Nazi Party, purchased the *Beobachter* from its eight shareholders. Together with Augsburg notary Gottfried Grandel, Eckart provided the money to buy out Bierbaumer and Kunze. Eckart bonded his belongings and raised additional collateral from his cousin, Simon Eckart. Eckart secured an additional sixty thousand marks from Ritter von Epp, presumably from a special Reichswehr fund.[69] In November 1921, ownership of the *Beobachter* was transferred to Hitler.

After the paper's purchase by the Nazis, Eckart became editor with Rosenberg as his associate. Focused on the *Beobachter*, and beset by financial and personal woes (including a divorce from his wife), Eckart discontinued *Auf gut deutsch* in May 1921. Its final issue was filled with contributions from the indefatigable Rosenberg. As Eckart declined, Rosenberg took increasing responsibility for the *Beobachter*, the party's chief organ, and became editor in 1922, though the ailing Eckart continued to write for it until his death.

Under attack from the left and from within his own camp in the summer of 1919, Sebottendorff left Munich for Konstanz, a resort town near the Swiss border, and to the resort at Bad Saeckingen.[70] In November of that year he moved to Freiburg, where he joined the local militia, the Volkswehr. With his usual sense of high style, Sebottendorff lived in a grand villa with Kathe Bierbaumer. His conspiratorial nature led him to organize a secretive, short-lived storm battalion within the militia. As usual, Sebottendorff is a furtive presence at best in the official records of the Volkswehr and of Freiburg. When registering as a resident of the town he signed himself Rudolf Glandeck von Sebottendorff, a citizen of Prussia. In April 1920 a local official made marginal additions to his registration forms, altering his name to Rudolf Glauer Sebottendorff, adding that he falsely carried the name of von Sebottendorff and cross-referencing him to the registration of Rudolf Glauer.[71]

A conservative politican, Dr. Otto Bielefeld of the Freiburg Citizen's Council, which represented the interests of local merchants, became suspicious of Sebottendorff's activities and wrote his counterpart at the Munich Citizen's Council for information. The reply is interesting for the light it shines on Sebottendorff's murky reputation, if not the facts of his career in counterrevolution:

> Confidential
>
> Upon your inquiry of 15 November regarding Mr. von Sebottendorff, I allow myself to respond that I do not have clear knowledge of Mr. Von Sebottendorff. I have only met Mr. von Sebottendorff a few times on occasion of my work as recruiter for the Reichswehr and my stay in Bamberg. As far as I know, Mr. von Sebottendorff, at the time of the soviet republic in Munich, was instrumental in gathering forces against the dictators. As far as we know, Mr. von Sebottendorff was associated with an anti-Semitic organization in Munich. We would not appoint Mr. von Sebottendorff as our treasurer. About the military proficiency of Mr. von Sebottendorff nothing is known.
>
> One hears here that Mr. von Sebottendorff in reality has a different name and is not a member of the nobility.
>
> With German citizen's greetings,
>
> Citizens Council Munich
> Meyer-Absberg
> Chairman[72]

Eventually Sebottendorff settled in Bad Sachsa, where in October 1920 he assumed editorship of *Astrologische Rundschau* and wrote several astrological textbooks that "enjoyed a high prestige among contemporary German astrologers for their empirical precision and clarity."[73]

Astrology persisted in Europe on the level of carnival fortune telling through the nineteenth century, until a revival of interest among the educated public was spurred by the growth of the Theosophical movement after the 1880s. A new generation of astrologers, armed with weighty books and periodicals concerned with the esoteric dimension of astrological symbolism, emerged in large part from the ranks of Theosophists, where appetites for astrology may have been wetted by Blavatsky's teachings.[74] One of the leading figures in the German astrological revival, Hugo Vollrath, was a disciple of Franz Hartmann, who served as the link between the inner circles of the Theosophical Society and Ariosophy's founder, Guido von List. Vollrath established the Theosophical Publishing House in Leipzig in 1906, which published an array of occult and astrological texts.

In Germany, a succession of seemingly inexplicable events beginning with defeat in World War I and continuing through the political and economic turmoil that followed encouraged astrology's popularity as Germans devoured horoscopes in search of things to come. Ernst Tiede, editor of the Theosophical Publishing House's flagship periodical, *Astrologische Rundschau,* had been a correspondent of List and Lanz, and penned a book steeped in Ariosophy, *Ur-Arische Gotteserkenntnis* (1917). In autumn of 1920 Sebottendorff succeeded Tiede as editor of the *Rundschau.* He continued as editor in chief through 1930, despite notations on the masthead after 1925 identifying him as "temporarily in Lugano, Switzerland" or "temporarily residing in a foreign country."[75]

During his tenure under Vollrath, Sebottendorff became "one of Germany's most prolific and, indeed, widely read astrological authors," writing or editing at least half a dozen books, including a 1921 translation from English, *Die Botschaft der Sterne,* by Max Heindel, a California-based Rosicrucian astrologer. "While the Freiherr's name soon became a household word in German astrological circles he lived and worked in the strictest privacy and avoided all personal contacts," according to a chronicler of prominent European astrologers from the early twentieth century.[76] One curious story about Sebottendorff and the alleged influence of astrology over Hitler was put forward, with no supporting evidence, by Louis de Wohl, a refugee German astrologer in the pay of British intelligence during World War II. Wohl asserted that Sebottendorff warned Hitler that November 1923 was inauspicious for a putsch, and that in the aftermath and under the influence of Hess, Hitler began to enlist the services of astrologers.[77] While the story may have no basis, its existence indicates that Sebottendorff enjoyed recognition in occult circles and a reputation for early ties with the Nazis.

During this time Sebottendorff maintained contact with Thule's parent organization, the Germanenorden, as a contributor to the Orden's publication *Rigende Jugend* (1920–1921). Early in 1923, Sebottendorff left Bad Sachsa for a third Turkish sojourn, described by him as a quest for occult knowledge.[78] Early in 1924 he was in Switzerland for what he cryptically called "a not completely voluntary stay" in a book he authored on the secrets of Freemasonry and the occult. He claimed he was commanded to write the book by the chiefs of an esoteric order, probably the Rite of Memphis lodge with which he was affiliated in prewar Turkey.[79] According to Sebottendorff, he served as Mexico's consul in Constantinople from 1926 to 1928, although Turkish records indicate that he was removed from this post in 1926 at the behest of the Atatürk regime.[80] Following his 1928 divorce from Anna Iffland, Sebottendorff claimed to have traveled through Central America, Mexico, and the United States between 1929 and 1931. He became a knight in the Imperial Order of the Knights of Constantine and St. George, a chivalric order whose fanciful lore claimed Constantine the Great as its founder. According to Sebottendorff, the Order was involved in the aftermath of the Bolshevik Revolution in anti-Communist intrigue.[81]

Meanwhile, the Thule Society's Rudolf John Gorsleben (1883–1930), a playwright, occultist, and journalist before World War I, who served as an adviser to Turkish troops fighting T. E. Lawrence's Bedouins during the war, founded the Edda Society (1925). Named for the Icelandic sagas that inspired List's neo-Wodanism, the Thulist offshoot numbered among its members Ludendorff's notoriously eccentric spouse, Mathilde von Kemnitz, and Werner von Bulow, from a politically prominent family that had produced a chancellor under Wilhelm II and a state secretary in the foreign ministry under Hitler.[82] The Thule Society's parent organization, the Germanenorden, was in existence as late as 1934 under the leadership of Philipp Stauff and General von Brockhusen.[83]

By the time Sebottendorff returned to Munich after Hitler's appointment as chancellor (1933), several of Thule's members had risen in the Nazi ranks with Rosenberg and Hess. The most prominent, Dr. Hans Frank, was condemned to death at Nuremberg for his role in the Holocaust and the enslavement of Poles. As governor-general of Poland (1939–1945), Frank presided over his fiefdom in regal splendor from Cracow Castle, but his authority was continually undermined by the SS. Joaquim Fest memorably called him an "imitation of a man of violence,"[84] torn between an ideal of justice and the need to prove himself as a strongman among the toughs of the Nazi movement. His legal principles were rooted in Thule's call to replace jurisprudence based on Roman law, the Code Napoléon, or written constitutions, with ancient Nordic common law. With Germany's monarchies swept away and replaced by a hated republic, Thule's interest in overturning the legal system in favor of an organic law rooted in the *Volk* became more than an academic topic. Frank's worldview aided his rise as the Nazi Party's most successful attorney during its brawling years in the late 1920s and early 1930s. It emboldened him to advocate the destruction of the Jews, yet it also led to his proclamation in a 1942 lecture at Berlin's Friedrich-Wilhelm University that "no empire has ever been conceivable without justice—or contrary to justice."[85] In his capacity after 1933 as Reich Commissioner for the Coordination of Justice in the German States and the Renovation of the Administration of Law, Frank was placed in charge of the German Juridical Front, to which all court officials and attorneys were required to belong. Through his office, the theories expounded by the Thule Society had a practical effect.

Frank is usually dismissed as a vacillating personality, but perhaps his apparent shifts between idealism and mayhem were the logical outcome of a mind-set developed during his time as a youthful member of the Thule Society. There are curious parallels between his behavior and that of his fellow Thule alumnus, Rosenberg. Both men tried to resign their high offices in the occupied east when it became clear that their counsel was being ignored. Albert Speer contrasted the cowardly, braggardly, or evasive response of most Nuremberg defendants with the behavior of Rosenberg and Frank, who gave "an impression of honesty and consistency."[86]

Other members of the Thule Society took their place in the Nazi ranks. Hans Bunge was an officer in Hitler's SS bodyguard, the Leibstandarte Adolf Hitler. Karl Fiehler was lord mayor of Munich.[87] Wilhelm LaForce marched with Hitler in the Beer Hall Putsch and was incarcerated with the führer at Landsberg. In the putsch's aftermath, when the Nazi Party was proscribed, Max Sesselman represented the party as a deputy of the Völkischen Bloc in Bavaria's provincial assembly, the Landtag.

Sebottendorff claimed that a power struggle ensued between himself and Sesselman in spring of 1933 for control of an organization that no longer existed, but whose old membership clamored for a regrouping. Hering later recalled a legal challenge by Sesselman for use of the name Thule Society. A Thulist attorney, Dr. Gaubatz, argued Sebottendorff's case successfully in court, and the Society was officially reorganized with Gaubatz as president on July 25, 1933. Only weeks later Sebottendorff was listed on the city register as president (August 18) with longtime member Hans Riemann, an engineering teacher and Nazi organizer in Mittweida, as his deputy.[88] Apparently by 1934 Franz Dannehl, a well-known explorer and butterfly collector, assumed at least titular leadership of the Society.[89] Sebottendorff's presence galvanized the Thule Society, or at least raised its visibility. Records from this period show regular meetings at the Society's old headquarters, the Four Seasons, including a lecture by Sebottendorff on astrology as a method of determining the age of prehistoric stone circles. The Society had become active enough to encourage Sebottendorff to publish at least two numbers of a journal, *Thule-Bote.*[90] Late in 1933, Sebottendorff's account of Thule's glory years, *Bevor Hitler kam,* was published in Munich by H. G. Grassinger Verlag. That the Thulist Hans Georg Grassinger, a former editor of the *Beobachter* and cofounder of the German Socialist Party, brought the book to press indicates the persistence of the network Sebottendorff had begun to gather around himself in the waning months of World War I. A first edition of three thousand copies was greeted with lively interest. Early in

1934, a second illustrated and expanded edition of five thousand copies was published.[91]

Although unverifiable, assertions by Sebottendorff's associates, made thirty years after the fact, cast his activities upon returning to Germany in an interesting light. One intimate claimed he did not know "whether the motives that brought Sebottendorff back to Munich were primarily connected with business affairs or politics," adding that he "was not so well off" as he had been in 1918–1919. This same associate also said that Sebottendorff had been in contact with Himmler but failed to interest the Reichsführer-SS in a scheme to establish a Masonic lodge in Vienna as a cover for intelligence operations.[92]

Despite his profession of loyalty to the Nazi movement, Sebottendorff attracted unfavorable attention from Germany's new rulers. He succeeded in joining the Nazi Party after his return to Germany but was expelled by fall of 1933, having been accused of a curious offense, the intent of traveling to Palestine "to spread atrocity stories," presumably about the status of Jews in the Reich.[93] Long after the demise of the Third Reich, Grassinger called *Bevor Hitler kam* "a veiled attack on Hitler," cleverly designed to subvert his claims as originator of the Nazi movement.[94]

As early as September 13, 1933, a bulletin from the Reich Ministry of the Interior alerted the Bavarian Political Police (known as the Baypopo before its formal incorporation into the national Gestapo) to the "political impostor" at large in their jurisdiction. In November, Captain Kraus of the political police was ordered to place Thule under surveillance and "to study all documents pertaining to von Sebottendorff and to assist in gathering information against Sebottendorff." That Kraus was a veteran of the Thule Society, a fact of which his superiors could not have been ignorant given his mention in *Bevor Hitler kam,* leads to speculation that some level of collusion existed between Thule and at least the middle tier of the Nazi police state.

Aware that the net was tightening around him, Sebottendorff took delaying actions. On November 24 he filed a complaint against Kraus with the Munich office of the Bavarian State Police. Although Nazi Germany was well on its way toward totalitarianism, the inspector of police initiated an investigation of Sebottendorff's accusations that certain officers had abused their authority. At best Sebottendorff's moves only slowed the gears of the police state. According to a memo from the political police dated February 12, 1934, Sebottendorff was "presently in custody. The charges against him are pending, regarding the spreading of malicious rumors. Also there are charges of fraud pending with several state's attorneys. These proceedings have not been concluded."[95] On March 1, 1934, the Bavarian Political Police notified Grassinger that *Bevor Hitler kam* was banned and confiscated, informing him that "the whole tendency of the book is in general—contrary to fact—to give the chief credit for the national renewal of Germany to the Thule Society."[96] The Baypopo seized most copies of the book's second edition; at least one was preserved and housed in the restricted section of the Nazi Party's Central Archive, stamped with a large red V for *Volkswiderlich* (Against the People). It was the same treatment given to books by Ernst Röhm and other Nazis who had fallen from favor with the regime.[97] By some accounts Grassinger was briefly taken into custody by the Baypopo. Also arrested was longtime *völkisch* activist Bernhard Stempfle, whom the Nazis suspected of having contributed in some way to *Bevor Hitler kam.* Stempfle had also helped edit *Mein Kampf,* but his contribution to Nazism was accounted for nothing. He was murdered during the Night of the Long Knives, when Hitler and the SS silenced opponents within and outside of the Nazi movement.[98]

The trail of Sebottendorff goes cold with his disappearance inside the labyrinth of the Nazi police state, an edifice whose theory rested on the non-Roman legal system advocated by the Thule Society as early as November 1918. Grassinger later claimed that Sebottendorff was killed by the Nazis, but offered no proof.[99] Although the circumstances remain unclear, the Nazis apparently released Sebottendorff, who returned to his beloved Turkey. Germany's intelligence chief in Istanbul from the middle of World War II, Herbert Rittlinger, claimed that the aging Ariosophist, by then a man of seventy, was one of his operatives, an inheritance from his predecessor's list of spies. In Rittlinger's memory, Sebottendorff was a kindly, penurious gentleman, an amiable companion ("I did not find his humorous bonhomie unsympathetic"), who spoke more of Tibet and Rosicrucianism than Nazi Germany, but not a good spy: "As an agent, he was a zero." Unfamiliar with Sebottendorff's past, Rittlinger later wondered whether highly placed friends arranged his release from imprisonment. He was also concerned that Sebottendorff may also have been working for the Allies, commenting years after the war, "Our counterintelligence man thought it was certain but could never prove it, and I myself thought it was quite possible." Nonetheless, he paid Sebottendorff 250 Turkish pounds and later 400 Turkish pounds a month, a sum not inconsiderable. In September 1944, with the Nazis wheeling from defeat after defeat, Turkey finally expelled the German consulate from Istanbul. His handlers left Sebottendorff with enough money to keep him modestly for one year. After the war, Rittlinger was told that Sebottendorff threw himself into the Bosporus on May 9, 1945. Another rumor claimed Sebottendorff was murdered.[100] If either account of his demise were true, his death occurred only two days after the Ariosophical dream of an Aryan millennium was shattered. Hitler was dead, and Germany had unconditionally surrendered to the twin forces regarded by Ariosophy as the principal manifestations of the Jewish world menace, the Bolshevik Slavs and capitalist Anglo-Saxons.

10

Thule.org

Maybe only cheap fiction gives the true measure of reality.

—Umberto Eco, *Foucault's Pendulum*

The Thule Society was probably dispersed once and for all by the Nazi regime before the end of 1934; Sebottendorff probably ended his own life after the defeat of the Third Reich in 1945. There is no evidence that either Thule or Sebottendorff outlived the regime they helped inspire, but their legend has survived and proliferated in recent decades through the medium of dubious books and the World Wide Web. The reemergence of Thule from the obscurity to which the Nazis consigned it warrants attention. Ironically, neo-Nazis, the self-styled heirs to the Third Reich, are among those who have kept the Society's name in circulation. For many latter-day partisans of the Third Reich, the legend of Thule lends intrigue to their project of racism and animosity against liberal institutions.

In embracing the colorful lore that has grown up around the Thule Society, the largely powerless neo-Nazis have compensated themselves for their place in political limbo. The early Nazis under Hitler had no such need for compensation and considered Thule a political embarrassment. Hitler was careful to cover any link between the Thule Society and the birth of the Nazi movement when he wrote *Mein Kampf* (1925), casting aspersions on the founders of the German Workers' Party and men of their sort without mentioning names. In rewriting the history of their movement and the postwar counterrevolution against the left, the Nazis relegated Thule to the footnotes, while dissociating Eckart, Rosenberg, and Hess from its circles. Eckart was honored posthumously as a forerunner to the führer. Sebottendorff was forgotten.

Muted references to the Society can nonetheless be found in chronicles of postwar Munich published after the Nazis seized power. The infamy of the Luitpold Gymnasium massacre was so widespread, and the connection between its prominent victims and Thule so well known, that the Nazis found it impossible to entirely erase the Society from the annals of the 1919 counterrevolution. Ernst von Salomon, a famous Freikorps commander, was the most prominent author of the Nazi period to include the Thule Society among the forces struggling against the Bavarian Soviet Republic.[1]

The West began to hear of the Thule Society before the end of World War II, especially in the popular accounts of Konrad Heiden, a refugee German journalist and eyewitness to many events in Munich. Heiden placed Thule at the forefront of the "armed intellectuals" who opposed Bavaria's leftist regimes, and sketched out the Society's role in terrorism and paramilitary action. He also proposed Thule as prominent in the dissemination of *The Protocols of the Elders of Zion.* Heiden traced the group's influence on Hitler through his two intellectual mentors, Eckart and Rosenberg.[2] Similarly, Peter Viereck's influential critique of German culture, *Metapolitics: From the Romantics to Hitler* (1941), identified Thule, especially Eckart, Hess, and Rosenberg, as crucial to the development of the Nazi party.[3]

Esoteric groups from around the world may also have known of the Thule Society in those years. According to Nicholas Goodrick-Clarke, interest in Thule could be found among India's fringe nationalists in the waning years of the British raj. The pro-Nazi Hindu activist Asit Krishna Mukherji was by 1938 an enthusiastic devotee of Eckart and "saw the Thule Society with its pan-Aryan ideas as the secret initiatory society behind the open political movement of National Socialism."[4]

The Thule Society's significance escaped the attention of the earliest Allied investigators and Western historians to sift through the rubble of the Third Reich. As the mountains of information left behind by the

Nazis began to be scaled, glimpses of Thule found their way to the great early biographers of the Nazi movement, Alan Bullock, Joachim Fest, and John Toland, and into George Mosse's seminal investigation of the *völkisch* subculture, *The Crisis of German Ideology* (1964). Detailed scholarly analysis waited until Goodrick-Clarke's pathfinding study of cultural undercurrents in German-speaking Europe, *The Occult Roots of Nazism* (1992).[5] The lacuna in scholarship attracted the interest of fantasists and frauds, imaginatively coloring the blank spaces with lurid depictions of the Thule Society as a nexus of Satanism, politics, and conspiracies stretching across time and space. The Third Reich was so aberrant and, for many, so perversely intriguing, that irrational explanations have been eagerly and often carelessly embraced by popular audiences as supplement or substitute for the economic and political rationales of mainstream historians. Lending a false note of credence to a farrago of ungrounded speculation, the Thule Society gained a prominent place in the legend of an "occult Reich" after being cited in several prominent pseudo-histories. In the pantheon of popular culture Thule became evil incarnate, a shadow in the dark zone where fantasy eclipsed facts.

Imaginary History

The construction of a body of doubtful lore surrounding the Thule Society began in 1960 with *Le Matin des Magiciens*, published in Great Britain as *The Dawn of Magic* and the United States as *The Morning of the Magicians.*[6] In its embrace of esotericism of all sorts, the book resonated loudly within the 1960s counterculture. *The Morning of the Magicians* was an imaginative series of associations, linking alchemy and quantum physics, Jung and Gurdjieff, and like the science fiction stories of the previous generation, it became an unlikely stimulant for the dreams of many artists and intellectuals. It was a best seller in the 1960s and early 1970s, appearing in paperback editions with psychedelic covers. "Few books that followed in the sixties occult revival weren't indebted to it in some way," wrote a chronicler of the counterculture's intellectual concepts.[7] It was also careless with facts, sloppy with evidence.

The authors of *The Morning of the Magicians*, Louis Pauwels and Jacques Bergier, were members of the French intelligentsia who wrote their magnum opus of "fantastic realism" in the spirit of the Surrealist manifestos of earlier decades. Pauwels had edited Albert Camus's influential newspaper *Combat*; Bergier, a physicist, had worked for Allied intelligence.

The idea of the occult as a backdrop to Hitler had already been introduced to English-speakers through Hermann Rauschning's *Hitler Speaks* (1939), which raised the specter of black magic and contained quotes from Hitler echoing Ariosophical premises without mentioning Thule or any specific source. At the time Rauschning's implications were too outré to be considered as anything but metaphor. The sections of *The Morning of the Magicians* having to do with Nazism and its links to rejected cosmologies, pseudo-sciences, and the occult illustrated the authors' position on the relativity of human experience, the ways in which even outrageous worldviews can frame the vast and unruly material of reality. *The Morning of the Magicians* popularized the theory of the Third Reich as the project of black occultists, a "magic socialism" warring against Western science, the Judeo-Christian tradition, and the rule of reason. Although Pauwels and Bergier proposed Thule as only one node in the plurality of "subterranean Germany," they brought the group to the attention of millions of readers and into the demonology of pop culture. In *The Morning of the Magicians,* Eckart is Thule's leading personality, espousing a cosmology as redolent of H. P. Lovecraft as H. P. Blavatsky. According to the authors, Eckart and his compatriots believed that "Beings intermediate between man and other intelligent beings from Beyond, would place at the disposal of the Initiates a reservoir of force," enabling Germany to conquer the world and become the cradle for the coming race of supermen, "guided by the Great Ones of the Ancient World."[8]

Pauwels and Bergier introduced the error, often repeated in crank books and cyberspace, that Karl Haushofer belonged to Thule. *The Morning of the Magicians* painted Haushofer as a black magician and Hitler as his medium, the channel through which malign forces exerted their influence on the world of men. In this instance a grain of fact was transformed into a granary of fantasy. Haushofer's geopolitical theories did help to shape Hitler's obsession with subjugating Russia, yet there is no evidence that the Munich professor intersected with the occult underground except through academic mentorship of his student, Rudolf

Hess, or had any interest in occultism. This did not prevent Pauwels and Bergier from asserting that Hitler's mania for conquering the Soviet Union came from the alleged esoteric side of Haushofer, who in their account expounded on Central Asia as the ancestral home of the Aryans, the "central core" of the world, where the Hidden Masters secreted themselves.[9]

The Morning of the Magicians opened the way for hysterical fantasy presented as fact in Trevor Ravenscroft's *The Spear of Destiny* (1973). The British author claimed that the Spear of Longinus, one of several lances said to have pierced the side of Christ on the cross and preserved as religious relics in various locations, was an instrument of power influencing the course of European history. Hitler, identified once again as a medium for occult forces, was convinced of victory so long as he held possession of the relic. The spear in question had been kept among the Hapsburg crown jewels since the Napoleonic era and was on display in Vienna at the time of Hitler's sojourn. Ravenscroft's thesis rests on one slender reed of truth. The Ariosophists advocated returning the Hapsburg regalia, including the Spear of Longinus, to its pre-Napoleonic home in the medieval imperial city of Nuremberg, a transfer accomplished by the Nazis after the Anschluss. Ravenscroft may also have been correct in speculating that the Thule Society included a core of dedicated occultists inside a wider outer circle whose interests were political, cultural, or exclusively anti-Semitic.

In all other respects *The Spear of Destiny* was pulp fiction in the guise of history read through an extrasensory lens. Borrowing liberally from *The Morning of the Magicians* along with occult novels such as Edward Bulwer-Lytton's *Zanoni* and Aleister Crowley's *Moonchild*, Ravenscroft proposed Hitler as an initiate of the List Society while in Vienna, where he accessed higher consciousness through the psychedelic effects of peyote. The führer was depicted as the reincarnation of Landulf II of Capua, a ninth-century sorcerer. Haushofer stands accused of being the guiding hand of the Thule Society, which Ravenscroft pictured as being absorbed wholesale into the SS during the Third Reich.

The Spear of Destiny was the bestseller among a gaggle of pseudo-histories of Nazi Germany involving the Thule Society, which followed in the wake of *The Morning of the Magicians.* In Jean-Michel Angebert's *The Occult and the Third Reich* (1974), Nazism was interpreted as a Gnostic conspiracy and Eckart anointed as "high priest" of Thule. Spurious accounts of the Nazi-Thule axis were prominent in Werner Gerson's *Le Nazisme, société secrète* (1969), Elisabeth Antébi's *Ave Lucifer* (1970), J. H. Brennan's *Occult Reich* (1974), and Jean Claude Frère's *Nazisme et sociétés secrètes* (1974). The story continues to be retold and developed like an ancient legend that collects new details with every generation. Although major publishers have proven less interested in the "Occult Reich" since the 1970s, some indefatigable authors have turned to small presses and self-publishing, as well as the Internet. Rock musician and conspiracy theorist George Picard and his collaborator Jerry E. Smith have added their own bloodcurdling elaboration on Ravenscroft with their *Secrets of the Holy Lance* (2005). Alec Maclellan is only one conspiracy writer who continues to link the Spear of Longinus with Vril, the Thule Society, and the theories of advanced cultures hidden inside a hollow earth in books such as *The Hollow Earth Enigma* (1999) and *The Secret of the Spear* (2004). Many of these books professed horror at the dark doings of Nazi occultists while offering titillating glimpses into their secrets. Building on those fantasies, a new generation of neo-Nazis wrote their own approving pseudo-histories of the Thule Society.

Children of Aldebaran

Prominent among the pro-Nazi fantasists of Thule are a pair of Austrian writers. Norbert Jürgen-Ratthofer and Ralf Ettl emerged from a neo-Nazi subculture obsessed with the notion that UFOs were German V-weapons, developed before the close of World War II and shipped to bases hidden in the Arctic, South America, and Antarctica. In *Das Vril-Projekt* (1992), they set forth the idea that the Thule Society and its confederates established contact with extraterrestrials and channeled alien technology to the German military.[10]

The book's title refers to the Vril Society, an obscure Berlin occult lodge whose existence was first publicized after World War II by refugee German rocket engineer Willy Ley and later popularized by *The Morning of the Magicians.*[11] In another example of fiction embraced as reality,

Vril, a supposed natural force of enormous potential when harnessed by adepts, originated in Bulwer-Lytton's novel *The Coming Race* (1871) and passed from there into Blavatsky's *Isis Unveiled* (1877). It has only recently been established that the long-disputed Vril Society actually existed.[12]

In *Das Vril-Projekt,* members of the Thule and Vril groups met near Berchtesgaden in December 1919 with the Croatian medium Maria Orsic. They listened as Orsic delivered telepathic messages in Sumerian from the planet Sumi-Er, orbiting Aldebaran in the constellation of Taurus. Among the revelations was a new theory on the origins of the Aryan race. Orsic's messages called them descendants of ancient colonists from Sumi-Er. Jürgen-Ratthofer and Ettl were probably indebted to the pseudohistory of Germany's Erich von Danikin, who sold many books and kindled great popular speculation in the wake of his international bestseller *Chariots of the Gods?* (1968), which attributed much of ancient history to the intervention of colonists from other worlds.

Das Vril-Projekt asserts that Sebottendorff had already immersed himself in Babylonian and Sumerian lore before the session near Berchtesgaden and had published his findings on Mesopotamian evidence for a Manichean struggle between light and darkness, represented by the Aryans and the Jews, in *Der interkosmische Weltenkampf* (1919), a book whose existence is doubtful. The Babylonian aspect was probably suggested by the writings of Lanz, who based many of his Ariosophical speculations on bizarre interpretations of ancient texts from Mesopotamia.

Haushofer figures in *Das Vril-Projekt*'s account. He was cited as a participant in an August 1917 discussion of Sumerian lore at a Vienna cafe with Sebottendorff, Orsic, the pilot Lothar Waiz, and a man called Gernot, prelate of a secret Templar order called the Herren vom Schwarzen Stein (Lords of the Black Stone). The Black Stone lodge sought to harness the power of the "Black Sun," an energy accessible by initiates that has become part of the legendry of esoteric neo-Nazis since the 1950s.

Through Orsic, the alliance of occultists led by Sebottendorff began to receive instructions for the construction of flying machines operating with electromagnetic fields and antigravity. In 1934 Waiz flew the first of these machines; afterward, the Thule Society helped establish SS Development Department E-IV to test saucer-shaped aircraft powered by a

Thule-Tachyonator engine. By the end of the war E-IV had flown a variety of craft. Among the arsenal of experimental craft were the Vril-1 and -2 fighters; the larger Haunebau I, Haunebau II, and Haunebau III, the last of which carried a crew of thirty-two and reached speeds of 40,000 kilometers per hour; and the Andromeda, a mother ship with room for several of the smaller craft in its hanger. Worried by the faltering German war effort at the end of 1943, Thule and Vril leaders decided to develop the Vril-Odin, a faster-than-light starship. Its mission was to reach Aldebaran by 1967, with an urgent request for help in the war against the Allies. Why the occultists were unable to send an SOS telepathically is not explained. Aldebaran supposedly responded by dispatching a star fleet, which should have arrived on earth between 1992 and 2005, to restore Aryan dominance.

Das Vril-Projekt and similarly themed video "documentaries" by Jürgen-Ratthofer have circulated beyond the neo-Nazi milieu, attracting interest among New Age and UFO circles. Its core ideas have found their way into the work of other authors, among them, German anti-Semitic conspiracy theorist Jan van Helsing, who also brought Lanz's pseudohistory into the space age, positing that in primordial times Aldebaran colonists had bred Tschandala as slaves. After the Tschandala revolted, the submen mixed with other races and commenced an age-old struggle with the Aryans, the children of Aldebaran, for mastership of the earth.[13]

World Wide Web

The legend of Thule journeyed from outer space to cyberspace without difficulty. Beginning in the 1990s, the Society became a hot topic on the Internet for amateur history detectives and cranks, many of them cribbing from Ravenscroft, elaborating on *The Spear of Destiny* from their own perspectives. Others worked from the facts as reported by Goodrick-Clarke but often cast them according to their own lights. Many websites assumed that "the planning of the Second World War started when Adolf Hitler joined a secret society called the Thule Society."[14]

A recent Google search found over 399,000 results for the Thule Society. The levels of writing and logic from the often-anonymous cyberscribes range from erudite to subliterate and are as varied as their agendas.

On its site, the Grand Lodge of British Columbia and Yukon was keen to dissociate Freemasonry from Sebottendorff, conceding only that he had been initiated into "an irregular body of the Rite of Memphis under the Grand Orient of France."[15] One can understand the Grand Lodge's concern over any connection between its fellowship and the birth of Nazism, especially given the wide network of Internet sites dedicated to exposing the supposed machinations of Masonry. The *Illuminati News* recapitulated *The Spear of Destiny* with a few new stitches, claiming Hitler was a member of the Vril Society as well as Thule.[16] Conspiracy theorists who believe history has been manipulated by secret societies controlled by Europe's old aristocratic families have found room in their demonology for the Thule Society.[17]

Websites can be found that are anti-Nazi but pro-Sebottendorff. One claims that "corrupt and sinister forces tried to invert the original mission of Thule," leading to Sebottendorff's flight from Germany in the 1920s.[18] Another sympathetically explicates Sebottendorff's writings on Sufism and claims that after his return to Germany, "he had to defend himself from racist and xenophobic attitudes" because of his Turkish citizenship.[19] In the eyes of other commentators, Sebottendorff's Turkish citizenry is evidence of his malice. On a site dedicated to the proposition that an Ottoman Turkish conspiracy against the Judeo-Christian tradition was at the bottom of Nazism, Sebottendorff's Turkish connections are cast in a sinister light.[20]

Aptly summarizing the viral spread of online misinformation on Thule, British cultural critic Joanna Kavenna mocked the subliteracy of many sites, whose keepers were unable even to spell "Sebottendorff" correctly or establish the date of the Society's foundation. "'Thuel Gessollshlock was the mother of Nazism,' they concluded, with learned authority," she wrote. "They still thought Thule was a code word for their 'Aryan cult.'"[21]

Fictional Worlds

While the Internet has given rise to the most numerous references to Thule, the Society has also found its way into popular consciousness through fictional worlds in literature, film, and video games. In *Foucault's Pendulum* (1988), a comedic novel of ideas, the great Italian writer and intellectual

Umberto Eco imagines the staff of a publishing house gradually drawn into the secretive underground of the Knights Templar. Both the Thule Society and Sebottendorff are mentioned as links between the centuries-old Templar conspiracy and Nazi Germany. Best-selling British horror novelist James Herbert took up the survival of Thule and wrapped it in Ravenscroft's lore in *The Spear* (1978), which depicts the Society as drawing from the power of the Spear of Longinus while engaged in an apocalyptic international conspiracy.

Among the most widely circulated representations of Thule are the *Hellboy* graphic novels by American illustrator Mike Mignola, adapted into a Hollywood movie by Mexican director Guillermo del Toro (2004). One of the secondary villains of the books, transformed into a principal malefactor for the film, is the sadomasochistic Karl Ruprecht Kroenen, SS officer and master of the Thule Society. In the movie, Kroenen constructs a device to conjure up the apocalyptic Scarlet Beast, the Hellboy of the story's title.

The Thule Society and a beautiful, evil woman called Dietlinde Eckart figure in the Japanese anime (animated) film *Fullmetal Alchemist the Movie: The Conquest of Shamballa* (2005), whose story was drawn from a popular manga (graphic novel). Set in 1923, the characters find their way to Munich and the Thule Society, which in keeping with ideas found in *The Morning of the Magicians* is trying to establish contact with the hidden lords of Shamballa. In this rendering, Thule uses the Nazis as a tool for world domination. The Thule Society also appears in the video game *Bloodrayne*, which was transformed into a poorly received movie (2005). Its story concerns a conspiracy by evil vampires, in league with the Nazis, to conquer the world. In the conspiracy-driven video game *Secret Societies*, Thule keeps company with Aum Shinrikyo, the Mossad, the Knights Templar, and the Freemasons.

The Survival of Thule

In its entry on the Thule Society, Wikipedia solemnly reports a rumor that the esoteric lodge resumed activity in 1966, during the Wagner festival in Bayreuth: "Among the participants was an American exchange student, Gene A. Statler, a distant relative of Gauleiter Hans-Arnold Stadler."

The origins of the legend may rest in the continued interest shown by the German far right in Bayreuth, especially the leaders of the National Democratic Party, whose leaders were often on hand for the festival.[22] Wikipedia claims Statler left an account of the Thule conclave in his diary, which came into possession of Raymond Palmer, identified only as a "magazine editor." Palmer was actually a conspiracy theorist who began his career writing science-fiction stories for 1930s fanzines before rising to the editorship of the pulp magazine *Amazing Stories.* After World War II, Palmer was involved in spreading the tale of malevolent robots called Deros who dwelled below the earth's surface.[23] Palmer soon turned his attention skyward, editing a magazine called *Flying Saucers* and another publication, *Fate*, concerned with paranormal phenomena.

Other intriguing but unproven references have been made by more reputable writers. It has been reported that "a secret neo-Nazi lodge" in Bolivia calling itself Thule met in candlelit sessions during the 1950s. Among its members were Bolivian military leaders and fugitive Gestapo Capt. Klaus Barbie, the "Butcher of Lyon."[24]

Whether anyone associated with the Thule Society ever attempted to reorganize the group, Thule has become a brand name for neo-Nazi activism in the United States and elsewhere among younger militants drawing from the Nordic mythology associated with Ultima Thule as well as Sebottendorff's society. Because of widespread social disapproval, cyberspace has provided Nazis with a convenient meeting ground for conducting their activities and spreading propaganda outside of traditional public spaces. The Thule Network links dozens of electronic bulletin boards posting information on political rallies, bomb making, and the "persecution" of Nazis. On its website, the American Thule Society identifies itself as "a focused political activism organization comprised of like-minded individuals from all walks of life. Our mission is to secure a future for white children through political activism and the education of the masses."[25] The site is a clearinghouse for news of racist and Nazi agitation from around the world and maintains the online Radio Thule for audio streaming.

Even in Germany and Austria, where strict laws against Holocaust denial and the display of Nazi symbols remain in force, the quasi-scholarly

Thule-Seminar publishes a journal called *Elemente.* Its cover shows the Wewelsburg sun wheel, an SS symbol that may have been devised by Karl Maria Wiligut, a follower of List and Lanz in Himmler's circle.

Along with the rumored survival of Hitler and other Nazi leaders following Germany's defeat, hidden troves of Nazi gold, the esoteric objectives of the SS, and the outer fringes of Germany's wartime weapons research, the invocation of the Thule Society became part of the popular mystique Nazism acquired among detractors and supporters beginning in the 1960s. Nazism has become inescapable in popular culture, where it often serves as shorthand for pure evil. Rumors and legends of occult Nazism can be found everywhere from obscure paperback fiction to one of the most popular Hollywood movies of recent decades, *Raiders of the Lost Ark.* Thule remains an element in the worldwide obsession with Nazism, an unhealthy fascination for those who continue to extol the Nazi project, but also for those who understand Nazism as comic book villainry, a fantasy of evil overlooking the complexity of its origins, its rise to power, and the toll it exacted on humanity.

Notes

Introduction

1. From a 1931 interview with a Leipzig newspaper editor, quoted in Breiting, *Secret Conversations*, 68.
2. As to the question of the "intentionality" of the Holocaust, a debate that occupied many historians during the 1970s and 1980s, Ian Kershaw's summation on the matter reflects the best contemporary thinking. "Hitler's fixed points of ideology—'removal of the Jews' and preparations for a future titanic struggle to attain 'living space'—acted as such broad and compelling long-term goals that they could easily embrace the differing interests of those agencies which formed the vital pillars of the Nazi regime." *Nemesis*, xlv. The inherent racism of many Germans must be contrasted with the apathy of most Germans toward the militant anti-Semitism of Nazi Party cadres. Kershaw, *Hubris*, 561–62.

   There has also been a shift in historical understanding as to whether Hitler possessed a genuine belief system. In his pathfinding 1952 work, *Hitler: A Study in Tyranny*, Alan Bullock maintained that Hitler was nothing more than a cynical Machiavellian figure, virtually devoid of beliefs, for whom power was its own end. In *Hitler and Stalin*, 139ff., 341, 937ff., he conceded in the face of mounting evidence that National Socialism was a coherent ideology, *Mein Kampf* was a political program, and Hitler was possessed by genuine convictions.
3. Hitler, *Mein Kampf*, 399.
4. Hamann, *Hitler's Vienna*, 135, 141. By November 18, 1908, Hitler registered with the Vienna police as a "student" (a false representation of his status) living at Felberstrasse 22. "There are no witnesses to Hitler's activity during the nine months that he stayed in Felberstrasse. . . . It has often been presumed, nevertheless, that it was in precisely these

months that he became an obsessive racial antisemite." Kershaw, *Hubris*, 49. During the closing months of 1909 Hitler had no known address and may have been a homeless person. A number of eyewitness accounts, not all of them entirely credible, address his 1910–1911 period as the resident of a men's shelter. "Hitler's life recedes into near obscurity for two years or so," until 1912, when begins another set of recollections from his life in the men's shelter. Ibid., 56.

5. Hamann, *Hitler's Vienna*, 56–59.
6. Fest, *Hitler*, 115–117.
7. Mitchell, *Revolution in Bavaria*, 272.
8. Mosse, *Crisis of German Ideology*, 229.
9. Cordes, "Thule-Gesellschaft."
10. Hillmayr, *Roter und Weisser Terror*, 32.
11. Goodrick-Clarke, *Occult Roots*, 146–52.
12. Sebottendorff, "Erwin Haller." Sebottendorff's autobiographical account of his Turkish period in the form of a serialized novel is examined by Goodrick-Clarke (*Occult Roots*, 135) who confirms many of the novel's details by comparison with independent sources.
13. For a discussion of Hitler's quote, see Smith, Markusen, and Lifton, "Armenian Genocide," 292 fn. 21.
14. Mosse, *Crisis of German Ideology*, 297.
15. Hitler, *Mein Kampf*, 224.
16. Ibid., 363.
17. Phelps, "Anton Drexler," 1134.

Chapter 1. The Coming Race

1. Webb, *Occult Underground*, 5.
2. Among artists and intellectuals, occultism often "became the language of radical counter-culture" in the late nineteenth century, "which could be taken up by radicals on both the left and the right." Hutton, *Triumph of the Moon*, 72.
3. Clarke, *Oriental Enlightenment*, 89.
4. Ibid., 16.
5. As early as 1808, French translator Anquetil-Duperron compared the recovery of Indian spirituality with the rediscovery of Greco-Roman classics that helped inspire the Renaissance. Webb, *Flight from Reason*, 29.
6. The idea may have been suggested to Blavatsky by Masonic legendry concerning "Secret Chiefs" or "Unknown Superiors" who "held themselves aloof from the normal affairs" of the lodges and "were in possession of the ultimate secrets" of Masonry. Some lodges believed that their Unknown Superiors were of supernatural origin. Webb, *Flight from Reason*, 147.

7. Conze, *Buddhism*, 211.
8. Nehru, *Toward Freedom*, 28.
9. Blavatsky, *Secret Doctrine*, 779–80.
10. Ibid., 812. Blavatsky's follower Annie Besant elaborated: "The fifth or Aryan race now leading human evolution was evolved from the fifth sub-race of the Atlantean." *Ancient Wisdom*, 360. Mainstream Theosophists believed that races supplanted one another through an evolutionary process guided by divine forces. They did not envision, as would the Ariosophists, a violent manmade program based on the premise of hurrying evolution process forward.

    Many earlier nineteenth-century German and European exponents of Aryans as an Ur culture, including philologist Friedrich Schlegel and geographer Karl Ritter, believed that the Aryans had originated in India and migrated to northern Europe. Only gradually was the Aryan ideal set against a negative representation of the Jew. Poliakov, *Aryan Myth*, 190–99.
11. Sebottendorff, *Bevor Hitler kam*, 223–24.
12. The invasion of the Soviet Union in 1941 afforded the SS a unique opportunity to collect the skulls of "Jewish Bolshevist commissars, who embody a repulsive but characteristic subhumanity." From a report by Haupsturmführer Hirt, an SS officer and professor of anatomy at the Reich University of Strasburg, February 9, 1942, quoted in Hilberg, *Destruction of the European Jews*, 608.
13. Barzun, *Race*, xiv.
14. Galton, *Hereditary Genius*, 45.
15. Barzun, *Race*, 133.
16. Hutton, *Triumph of the Moon*, 74–77.
17. King, *Magical World*, 192. Another member of Crowley's circle, German Theosophist Martha Kuntzel, believed that Hitler was her "magical son." She also discovered many parallels between Crowley's *The Book of the Law* and statements by Hitler as recorded by Hermann Rauschning in *Hitler Speaks*. Judging by Crowley's annotated copy of *Hitler Speaks*, preserved in the library of the Warburg Institute, the British occultist shared not only Kuntzel's opinion of the influence of his work on Hitler, but also many of the führer's views. King, *Magical World*, 161.

    One member of Crowley's inner circle claimed several meetings between the magician and Hilter. See Symonds, *Medusa's Head*. French philosopher René Guénon, influential among Europe's mystical nationalists, believed this as well. In a letter to the Italian neopagan Julius Evola, he asserted Crowley "had probably gone to Berlin to assume the role of Hitler's secret advisor." Guénon, *Lettres à Julius Evola*, 112. While there is no documented evidence of contact between Crowley and Nazi leaders, the magician's papers from his Berlin sojourn (1930–1932) are missing. Marco Pasi, "Aleister Crowley," 224f.

18. Crowley, *Magick*, 230ff.
19. Apocalyptic themes involving the destruction of the world as it was known and the start of a new human race haunted a trilogy of speculative fiction authored by Shiel. His trio of novels—*The Purple Cloud* (1901), *The Lord of the Sea* (1901), and *The Last Miracle* (1906)—were presented as if they had been dictated by a woman in a mediumistic trance. As one commentator wrote, "This was the age of Madame Blavatsky." Hartwell in Shiel, *Purple Cloud*, ix.
20. Quoted in Panshin and Panshin, *World Beyond the Hill*, 80. Theosophists believe that Bulwer-Lytton was at the center of a small circle whose members experimented with magic, among them the great French occultist Eliphas Lévi. Fuller, *Blavatsky and Her Teachers*, 83–84.
21. From a manifesto issued by Mathers, October 1896, quoted in King, *Magical World*, 17.
22. Webb, *Occult Underground*, 317. Mathers, the Golden Dawn's grandmaster, was involved in organizations dedicated to the Stuart restoration, which would have necessitated the overthrow or abdication of the present royal house. Included in Mathers' circle were such forerunners of the animal rights movement as Anna Kingsford, who claimed to have killed by occult means several scientists who conducted experiments on animals. Webb, *Flight from Reason*, 231–32.
23. King, *Magical World*, 6–7.
24. Boyd, *Ireland's Literary Renaissance*, 212–52.
25. Mann, *History of Germany*, 45.
26. Similar phenomena accompanied the quest for nationhood by Irish and Polish intellectuals, artists, and mystics during the nineteenth century, when neither nation enjoyed an independent political existence. Webb, *Flight from Reason*, 155–70, 206–17. Douglas Hyde, Eire's first president, began his public life as a folklorist and collector of Irish fairy tales.
27. Davenport-Hines, *Gothic*, 2–3, 180.
28. Barzun, *Race*, 22–23.
29. Ibid., 49–62.
30. For a discussion of the gradual penetration of racism into German social sciences, see Massin, "From Virchow to Fischer," in Stocking, ed., *Volksgeist as Method and Ethic*, 74–154.
31. Mann, *History of Germany*, 296.
32. Mosse, *Crisis of German Ideology*, 5.
33. Chamberlain, *Foundations of the Nineteenth Century*, xxviii, 484ff.
34. Wagner, *Prose*, 269ff.

35. For a careful assessment of Wagner's anti-Semitism and its influence, see Magee, *The Tristan Chord*, 343–80. Alfred Rosenberg summed up the Nazi position on Wagner when he wrote that the composer "foresaw the dawn" of Nazism. *Der Mythus des 20. Jahrhunderts*, 443.
36. Mosse, "Mystical Origins," 81.
37. Mosse, *Crisis of German Ideology*, 42.
38. Webb, *Occult Establishment*, 42.
39. Ibid., 44ff. The author relies on Eckstein's autobiography *Alte unnennbare Tage* (Vienna, 1936) for his account of Viennese Theosophists, and an essay by Robert Brauin in the collection *Der Aufsteig der Frau* (Jena, 1925) for Mayreder's feminism. Eckstein recalled, "It was mostly young people who met there and took part in the collective exchange of views . . . most of us had shoulder-length hair and full beards, our lunch table might have reminded spectators not a little of Leonardo's *Last Supper*." Eckstein, *Alte unnennbare Tage*, 105–6. The writer Richard von Kralik, later a member of a writers' circle with Guido von List, was also one of Eckstein's associates.
40. Ibid., 46.
41. Morton, *Nervous Splendor*, 4
42. Hitler, *Mein Kampf*, 23.
43. For accounts of Hartmann and his adventures among the Theosophists in the United States and India, see Johnson, *Initiates of Theosophical Masters*, 44; Barborka, *H. P. Blavatsky*, 402; Fuller, *Blavatsky and Her Teachers*, 122.
44. Quoted in Barborka, *H. P. Blavatsky*, 271, from *Lotusblüten* LXV, 142.
45. Goodrick-Clarke, *Occult Roots*, 23.
46. Similar convergences occurred throughout the Western world. Occultists "shared a collection of convictions all of which were rejected by the Establishment of Rationalism and right order, and all of which had some flavor of the idealistic. . . . Indeed, if one is hunting occultists, it is no bad way to begin by analyzing vegetarians." Webb, *Flight From Reason*, 228. Hitler's recorded statements on the subject of diet and health are legion. Hitler, *Hitler's Secret Conversations*, 94.
47. Green, *Mountain of Truth*, 1, 119ff.
48. Webb, *Flight from Reason*, 55.
49. Goodrick-Clarke, *Occult Roots*, 59.
50. Reuss also numbered many influential followers, including Rudolf Laban, an esteemed exponent of modern dance. See Green, *Mountain of Truth*, 104, for an uncritical view of the Non-National Congress as a pacifist assembly, and Howe, "Theodor Reuss," for evidence linking the event to German war aims.
51. Green, *Mountain of Truth*, 105.

52. For a thoughtful sifting of the evidence relating to Reuss's peripatetic life, see Howe, "Theodor Reuss."
53. Crowley was himself a paid agent of the German government during his World War I sojourn in the United States. After suffering a stroke in 1922, Reuss intended Crowley to take charge of OTO, but the order splintered in acrimony over the controversial Englishman. One of OTO's more enthusiastic supporters of Crowley, Karl Germer, lived with and financially supported Crowley for several years before his ten-month imprisonment by the Gestapo (1935) as part of a crackdown against OTO and related occult groups. After his unexplained release from Esterwegen concentration camp, Germer made his way to the United States, where he became active in OTO circles. King, *Magical World*, 77–78, 80–81, 149–54, 160–61. Crowley sat out World War II in obscurity, living quietly in England while continuing to correspond with occultists from around the world.
54. Fuller, *Blavatsky and Her Teachers*, 185.
55. Blavatsky, *Letters*, 118.
56. Green, *Mountain of Truth*, 119.
57. Goodrick-Clarke, *Occult Roots*, 24ff.
58. Cited in Hamann, *Hitler's Vienna*, 209.
59. Schliemann, *Troy and Its Remains*, 102, 105.
60. For example, Hartmann noted that both Blavatsky and List rejected the Jewish origin of the Kabbalah, a body of mystical traditions first codified among the Jewish community of Islamic Spain in the thirteenth century. Mosse, "Mystical Origins," 86. According to List, the beleagued priesthood of the old gods entrusted their secrets to the rabbis of eighth-century Cologne, who transcribed their teachings into the Kabalah. List, *Die Armanenschaft*, 90–96. List's final work, uncompleted at death, was *Armanismus und Kabbala*. According to rumor, the manuscript was circulated among members of List's inner circle, the occult lodge HAO, Flowers, "The Works of Guido von List" in List, *Secret of the Runes*, 17.

Chapter 2. Shadows on the Danube

1. May, *Vienna*, x.
2. Hitler, *Mein Kampf*, 56.
3. May, *Vienna*, 39–40.
4. List had occasionally used the title "von" since 1903 but only called himself von List consistently after 1906. In October 1907, at a legal inquest initiated by the Austrian association of nobles, List asserted that his great-grandfather had forsworn the title after entering the middle-class innkeeper's trade. As evidence of his aristocratic claims, he produced a

coat of arms emblazoned with a pair of rampant foxes and cited nobles called von List from medieval chronicles. Balzli, *Guido von List*, 11–12. Balzli was secretary of the List Society and editor of *Prana*, a periodical published by the Theosophical publishing house at Leipzig whose contributors included List, Franz Hartmann, the illustrator Fidus, and renegade Anglican cleric C. W. Leadbetter, an intimate of Madame Blavatsky and Annie Besant. *Prana*'s list of contributors testifies to the complicated, international web of which List was an important nexus.

5. "God created us in several kinds of branches, or tribes, from which the various peoples arose—just as he had caused plants and animals to come into being in many different kinds from the beginning of time. . . . Each greater unity of humans, which has its own language, writing system and history, unique in its sense, customs and way of thinking, is called a Folk." List, *The Invincible*, 19. A pamphlet in the form of a *völkisch* catechism with Art Nouveau illustrations, *The Invincible* was penned in opposition to a law mandating religious instruction in the schools of Lower Austria. After formulating Ariosophy, List dismissed the pamphlet as only a rough sketch, "superseded by much deeper knowledge."
6. A portrait of List at age three is reproduced in Balzli, *Guido von List*, facing 5.
7. Ibid., 15–17.
8. List, *Deutsch-Mythologische Landschaftsbilder*, 592.
9. Ibid., 562–91. List also published a short story based on the evening, "Eine Zaubernacht" ("A Magic Night"), whose protagonist invokes a seeress who reveals to him that he is not to be the liberator of the Germans but a skald of prophesy. List, *Alraunenmaren*, 397–415.
10. Goodrick-Clarke, *Occult Roots*, 199.
11. Hutton, *Triumph of the Moon*, 28.
12. List, *Deutsch-Mythologische Landschaftsbilder*, 125.
13. List, *The Invincible*, 8.
14. Goodrick-Clarke, *Occult Roots*, 9. The mountaineering publication List wrote for was called *Neue deutsche Alpenzeitung*.
15. Balzli, *Guido von List*, 19.
16. The Pan-German newspapers that published List's articles included *Heimat*, *Neue Welt*, and *Deutsche Zeitung*.
17. The Pan-German Association, the most powerful organization produced by the movement, was founded in 1890 as a pressure group for German imperialism "based on a *völkisch* rationale." Mosse, *Crisis of German Ideology*, 219–22.
18. Liebenfels, "Bismarck und Schönerer."
19. Hitler, *Mein Kampf*, 95ff., 105.
20. With *Carnuntum* and his other novels, List was working within an already established genre of Germanic historical fiction dealing with antiquity

and the early Middle Ages. Nagl and Zeidler, *Deutsch-österreichesche Literaturgeschichte*, 1935.

21. Goodrick-Clarke, *Occult Roots*, 36ff.
22. Ibid., 37. From 1891 to 1893 List was involved in a writers' group for which he supplied the name, Iduna, after the German goddess of youth. Taking part in its meetings were Rudolf Steiner, Fritz Lemmermayer, Marie Eugene delle Grazzie, Karl Maria Heidt, Richard von Kralik, and Joseph Kalasanz Poestion. After Iduna broke up, List and Fanny Wschiansky organized the Literarische Donaugesellschaft (Danube Literary Society). Flowers, "The Life of Guido von List" in List, *Secret of the Runes*, 6.

    Steiner later founded his own version of Theosophy, called Anthroposophy, and established the first Waldorf school. Shortly after Iduna ended, he was on opposite ends with List's close associate Franz Hartmann in an earlier schism within Theosophy. Hartmann established the German branch of the International Theosophical Brotherhood at Leipzig in 1896, while Steiner remained loyal to Theosophy's London office. Later embroiled in other obscure disputes with Ariosophists, Steiner was accused by the Thule Society's founder of using his influence against Germany during World War I. Sebottendorff, *Bevor Hitler kam*, 77. Thule member Dietrich Eckart denounced Steiner as a Jew and claimed he rebuffed advances by his agents, who sought an alliance between Ariosophy and Anthroposophy. Webb, *Occult Establishment*, 286, citing Eckart, "Ein eigentümlicher Theosoph," *Auf gut deutsch* (July 11, 1919). Oddly, the most prominent graduate of Thule, Hitler's deputy Rudolf Hess, continued to cite Steiner positively on medicine, astrology, and the benefits of organic produce. Webb, *Occult Establishment*, 308.

    Aside from Steiner, Kralik was the most prominent of List's literary colleagues, a cultural historian, and polymath ranked in Vienna alongside Wagner, Nietzsche, Mahler, and Social Democratic leader Viktor Adler. See Fischer, *Fin de Siècle*, 27; and Gehr, *Karl Lueger*, 312.
23. Balzli, *Guido von List*, 30. Among his talks were lectures on Wodanism in 1892 and 1893 before the Verein Deutsches Haus and the German Historical Union (Verein Deutsche Gesichte). List also spoke to the Deutscher Turnverein.
24. Goodrick-Clarke, *Occult Roots*, 40.
25. List, *Secret of the Runes*, 81.
26. Quoted in Balzli, *Guido von List*, 18.
27. Lethaby, *Architecture, Mysticism, and Myth*, 1.
28. List, *Secret of the Runes*, 77ff.
29. See an address by Nazi minister of agriculture and Reich farm führer Walther Darre, "The German Peasant Formed German History," reprinted in Mosse, *Nazi Culture*, 147–50. An indirect connection can be

traced between Darre and the Thule Society through *Die Sonne*, a Nordic journal for which he wrote in the 1920s along with anthropologist Hans F. K. Gunther, a leading proponent of racist science who accepted a professorial chair for racial studies at Jena in 1930. Gunther also wrote for *Deutsche Freiheit*, a Munich weekly acquired in 1920 by Thule associate Rudolf John Gorsleben, who later founded his own esoteric group, the Edda Society. *Die Sonne* continued to be published at least through 1937, when it was accused by factions within the Nazi party of being a mouthpiece for "complainers." Kater, *Das Ahnenerbe der SS 1935–1945*, 125.

30. Goodrick-Clarke, *Occult Roots*, 39, working from articles in *Ostdeutsche Rundschau*, December 3 and 4, 1884, 2–3, 5.
31. Ibid., 40.
32. Ibid., 41.
33. In 1907 List's follower Ernst Wachler, a playwright and novelist, founded the Mountain Theater (Berg Theater) in the Harz Mountains. Its productions "were embodiments of rites which would dramatize Volkisch Weltanshauung," its repertoire included Wachler's *Hohenstaufen* and *Walpurgis*. "National Socialism, in time, adopted and implemented Wachler's ideas on a more ambitious scale," staging public spectacles with Nordic themes and founding many outdoor stages and amphitheaters on his model. Wachler's novel *Osning* (1914) depicted a neopagan secret society named for the ancient Teutonic hero Arminius, whose master leads a revival of the Volk from a cave in the Teutoberger woods, a place where Germans had once defeated the Roman legions. Mosse, *Crisis of German Ideology*, 80–81. As with many of List's followers, Wachler circulated widely in the occult underground. By the 1930s he became a contributor to *Asgard*, a magazine published by the influential *völkisch* occultist Georg Lomer, whose solar worship included the idea of the sun as symbol of Aryan masculinity and the moon, reflecting but not giving light, a symbol of Jewish femininity. Ibid., 215.
34. List, *Secret of the Runes*, 41. In September 1903 List's article on the esoteric meaning of religious symbols was published in the Viennese Theosophical magazine *Die Gnosis*, his first appearance in an explicitly occult periodical. *Die Gnosis* later merged with Rudolf Steiner's Berlin-based publication, *Luzifer*.
35. List, *Die Religionen der Ario-Germanen*, 91–93.
36. List, *Die Rita der Ario-Germanen*, 15–16, 19–23. "Rita" was adapted from the Sanskrit *rta*, meaning cosmic order.
37. List, *Die Bilderschaft der Ario-Germanen*, 30.
38. List, *Die Ursprache der Ario-Germanen*, 19–24.

39. List, *Secret of the Runes,* 74. List believed that Roman writers drew a false picture of Germans as a lesser civilization.
40. List, *Die Armanenschaft der Ario-Germanen,* vol. 1, 20.
41. List, *Secret of the Runes,* 67.
42. Ibid., 53.
43. Ibid., 46.
44. Ibid., 95–96.
45. Ibid., 54.
46. List, *Die Armanenschaft der Ario-Germanen,* vol. 2, 70ff.
47. List, *Der Ubergang vom Wotanstum zum Christentum,* 106.
48. List, *The Invincible,* 8. List added that "the highest goal of the education of the folk, is only attainable when the irrevocable laws of evolution, according to which the All is formed, whereby each advances the development of its own kind and race, are taken into account."
49. List, *Secret of the Runes,* 76–77. A rich literature of German historical fiction rooted in Gothic medievalism concerning the Vehmgericht probably fed List's imagination. Goodrick-Clarke, *Occult Roots,* 75–76.
50. List, *The Invincible,* 26, 28.
51. List, *Die Armanenschaft der Ario-Germanen,* vol. 2, 107.
52. English author George T. Chesney's *The Battle of Dorking* (1871) inaugurated the genre by imagining a future defeat of Britain at the hands of Germans armed with advanced weapons. His influential story, which prompted many imitations and responses, was translated into German by the prominent Theosophist Wilhelm Hubbe-Schlieden. Another example, George Griffith's *The Angel of the Revolution* (1893), foresaw a world war fought with submarines and airships. Panshin and Panshin, *World Beyond the Hill,* 73.
53. Ernst Lauterer (aka Tarnhari) first contacted List by a letter dated November 11, 1911. He published several pamphlets, collaborated with the Thule Society's Dietrich Eckart and became a frequent guest in the Berlin home of the Germanenorden's Philipp Stauff. List, *Der Armanenschaft der Ario-Germanen* (2nd ed., Leipzig, 1913), 98ff.
54. Mosse, *Crisis of German Ideology,* 77. Tarnhari would be imprisoned for obscure reasons during the Third Reich.
55. Goodrick-Clarke, *Occult Roots,* 86, citing an article by List in Ostarrede (April 21, 1915); Balzli, *Guido von List,* 125–33. List borrowed the image of Starke von Oben from prophetic passages of the Edda. He did not possess perfect foresight. Witness List's predictions of Allied defeat during World War I, published in Balzli's Theosophical monthly, *Prana.* Goodrick-Clarke, *Occult Roots,* 47.
56. List, *Secret of the Runes,* 77–78. The essence of List's essay became the first publication by the List Society, *Die Geheimnis der Runen* (Gross-

Lichterfelde: Guido-von-List-Gesellschaft, 1908). The word *kala* is Sanskrit in origin, referring to time or measures.

57. Among the signatories were List's patron, the industrialist Friedrich Wannieck, and his son, Friedrich Oskar; List's colleague Jörg Lanz von Liebenfels; Ludwig von Bernuth, chairman of a *völkisch* health organization; Adolf Harpf, editor of the *Marburger Zeitung*; Herman Pfister-Schwaighusen, linguistics lecturer at Darmstadt University; Wilhelm von Pickl-Scharfenstein, anti-Semitic publicist; Amand Freiherr von Schweiger-Lerchenfeld, an army officer and editor of the popular magazine *Stein der Weisen*; Ernst Wachler, author and impresario; Aurelius Polzer, editor of newspapers at Graz and Horn; Fritz Winterstein, a leader of the anti-Semitic Deutsche Social Partei in Kassel; Wilhelm Rohmeder, a Pan-German education reformer in Munich who later joined the Thule Society; Arthur Schulz, a Berlin educational reformer; Friedrich Wiegershaus, an officer with the influential white-collar union Deutschnationale Handelsgehilfen-Verband; Hugo Göring, a Theosophical editor in Weimar; Harald Arjuna Graevell van Jostenoode, a Heidelberg Theosophical author; Max Seiling, a Munich occult pamphleteer; and Paul Zillman, editor of *Metaphysische Rundschau* and a member of a Berlin occult lodge. List, *Die Rita der Ario-Germanen*, 197–98. For Rohmeder's membership in Thule, see Sebottendorff, *Bevor Hitler kam*, Membership List, 218ff.

58. For the favorable impression Lüger made on Hitler, see Hitler, *Mein Kampf*, 71ff. From the evidence of his public life, Lüger seems an uncomfortable bedfellow with List. Although the two men shared a disdain for Jews, capitalists and leftists, and a love for nature, the demagogic Lüger was an ardent champion of the Hapsburgs and a devout Roman Catholic. Despite List's disdain for the Roman Church and his marriage-day flirtation with Protestantism, he was, unlike many Pan-Germans, devoted to the Hapsburgs, regarding them as heirs to the ancient Armanenschaft rulers of Germany. List, *Die Bilderschaft der Ario-Germanen*, 295.

    Close examination of the circles surrounding List and Lüger suggests an overlap. Lüger's vice mayor, Josef Neumayer, was a member of List's secretive occult lodge, Hoher Armanen-Orden. Neumayer once told the city council that "all Jews could be burned alive" and later complained of Jewish judges, declaring they lacked "the understanding, the feeling for moral-religious and national requirements and viewpoints of the Aryan nations." When liberal councilors loudly objected, Lüger had them expelled from the meeting. Gehr, *Karl Lueger*, 96, 360 fn 113, citing Amtsblatt 75 (September 19, 1905), 1908, and Amtsblatt 80 (October 5, 1897), 1973–74. List's literary companion, Richard von Kralik, wrote for the Christian Socialist children's magazine, *Wiener Kinder*. Ibid., 177.

59. Known members of the List Society include Theosophist leader Franz Hartmann; Johannes Balzli, secretary of the Leipzig Theosophical Society; Rudolf Berger, officer of the German National Socialist Workers' League in Vienna; rabbinical scholar Moritz Altschuler; Hermann Brass, chairman of the German League in Moravia; Wagner biographer Conrad Glasenapp; Col. Karl Hellwig, a *völkisch* activist in Kassel; popular genealogist Bernhard Koerner; Theosophical editor Arthur Weber; Karl Heise, organizer of a vegetarian commune near Zurich; Dankwart Gerlach, a champion of the *völkisch* youth movement; Josef Ludwig Reimer, a Viennese Pan-German author; Philipp Stauff, an anti-Semitic journalist in Berlin who became prominent in the Germanenorden, the Thule Society's parent organization; Gen. Blasius Count von Schemua of the Austro-Hungarian general staff; Ellegaard Ellerbek, a novelist who later wrote for Thule member Dietrich Eckhardt's newspaper *Auf gut deutsch*; Friedrich Freiherr von Gaisberg, a Wurttemberg nobleman and founder of the St. Michael Association, dedicated to preserving the peerage's special interests; Karl Herzog, officer of Deutsche Haus Verein; Friedrich Schwickert, an astrologer who joined Lanz's ONT in the 1920s; and Karl Hilm, an occult novelist. List, *Der Armanenschaft der Ario-Germanen*, 71–4; and List, *Der Bilderschrift der Ario-Germanen*, 384–89.

    Ellerbeck was associated with Alfred Schuler, a devotee of List and prominent bohemian in Munich literary life before and after World War I, but did not become important until the publication of *Sönne Sönnings Söhne and Sönnensee* (1919). His extreme views gained public attention when he declared that a frieze in the home Germany's Jewish finance minister, Walther Rathenau, depicted the execution of Europe's crowned heads. As he awaited his death sentence at Nuremberg, one-time Thule Society member Alfred Rosenberg praised Ellerbeck. Rosenberg, *Letzte Aufzeichnungen*, 95.

    Count Schemua, a "suave and tactful" associate of Hapsburg heir Francis Ferdinand, was named chief of staff of the Austro-Hungarian army in 1911. May, *Hapsburg Monarchy*, 456.

60. Goodrick-Clarke, *Occult Roots*, 44. An unexplained transition apparently occurred between the original Vienna Theosophical Society founded in 1887 with a Jewish president, Friedrich Eckstein, and the Vienna Theosophists who enrolled in the List Society. Goodrick-Clarke believes that the original Vienna Theosophical Society lapsed in the 1890s, but he argues from negative evidence, a lack of records regarding the Vienna branch in Theosophy's London office. Goodrick-Clarke, "The Mod-

ern Occult Revival in Vienna, 1880–1910," in Pynsent, ed., *Decadence and Innovation*, 106–8.

61. Goodrick-Clarke, *Occult Roots*, 44. For an extensive List bibliography, see ibid., 272–74.
62. List, *Deutsch-Mythologische Landschaftsbilder*, 591–602. HAO members included Anna Witteck, Wilhelm Kochne and his wife, Rudolf Janko and his wife, Friedrich Oskar Wannieck, Heinrich Winter, Eugen Mertens, Philipp Stauff of the Germanenorden, Blasius von Schemua, Viennese Christian Socialist politician Josef Neumayer, Austrian Privy Councilor Franz Lang, Friedrich J. Bieber, Franz Zenkl, author Emmerich Boyer von Berghof, A. Blaumauer, Rudolf Janako, Heinrich Franz Lang, Walter Felner, and Baron Skal. As Lanz falsely claimed mother's maiden name as Skala, and was given to altering his name and at times posed as a baron, perhaps Baron Skal was a pseudonym.

    List was HAO's grandmaster; in that capacity he called himself Arz-Wiho-Aithari, in keeping the practice of hierarchical occult lodges whose members adopted fraternal names. As HAO members died, their tombstones were often carved with swastikas. Balzli, *Guido von List*, 148ff., 183–86. List, *Deutsch-Mythologische Landschaftsbilder*, plate facing 600, 650. Neumayer was Vienna's second and later first vice mayor under Karl Lüger; he succeeded Lüger as lord mayor in 1910 but resigned two years later after being spotted in a bordello wearing only a beribboned medal. Gehr, *Karl Lueger*, 95, 386 fn 55.
63. Maranci, *Medieval Armenian Architecture*, 153–55.
64. Mosse, *Crisis of German Ideology*, 120.
65. Goodrick-Clarke, *Occult Roots*, 44–45. Among authors who dedicated their books to List were Jerome Bal, B. Hanftmann, Karl Heise, Ernst von Wolzogen, and Karl Engelhardt.
66. Ewers, *Sorcerer's Apprentice*, in "About the Author"; Flowers, "The Life and Times of Hanns Heinz Ewers," in Ewers, *Strange Tales*, 1–22. Flowers claims that Ewers wrote for a journal published by List called *Der Scherer*. Evidence of Sebaldt's influence on List can be discerned in the latter's interest in the "old Aryan sexual religion," and the origins of the swastika in the fire whisk (Feuerquirl) with which the god Mundelfori brought the universe into existence. List, "Die esoterische Bedeutung religiösen Symbole," *Die Gnosis* 1 (1903), 323–27. Evidence for personal contact can be found on Sebaldt's handwritten inscription on the flyleaf of his book, *Mythologie des Diaphetur* (Leipzig, 1905), found in List's library. Goodrick-Clarke, *Occult Roots*, 293, fn. 6.
67. Gorsleben served as the Edda Society's chancellor. Its grandmaster, the retired civil servant Werner von Bulow, had designed a "runic world

clock" inscribed with Listian devices. Other known members include Mathilde von Kemnitz, who later married Gen. Erich Ludendorff, the pro-Nazi hero of World War I; esoteric writers Martin Brucher, Albert March, and Karl Nuse; Otto Siegfried Reuter, prolific author on the subjects of astrology, prehistory, and paganism, as well as leader of the German Belief Fellowship; Carl Reinhold Petter, an Aryan activist in Danzig; and the Society's treasurer, Friedrich Schaefer, whose wife, Kathe, played host for a circle surrounding the ONT's Karl Maria Wiligut, an occultist who later counseled SS leader Heinrich Himmler. Gorsleben's periodical *Deutsche Freiheit*, later *Arische Freiheit*, became the Edda Society's organ. In 1928 Gorsleben briefly merged his periodical with *Zeitschrift für Geistes-und Wissenschaftsreform*, published by Herbert Reichstein, a prominent Ariosophical publisher. Initiated under the name Fra Rig, Gorsleben also belonged to the Staufen priory of ONT, the secret order headed by Lanz.

Following Gorsleben's death, Bulow first renamed the periodical *Hag All All Hag* and then simply *Hagal*. Published through 1939, *Hagal* brought a Listian interpretive lens to Nordic mythology and literature, architecture and folklore. It also claimed Nazism as a positive manifestation of cosmic forces. Goodrick-Clarke, *Occult Roots*, 159–60, 171. One of Hagal's contributors was Josef Heinsch, whose writings on "heilige linien" paralleled theories by contemporary English folklorists on ley lines, a network of magical channels connecting sacred sites of primeval Europe. Heinsch is still cited in the twenty-first century on occult websites.

68. Marby, *Sonne und Planeten im Tierkreis*, 255 and dust jacket. Marby's occult practices were denounced for murky reasons by Karl Maria Wiligut, a Listian who attached himself to Heinrich Himmler. Letter of May 2,1934, from Weisthor (pseud. Wiligut) to Himmler, Bundesarchiv, Koblenz, Himmerl, Nachlass 19.
69. Marby, *Der Weg zu den Muttern* (Stuttgart, 1957), 65ff.
70. Goodrick-Clarke, *Occult Roots*, 161–62.
71. Several letters were published in Balzli, *Guido von List*, 167–74.
72. *Jahrbuch des Deutschnationalen Handelsgehilfen Verband* (1917), 203–6. Mosse, *Crisis of German Ideology*, 258.
73. Hamann, *Hitler's Vienna*, 206.
74. Jäckel and Kuhn, *Hitler*, 186.
75. Cited in Hamann, *Hitler's Vienna*, 212–13.
76. Flowers, "The Reception of List's Ideas" in List, *Secret of the Runes*, 35–36. Wotansvolk, a late-twentieth-century sect of Wodan worshippers headquartered in St. Maries, Idaho, have erected a wooden temple to List's memory. Goodrick-Clarke, *Black Sun*, 274–77.

77. Goodrick-Clarke, *Occult Roots*, 232, fn. 38. Lanz apparently met List in the company of Franz Kiessling, a noted Austrian folklorist.
78. For Lanz's strained assertions of aristocracy, see Daim, *Der Mann*, 44, and Goodrick-Clarke, *Occult Roots*, 240, fn. 2. Supporting evidence is lacking for a rumor reported as fact in Harmann, p. 216, that Lanz's mother was of Jewish ancestry. Lanz was actually the son of a Viennese schoolmaster, Johann Lanz.
79. Quoting from Blavatsky's *The Secret Doctrine*, Lanz claimed that paleontology supported her theories on the lost continents of Lemuria and Atlantis, and that her prehistoric monsters corresponded with the beast-men of his Theozoologie. Lanz, *Die Theosophie*, 5, 11ff., 28–32.
80. Goodrick-Clarke, *Occult Roots*, 227, fn. 1. After Lanz coined Ariosophy in 1915, the word displaced other terms for *völkisch* Theosophy including List's preference, Armanism, and Lanz's earlier coinage, Theozoology.
81. Even Ian Kershaw dismisses him. Lanz "managed the near-impossible and took List's zany notions a stage further." Kershaw, *Hubris*, 50.
82. Goodrick-Clarke, *Occult Roots*, 92ff. Lanz cited a doctorate as part of his credentials, a claim routinely scoffed at by historians. Although there is no record of Lanz's doctoral dissertation at the University of Vienna, the erudition shown in contributions to scholarly publications led Goodrick-Clarke (who, unlike most scholars of German history, bothered to read Lanz's work) to believe that he may have earned a doctorate from a smaller Austrian college.

    In any case, intellectuals took Lanz's academic credentials seriously in his day. In the first decade of the twentieth century, he was published in such scholarly journals as zoologist Ernst Haeckel's *Das freie Wort*, Social Darwinist Ludwig Woltmann's *Politisch-Anthropologische Revue*, and the *Vierteljahrschrift für Bibelkunde*, edited by the List Society's Moritz Altschuler. Lanz contributed to Monumenta Judaica, a multivolume scholarly study of Jewish canonical writings and traditions, and folkloric architectural studies for a book on Hapsburg crown lands. After World War I, Lanz published in such erudite journals as the *Zeitschrift für Menschenkenntnis und Schicksalforschung* (for which he wrote a tribute to List).

    The connection between Lanz and Haeckel (1834–1919), perhaps the most eminent German scientist of his day among the general public, raises intriguing questions, especially in light of a Thule Society membership list that included an unidentified Ernst Haeckel among the initiates. Sebottendorff, *Hitler*, Membership List, 218ff. Haeckel was Germany's leading proponent of Darwinism in biology as well as sociology. As such he is usually identified as a positivist and a materialist, albeit one who understood evolution as a cosmic force working through racial selection. Many of Haeckel's arguments were congenial to Ariosophical anthropology, including his anti-Semitism, support of eugenics to keep superior races from disintegrating, and lauding of Germans as the human line that had most progressed from the ape. Lanz's contribution to Haeckel's periodical is not proof of a profound linkage of ideas, since Haeckel's Monist League attracted a broad membership, including pacifists, free thinkers, women's rights advocates, homosexual activists, and uneven unconventional Marxists. Mosse, *Final Solution,* 86–87; Gasman, *Scientific Origins,* xiv, xxii, xxvi–xxvii.

83. An index of *Ostara* reveals reviews of popular German cowboy author Karl May, the publications of the Germanenorden's Theodor Fritsch and Theosophical astrologer Ernst Tiede, whom Sebottendorff later succeeded as editor of *Astrologische Rundschau;* articles on the "Jewish money monopoly," apologetics for war and the sexual, intellectual, and cultural differences between blond Aryans and dark "lower" races; essays on racial hygiene and the crass commercialization of the contemporary publishing industry; warnings against the peril from Asia, especially the "Mongrelized Russians," whose cruelty makes them dangerous opponents; the Aryans as creators of world culture; and essays extolling Wagner and condemning Charlemagne for slaughtering the pagan Saxons. Heer, *Der Glaube des Adolf Hitler,* 710–17.

Through his editorship of *Ostara,* Lanz became a key link in a network of writers associated with List. Before founding *Ostara,* Lanz contributed to Fritsch's Germanenorden organ *Hammer* (1902–1905). Among the contributors to *Ostara* were Dr. Adolf Harpf and Ludwig von Bernuth, signatories of the 1905 endorsement for the List Society; Adolf Hagen, R. Freydank, Dr. Eduard Ritter von Liszt, and Dr. Adolf Wahrmund. The prolific Lanz was the primary author for the eighty-nine issues of *Ostara* published through 1917, and continued to find time to write for other publications, including an essay on the Holy Grail for List Society signatory Amand Freiherr von Schweiger-Lerchenfeld's *Stein der Weisen.* For a partial but extensive Lanz bibliography, see Goodrick-Clarke, *Occult Roots,* 275–80. Lanz claimed *Ostara's* circulation reached a height of 100,000 in 1907, Daim, *Der Mann,* 114. The assertion is unverifiable, but reflects the magazine's widespread availability, especially in Vienna and Graz, where it was commonly sold at tobacco kiosks and widely read by college students.

Following World War I, *Ostara* resumed publication in Magdeburg, Saxony, under a new publisher, ONT member Detlef Schmude, (1922–1927). *Ostara*'s final publisher was Viennese industrialist and ONT member Johann Walthari Wölfl (1927–1931), who continued his Ariosophical publishing venture under the name *Ostara-Rundschau: Panarische Revue.* The new publication proposed a united front between Ariosophist, fascist, and racist groups throughout Europe and the United States. Goodrick-Clarke, *Occult Roots,* 118–19.

84. Inspired by Romantic-era literature, medievalism and monasticism were intimately joined in nineteenth-century Europe, often with significant results. Within Anglicanism, the Oxford Movement was powered in part by a desire to escape into an idealized vision of the Middle Ages. The Pre-Raphaelite Brotherhood was imbued with the complexion of a monastic order. Some occultists flirted with monasticism, including the Englishman Aelred Carlyle, who founded an irregular community of Benedictines (1896). Webb, *Occult Underground,* 124–28.

    In his elaboration of List's notion of the Armanenschaft's survival, Lanz imagined that early medieval monastics such as St. Benedict of Nursia, St. Bernard of Clairvaux, and St. Bruno preserved ancient Aryan precepts. From them, secret teachings passed down through such figures as Meister Eckart (c. 1260–1327), Paracelsus the alchemist (c. 1490–1541), the irrationalist seer of Romantic Sturm und Drang literature Johann Georg Hamann (1730–1788), the nineteenth-century mesmerist J. H. Jung-Stilling, and Baron Carl du Prel, whose *Philosophy of Mysticism* (1885) was included in the bibliography of Freud's seminal *The Interpretation of Dreams* (1900). Lanz, "Rassenmystik," 10ff.

85. Heiligenkreuz records accuse Lanz of "surrender to the lies of the world and carnal love." Cited in Goodrick-Clarke, *Occult Roots,* 92, along with rumors within Lanz's movement that he briefly embraced Protestantism, citing *Ostara* III, no. 1 (1930), v. According to unconfirmed rumor, he married upon leaving the order. Daim, *Der Mann,* 44. Lanz himself asserted the corruption of Roman Catholicism in a trio of anticlerical books published in Frankfurt (1903–1904).

86. Goodrick-Clarke, *Occult Roots,* 240 fn. 5, citing Fr. Georg [Lanz], "Berthold v. Treun," *Berichte und Mittheilungen des Alterthums-Vereins zu Wein* 30 (1894), 137–40; and Lanz, "Das Necrologium Sancrucense modernum," *Archiv für Österreichische Geschichte* 89 (1900), 247–354.

87. Quoted in Fest, *Hitler,* 36, probably from an *Ostara* editorial. Lanz's obsession with "beast-men" caused by primeval miscegenation continues to resonate in the more esoteric literature of neo-Nazism. Serrano, *Adolf Hitler,* 98, 183. Serrano was a Chilean poet and diplomat who cultivated contacts among Nazi exiles and Latin America and Europe, but he also corresponded with Hermann Hesse and Carl Jung. Serrano has also become influential on younger generations of neo-Nazis with his fantastic, magical vision of National Socialism. Goodrick-Clarke, *Black Sun,* 190–91.

88. Lanz was not the only occultist to find inspiration in Assyria. The novels of Josephin Peladan, an eccentric Roman Catholic Rosicrucian who went about Paris dressed in a medieval doublet, drew on Assyrian mythology. Webb, *Occult Underground*, 169, 171.
89. Lanz, *Theozoologie*, 113, 133ff. For Blavatsky on the third eye, see *Secret Doctrine*, 299ff.
90. Lanz, *Theozoologie*, 133.
91. Ibid., 135, 147–52.
92. Some neo-Nazis have revived the use of Tschandala as a term of abuse for other races. Goodrick-Clarke, *Black Sun*, 170. The great Swedish writer August Strindberg, with whom Lanz claimed to be associated, wrote a novel called *Tschandala* in 1888. It remained unpublished until a decade later, during the period when Lanz claimed to have met Strindberg.
93. Quoted in Goodrick-Clarke, *Occult Roots*, 98.
94. Ibid., 100–101. After the death of Franz Hartmann, Jostenoode took the editorship of Hartmann's Theosophical organ, *Neue Lotusblüten.*
95. Lanz's particular rendition of the swastika has become popular in recent decades among neo-Nazi youth groups in Germany and heavy metal bands in the United States. Goodrick-Clarke, *Black Sun*, 207, 209.
96. Herndl, *Die Trutzburg*, 251–52. Herndl writes of a festival at Burg Werfenstein (spring 1908) with several hundred guests arriving by steamboat from Vienna to the roar of cannons from the castle's flag-festooned battlements. Ibid., 257ff. Herndl, an occult novelist, founder of an occult study group called the Sphinx Reading Club, and apparent member of the List Society, lived in a hermitage on Wörth Island, near Burg Werfenstein.

    Lanz's claim of establishing ONT in 1900 are examined and dismissed in Goodrick-Clarke, *Occult Roots*, 245 fn. 12, though in a later work he cites 1900 as ONT's founding year. Goodrick-Clarke, *Black Sun*, 135.
97. Lanz, "Anthropozoon biblicum," *Vierteljahrschrift fur Bibelkunde* 1 (1903), 321, and *Vierteljahrschrift fur Bibelkunde* 2 (1904), 410.
98. J. von Lanzenfels [Lanz], "Die heilige Gral," 226.
99. Lanz produced an extensive literature of ritual books for ONT, one of which was later found in Adolf Hitler's library. Phelps "Der Hitler-Bibliothek," 923–31.
100. Goodrick-Clarke, *Occult Roots*, 113. Familiars included List; List Society member Blasius von Schemua; health reformers Wilhelm Diefenbach and Gustav Simons; and the Theosophical painter and illustrator Fidus (Hugo Höppener). Lanz claimed Swedish writer August Strindberg as a Familiar, but Goodrick-Clarke's careful appraisal is inconclusive, proving only that Strindberg had been in the neighborhood of Burg

Werfenstein, and that Lanz had written to the author. Ibid., 246 fn. 33. What is known is that the playwright became part of the occult underground in the 1890s as an intimate of occultists in Paris, where he published essays on alchemy and wrote for an anti-Semitic periodical; he also had ties to Austria, where he lived in 1893 with his second wife, the free-spirited Austrian journalist Frida Uhl. Since Strindberg flirted with Theosophy, Roman Catholicism, Swedenborg, and the black arts, it is plausible that he corresponded with Lanz, who then exaggerated the scope of their relationship.

Fidus was a prominent German illustrator, steeped in Nordic mythology and rooted in Art Nouveau, but reaching for surrealism and psychedelia. Swastikas and runic-style lettering were recurrent motifs from the artist, revealed in photographs as a long-haired, barefoot proto-hippie. Fidus designed covers for Hugo Vollrath's *Theosophie* magazine and the contents page for *Politisch-Anthropologische Revue*, a journal to which Lanz contributed essays. Frecot, Geist, and Kerbs, *Fidus*, 404, 407. Fidus was associated with a wide network of *völkisch* and occult groups, and was a champion of the Wandervögel. He endorsed the radical Wandervögel league, the Greifen (Hawks), to which Adolf Eichmann had belonged. Mosse, *Crisis of German Ideology*, 226.

101. Goodrick-Clarke, *Occult Roots*, 103–4.
102. Others who joined ONT after the war include the astrologer Friedbert Asboga, the Swabian forester Konrad Weitbrecht, Georg Hauerstein Jr. (son of Georg Hauerstein, a friend of List and prewar ONT initiate), Berlin palmist Ernst Issberner-Haldane, Walter Krenn, Austrian chemical engineer and prewar Pan-Germanist Albrecht Friedrich von Gröling, Theodor Czepl, and Richard Anders (later an SS officer who served as a link between Himmler and occultists). Lanz's brothers Herwik and Friedolin remained active. Hans Heinrich Prince von Pless was among the order's donors. Members established several priories in Germany, which continued after Hitler's ascent to power and through the late 1930s. During the 1920s and 1930s, ONT numbered several hundred members in Germany, Austria, and Hungary. Goodrick-Clarke, *Occult Roots*, 115–18. For Anders and Himmler, see Goodrick-Clarke, *Black Sun*, 136.

During the 1920s Lanz was published by Herbert Reichstein as part of the occult book series, *Ariosophische Bibliothek*. Reichstein was at the center of a German occult circle that included ONT member Issberner-Haldane as well as astrologer Wilhelm Wulff, whom Heinrich Himmler consulted as World War II ended. Reichstein also published a periodical, *Zeitschrift für Menschenkenntnis und Schicksalforshung*, to which

Sebottendorff's astrological collaborator Ernst Tiede contributed, and founded an Ariosophical Society. One member of Reichstein's society, Gregor Schwartz-Bostunitsch, also worked for Alfred Rosenberg's news service, Weltdienst, and later became an SS officer. Goodrick-Clarke, *Occult Roots*, 164–70.

103. Ibid., 119–20.
104. Ibid., 121, working from interviews with P. Miklos Kerper, Stephan Bodor, and P. Miklos Szalai, August 9, 10 and 13, 1978. At least one other priory was established in Hungary. After Lanz departed for Switzerland, Paul Horn, a member of Hungary's parliament, was left in charge of the Hungarian chapters.
105. The ONT regrouped in Vienna after World War II and maintains a shadowy existence. Goodrick-Clarke, *Black Sun*, 135. One of its recent priors published a book lauding Lanz. Mund, *Neue Templer Orden.*

Chapter 3. Munchhausen Incarnate

1. Ellic Howe, "Rudolf Freiherr von Sebottendorff," 40. The manuscript was privately published as a limited edition in 1989 in honor of Howe's seventy-ninth birthday by Albrecht Goetz von Olenhusen, Freiburg, e-mail from Olenhusen to author, December 31, 2004. Howe quoted a Thule Society member acquainted with Sebottendorff in 1918–19, who stated, "I had the impression that he was always an intelligence operative and worked for several different services, although doubtlessly never against German interests." Howe identified the man, a source for much of his speculation, only as "Herr N." Perhaps he was Paul Nagel, the only possible candidate whose surname began with "N" from the only published roster of Thule members. Sebottendorff, *Bevor Hitler kam*, Membership List, 218ff. Howe speculated that Sebottendorff may have been working for intelligence agencies in Turkey before 1914. He also quotes "N" on negative rumors regarding Sebottendorff's alleged career in espionage. "There were some who did not hesitate to describe him as an agent who could always be bought." Sebottendorff, *Bevor Hitler kam*, Membership List, 64–65.
2. Olenhusen, ed., *Wege und Abwege*, 125.
3. Howe, "Sebottendorff, " 38, 40.
4. Sebottendorff, *Die Praxis*, 1.
5. Rudolf was spelled Rudolph on his birth certificate, the first but not the last confusion over Sebottendorff's name. He was the second son in a family of six siblings, many of whom died in childhood. Olenhusen, "Zeittafel zur Biographie Rudolf von Sebottendorff (1875–1945)," appendix to Howe, "Sebottendorff," 1989 ed., 74.

6. Sebottendorff, *Talisman*, 7. *Talisman* describes the adventures of Erwin Torre, who later changed his name to Erwin von Neudorf. Howe believed that "the pseudonyms (and sometimes actual names) in the later chapters would have easily been recognized" by Sebottendorff's Munich associates. He added that Sebottendorff "demonstratively had no skill as a novelist, in the sense that he was not inventive" and concluded that "many of the events he described [in *Talisman*] actually happened." Ibid., 7. Setting aside the imaginative skills of its author, *Talisman* contains many obvious parallels to Sebottendorff's life, among them, Torre's birthplace, Alsenau, a real village near the Glauer family's hometown. The narrative of *Talisman* often closely coincides with Sebottendorff's ostensibly factual accounts of his life.

   The novel was published by Johannes Baum Verlag, a prominent German occult publisher. One of Baum's other authors, Georg Lomer, published the neopagan magazine *Asgard* (1929), with contributions by List Society member Ernst Wachler and the Ariosophist Gregor Schwartz-Bostunitsch, who became an SS officer. Nicholas Goodrick-Clarke, *Occult Roots*, 162, 165.
7. Sebottendorff, *Talisman*, 7–8.
8. Tiede, *Astrologisches Lexikon*, 279. This account also had Sebottendorff studying at Zurich Polytechnic sometime between 1900 and 1908.
9. Sebottendorff, *Talisman*, 8–12.
10. Ibid., 15–20. In fiction as well as in life, Sebottendorff apparently was something of a ladies' man. *Talisman* also details an affair in Berlin (1897) and another with a girl who lodged in the same rooming house as Torre in Hanover.
11. Ibid., 18–22. For corroboration of sailing dates with Lloyds Record Library, see Goodrick-Clarke, *Occult Roots*, 251.
12. Sebottendorff, *Talisman*, 22–25.
13. Ibid., 30–37.
14. Howe, "Sebottendorff," 12, referencing *Murray's Handbook for Travellers in Constantinople, Bursa, etc.* (London: J. Murray, 1893), which describes "the great park of Abraham Pasha, agent to the ex-Khedive of Egypt, Ishmael Pasha" at Beikos.
15. Tiede, *Astrologisches Lexikon*, 279.
16. Sebottendorff, *Talisman*, 31–32, 34–37.
17. Ibid., 31, 40–42, 46–58.
18. Howe, "Sebottendorff," 13, citing *Murray's Handbook.* The hotel mentioned in Talisman, operated by Frau Brotte, actually existed.
19. Sebottendorff, *Talisman*, 53–57, 65–68. Old Termudi had retired from business and devoted himself to occult studies. Abraham, his eldest son, managed the family's bank. It is likely that the Termudi name was

fictionalized by Sebottendorff, but that the family and circumstances he described were otherwise close to reality.

20. Sebottendorff, *Praxis*, 2ff. Sebottendorff's concerns echoed a split that began in Masonry with the formation of the United Grand Lodge in London (1717). Many existing lodges (terming themselves the "Ancients") rejected the Grand Lodge's new constitution and ceremonies and rebuffed its leadership.
21. Heckthorn, *Secret Societies*, 11, 44–46, 98.
22. Akerman, *Rose Cross*, 2–6.
23. Sebottendorff, *Praxis*, 10ff.
24. Goodrick-Clarke, *Occult Roots*, 139, working with Haupt Liste fuer den in Reichs-Aus-Lander No. 513699, Stadtarchiv, Munich.
25. Familienbogen Glauer (November 19, 1918), Stadtarchiv, Munich.
26. Mentioned in Tiede's *Astrologisches Lexikon* is a novel by Sebottendorff, *Der Magier*, supposedly published by Hummel's publishing house, Talis Verlag. Evidence for the book's publication is otherwise lacking, but the reference indicates that Sebottendorff stayed in touch with his mentor. Olenhusen, "Zeittafel," 95. For the 1905 encounter between Sebottendorff and Hummel, see Howe, "Sebottendorff," 17, citing an article by Martin Pfefferkorn in *Astrologische Gesellschaft in Deutschland Nachrictenblatt*, October–November 1933.
27. "Das Portrait eines hakenkreuzlerischen Hochstaplers," *Münchener Post*, March 14, 1923.
28. Sebottendorff, *Astrologie*, 5. Echoing the architectural interpretations of Guido von List, he also found esoteric significance in the hand gestures of carved figures in the vestibule. Sebottendorff, *Praxis*, 24ff.
29. Sebottendorff, "Erwin Haller."
30. Hanioğlu, *Preparation for a Revolution*, 260.
31. Poulton, *Top Hat*, 86.
32. Hanioğlu, *Young Turks*, 4. See also Poulton, *Top Hat*, 80.
33. Poulton, *Top Hat*, 86.
34. Macfie, *End of the Ottoman Empire*, 84–85.
35. Ibid., 86.
36. Fikret Adanir, "Kemalist Authoritarianism and Fascist Trends in Turkey During the Inter-War Period," in Larsen, ed., *Fascism Outside Europe*, 318.
37. Macfie, *End of the Ottoman Empire*, 89.
38. Poulton, *Top Hat*, 84, citing Arnold Toynbee, "Report on the Pan-Turanian Movement," London, Intelligence Bureau, Dept. of Information, Admiralty, L/MIL/17/16/23.
39. Members of this shadowy group were implicated in the attempted 1981 assassination of Pope John Paul II. Lee, *Beast Reawakens*, 202.
40. Walker, *Armenia*, 191; Balakian, *Burning Tigris*, 163–66.

41. Cited in Great Britain, Parliamentary Papers, Miscellaneous No. 31 (1916), 87.
42. Ibid., 84.
43. Toynbee, *Turkey*, 34.
44. Sebottendorff, "Erwin Haller."
45. Sebottendorff, *Talisman*, 78–79.
46. Sebottendorff, *Praxis*, 5ff. Sebottendorff's fictional alter ego, Erwin Torre, was initiated into the Sufi order. *Talisman*, 50–51. Sebottendorff was not the only European discovering Sufism. At the same time, bohemian Westerners associated with French leftist and Theosophical circles, including the feminist writer Isabelle Eberhardt and the painter Ivan Aguel, also found their way into Sufi orders. Sedgwick, *Against the Modern World*, 59–65. An embrace of Islam was understood by the intelligentsia of the time as a gesture against the status quo of Western Civilization.
47. Birge, *Bektashi Order of Dervishes*, 16–20, 78–81, 83–84, 213.
48. Trimingham, *Sufi Orders in Islam*, 254.
49. Sebottendorff, *Hitler*, 169, countering charges made in "Ein gewissenloses Herzblatt," *Münchener Post*, August 2, 1919. For confirmation of Sebottendorff's Turkish citizenship, see Goodrick-Clarke, *Occult Roots*, 252, citing a letter (February 21, 1969) from Zeki Kuneralp (Ministry of Foreign Affairs, Ankara) to John Jardine (British Consul, Ankara).
50. Sebottendorff, *Praxis*, 2ff.
51. Familienbogen Glauer.
52. *Genealogisches Taschenbuch*, 440–42. The Sebottendorffs were feudal lords in the Baltic during the Middle Ages and had been granted a coat of arms, bearing a cinnamon root, which Rudolf von Sebottendorff adopted as his own, by the Holy Roman Emperor Otto II (955–983).
53. *Wiesbadener Zeitung*, October 23, 1915, 6. Curiously, Rudolf Freiherr von Sebottendorff and his wife were identified in the obituary as Sigmund's cousins. The story of Sebottendorff's adoption is refracted at odd angles in his autobiographical novel. In the story, protagonist Erwin Torre had already changed his name to Neudorf before meeting an elderly retired Austrian cavalry captain, Baron von Neudorf, who adopted him as a son. Sebottendorff, *Talisman*, 84.
54. Curiously, Sebottendorff claimed that an official of the Holy Roman Empire named Sebottendorff authorized the publication in 1619 of Heinrich Khunrath's *Amphitheatrum Sapientiae Aeternae*, a work of esoteric Masonry. Sebottendorff, *Praxis*, 23. Perhaps the Sebottendorffs had enjoyed many centuries of occult activities before adopting Rudolf, an eager adept, into the family.

55. Howe, "Sebottendorff," 2–3. Howe discovered a police registration card in Freiburg where the Thule's grandmaster resided in 1920, in which he was identified as "von Sebottendorff, Glandeck Rudolf." Adding to the confusion, an official evidently crossed out Glandeck and wrote Glauer above it.
56. Sebottendorff, *Talisman,* 16. In evaluating the evidence, Howe speculated that Sebottendorff may have served with a unit from the similarly named village of Yenikoy, "Sebottendorff," 16. The fictional braiding may have been designed to strengthen the literary bonds between the protagonist and his loyal Turkish friends from Jenikioj.
57. Sebottendorff, *Talisman,* 80–81.
58. Ibid., 83.
59. Webb, *Occult Establishment,* 41. The Blue Star Lodge was founded by Baron de Leonhardi, a member of the Hungarian parliament, and numbered among its members Karel Weinfurter, A. Rimay de Gidofalva, and Gustav Meyer (aka Meyrink). Goodrick-Clarke, "The Modern Occult Revival in Vienna, 1880–1910," in Pynsent, ed., *Decadence and Innovation,* 107.
60. Frank, *Gustav Meyrink,* 40.
61. Lennhoff and Posner, *Internationales Freimauerlexicon,* 103–5. Soon after war's end, a Swiss member of the List Society published a book denouncing "Anglo-Jewish Masonry" for the war. Heise, *Die Entente-Freimaurerei.*
62. Mystery also surrounds Sebottendorff's wife. Born in 1876 in Shanghai to wealthy Berlin merchant Wilhelm Muller, she had probably been married prior to meeting Sebottendorff. Berta was described on her 1920 police registration card in Freiburg i. Br. as a Turkish citizen. Howe, "Sebottendorff," 6; Olenhusen's appendix to Howe, 76. She was divorced from Sebottendorff in 1928, but it is unclear if she followed her husband after his departure from Germany in 1923. Sebottendorff, *Hitler,* 250.
63. Olenhusen in "Zeittafel," 77, believes Sebottendorff was placed under court supervision due to "excessive spending," but he also cites a letter from Sebottendorff to Thulist Johannes Hering (December 7, 1922) in which the former claimed it was a legal maneuver to shield his wife's wealth from her avaricious executor.
64. Familienbogen Glauer (1917).
65. Sebottendorff, *Hitler,* 168.
66. Sebottendorff, *Talisman,* 86. The novel also describes the arrest of its protagonist on charges of using a false name, impersonating an aristocrat, and espionage. With the help of the Turkish counsel, a man called Nazim, Erwin von Neudorf cleared his name and was released.
67. Ibid., 101, 110–11. The mysterious "Herr N." also claimed that Sebot-

tendorff "was not an out-and-out 'Volkischer,' nor, was he anti-semitic." Howe, "Sebottendorff," 37.

68. Sebottendorff, *Astrologie*, 5.
69. Sebottendorff, *Hitler*, 31–32.
70. Ibid., 15.
71. Sebottendorff, *Astrologie*, 127.
72. Ibid., 129.
73. Sebottendorff, *Hitler*, 42.
74. Sebottendorff, *Astrologie*, 135–36.
75. Sebottendorff, *Hitler*, 58–59. Compare with List, "In the sign of the Ar the Aryans—the sons of the sun—founded their law [Rita], the primal law of the Aryans, of which the earn, or eagle [Aar], is the hieroglyph. It sacrifices itself, as it consecrates itself in a flaming death, in order to be reborn." List, *Secret of the Runes*, 57.
76. Sebottendorff, *Astrologie*, 130. Sebottendorff's position was in keeping with the Young Turks' disdain for their Bedouin subjects and may have been influenced by his exposure to the Bektashi dervishes, who admitted women to their lodges "on equality" with men. Birge, *Bektashi Order of Dervishes*, 211. List also had a few good words for women when he claimed that Wodanism "lifted women to the level of goddesses, and lifted the procreative act . . . to a sacrament." List, *Secret of the Runes*, 97.
77. Sebottendorff, *Hitler*, 21.
78. Tiede, *Astrologisches Lexikon*, 279. No copy has been located of Sebottendorff's book, *Deutsche Mystik* (Stamboul, 1915). See Goodrick-Clarke, *Occult Roots*, 252.
79. *Technik-Geschichte* 23 (1934), 102ff.; Sebottendorff, *Hitler*, 239. The tank, invented by Friedrich Wilhelm Göbel, was demonstrated in early 1914 but rejected by the German military. "If Sebottendorff 'financed' or attempted to procure financial backing for the Göbel tank, it cannot have been a financially rewarding venture." Howe, "Sebottendorff," 5–6. The tank was one of several prototype armored combat vehicles tested by British, French, and other armies in the years preceding World War I, but whose potential was ignored.
80. Sebottendorff, *Talisman*, 84ff.
81. Goodrick-Clarke, *Occult Roots*, 141, citing an April 20, 1980, letter to the author from Irmgard Uhlig (Kleinzschachwitz, Dresden).
82. Mosse, *Crisis of German Ideology*, 112.
83. Phelps, "Theodor Fritsch," 442.
84. Goodrick-Clarke, Occult Roots, 123–24. Fritsch edited the *Kleine Muhlen-Journal* (*Small Mills Journal*) beginning in 1880, launched a second periodical for millers in 1882 and organized the German Millers League.

85. Fritsch originally published the *Antisemiten Catechismus* under the pen name Thomas Frey. Phelps, "Theodor Fritsch," 443.
86. Phelps, "Theodor Fritsch," 442, quoted from *Hammer* (January 1931). The influence of Fritsch on Hitler's earliest public speeches as an orator for the Nazi Party has also been noted. Phelps, "Hitlers 'grundlegende Rede,'" 395–96.
87. Mosse, *Crisis of German Ideology*, 112.
88. Among Hammer Verlag's authors was Fritsch's close friend and collaborator, Willibald Hentschel, a pupil of eminent zoologist Ernst Haeckel. Hentschel's preoccupation with racial dynamism as an electrical current that animated history is comparable to Lanz's doctrine of Theozoology. His book *Varuna*, which enjoyed great influence on popular German thought, proposed a Utopian settlement called Mittgart, after a legendary place of origin for the Aryans. It was to be an agricultural colony, where the fittest human stock could flourish in the open air. Hentschel, *Varuna*, 602, 604.
89. Phelps, "Theodor Fritsch," 443; and Levy, *Downfall*, 166ff.
90. Fritsch, *Neue Wege*, 280.
91. Phelps, "Theodor Fritsch," 443, 445; see also Huttig, "Die politischen Zeitschriften," 17. With its association of the hammer with the Nordic deity Thor, periodicals called *Hammer* intersect *völkisch* circles more than once. List published an article (c. 1896) in a monthly called *Der Hammer*, the organ of an Austrian Pan-German group, the Nationalist Workers' League. The name *Hammer* was revived by the SS when it established a Dutch-language publishing house, Hammer Verlag, in occupied Holland. Kater, *Das Ahnenerbe*, 179.
92. Phelps, "Theodor Fritsch," 442, 446, 448. For an examination of Henry Ford's influence on the nascent Nazi movement and Theodor Fritsch's role as his German publisher, see Baldwin, *Henry Ford*, 172ff. Some of Fritsch's work was translated into English and published by the Britons, an English anti-Semitic group founded in 1918 and active in circulating the *Protocols of the Elders of Zion* in the United Kingdom. Webb, *Occult Establishment*, 130.
93. Phelps, "Theodor Fritsch," 445.
94. Fritsch, "Vom partei-politischen Antisemitismus," 153–58.
95. Apparently wheels were turning toward the establishment of the Reichshammerbund even before the March meeting. As early as February, Hellwig drew up a constitution for the organization. The roots of the Germanenorden extend to still earlier discussions. In 1910 Philipp Stauff, a journalist and List Society member, proposed the establishment of a secret anti-Semitic lodge in a letter to Heinrich Kraeger, who cofound-

ed the Deutsch-Sozialistische Party (1918), an organization associated with Thule that later amalgamated with the Nazis. The idea of an anti-Semitic lodge was taken up in 1911 by Johannes Herring. Herring was an associate of List and Lanz, and member of the Munich Hammer group, who later joined the Thule Society. In that same year Hermann Pohl circulated a letter, which included Fritsch's endorsement, about the possibility of founding a covert network on the model of the Wotan Lodge. Concealed within the Magdeburg Hammer group and with Pohl as its elected master, the Wotan Lodge conducted rituals based on ancient German paganism. Goodrick-Clarke, *Occult Roots,* 126–27, citing Bundesarchiv, Koblenz, NS26/887, NS26/512, and NS26/512a. See also *Allgemeine Ordens-Nachrichten* 14 (September 1918), 3–4.

96. Goodrick-Clarke, *Occult Roots,* 126, citing Bundesarchiv, Koblenz, NS26/888.
97. Ibid., 126–27, citing Karl August Hellwig, "Verfassung des R.H.B." and Theodor Fritsch, "Richtlinien für den Reichshammerbund," Bundesarchiv, Koblenz, NS26/888. Phelps, "Before Hitler Came," 248–49.
98. Goodrick-Clarke, *Occult Roots,* 126, citing Bundesarchiv, Koblenz, NS26/888.
99. Ibid., 128, citing Bundesarchiv, Koblenz, NS26/885.
100. Howe, "Sebottendorff," 26.
101. Gumbel, *Verschwörer,* 100.
102. Phelps, "Theodor Fritsch," 447. Howe, "Sebottendorff," 26–28.
103. Goodrick-Clarke, *Occult Roots,* 128, citing Bundesarchiv, Koblenz, NS26/852.
104. Ibid., 128, citing a circular by Pohl dated July 1912, Bundesarchiv, Koblenz NS26/492. Sebottendorff, however, claimed that by the summer of 1914 the Orden had several thousand members. Sebottendorff, *Bevor Hitler kam,* 34.
105. Sebottendorff, *Bevor Hitler kam,* 34.
106. Goodrick-Clarke, *Occult Roots,* 129, citing Bundesarchiv, Koblenz, NS26/852.
107. Ibid., 129 citing the leaflet "Anweisung zur Werbearbeit" (n.d.) deposited in Bundesarchiv, Koblenz, NS26/852.
108. *Allgemeine Ordens-Nachrichten* (March 1918), 3–4.
109. Goodrick-Clarke, Occult Roots, 129.
110. Sebottendorff, *Bevor Hitler kam,* 35.
111. Goodrick-Clarke, *Occult Roots,* 154–55. Kirchoff corresponded with Karl Maria Wiligut, a List follower who later became influential with Heinrich Himmler and contributed to *Hagal,* the publication of the Edda Society, yet another group steeped in List's neopagan perspective.
112. Ibid., 132–33, citing Bundesarchiv, Koblenz, NS26/510, NS26/852.

Other officers of the "original" Germanenorden included Dr. Gensch from Berlin, who acted as treasurer, and Regierungsrat Dr. Koerner, an official of the Prussian office of heraldry with a Listian interest in the runic symbolism of armorial devices.

113. Lohalm, *Völkischer Radikalismus,* 228–29; and Jasper, "Erzberger-Moerder," 430–53. The tireless Fritsch was one of the national leaders of the Schutz-und-Trutzbund, which grew from 25,000 members in 1919 to 110,000 by the following year. Among the leaders of the Schutz-und-Trutzbund's Munich chapter were such familiar associates of the Thule Society as Dietrich Eckart, Julius Lehmann, and Gottfried Feder, along with Max Sesselmann, an editor of the *Münchener Beobachter* who later marched with Hitler during the Beer Hall Putsch. Like the Thule Society, the Munich Schutz-und-Trutzbund met at Hotel Vier Jahreszeiten. Till, ed., *Munchen,* 55.
114. Sebottendorff, *Talisman,* 90–95.
115. Ibid., 95–98. The Germanenorden chief identified in the novel as Herr Lange seems identical to Walvater's chancellor Pohl. A few documents of the Germanenorden-Walvater were preserved in the Nazi Party archive. Among them, a membership application demanding information on the amount of hair on various parts of the body and an imprint of the sole of the applicant's foot, all this to screen out non-Aryans. NSDAP Hauptarchiv HA no. 851.
116. Sebottendorff, *Bevor Hitler kam,* 40.

Chapter 4. Hammer of the Gods

1. Sebottendorff, *Bevor Hitler kam,* 40–41.
2. Ibid., 41.
3. Sebottendorff, "Werbeblatt Germanenorden," vol. 1; and Sebottendorff, "Werbeblatt Germanenorden," vol. 2. For List's interpretation of Heil and Sieg as a "millennia-old Aryan greeting and battle-cry," see List, *Secrets of the Runes,* 57.
4. Franz, "Munich," 326.
5. Chickering, *We Men Who Feel Most German,* 242. The nature of Lehmann's association with the Thule Society is clouded by the omission of his name from the incomplete membership roster Sebottendorff included as an appendix to his memoirs, *Bevor Hitler kam.* As with the similarly omitted Gottfried Feder, most authorities assume Lehmann was a member of Thule because of his prolific work on its behalf. Lehmann was in all events a confirmed joiner. He served on the managing board of the Pan-German League, and as chairman the league's Munich branch. Lehmann also became a member of the nationalistic German

Naval Union and Thule member Wilhelm Rohmeder's Deutschen Schulverein. J. F. Lehmanns Verlag was one of Germany's most prominent publishing houses during the Third Reich and continued to exist until 1981. Till, ed., *Munchen*, 55–56, 132–33, 150.

6. Grunberger, *Red Rising*, 27; Flood, *Path to Power*, 519.
7. Franz, "Munich," 326.
8. Sebottendorff, *Hitler*, 218.
9. Franz, "Munich," 326.
10. Mitchell, *Revolution in Bavaria*, 215.
11. Sebottendorff, *Hitler*, 218.
12. Ibid., 222.
13. Balzli, *Guido von List*, 176–77.
14. Goodrick-Clarke, *Occult Roots of Nazism*, 143.
15. Sebottendorff, *Hitler*, 41, 223.
16. Phelps, "Before Hitler Came," 251, citing a letter by Nauhaus, NSDAP Hauptarchiv HA no. 886.
17. Sebottendorff, *Hitler*, 52. Howe, "Sebottendorff," 28.
18. Phelps, "Before Hitler Came," 252, citing NSDAP Hauptarchiv HA no. 865.
19. File #1483, Registergericht, Amstgericht Munich.
20. Franz, "Munich," 326.
21. Sebottendorff, *Hitler*, 41.
22. "Herr N.," quoted in Howe, "Sebottendorff," 39.
23. Sebottendorff, *Hitler*, 43.
24. Ibid., 52.
25. Goodrick-Clarke, *Occult Roots of Nazism*, 144, citing Bundesarchiv, Koblenz, NS26/865.
26. Sebottendorff, *Hitler*, 52, 220, 223.
27. Phelps, "Before Hitler Came," citing NSDAP Hauptarchiv HA no. 865.
28. Howe, "Sebottendorff," 35.
29. Sebottendorff, *Bevor Hitler kam*, 52.
30. Phelps, "Before Hitler Came," 255.
31. Sebottendorff, *Talisman*, 100.
32. Sebottendorff, *Hitler*, 44, 218–19, 231.
33. Goodrick-Clarke, *Occult Roots of Nazism*, 47.
34. Sebottendorff, *Bevor Hitler kam*, 63. Howe, "Sebottendorff," 32.
35. Sebottendorff, *Bevor Hitler kam*, 44.
36. Ibid., 45.
37. Ibid., 46.
38. Ibid., 49.
39. Ibid., 53.

40. Ibid., 194; and Cecil, *Myth of the Master Race*, 31.
41. Sebottendorff, op. cit., 55–56.
42. Ibid., 58, 50–61.
43. Ibid., 62.
44. Ibid., 61.
45. Ibid., 73; for Harrer's role in the establishment of the Nazi Party, see Fest, *Hitler*, 116; for Frank's membership in the Thule Society, see Fest, *Face of the Third Reich*, 213.
46. Hillmayr, *Roter und Weisser Terror*, 33.
47. Sebottendorff, *Hitler*, 62.

Chapter 5. The German Revolution

1. Bessel, *Germany*, 1.
2. Bouton, *Kaiser Abdicates*, 25.
3. Laqueur, *Young Germany*, 33, 74–76, 81ff. He quotes Gerlach from *Wandervögel Fuhrerzeitung* 4/5 (1914), 84. For Gerlach's membership in the List Society, see Goodrick-Clarke, *Occult Roots of Nazism*, 43. Rudolf Hess and Alfred Rosenberg, both former Thule Society members at the top of the Nazi regime, spoke favorably of the Wandervögel. Laqueur, *Young Germany*, 194.
4. Heller, "Brucke," 28–34.
5. Bouton, *Kaiser Abdicates*, 33.
6. Ibid., 39–40.
7. Audoin-Rouzeau and Becker, *14-18*, 34–35.
8. Quoted in Bessel, *Germany*, 2. The popular enthusiasm for the coming war has been criticized recently by some historians, who have tried to confine it to Europe's middle classes. Morrow Jr., *Great War*, 38–39. Nonetheless, enough anecdotal evidence exists to suggest that the fervor spilled over to industrial workers and farmers, regardless of their special anxieties over the war's economic impact.
9. Although Ludendorff marched at Hitler's side during the failed Beer Hall Putsch against the Bavarian government in November 1923, by 1927 Hitler broke with the general, accusing him of Freemasonry. Kershaw, *Hitler*, 195, 269.
10. For the general's initial encounters with Kemnitz, see Ludendorffs, *Ihr Werk und Winken*, 40–41. He charged that "the Christian doctrine and the way of life it has given to the people was . . . the means for obtaining for the Jew the mastery of the world." Ludendorff, *Vom Feldernn zum Weltrevolutionar*, 13.

    The old general divorced his first wife and married Kemnitz on September 14, 1926. Afterward Kemnitz, with her famous husband as occasional coauthor, issued a stream of pamphlets and books under their own imprint, Ludendorffs Verlag, in Munich. When Hitler and Kemnitz engaged in heated discussions on the philosophical structure of Nazism at Feder's home, the führer became annoyed at her presumption. Hanfstaengl, *Hitler*, 84–85. In 1933 the Nazis banned one of the Ludendorffs' organizations, the Tannenbergbund, but their other association, the Deutsche Gotterkenntnis, was tolerated during the Third Reich.

11. For an account of the war's impact on Germany's society and economy, see Bessel, *Germany*, 8–22.
12. Bouton, *Kaiser Abdicates*, 66.
13. Trotsky, *Russian Revolution*, 223.
14. Carr, *Russian Revolution*, 10.
15. Bouton, *Kaiser Abdicates*, 66ff.
16. Sebottendorff, *Bevor Hitler kam*, 49.
17. Ryder, *German Revolution*, 7.
18. Quoted in Bouton, *Kaiser Abdicates*, 91.
19. Sebottendorff, *Bevor Hitler kam*, 36.
20. Bouton, *Kaiser Abdicates*, 83.
21. Ryder, *German Revolution*, 130; and Bouton, *Kaiser Abdicates*, 98–100.
22. Ryder, *German Revolution*, 129.
23. Ibid., 4.
24. Groener, *Lebenserinnerungen*, 467.
25. Watt, *Kings Depart*, 160.
26. Ryder, *German Revolution*, 201.
27. Noske, *Von Kiel bis Kapp*, 67.
28. Ryder, *German Revolution*, 203.
29. Ibid., 204.
30. In a letter (December 1914) to List from his patron Friedrich Wannieck, the latter wrote of seeking consolation from a medium over the death of his son in the war. The medium was a Miss von Rantzau, an associate of List Society member Franz Hartmann. Both Wannieck's son and Hartmann spoke through her, commending List's work. Balzli, *Guido von List*, 184–85.
31. Deuerlein, ed., *Der Aufstieg der NSDAP*, 59.

Chapter 6. The Bavarian Socialist Republic

1. Hitler, *Mein Kampf*, 126.
2. Haffner, *Failure of a Revolution*, 163.
3. Mann, *History of Germany*, 521.
4. Gentizon, *La Revolution allemande*, 22.
5. Watt, *Kings Depart*, 281ff.
6. Ryder, *German Revolution*, 212.

7. Quoted in Mitchell, *Revolution in Bavaria,* 120.
8. Hitler, *Mein Kampf,* 207.
9. Gentizon, *La Revolution allemande,* 99–100.
10. Watt, *Kings Depart,* 325.
11. Nettl, *Rosa Luxemburg,* 21.
12. Fest, *Hitler,* 109. Even Thomas Mann complained of the "Jewish scribblers" who suddenly ruled in Munich. *Diaries 1918–1939,* 19.
13. Franz, "Munich," 323.
14. Ibid., 326.
15. According to one historian, the first Freikorps was Maercker's Volunteer Rifles, established December 22, 1918 in Westphalia. See Watt, *Kings Depart,* 250ff. The Thule Combat League was already in operation by the beginning of December.
16. Among Lehmann's projects was a periodical, *Deutschlands Erneuerung,* which included articles by Thulist Alfred Rosenberg, geneticist Fritz Lenz, Max von Gruber (professor of hygiene at the University of Munich), and the American eugenicist Lothrop Stoddard. In the 1920s Lehmann published books by racial theorists Hans F. K. Gunther and Ludwig Schemann. Lehmann joined the Nazi Party in 1920 and sent Hitler books on eugenics and race. Weikart, *From Darwin to Hitler,* 222–23.
17. Sebottendorff, *Bevor Hitler kam,* 63, 259; Franz, "Munich," 326.
18. Hillmayr, *Roter und Weisser Terror,* 33.
19. Sebottendorff, *Bevor Hitler kam,* 63.
20. Ibid., 65.
21. Franz, "Munich," 30; and Hillmayr, *Roter und Weisser Terror,* 33–34.
22. Sebottendorff, *Bevor Hitler kam,* 54.
23. Mitchell, *Revolution in Bavaria,* 182.
24. Ibid., 77–81.
25. Sebottendorff, *Bevor Hitler kam,* 49.
26. Quoted in Mitchell, *Revolution in Bavaria,* 91.
27. Ibid., 103.
28. Ibid., 168–175.
29. Engelman, "Dietrich Eckart," 150.
30. Sebottendorff, *Bevor Hitler kam,* 64–67, 224; for confirmation of the principal points of Sebottendorff's account, see Hillmayr, *Roter und Weisser Terror,* 34.
31. Mitchell, *Revolution in Bavaria,* 200.
32. Sebottendorff, *Bevor Hitler kam,* 68.
33. Ibid., 68; for confirmation of the principal points of Sebottendorff's account, see Hillmayr, *Roter und Weisser Terror,* 31.
34. Sebottendorff, *Bevor Hitler kam,* 69; for confirmation of the raid on

the Four Seasons Hotel, see Mitchell, *Revolution in Bavaria,* 202, and Phelps, "Before Hitler Came," 252.

35. Zittel, "Raetemodell Muenchen," 26.
36. Phelps, "Before Hitler Came," citing *Münchener-Augsburger Abendzeitung,* December 27–31, 1918.
37. Mitchell, *Revolution in Bavaria,* 202–3.
38. Ibid., 267.
39. Ibid., 268; Hillmayr, *Roter und Weisser Terror,* 34; for Kraus's Thule membership, see Sebottendorff, *Bevor Hitler kam,* 221.
40. Sebottendorff, *Bevor Hitler kam,* 92–93.
41. "Herr N." gathered that Sebottendorff "had considerable means at his disposal and that he was apparently not required to account for the expenditure of these funds. . . . He had no desire to make any political or economic profit from his activity." Howe, "Sebottendorff," 39–40.
42. Sebottendorff, *Bevor Hitler kam,* 62; and Grunberger, *Red Rising,* 153–54.
43. Engelman, "Dietrich Eckart," 103. "Herr N." recalled that Eckart praised Sebottendorff for his gift of simplifying complicated issues for the common man and admiringly referred to him as a "drummer," a compliment he also bestowed on Hitler. Howe, "Sebottendorff," 38.
44. Hillmayr, *Roter und Weisser Terror,* 33.
45. Franz, "Munich," 326.
46. Oddly, the name "Arco" turned up in occult literature several years prior to the young man's frustrated attempt to join the Thule Society. In "From the Diary of an Orange Tree" (1905), a short story by List's associate Hanns Heinz Ewers, one of the characters is a cavalry officer called Count Arco. Bewitched, the fictional Arco loses his reason to an enchanting sorceress.
47. Sebottendorff, *Bevor Hitler kam,* 76.
48. Ryder, *German Revolution,* 212–13.
49. Hillmayr, *Roter und Weisser Terror,* 35.
50. Sebottendorff, *Bevor Hitler kam,* 49.
51. Ibid., 83; for confirmation of the plausibility of Sebottendorff's assertion, see Mitchell, *Revolution in Bavaria,* 272.
52. Sebottendorff, *Bevor Hitler kam,* 84.
53. Large, *Where Ghosts Walked,* 92.
54. Watt, *Kings Depart,* 244.
55. Sebottendorff, *Bevor Hitler kam,* 83.
56. Ibid., 67.
57. Mitchell, *Revolution in Bavaria,* 314.
58. Hanser, *Putsch!,* 167.
59. Ibid., 170. Like many German soldiers who encamped on the far right upon their return home, Ernst Toller was deeply affected by his war-

time experience. His response, however, was a distrust of violence coupled with disillusionment over the old social order. "The war itself had turned me into an opponent of war," he wrote, and "I felt that the land I loved had been betrayed and sold. It was for us to overthrow these betrayers." Toller, *I Was a German*, 100–101.

60. Ryder, *German Revolution*, 213.
61. Hanser, *Putsch!*, 170.
62. Ibid., 172–73; Mitchell, *Revolution in Bavaria*, 328.
63. Sebottendorff, *Bevor Hitler kam*, 62.

Chapter 7. The Battle for Munich

1. Quoted in Mitchell, *Revolution in Bavaria*, 314–15.
2. Decree quoted in Sebottendorff, *Bevor Hitler kam*, 106.
3. Kuron, "Freikorps und bund Oberland," 16, citing Official News Bulletin of the Archdiocese of Bamberg (April 30, 1919).
4. Sebottendorff, *Bevor Hitler kam*, 95–6.
5. Ibid., 102.
6. Beyer, *Die Revolution*, 144, citing Bavarian Haupstaatsarchiv MA 99902.
7. Hillmayr, *Roter und Weisser Terror*, 88.
8. Sebottendorff, *Bevor Hitler kam*, 220.
9. Beyer, *Die Revolution*, 156.
10. Sebottendorff, *Bevor Hitler kam*, 107.
11. Kuron, "Freikorps und bund Oberland," 16.
12. Sebottendorff, *Bevor Hitler kam*, 106–7.
13. Epp's aide-de-camp, Ernst Röhm, joined the Nazis much earlier than his commander. Röhm welded the brown-shirted SA into the Nazi Party's original contingent of storm troopers, which grew into a three-million-man militia before his murder in 1934 after the Night of the Long Knives. Epp's adjutant, Karl Wolff, later became Heinrich Himmler's SS chief of staff. Jones, *Hitler's Heralds*, 139–40, 252, 267.
14. Sebottendorff, *Bevor Hitler kam*, 106–7.
15. Ibid., 109.
16. Ibid., 124.
17. Mitchell, *Revolution in Bavaria*, 306–7.
18. Ibid., 317.
19. Quoted in Sebottendorff, *Bevor Hitler kam*, 110–11.
20. Grunberger, *Red Rising*, 112–13.
21. Phelps, "Before Hitler Came," 252–53, citing an anonymous typescript in NSDAP Hauptarchiv no. 72.
22. Sebottendorff, *Bevor Hitler kam*, 112–13.
23. Mitchell, *Revolution in Bavaria*, 317–18.

24. Fest, *Hitler*, 85, citing Thor Goote, *Aus der Gesichte der Bewegung*, a November 1934 publication of the official German Labor Front, and a letter from Hitler's army friend Ernst Schmidt to Hitler biographer Werner Maser.
25. Hitler, *Mein Kampf*, 207–8. In *Hubris* (639), Kershaw dismisses Hitler's account of his attempted arrest by pointing out that the "Central Council" had already been dissolved on April 13, but this may be a matter of imprecision rather than deception. By using the term "Central Council," Hitler could have referred generically to the Red authorities clinging to power in Munich through the end of April.
26. Hitler's activities from his return to Munich in March through the city's liberation from the Reds in May remain obscure and subject to speculation. In *Hitler* (84), Fest wonders about the odd "political indolence" of Hitler, who returned to a barracks flying the red flag rather than joining a Freikorps. Hitler was arrested by Freikorps Epp after the battle for Munich in early May, but according to Fest, "some officers who knew him intervened, and he was released again." Hitler claims, "A few days after the liberation of Munich, I was ordered to report to the examining commission concerned with revolutionary occurrences in Second Infantry Regiment." *Mein Kampf*, 208. Were those officers known to him from wartime service, or was he familiar with them from a connection through the Thule Society? Could Hitler have been masking his early *völkisch* ties by obscuring his activities under the Soviet Republics?

    In *Legend, Myth & Reality* (101–3), Maser takes the conventional, entirely plausible position that Hitler "remained in barracks, awaiting developments" and even adapted himself to circumstances by wearing a red armband. Maser derives this from a 1952 letter to him by Otto Strasser, a leader of the left socialist wing of the Nazi Party. As his brother, Gregor Strasser, was murdered on Hitler's orders during the Night of the Long Knives, his recollections may not be entirely disinterested. Rumors had long placed Hitler in the Social Democratic camp during the early months of 1919. Heiden, *Hitler*, 54.

    More recent research uncovers a more interesting, if still tantalizingly incomplete picture. A routine military order of April 3, 1919, referred to Hitler as the representative (Vertrauensmann) of his company, a task apparently involving the distribution of Social Democratic materials to the troops. On April 15, Hitler was elected deputy battalion representative. Kershaw, *Hubris*, 117–18, citing Bavarian Hauptstaatsarchiv Abt. IV, 2 I.R. Batl. Anordnungen Bl. 1504/1505/1516. "How to interpret this evidence is, nevertheless, not clear," Kershaw, *Hubris*, 118. Given the Thule Society's admitted cooperation with the Social Democrats beginning in the early weeks after the November revolution, it is possible that Hitler was acting in concert with a Thule front group, which would explain his hasty release from captivity by investigators from Freikorps Epp.

27. Grunberger, *Red Rising*, 136.
28. Kuron, "Freikorps und bund Oberland," 17; Hillmayr, *Roter und Weisser Terror*, 88.
29. Sebottendorff, *Bevor Hitler kam*, 107–8.
30. Kuron, "Freikorps und bund Oberland," 17.
31. Schwarzwaller, *Rudolf Hess*, 58, 63.
32. Sebottendorff, *Bevor Hitler kam*, 108, 224, 250.
33. Ibid., 109.
34. Jones, *Hitler's Heralds*, 142–43.
35. Sebottendorff, *Bevor Hitler kam*, 117.
36. Kuron, "Freikorps und bund Oberland," 18.
37. Sebottendorff, *Bevor Hitler kam*, 116.
38. Schmidt-Pauli, *Geschichte der Freikorps*, 360.
39. Kuron, "Freikorps und bund Oberland," 18–21.
40. Oberland Central consisted of Sebottendorff and a staff including the Thule members Lt. Edgar Kraus, Lt. Karl Schwabe, Lt. Dr. Julius Arndt, and Lt. Franz Freiherr von Felitzch along with Sebottendorff's chauffeur Schödel. Schwabe became an aviator in Africa. Schödel would become a motorcycle manufacturer in Erlangen. Sebottendorff, *Bevor Hitler kam*, 120, 127, 130, 134, 218, 219. Freikorps Chiemgau continued to exist for many months following the fall of Munich as a home guard financed by the Hoffmann government. Kanzler, *Bayerns Kampf*, 24ff.
41. Mitchell, *Revolution in Bavaria*, 322. The higher number is indicated in Bavarian Haupstaatsarchiv, Munich, IV, Gruppenkommando 4, vol. 1/2. Confusion over the exact number of "Prussians" engaged in the battle for Munich may be the result of a stream of reinforcements reaching Bavaria at different times.
42. Jones, *Hitler's Heralds*, 139.
43. Ibid., 161. Many members of the Erhardt Brigade later affiliated themselves with the Nazis by joining the SA.
44. Koch, *Der deutsche Bürgerkrieg*, 116.
45. Ryder, *German Revolution*, 213.
46. Haffner, *Failure of a Revolution*, 171.
47. Got, *La Terreur en Bavière*, 177.
48. Hanser, *Putsch!*, 174.
49. Grunberger, *Red Rising*, 137.
50. Hanser, *Putsch!*, 175.
51. Mitchell, *Revolution in Bavaria*, 320–21; Watt, *Kings Depart*, 325.

52. Sebottendorff, *Bevor Hitler kam*, 114.
53. Mitchell, *Revolution in Bavaria*, 323–24.
54. Grunberger, *Red Rising*, 116–17, 123–25.
55. Ibid., 137.
56. Hillmayr, *Roter und Weisser Terror*, 99.
57. Sebottendorff, *Bevor Hitler kam*, 136; Hillmayr, *Roter und Weisser Terror*, 100–101.
58. Salomon, *Das Buch vom deutschen Freikorpskaempfer*, 101.
59. Sebottendorff, *Bevor Hitler kam*, 138.
60. Ibid., 135, 138; Hillmayr, *Roter und Weisser Terror*, 100–102.
61. Gustav Franz Maria, Prince von Thurn und Taxis, was not the first member of his family to join a secretive lodge. His ancestor, Carl Anselm, Prince von Thurn und Taxis, established a Masonic lodge at the family's seat in Regensburg in 1765. See Frick, *Die Erleuchteten*, 350.
62. Sebottendorff, *Bevor Hitler kam*, 128.
63. Cronauer was either in collusion with anti-Soviet forces or tried to apply fairness and the rule of law to the usually polemical field of "revolutionary justice." In an article written only days after the fall of Munich for the *Neuen Zeitung*, mouthpiece of the Munich Independent Socialists (May 10, 1919), Cronauer pointed to cases in which he acquitted suspected anti-Communists of espionage and counterrevolutionary activities. Cited in Beyer, *Novemberrevolution*, 172–73.
64. Hillmayr, *Roter und Weisser Terror*, 101–2.
65. Bavarian Hauptstaatsarchiv Munich, Kriegsarchiv, Handschriften no. 2416.
66. Hillmayr, *Roter und Weisser Terror*, 102–3; Sebottendorff, *Bevor Hitler kam*, 138.
67. Sebottendorff, *Bevor Hitler kam*, 135, 138–39.
68. Beyer, *Novemberrevolution*, 144–45, citing Stadtarchiv Munich, Zeitgeschichte Sammlung (Revolution 1918–1919).
69. Folsing, *Albert Einstein*, 17ff.
70. For a colorful but plausible account of the mistreatment of Thule prisoners by Seidel, see Salomon, *Das Buch vom deutschen Freikorpskaempfer*, 101. Reading like a piece of New Journalism by Tom Wolfe or Norman Mailer, Salomon's rendition includes much alleged dialogue from the event, including the following threat by a "ragamuffin soldier" to Countess Westarp: "A bullet is too good for you. A knife should be plunged into your bodies to exit on the other side. Too bad, mine is too short." According to Salomon, when Daumenlang arrived at Luitpold Gymnasium with broken glasses and face covered with blood, one of the Red Guards, his "heart touched" by the brutal beating, brought him a stool. Salomon was a veteran of Freikorps campaigns in the Baltic and Upper

Silesia and was complicit in the 1922 assassination of Germany's foreign minister, Walter Rathenau.

71. Grunberger, *Red Rising*, 134–35.
72. Seidel gleefully reported to Egelhofer that he had killed "the gentlemen of the Thule Society." Got, *La Terreur en Bavière*, 276.
73. Given the confusion of the soviet regime's final hours, the origin of the orders to kill the Thule members cannot be traced. It is possible that Seidel was pleading the responsibility of a soldier to obey his superiors by blaming Egelhofer. Writers during the Nazi period claimed that Egelhofer, the only "German" among the regime's leadership, was "not very interested" in the anti-Semitism of the Thule Society, and that it was Levien who was preoccupied with punishing Thule for its anti-Jewish agitation. See Salomon, *Das Buch vom deutschen Freikorpskaempfer*, 101.
74. Hillmayr, *Roter und Weisser Terror*, 104–11; for a more colorful account based on contemporary testimony, but concurring on the essential points, see Salomon, *Das Buch vom deutschen Freikorpskaempfer*, 101–4. Salomon's rendition includes such details as the shouts of "To the wall with the whore!" by Red Guards as Countess Westarp was led to the place of execution.

    Likewise, Sebottendorff includes an account of Westarp writing a farewell letter against the back of a Red Guard and pleading, "I am innocent! Do not turn me into a corpse!" He claims Thurn und Taxis was the last to be executed. *Bevor Hitler kam*, 146–47. Interestingly, at the Munich trial (September–October 1919) of those accused of taking part in the Luitpold execution, defense attorneys called for an examination of the Thule Society, a request denied by the court, which "anxiously tried to protect the public image of the Thule Society . . . as a harmless Germanic lodge." Hillmayr, *Roter und Weisser Terror*, 32. For the summary executions of Reds by Whites approaching Munich, see Grunberger, *Red Rising*, 134–35.
75. Mitchell, *Revolution in Bavaria*, 326–27.
76. Ibid., 327–28.
77. Haffner, *Failure of a Revolution*, 175.
78. Mitchell, *Revolution in Bavaria*, 329.
79. Grunberger, *Red Rising*, 134–35; Hanser, *Putsch!*, 187.
80. Jones, *Hitler's Heralds*, 142.
81. Bavarian Haupstaatsarchiv Munich, Kriegsarchiv, Handschriften no. 2416.
82. Ernst Röhm, *Hochverraters*, 100–101.
83. *The Times* (London) front-page headline for May 5, 1919, read, "Shooting of Hostages/Munich Savagery."
84. The city of Munich assumed the cost of funerals for Walter Nauhaus

and Walter Deicke. On June 25, 1919, the Thule Society wrote the Munich council asking that the cost of installation and upkeep of gravestones also be borne by the city. Neue Schriftenreihades Stadtarchivs Munchen, vol. 29 (Munich, 1968), 83.

85. Beyer, *Novemberrevolution*, 155.
86. Koch, *Der deutsche Bürgerkrieg*, 117.
87. Bavarian Haupstaatsarchiv Munich, Kriegsarchiv, Handschriften no. 2416.
88. What was thought to be genitals of the victims found at Luitpold proved to be pig offal. Grunberger, *Red Rising*, 149.
89. Sebottendorff, *Bevor Hitler kam*, 147.
90. Ibid., 110.
91. One member of the Thule Combat League, Karl Stecher, died in street fighting. Ibid., 129.
92. Grunberger, *Red Rising*, 140; Kuron, "Freikorps und bund Oberland," 24.
93. Grunberger, *Red Rising*, 136.
94. Bavarian Haupstaatsarchiv Munich, Kriegsarchiv, Handschriften no. 2416.
95. Hanser, *Putsch!*, 190.
96. Ibid., 176.
97. Mitchell, *Revolution in Bavaria*, 338.
98. During the fight for Haar, a member of the Thule Combat League who had transferred to Freikorps Chiemgau, Lieutenant Wiedemann, was killed. Sebottendorff, *Bevor Hitler kam*, 130.
99. Ibid., 129.
100. Grunberger, *Red Rising*, 138.
101. Mitchell, *Revolution in Bavaria*, 337.
102. Axelrod was sentenced by a Munich court to fifteen years hard labor but was extradited to the Soviet Union under intense diplomatic pressure from Moscow. Levine shouted, "Long live the world revolution!" before falling to the bullets of his firing squad. Sebottendorff, *Bevor Hitler kam*, 133–34; and Mitchell, *Revolution in Bavaria*, 338.
103. According to Stauff, List and his wife arrived by train in Berlin en route to the Landen, Brandenburg, home of List Society member Eberhard von Brockhusen. Too sick to continue, List died in a Berlin guesthouse with Stauff at his side. "Guido von List gestorben," *Münchener Beobachter*, May 24, 1919, 4. Another account, however, places his death in Vienna on May 21. Nagl and Zeidler, *Deutsch-österreichesche Literaturgeschichte*, 1935. Stauff's obituary appears credible, given its proximity in time to List's demise, but Nagl-Zeidler's report of death in List's hometown is also plausible, considering the difficulty of an ailing seventy-year-old man in traveling by train across a country where civil war still simmered.

It is possible that Stauff falsified his account of List's death in order to arrange a kind of apostolic succession for himself as head of the List Society. List was cremated and his ashes placed in an urn at Vienna's Central Cemetery.

104. Sebottendorff, *Bevor Hitler kam*, 129.
105. Freikorps Oberland fought against the Poles in Upper Silesia in the 1921 rebellion by Germans against the province's new Polish rulers. Elements of Freikorps Oberland become the 3rd Battalion, 42nd Rifle Regiment. Schmidt-Pauli, *Geschichte der Freikorps*, 360. Other members continued an independent existence as Bund Oberland, whose leader was arrested and convicted in 1922 on charges of plotting to raise funds by robbing travelers to Oberammergau's Passion Play. In February 1923 Bund Oberland loosely confederated with other right-wing paramilitiaries (including the SA) as part of the Arbeitsgemeinschaft der Vaterländischen Kampfverbände (Working Community of Patriotic Combat Groups) under the leadership of SA leader Ernst Röhm. In the murky political atmosphere of Munich, this association received training from Reichswehr District VII with a view toward a coming conflict with the central government in Berlin. In September 1923 Bund Oberland joined with the SA and the Reichsflagge in a more closely aligned federation called the Deutsche Kampfbund (German Combat League). It was as part of this association that Bund Oberland took part in Hitler's unsuccessful putsch against the Munich government in November 1923. In the aftermath of the Beer Hall Putsch, Bund Oberland was banned by Bavaria's government and never reemerged as a distinct entity. Gumbel, *Verschwörer*, 237ff.

Chapter 8. Thule and the Nazi Circle

1. Sebottendorff, *Bevor Hitler kam*, 13. *Bevor Hitler kam* was published in two editions, one in 1933 and a second expanded edition in 1934. The greater length of the 1934 version resulted from the addition of photographs and the enlargement of index notes. Both editions were dedicated to the memory of the seven Thule Society members who died at Luitpold Gymnasium.
2. Ibid., 167. Sebottendorff gave no precise date for his resignation but his chronology is congruent with the June 22, 1919, departure date given by Goodrick-Clarke, *Occult Roots of Nazism*, 51.
3. Sebottendorff, *Bevor Hitler kam*, 220.
4. His offer was rejected. Phelps, "Before Hitler Came," 256.
5. Maser, *Legend, Myth & Reality*, 113.
6. Hitler, *Mein Kampf*, 217.

7. In May 1919 District IV Command established an "Information Department" to inculcate troops in an anti-Communist, pro-nationalist manner. Hitler was one of several promising orators recruited by the army for its education campaign. From June 5 to June 12, 1919, Hitler was sent to Munich University for courses in history, economics, and political science conducted by historian Karl Alexander von Mueller, who knew the Information Department's commanding officer, Capt. Karl Mayr, and by Mueller's brother-in-law, the Thule confederate Gottfried Feder. Under Mayr's orders, Hitler conducted a five-day course at Camp Lechfeld designed to combat political unreliability among the troops. Hitler continued to give talks to soldiers, often in the company of Mueller, into the early months of 1920. He remained on the army payroll until March 31, 1920. Kershaw, *Hubris*, 123.
8. Letter to fellow a V-Mann, Adolf Gemlich. Jäckel and Kuhn, *Hitler*, 88–90.
9. Sebottendorff, *Bevor Hitler kam*, 62, 233.
10. Hale, "Feder Calls Hitler to Order," 358; and Sebottendorff, *Bevor Hitler kam*, 73.
11. Hitler, *Mein Kampf*, 215, 210. Feder became a Nazi member of the Reichstag in 1924 and headed a party economic planning group whose elaborate scheme for socializing Germany was shelved by Hitler. From 1933 to1934, Feder served as undersecretary of Labor, and then took a position as economics professor at the Technische Hochschule in Charlottenburg.
12. Toland, *Adolf Hitler*, 87.
13. Engelman, "Dietrich Eckart," 156, citing Bavarian Hauptstaatsarchiv Division IV, Munich, Reichswehrgruppenkommando 4, Band 50, Akte 8. Mayr later turned on the far right and became active in the Social Democratic Party militia, the Reichsbanner. He fled to France in 1933, was captured by the Germans after the French surrender in 1940, and died at Buchenwald in 1945. Mayr would later claim that he ordered Hitler to join the German Workers' Party to foster its growth. Mayr, "I Was Hitler's Boss," 193–99.
14. Toland, *Adolf Hitler*, 88; Mayr, "I Was Hitler's Boss,"195–96; and Kershaw, *Hubris*, 155.
15. Hitler, *Mein Kampf*, 222.
16. Ibid., 220.
17. Flood, *Path to Power*, 65–66.
18. Orlow, *History of the Nazi Party*, 13.
19. Phelps, "Anton Drexler," 1135.
20. Heinz, *Germany's Hitler*, 116–120. The author interviewed Drexler at length shortly after the Nazi takeover.

21. Phelps, "Anton Drexler," 1135.
22. Heinz, *Germany's Hitler*, 121.
23. Sebottendorff, *Bevor Hitler kam*, 73.
24. Duerlin, ed., *Der Aufstieg*, 59
25. Phelps, "Anton Drexler," 1135.
26. Sebottendorff, *Bevor Hitler kam*, 219; Franz, "Munich," 328.
27. Heinz, *Germany's Hitler*, 121.
28. Cited in Toland, *Adolf Hitler*, 86.
29. Sebottendorff, *Bevor Hitler kam*, 81; and Toland, *Adolf Hitler*, 86.
30. Orlow, *History of the Nazi Party*, 11.
31. Ibid., 12. For the regularity of Workers' Circle meetings, the author cites NSDAP Hauptarchiv Roll 3, Folder 78.
32. For an essay on the significance of the number, see Crowley, *777*, 42–43. According to Crowley, seven is a number of "peculiar importance and sanctity" but also "a most evil number whose perfection is impossible to attack." For Crowley's ties to German Theosophical groups contemporary with the Thule Society, see Webb, *Occult Establishment*, 61.

    The significance of the number seven has also been much discussed in connection with Hitler's membership number in the German Workers' Party. Confusion continues to hang over this question. According to a 1940 letter from Anton Drexler, Hitler joined the DAP as member 555 but later changed his membership card to indicate that he was number seven, which could suggest that the rising führer attached significance to the number. But in a 1941 letter DAP's first secretary, Michael Lotter, recalled that Hitler was the seventh member of the Political Workers' Circle, the leadership component of the party most directly connected with the Thule Society. Kershaw, *Hubris*, 127, citing Bavarian Haupstaatsarchiv, Abt. V, P 3071, Slg. Personen, Anton Drexler, and Institute fuer Zeitgeschichte, Munich, Fa 88/Fasz. 78, Fol. 11–12.

    Writers with an occult perspective have noted the recurrence of the number seven in connection with the Nazi movement by pointing to Hitler's confinement in cell no. 7 at Landsberg, and after his sentencing at Nuremberg, Rudolf Hess became prisoner no. 7 at Berlin's Spandau prison.
33. Phelps, "Anton Drexler," 1136. The article is not footnoted but the author claimed as his source the NSDAP Hauptarchiv.
34. Ibid., 1136–37.
35. Fest, *Hitler*, 117.
36. Hitler, *Mein Kampf*, 687.
37. Heiden, *Der Fuehrer*, 373.
38. Mosse, *Crisis of German Ideology*, 297.

39. Rosenberg, ed., *Dietrich Eckart,* 13.
40. Toland, *Adolf Hitler,* 99.
41. Dresler, *Dietrich Eckart,* 36.
42. Engelman, "Dietrich Eckart," 95–96.
43. This despite a dispute between Sebottendorff and Eckart over who would finance the paper. Eventually Eckart received 10,000 marks from Hans Duchner, publisher of the *Münchener Zeitung.* The industrialist Wolfgang Kapp, who would lead a failed putsch against the Weimar Republic, donated 1,000 marks. Other funds were provided by the tireless Captain Mayr through the good offices of the Reichswehr's District IV Command. An additional 25,000 marks came from the printer of *Auf gut deutsch,* who in exchange was made a partner in Eckart's Hoheneichen Verlag. The premiere issue of *Auf gut deutsch* was mailed to 25,000 addresses. Plewnia, *Auf dem Weg zu Hitler,* 33; Sebottendorff, *Bevor Hitler kam,* 77–78; Engelman, "Dietrich Eckart," 103–4.

    Auf gut deutsch attracted such writers as the Germanenorden's founder, Theodore Fritsch; dramatist Ernst Wachler, a List Society member; and List's ardent admirer, the *völkisch* author Ellegaard Ellerbek, who claimed that Germans were descendants of the old Nordic gods.
44. Engelman, "Dietrich Eckart," 125. For texts of early issues of *Auf gut deutsch,* see Rosenberg, ed., *Dietrich Eckart,* 193–230. For Eckart's occult inclinations, which possibly drew him to the Thule Society rather than a more conventional rightist political association, see Rosenberg, ed., *Dietrich Eckart,* 22–23. Eckart was scornful of mainstream Theosophy, writing of the "Theosophical Society . . . which never knew—and still does not know—what Theosophy really means." Webb, *Occult Establishment,* 285, citing Eckart, "Der Adler des Jupiters," *Auf gut deutsch* (December 12, 1919).
45. Grassinger proposed the union of his German Socialist Party with Kahr's Bavarian People's Party. Engelman citing a letter (December 19, 1969) from Grassinger to the author. "Dietrich Eckart," 106.
46. Franz, "Munich," 327. Following the Germanenorden's winter solstice conclave in Berlin, December 1918, Sebottendorff brought the program of the Deutsche-Sozialistische Partei back with him to Munich. Sebottendorff, *Bevor Hitler kam,* 171, 223–24, 235.
47. Orlow, *History of the Nazi Party,* 27, 42.
48. Engelman, "Dietrich Eckart," 115.
49. Ibid., 128.
50. Euringer, *Leben eines deutschen Dichters,* 27.
51. Engelman, "Dietrich Eckart," 129, citing Bavarian Haupstaatsarchiv Division IV, Munich, Reichswehrgruppenkommando 4, Band 42, Akte 2.

52. Engelman, "Dietrich Eckart," 133ff. Eckart made an anti-Semitic speech to his fellow passengers, one of whom, Berlin theater critic Stefan Grossman, recognized the author of the German *Peer Gynt,* and reported on the speech in his newspaper. *Vossische Zeitung,* evening edition, April 22, 1919.
53. Engelman, "Dietrich Eckart," 135.
54. Ibid., 135.
55. Hitler, *Mein Kampf,* 219.
56. Ay, ed., *Appelle einer Revolution,* 36.
57. Engelman, "Dietrich Eckart," 143–44.
58. Treutzscher, *Armes Volksturm!,* 38–40, 66, 69.
59. Engelman, "Dietrich Eckart," 146.
60. Ibid., 146–47, 159, citing NSDAP Hauptarchiv HA 80, B1, 3-3a-i. According to Orlow (*History of the Nazi Party,* 13), four hundred invitations were sent out for Eckart's speech, citing NSDAP HA, Roll 3, Folder 76. Orlow sees Eckart's appearance as a sign of the party's increasing strength. While it is true that the party was growing, the appearance of Eckart and Feder as speakers becomes less remarkable if one is cognizant of the role of the Thule Society as the network connecting Eckart and Feder with Drexler and Harrer.
61. Engelman, "Dietrich Eckart," 158.
62. Ibid., 160.
63. Cohn, *Warrant for Genocide,* 109–10.
64. Heiden, *Der Fuehrer,* 1–4. The book by Sergei Nilus (1862–1929) was first published in 1905 as *The Great in the Small and Antichrist as an Imminent Political Possibility.* In the introduction to the 1911 edition, Nilus claimed to have received a copy of the *Protocols* from an official in the czarist court. Nilus was not the first to publicize the *Protocols* in Russian, but he was the first to present it between the hard covers of a book. An expanded 1917 edition under a new title, *He Is Near, at the Door . . . Here Comes the Antichrist and the Reign of the Devil on Earth,* may have been the version that came to Rosenberg if the legend is true. *He Is Near* has been republished in post-Soviet Russia.
65. Cohn, *Warrant for Genocide,* 130.
66. Ibid., 129–38.
67. Toland, *Adolf Hitler,* 102.
68. Rosenberg, *Memoirs,* 48.
69. Cecil, *Myth of the Master Race,* 22.
70. Fest, *Face of the Third Reich,* 166.
71. Hart, *Alfred Rosenberg,* 37–38.
72. Rosenberg, ed., *Dietrich Eckart.*

73. Oddly, with the gallows confronting him, Rosenberg held to the cover story when composing his memoirs that the Thule Society was a club studying German prehistory, although he did reference the influence of Theodor Fritsch's *Hammer*. Rosenberg, *Letzte Aufzeichnungen*, 8, 79; and Rosenberg, *Memoirs*, 41. Rosenberg's involvement in circles surrounding the Thule Society can be seen in his contributions to *Deutsche Republik*, published by Thule member R. J. Gorsleben. Cecil, *Myth of the Master Race*, 31.
74. Toland, *Adolf Hitler*, 78.
75. Engelman, "Dietrich Eckart," 114–15.
76. Kershaw, *Hubris*, 152–53.
77. Hitler, *Hitler's Table Talk*, 472. According to Rosenberg, Hitler said of the *Mythus*, "It is a very clever book, only I ask myself who today is likely to read and understand such a book." Rosenberg, *Grossdeutschland*, 95.
78. Hanfstaengle, *Missing Years*, 41. Hanfstaengl quoted Oswald Spengler, who condemned Hitler's intellect because of his devotion to the *Mythus*, in *Zwischen Weissen*, 102.
79. Phelps, "Hitlers 'grundlegende' Rede ueber den Antisemitismus,'" 398.
80. Breiting, *Unmasked*, 79.
81. Nova, *Nazi Theorist*, 82–83.
82. Quoted in Cecil, *Myth of the Master Race*, 33–34.
83. Blavatsky, *The Secret Doctrine* II (London: Theosophical Publishing Co., 1888), 812.
84. Rosenberg, *Mythus*, 25.
85. Houston Stewart Chamberlain, *Foundations of the Nineteenth Century*, 498. Chamberlain also rejected the word "Aryan" except in a linguistic context, 264.
86. Rosenberg, *Mythus*, 114.
87. Chamberlain, *Foundations*, lxxvii.
88. Rosenberg, *Mythus*, 26–29.
89. Ibid., 2.
90. Rosenberg, *Selected Writings*, 101, 108.
91. Rosenberg, *Mythus*, 614–15.
92. According to Hitler, "Christianity is the worst of the regressions that mankind can ever have undergone." See Hitler, *Hitler's Secret Conversations*, 262.
93. Gross, *850 Worte.*
94. Griessdorff, *Unsere Weltanschauung*, 12.
95. Rosenberg, *Mythus*, 135–36.
96. Rosenberg, *Weltanschauung und Glaubenslehre*, 9.
97. Kershaw, *Hubris*, 225–26.

98. Stephen E. Flowers, "The Reception of List's Ideas" in List, *Secret of the Runes*, 34.
99. Cecil, *Myth of the Master Race*, 1.
100. Rosenberg, *Memoirs*, v.
101. Ibid., 90.
102. Nazi Conspiracy and Aggression (Washington, 1946) Suppl. A, 26–27.
103. Speer, *Spandau*, 108, 381.
104. Schwarzwäller, *Rudolf Hess*, 58, 60–61, 63–66, 70–74.
105. Quoted in Fest, *Face of the Third Reich*, 188, citing John Rawlings Rees, ed., *The Case of Rudolf Hess: A Problem in Diagnosis and Forensic Psychiatry* (London, 1947).
106. Hess, *Ein Schicksal*, 43.
107. Fest, *Face of the Third Reich*, 187–97.
108. Karl Mayr, "I Was Hitler's Boss," 198.
109. Haushofer had been imprisoned at Dachau following the failed July 1944 coup against Hitler. Albrecht died in SS custody. Kershaw, *Hubris*, 248–49.
110. Quoted in Jacobsen, *Karl Haushofer*, 231.
111. Hitler, *Hitler's Secret Conversations*, xxvii.
112. Hutin, *Unsichtbare Herrscher*, 167.
113. Stafford, ed., *Flight from Reality*, 10–13, 16. In another assertion, Fleming, who authored the James Bond stories after his wartime service with naval intelligence, devised a scheme to lure Hess to Britain, possibly involving the offices of occultist Aleister Crowley. A handwritten letter from Crowley, offering to interrogate Hess, has survived. No record has survived indicating his offer was accepted. Pasi, "Aleister Crowley," 158f.
114. *Völkischer Beobachter*, May 14, 1941.
115. Goebbels, *Goebbels Diaries*, 363–75, 424, 440.
116. Howe, *Astrology*, 117–19, 192–95, 225–26.
117. Toland, *Adolf Hitler*, 666.
118. Fest, *Face of the Third Reich*, 120–21.
119. Orlow notes that as early as December 1919, Hitler demanded the dissolution of links between the party and the Workers' Circle, and strengthening the power of the party's executive committee, thereby increasing his own position at Harrer's expense. *History of the Nazi Party*, 15. Orlow cites "Organisation des Ausschusses der Ortsgruppe Muenchen und seine Geschäftsordnung," NSDAP HA, Roll 3, Folder 76. See also Hitler, *Secret Conversations*, 365.
120. Fest, *Face of the Third Reich*, 121, 140–42. The circumstances surrounding Harrer's departure remain obscure. Drexler did not surrender without a fight at the end but was persuaded to step down by fellow Thulist Eck-

art. After the Nazi takeover of Germany, Drexler was appointed chief inspector to the Reichsbahn, the state-owned railroad, an insignificant post for one of the founders of the Nazi Party.

121. Heiden, *Hitler*, 76. Heiden writes of Eckart: "From him Hitler learnt to write and even to speak, if by this be understood not merely spirited ranting but the forming of sentences and the building up of a sequence of ideas."
122. Kershaw, *Hubris*, 155; Fest, *Face of the Third Reich*, 133; and Toland, *Adolf Hitler*, 99.
123. Heiden, *Adolf Hitler*, 1, 57–58; in an article in the *Völkischer Beobachter* (August 1921), Eckart proclaimed Hitler as the awaited German messiah, cited in Fest, *Face of the Third Reich*, 133.
124. The great sociologist Max Weber, who died in 1920 after participating in the German delegation to the Versailles conference, had warned of the inherently unstable character of "charismatic rule," a dangerously extra-legal and unbureaucratic model of leadership, which tends to arise in times of crisis. Weber, *Economy and Society*, 241–46.
125. Kershaw, *Hitler*, 17. Hitler's unpromising appearance did not dissuade artists under the Third Reich from depicting him as a knight in white armor, notably Hubert Lanzinger's painting for the infamous German art exhibition in Munich (1937).
126. Hitler and Eckart vacationed together in Berchtesgaden in 1923, four years before Hitler purchased the house that would later be transformed into his mountain aerie. Perhaps the site was not chosen by Hitler only for its scenery, but because it loomed in Germany's neopagan imagination. In "Berchtesgaden . . . among its limestone crags, in a spot scarcely accessible to human foot, the peasants of the valley point out to the traveller the black mouth of a cavern and tell him that, within, Barbarosa lies in an enchanted sleep . . . waiting to descend with his crusaders and bring back to Germany the golden age." Bryce, *Holy Roman Empire*, 180–81. Wagner declared the medieval Holy Roman Emperor Frederick I, called Barbarosa ("Red Beard"), the reincarnation of Siegfried, and asserted that one day he would return. Wagner, *Prose Works* VII, 257–99. Barbarosa was also the code name chosen by Hitler for his assault on the Soviet Union in 1941. See also Kershaw, *Hubris*, 154–55. Eckart quoted in Toland, *Adolf Hitler*, 142.
127. Heiden, *Der Fuehrer*, 92.
128. Phelps, "Hitler and the Deutsche Arbeiterpartei," 982.
129. Flood, *Path to Power*, 80–81.
130. Hitler's first speech before a meeting of the German Workers' Party occurred on October 16, 1919, in the smaller Hofbräuhauskeller, which

seated around 130 people. Hitler, *Secret Conversations*, 354–55. His passionate oratory was applauded by the party leadership, who by November would give him the title of Werbeobmann or "publicist."

131. Kershaw, *Hubris*, 144–46, 647 fn. For Dingfelder's membership in Thule, see Sebottendorff, *Bevor Hitler kam*, 218. For Hitler's quote, see Hitler, *Secret Conversations*, 369–70.
132. Hitler, *Secret Conversations*, 155.

Chapter 9. Trail of the Crooked Cross

1. Kershaw, *Hitler*, 17–18.
2. Ibid., 19.
3. Fest, *Inside Hitler's Bunker*, 40–41.
4. Kershaw, *Hubris*, 62.
5. Albert Speer, *Erinnerungen* (Frankfurt am Main: Ullstein, 1969), 112.
6. Hitler, *Mein Kampf*, 59.
7. Kershaw, *Hubris*, 63–64, citing Reinhold Hanisch, "I Was Hitler's Buddy," *New Republic*, April 5, 12, and 19, 1939, 239–42.
8. Ibid., 66–67.
9. Calic, *Unmasked*, 49. The quote was given during an interview with Richard Breiting, editor of the conservative *Leipziger Nueste Nachrichten.* Breiting died after Hitler came to power, probably as the result of the Gestapo's efforts to suppress his unpublished notes from the interview.
10. Kershaw, *Hubris*, 125, citing Bavarian Haupstaatsarchiv, Abt. IV, RW-GrKdo 4, no. 314.
11. Hitler, *Hitler's Secret Conversations*, 281–82.
12. Daim, *Der Mann*, 12, citing a letter (22 February 1932) from Lanz to his fellow initiate, Frater Aemilius.
13. "That Hitler was acquainted with List's ideas is certain, although it is impossible to determine how much of it Hitler believed." Kershaw, *Hubris*, 50–51.
14. Daim, *Der Mann*, 14–34.
15. Kershaw, *Hubris*, 49.
16. Hitler, *Mein Kampf*, 73–74.
17. Rauschning, *Hitler Speaks.*
18. Hitler, *Hitler's Secret Conversations*, 51. Compare with Rosenberg, "Wodan, as a religious form, is dead ... he completed the decline of the gods of a mythological epoch." *Mythus*, 219.
19. Hitler, *Hitler's Table Talk*, 251; and Rauschning, *Hitler Speaks*, 220.
20. Hitler, *Mein Kampf*, 383.
21. Blavatsky, *Secret Doctrine*, 302ff.
22. Rauschning, *Hitler Speaks*, 240. Rauschning claimed to have reconstructed Hitler's quotes from remarks made at various private conferences

and meetings from 1932 through 1934. His recollections of conversations with Hitler have been dismissed by some historians, notably Kershaw, while others believe that he captured the spirit of the discussions in question. See Schieder, *Hermann Rauschnings*; Trevor-Roper, "The Mind of Adolf Hitler," introduction to Hitler, *Hitler's Secret Conversations*; and Conway, "Opponent of Nazism," 67–78.

23. Ibid., 241.
24. Blavatsky, *Secret Doctrine*, 439.
25. Rauschning, *Hitler Speaks*, 241.
26. Hitler, *Mein Kampf*, 296. Compare with Rosenberg's remark that the rise and fall of ancient Greece involved "a constant battle with others, with mythically as well as intellectually different blood arising from the swamps of the Nile, the waters of Asia Minor and the deserts of Libya," which eventually destroyed "the Nordic appearance of the Greeks." *Gestaltung der Idee*, 50.
27. Ibid., 300
28. Ibid., 579. Compare with Rosenberg's remark that the state was the "tool for National Socialist securing of soul, mind and blood." Rosenberg, *Gestaltung der Idee*, 22.
29. Ibid., 394.
30. Rauschning, *Hitler Speaks*, 227.
31. Padfield, *Himmler: Reichsführer-SS*, 36.
32. Carl Jung in *Schweizerland* 4, no. 9 (June 1918): 470; "Wodan," *Neue Schweizer Rundschau*, March 1936.
33. Mund, *Der Rasputin Himmlers*, 38–43.
34. Koehl, *The SS*, 127–28.
35. Flowers, *Secret King*, 20, 22, 31–32; and Mund, *Der Rasputin Himmlers*, 98–103.
36. Daim, *Der Mann*, 16, 162–63.
37. NSDAP Hauptarchiv T 581, No. 1229, Reel 52: Johannes Hering, "Dr. Jorg Lanz von Liebenfels und sein Orden des neuen Tempels."
38. Phelps, "Der Hitler-Bibliothek," 923–31.
39. Hitler's library included an eighteenth-century work on magic; a contemporary account of the Holy Grail; *Das Gebet* (*The Prayer*) by the popular esoteric author Bo Yin Ra, inscribed "Those able to shape the future are those able to pray"; and *Was heisst deutsch?* by Herman Wirth, chief of the Ahnenerbe. Miskolczy, *Hitler's Library*, 84–86.
40. Hamann, *Hitler's Vienna*, 212, citing a 1995 interview by Wilfried Daim with Schmidt-Falk.
41. Goodrick-Clarke, *Occult Roots of Nazism*, 199–200, citing Inge Kunze, "Herrenmenschentum, Neugermanen und Okkultismus: eine soziolo-

gische Bearbeitung der Schriften von Guido List," (Dissertation, University of Vienna, 1961), 4–6, 9, 11.

42. Kubizek, *Young Hitler,* 110–11.
43. Quoted in Toland, *Adolf Hitler,* 64.
44. Hitler, *Hitler Reden and Proklamationen,* 2269.
45. Mosse, *Crisis of German Ideology,* 75–76.
46. Baigent and Leigh, *Secret Germany,* 268.
47. Speer, *Erinnerungen,* 122ff.
48. Zmigrodski, *Historie du Svastika,* 18. Zmigrodski organized a swastika exhibition in Paris, 1889, at Palais des Artes Liberaux with three hundred drawings of swastikas from around the world.
49. Maser, *Legend, Myth & Reality,* 120.
50. Franz-Willing, *Ursprung der Hitler bewegung,* 84–85, citing interviews and correspondence with Krohn, Hanfstaengl, and other witnesses. Krohn was not the only member of the Thule Society to publicly advocate the swastika. In early summer of 1919 Fritz von Truetzschuler circulated a pamphlet in Munich proclaiming the swastika as "the symbol of the future."
51. Hitler, *Mein Kampf,* 496.
52. Franz-Willing, *Ursprung der Hitler bewegung,* 84.
53. Kershaw, *Hubris,* 648.
54. Sebottendorff, *Bevor Hitler kam,* 166–67.
55. *Allgemeine Ordens Nachrichten,* Ostaring [Eastertime] 1919.
56. Phelps, "Before Hitler Came," 260, citing Bavarian Haupstaatsarchiv Reichswehr Gruppenkommando 4, Band 46, Akte 9; and Bavarian Haupstaatsarchiv Schuetzenbrigade 21, Band 246, Akte 1.
57. Sebottendorff, *Bevor Hitler kam,* 167–70.
58. Phelps, "Before Hitler Came," 259, citing NSDAP Hauptarchiv no. 865.
59. Sebottendorff, *Bevor Hitler kam,* 116–17.
60. Ibid., 167–68.
61. Sebottendorff retained supporters in the Thule Society. "His patriotism cannot be doubted and for that he was ready to go through fire," said "Herr N." Howe, "Sebottendorff," 41.
62. Sebottendorff, *Bevor Hitler kam,* 170.
63. Phelps, "Before Hitler Came," citing NSDAP HA 865.
64. Gumbel, *Verschwörer,* 162.
65. Citing the diary of Johannes Hering, Howe lists such activities as lectures on megalithic culture, Oswald Spengler's *The Decline of the West,* and Rudolf John Gorsleben on "The Aryan Man." Thule celebrated the solstice and collected money for a pair of needy members, the actor Max Bayrhammer and former schoolmaster and rune enthusiast Dr. Schuster. Howe, "Sebottendorff," 62–63.

66. The letterhead still gives Thule's address and office phone number at the Four Seasons and indicates that meetings were held every Saturday. Neue Schriftenreihe des Stadtarchivs Munchen, vol. 29 (Munich, 1968), 83.
67. Sebottendorff, *Bevor Hitler kam,* 197–98. Testimony backing Sebottendorff's claim that the Thule Society became one of the front organizations for Nazi activists following the November 1923 putsch is found in a deposition Johannes Hering prepared for the Nazi Party archives, "Beiträge zur Geschichte der Thule-Gesellschaft," NSDAP Hauptarchiv no. 865.
68. Sebottendorff, *Bevor Hitler kam,* 192–96. Sebottendorff's sister, Dora Kunze, died August 13, 1921, at Lauban near the Glauer home at Görlitz. Howe, "Sebottendorff," 8.
69. Engelman, "Dietrich Eckart," 186, citing a letter (December 1921) from Epp to Eckart in the Eckart Estate.
70. Sebottendorff, *Bevor Hitler kam,* 194.
71. Albrecht Gotz von Olenhusen, "Burgerrat, Einwohnerwehr und Gegenrevolution, Freiburg 1918–1920" in Olenhusen, ed., *Wege und Abwege,* 115, 124–27, 130. In Sebottendorff's autobiographical novel, *Der Talisman des Rosenkreuzers,* the protagonist, Irwin Torre, leaves Munich in the middle of 1919 and after short stays at Badensee, Munich, and Berlin, sets himself up as a writer in a small village near Freiburg. Torre bemoans the loss of ideals and money he had endured in Munich, and philosophizes about the evanescence of life.
72. Olenhusen, ed., *Wege und Abwege,* 128, quoting from a letter dated November 25, 1919. That Bielefeld was Jewish may have been a factor in arousing his interest in Sebottedorff.
73. Goodrick-Clarke, *Occult Roots of Nazism,* 151–52, citing a letter from the Duke of Gothien to SS Obersturmbahnfuehrer Theodore Christensen, Bundesarchiv Koblenz, EAP 173-6-20-16/19a. The duke was a member of the Imperial Order of the Knights of Constantine and St. George, to which Sebottendorff also belonged.
74. Howe, *Astrology,* 54ff.
75. Olenhusen, "Zeittafel zur Biographie Rudolf von Sebottendorff (1875–1945)," appendix to 1989 edition of Howe, "Sebottendorff," 94.
76. Howe, *Astrology,* 87.
77. Ibid., 206.
78. Sebottendorff, *Geschichte der Astrologie,* 5.
79. Sebottendorff, *Die Praxis,* 1ff.
80. Sebottendorff, *Bevor Hitler kam,* 267. Howe secured information on Sebottendorff's removal as consul in a letter from the archivist of the

Turkish foreign ministry to the British Council Representative at Ankara. Howe, "Sebottendorff," 61.

81. Sebottendorff, *Bevor Hitler kam,* 243, 253
82. Goodrick-Clarke, *Occult Roots of Nazism,* 153–59, 182–83. Other members included Kathe Schaefer-Gerdau and SS officer Richard Anders.
83. Sebottendorff, *Bevor Hitler kam,* 238.
84. Fest, *Face of the Third Reich,* 209.
85. Quoted in ibid., 210.
86. Speer, *Inside the Third Reich,* 608.
87. Fiehler was detained by the Americans who occupied Munich at the end of World War II and was brought before a de-Nazification commission. Bauer, *Geschichte der Stadt Muenchen,* 399.
88. Howe, "Sebottendorff," 65, citing *Thule-Bote* October 1, 1933; Hering deposition, Sebottendorff, *Bevor Hitler kam,* 199.
89. Sebottendorff, *Bevor Hitler kam,* 218.
90. Phelps, "Before Hitler Came," 245, citing Rehse Collection No. 431, Manuscript Division, Library of Congress.
91. An unfavorable review of *Bevor Hitler kam* was published in Ludendorff's journal, *Am Heiligen Quell* IV (February 5, 1934), 482–84.
92. Howe, "Sebottendorff," 64, quoting "Herr N."
93. Ibid., quoting a "Warning Card" against Sebottendorff issued by the Bavarian Political Police, American Document Center, Berlin.
94. Ibid., 66–67, citing a January 1966 letter from Grassinger.
95. Bayerisches Hauptstaatsarchiv Landespolizei Munich II # 170 pers./3027; Bavarian Haupstaatsarchiv Munich, Kriegsarchiv Landespolizei insp. no. 76326.
96. Phelps, "Before Hitler Came," 245, citing Rehse no. 43.
97. Wait, *Vanguard of Nazism,* 81.
98. Howe, "Sebottendorff," 66–67, 69.
99. Phelps, "Before Hitler Came," 247, citing a letter to the author from Grassinger.
100. Rittlinger, *Bericht von Bosporus,* 184–85, 326; Goodrick-Clarke, *Occult Roots of Nazism,* 152, and Howe, "Sebottendorff," 71–73, citing a letter from Rittlinger (June 20, 1968). Rittlinger also recalled that Sebottendorff was demonstrably disappointed at the failure of the July 20, 1944, military coup against Hitler. It was "Herr N." who informed Howe of Sebottendorff's rumored murder.

Chapter 10. Thule.org

1. Salomon, *Das Buch vom deutschen Freikorpskaempfer,* 101–4. Reich and Achenbach references Thule in the struggle against the left (*Vom 9 November,* 20). Reich, a painter, was a friend of Eckart.

2. Heiden, *Der Fuehrer*, 19–22, 31; Heiden, *Adolf Hitler*, 58–59; and Heiden, *Hitler*, 48.
3. Viereck, *Metapolitics*, 254.
4. Goodrick-Clarke, *Hitler's Priestess*, 69. Goodrick-Clarke may have derived his information from his 1978 interviews with Mukherji's wife, Savitri Devi, who after World War II became globally prominent among neo-Nazis.
5. Several works in German have followed, including Hermann Gilbhard's *Die Thule-Gesellschaft: vom okkulten Mummenschanz zum Hakenkreuz* (Munich: Kiessling Verlag, 1994) and Detlev Rose's *Die Thule-Gesellschaft: Legende, Mythos, Wirklichkeit* (Tübingen: Grabert, 1994).
6. The authors of *The Morning of the Magicians* probably drew inspiration from speculations on Hitler as the medium for dark forces, and the role of the occult in German politics, published in France from the 1930s through 1940. For a survey of this literature, see Hakl, *Unknown Sources*, 22–27.
7. Lachman, *Turn off Your Mind*, 18.
8. Pauwels and Bergier, *Morning of the Magicians*, 193–94.
9. Ibid., 197–98.
10. Jürgen-Ratthofer and Ettl, *Das Vril-Projekt*, 10–31ff.
11. Lee, "Pseudoscience," 90–98; Pauwels and Bergier, *Morning of the Magicians*, 146–52.
12. Bahn and Gehring, *Der Vril-Mythos*, 91–111.
13. Helsing, *Unternehmen Aldebaran*, 12, 39ff.
14. "Tell Me More About Adolf Hitler and WWII," Three World Wars (2006), http://www.ThreeWorldWars.com/world-war-2/adolf-hitler.htm/.
15. "Rudolf Glandeck von Sebottendorff," Grand Lodge of British Columbia and Yukon (2003), http://www.freemasonry.bcy.ca/anti-masonry/sebottendorff_r.html/.
16. Wes Penre, "Hitler and the Secret Societies," Illuminati News (1999), www.illuminati-news.com/hitler-occult.htm/.
17. "New World Order: The Secret History" (n.d.), http://www.geocities.com/newworldorder_themovie/theosophy.html/. Author accessed online in 2007, but the website was removed prior to the publication of this book.
18. M. Sabeheddin, "Hitler, Nazis & the Occult," *New Dawn* 41 (March 1997), http://www.newdawnmagazine.com/. Author accessed online in 2007, but the article was removed from the website prior to the publication of this book.
19. "Von Sebottendorff," Lucid Zahor (n.d.), http://www.lucidzahor.1hwy.com/von.htm/.
20. "The Hidden Origins of Nazism," BlackRaiser (n.d.), http://www.blackraiser.com/nazorig.htm/.

21. Kavenna, *Ice Museum*, 141–43.
22. Hamann, *Winifred Wagner*, 479–80.
23. *The Morning of the Magicians* includes a chapter on the fascination by some Nazis with Hollow Earth theories, 185–90.
24. Lee, *Beast Reawakens*, 184. Barbie was recruited by U.S. Army counterintelligence after World War II and made his way to South America in 1951, despite French demands for extradition. He became part of a shadowy network peddling arms in the Middle East.
25. American-thule-society.org.

Bibliography

Books and Periodicals

Akerman, Susanna. *Rose Cross Over the Baltic: The Spread of Rosicrucianism in Northern Europe.* Boston: Brill, 1998.

Audoin-Rouzeau, Stéphane, and Annette Becker. *14-18: Understanding the Great War.* Translated by Catherine Temerson. New York: Hill & Wang, 2002.

Ay, Karl-Ludwig, ed. *Appelle einer Revolution.* Munich: Suddeutscher Verlag, 1968.

Bahn, Peter, and Heiner Gehring. *Der Vril-Mythos: Eine geheimnisvolle Energieform in Esoterik, Technik und Therapie.* Dusseldorf: Omega Verlag, 1997.

Baigent, Michael, and Richard Leigh. *Secret Germany: Stauffenberg and the Mystical Crusade against Hitler.* London: J. Cape, 1994.

Balakian, Peter. *The Burning Tigris: The Armenian Genocide and America's Response.* New York: HarperCollins, 2003.

Baldwin, Neil. *Henry Ford and the Jews: The Mass Production of Hate.* New York: PublicAffairs, 2001.

Balzli, Johannes. *Guido von List: Der Wiederentdecker uralter arischer Weisheit.* Vienna: Guido-von-List Gesellschaft, 1917.

Barborka, Geoffrey A. *H. P. Blavatsky: Tibet and Tulku.* Adyar, India: Theosophical Publishing House, 1966.

Barzun, Jacques. *Race: A Study in Superstition.* New York: Harper & Row, 1965.

Bauer, Richard. *Geschichte der Stadt Muenchen.* Munich: Beck, 1992.

Besant, Annie. *The Ancient Wisdom: An Outline of Theosophical Teachings.* Adyar, India: Theosophical Publishing House, 1966.

Bessel, Richard. *Germany after the First World War.* Oxford: Oxford University Press, 1993.

Beyer, Hans. *Von der Novemberrevolution zur Raterepublik in Munchen.* Berlin: Rutten & Loening, 1957.

———. *Die Revolution in Bayern 1918/1919.* Berlin: Deutscher Verlag der Wissenschaften, 1988.

Birge, John Kingsley. *The Bektashi Order of Dervishes.* London: Luzac Oriental, 1937.

Blavatsky, H. P. *The Secret Doctrine: The Synthesis of Science, Religion, and Philosophy.* London: Theosophical Publishing Co., 1888.

———. *The Letters of H. P. Blavatsky to A. P. Sinnett, and Other Miscellaneous.* Transcribed, compiled, and with an introduction by A. T. Barker. Pasadena, CA: Theosophical University Press, 1973.

Bouton, Stephen Miles. *And the Kaiser Abdicates: The Story of the Death of the German Empire and the Birth of the Republic Told By an Eye-Witness.* New Haven, CT: Yale University Press, 1920.

Boyd, Ernest. *Ireland's Literary Renaissance.* New York: Knopf, 1968.

Breiting, Richard. *Secret Conversations with Hitler: The Two Newly-Discovered 1931 Interviews.* Edited by Edouard Calic. Translated by Richard Barry. New York: John Day, 1971.

———. *Unmasked: Two Confidential Interviews with Hitler in 1931.* Edited by Edouard Calic. Translated by Richard Barry. London: Chatto & Windus, 1971.

Bryce, James. *The Holy Roman Empire.* London: Macmillan, 1871.

Bullock, Alan. *Hitler: A Study in Tyranny.* New York: Harper, 1952.

———. *Hitler and Stalin: Parallel Lives.* New York: Knopf, 1992.

Carr, Edward Hallett. *The Russian Revolution: From Lenin to Stalin.* New York: Free Press, 1979.

Cecil, Robert. *The Myth of the Master Race: Alfred Rosenberg and Nazi Ideology.* London: Batsford, 1972.

Chamberlain, Houston Stewart. *Foundations of the Nineteenth Century.* Translated by John Lees. New York: J. Lane, 1911.

Chickering, Roger. *We Men Who Feel Most German: A Cultural Study of the Pan-German League, 1886–1914.* Boston: Allen & Unwin, 1984.

Clarke, J. J. *Oriental Enlightenment: The Encounter between Asian and Western Thought.* London: Routledge, 1997.

Cohn, Norman. *Warrant for Genocide: The Myth of the Jewish World-Conspiracy and the Protocols of the Elders of Zion.* New York: Harper & Row, 1967.

Conway, J. S. "Hermann Rauschning as Historian and Opponent of Nazism." *Canadian Journal of History* 8 (1973).

Conze, Edward. *Buddhism: Its Essence and Development.* New York: Harper & Row, 1975.

Cordes, Guenter. "Thule-Gesselschaft." *Lexikon der deutschen Geschichte.* Stuttgart: Kroner, 1977.

Crowley, Aleister. *777 and Other Qabalistic Writings of Aleister Crowley: Including*

Gematria & Sepher Sephiroth. Edited by Israel Regardie. Binghampton, NY: Weiser, 1977.

———. *Magick in Theory and Practice.* New York: Castle, n.d.

Daim, Wilfried. *Der Mann, der Hitler die Ideen gab: Joerg Lanz von Liebenfels.* Munich: Isar Verlag, 1958.

Daraul, Arkon. *A History of Secret Societies.* New York: Citadel Press, 1962.

Davenport-Hines, R. P. T. *Gothic: Four Hundred Years of Excess, Horror, Evil, and Ruin.* New York: North Point Press, 1999.

Davidson, Eugene. *The Making of Adolf Hitler.* New York: Macmillan, 1977.

Deuerlein, Ernst, ed. *Der Aufstieg der NSDAP in Augenzeugenberichten.* Munich: Atheneum Verlag, 1982.

Diehl, James M. *Paramilitary Politics in Weimar Germany.* Bloomington: Indiana University Press, 1977.

Dresler, Adolf. *Dietrich Eckart.* Munich: Deutscher Volksverlag, 1938.

Eckstein, Friedrich. *Alte unnennbare Tage.* Vienna, 1936.

Engelman, Ralph Max. "Dietrich Eckart and the Genesis of Nazism." PhD diss., Washington University, 1971.

Euringer, Richard. *Dietrich Eckart: Leben eines deutschen Dichters.* Hamburg: Hanseatische Verlag, 1935.

Ewers, Hanns Heinz. *The Sorcerer's Apprentice.* Translated by Ludwig Lewisohn. New York: John Day, 1927.

———. *Strange Tales.* Edited by Stephen Flowers. Smithville, TX: Runa-Raven Press, 2000.

Fest, Joachim C. *The Face of the Third Reich: Portraits of the Nazi Leadership.* Translated by Michael Bullock. New York: Pantheon, 1970.

———. *Hitler.* Translated by Richard and Clara Winston. New York: Harcourt Brace Jovanovich, 1974.

———. *Inside Hitler's Bunker: The Last Days of the Third Reich.* Translated by Margot Bettauer Dembo. New York: Farrar, Strauss & Giroux, 2004.

Fischer, Jens Malte. *Fin de Siècle: Kommentar zu einer Epoche.* Munich: Winkler, 1978.

Flood, Charles B. *Hitler: The Path to Power.* Boston: Houghton Mifflin, 1989.

Flowers, Stephen E. *The Secret King: Karl Maria Wiligut, Himmler's Lord of the Runes.* Smithville, TX: Runa-Raven Press, 2001.

Folsing, Albrecht. *Albert Einstein: A Biography.* Translated by Ewald Osers. New York: Viking, 1997.

Frank, Eduard. *Gustav Meyrink, Werk und Wirkung.* Buedingen-Gettenbach: Avalun-Verlag, 1957.

Franz, Georg. "Munich: Birthplace and Center of the National Socialist German Workers' Party." *Journal of Modern History* 29 (1957).

Franz-Willing, Georg. *Ursprung der Hitler bewegung.* Hamburg: Verlag K. W. Schutz, 1962.

Frecot, Janos, Johann Friedrich Geist, and Diethart Kerbs. *Fidus: Zur asthetischen Praxis burgerlicher Fluchtbewegungen.* Munich: Rogner & Bernhard, 1972.

Frick, Karl R. H. *Die Erleuchteten.* Graz: Akademische Druck & Verlagsanstalt, 1973.

Fritsch, Theodor. *Neue Wege.* Leipzig: Hammer Verlag, n.d.

———. "Vom partei-politischen Antisemitismus." *Hammer* 11 (1912).

Fuegi, John. *Brecht & Co.: Sex, Politics, and the Making of the Modern Drama.* New York: Grove Press, 1994.

Fuller, Jean Overton. *Blavatsky and Her Teachers.* London: East-West Publications, 1988.

Galton, Francis. *Hereditary Genius: An Inquiry into Its Laws and Consequences.* Gloucester, MA: Peter Smith, 1972.

Gasman, Daniel. *The Scientific Origins of National Socialism: Social Darwinism in Ernst Haeckel and the German Monist League.* London: Macdonald & Co., 1971.

Gehr, Richard S. *Karl Lueger: Mayor of Fin de Siècle Vienna.* Detroit: Wayne State University Press, 1990.

Gentizon, Paul. *La Revolution allemande.* Paris: Payot & Cie, 1919.

Goebbels, Joseph. *The Goebbels Diaries 1939–1941.* London: H. Hamilton, 1982.

Goldstein, Jeffrey A. "On Racism and Anti-Semitism in Occultism and Nazism." *Yad Vashem Studies on the European Jewish Catastrophe and Resistance* 13 (1979).

Goodrick-Clarke, Nicholas. *The Occult Roots of Nazism: The Ariosophists of Austria and Germany 1890–1935.* Wellingborough, Northamptonshire, UK: Aquarian Press, 1985.

———. *Hitler's Priestess: Savitri Devi, the Hindu-Aryan Myth, and Neo-Nazism.* New York: New York University Press, 1998.

———. *Black Sun: Aryan Cults, Esoteric Nazism, and the Politics of Identity.* New York: New York University Press, 2002.

Got, Ambroise. *La Terreur en Bavière.* Paris: Perrin & Cie, 1922.

Gray, Cecil. *Musical Chairs.* London: Chatto & Windus, 1985.

Green, Martin. *Mountain of Truth: The Counterculture Begins, Ascona, 1900–1920.* Hanover, NH: University Press of New England, 1986.

Griessdorff, Harry. *Unsere Weltanschauung.* Berlin: Nordland Verlag, 1941.

Groener, Wilhelm. *Lebenserinnerungen.* Gottingen: Vandenhoeck & Ruprecht, 1957.

Gros, Otto. *850 Worte Mythus des 20. Jahrhunderts.* Munich: Hoheneichen Verlag, 1938.

Grunberger, Richard. *Red Rising in Bavaria.* London: Barker, 1973.

Guénon, René. *Lettres à Julius Evola (1930–1950).* Bolzano: SEAR Edizion, 1996.

Gumbel, Emil Julius. *Verschwörer: Zur Geschichte und Soziologie der deutschen Nationalistischen Geheimbuende 1918–1924.* Frankfurt: Fischer Taschenbuch Verlag, 1984.

Haffner, Sebastian. *Failure of a Revolution: Germany 1918–1919.* Translated by George Rapp. Chicago: Banner Press, 1986.

Hakl, Hans Thomas. *Unknown Sources: National Socialism and the Occult.* Translated by Nicholas Goodrick-Clarke. Edmonds, WA: Holmes, 2000.

Hale, James. "Gottfried Feder Calls Hitler to Order: An Unpublished Letter on Nazi Party Affairs." *Journal of Modern History* 30 (1958).

Hamann, Brigitte. *Hitler's Vienna: A Dictator's Apprenticeship.* Translated by Thomas Thornton. New York: Oxford University Press, 1999.

———. *Winifred Wagner: A Life at the Heart of Hitler's Bayreuth.* Translated by Alan Bance. Orlando, FL: Harcourt Brace, 2006.

Hanfstaengl, Ernst. *Hitler: The Missing Years.* London: Eyre & Spottiswoode, 1957.

———. *Zwischen Weisssen und Braunen Haus.* Munich: R. Piper, 1970.

Hanioğlu, M. Şükrü. *The Young Turks in Opposition.* New York: Oxford University Press, 1995.

———. *Preparation for a Revolution: The Young Turks, 1902–1908.* New York: Oxford University Press, 2001.

Hanser, Richard. *Putsch! How Hitler Made Revolution.* New York: P. H. Wyden, 1970.

Hart, F. T. *Alfred Rosenberg: Der Mann und Sein Werk.* Munich: J. F. Lehmann, 1939.

Heckethorn, Charles William. *The Secret Societies of All Ages and Countries,* vol. 2. New Hyde Park: New York University Press, 1965.

Heer, Friedrich. *Der Glaube des Adolf Hitler: Anatomie einer Politischen Religiositaet.* Munich: Bechtle, 1968.

Heiden, Konrad. *Hitler: A Biography.* London: Constable, 1936.

———. *Adolf Hitler.* Zurich: Europa Verlag, 1937.

———. *Der Fuehrer: Hitler's Rise to Power.* Translated by Ralph Manheim. Boston: Houghton Mifflin, 1944.

Heinz, Heinz A. *Germany's Hitler.* London: Hurst & Blackett, 1934.

Heise, Karl. *Die Entente-Freimaurerei und der Weltkrieg.* (Basel 1919).

Helsing, Jan van. *Unternehmen Aldebaran: Kontakte mit Menschen aus einem anderen Sonnensystem.* Gran Canaria, Spain: Ewertverlag, 1997.

Hentschel, Willibald. *Varuna.* Leipzig: T. Fritsch, 1907.

Herndl, Franz. *Die Trutzburg.* Leipzig: Altmann, 1909.

Hess, Ilse. *Ein Schicksal in Briefen: England, Nurenberg, Spandau: Gefangener des Friedens, Antworte aus Zelle Sieben.* Leoni am Starnberger, Germany: Druftel, 1971.

Hilberg, Raul. *The Destruction of the European Jews.* Chicago: Quadrangle Books, 1961.

Hillmayr, Heinrich. *Roter und Weisser Terror in Bayern nach 1918.* Munich: Nusser, 1974.

Hitler, Adolf. *Mein Kampf.* Translated by Ralph Manheim. Boston: Houghton Mifflin, 1943.

———. *Hitler's Secret Conversations.* Translated by Norman Cameron and R. H. Stevens. New York: Farrar, Straus & Giroux, 1953.

———. *Hitler's Table Talk, 1941–44: His Private Conversations.* Translated by Norman Cameron and R. H. Stevens. London: Weidenfeld and Nicholson, 1953.

———. *Hitler Reden and Proklamationen 1932–1945*, vol. 2. Edited by Max Domarus. Wuerzburg: Suddeutscher Verlag, 1963.

Hovannisian, Richard G., ed. *Remembrance and Denial: The Case of the Armenian Genocide.* Detroit: Wayne State University Press, 1999.

Howe, Ellic. *Astrology: A Recent History Including the Untold Story of Its Role in World War II.* New York: Walker, 1968.

———. "Rudolf Freiherr von Sebottendorff." Dissertation: Institut fur Zeitgesichte, Munich, 1968.

———. "Theodor Reuss: Irregular Freemasonry in Germany, 1900–1923." *Ars Quatuor Coronatum* 91 (February 1978).

Hughes, Robert. *The Shock of the New.* New York: Knopf/Random House, 1981.

Hutin, Serge. *Unsichtbare Herrscher und geheime Gesellschaften.* Bonn: Bucherei Hieronimi, 1973.

Huttig, Helmut. "Die politischen Zeitschriften der Nachkriegszeit in Deutschland." PhD diss., University of Leipzig, 1928.

Hutton, Ronald. *The Triumph of the Moon: A History of Modern Pagan Witchcraft.* Oxford: Oxford University Press, 1999.

Jäckel, Eberhard, and Axel Kuhn, eds. *Hitler: Sämtliche Aufzeichnungen 1905–1924.* Stuttgart: Deutsche Verlags-Ansstalt, 1980.

Jacobsen, Hans Adolf. *Karl Haushofer: Leben und Werk*, vol. 1. Boppard am Rhein: Boldt, 1979.

Jasper, Gotthard. "Aus den Akten der Prozesse gegen die Erzberger Moerder." *Vierteljahrschefte fuer Zeitgeschichte* 10 (1962).

Johnson, K. Paul. *Initiates of Theosophical Masters.* Albany: State University of New York Press, 1995.

Jones, Nigel H. *Hitler's Heralds: The Story of the Freikorps, 1918–1923.* London: Murray, 1987.

Jonge, Alex de. *The Weimar Chronicle: Prelude to Hitler.* New York: Paddington Press, 1978.

Jung, Carl. "Wotan." *Neue Schweizer Rundschau* 3 (March 1936).

Jürgen-Ratthofer, Norbert, and Ralf Ettl. *Das Vril-Projekt.* Ardagger, Austria: Michael Dambock, 1992.

Kanzler, Rudolph von. *Bayerns Kampf gegen den Bolschewismus.* Munich: Verlag Parcus, 1931.

Kater, Michael H. *Das Ahnenerbe der SS, 1935–1945: ein Beitrag zur Kulturpolitik des Dritten Reiches.* Stuttgart: Deutscher Verlags-Anstalt, 1974.

Kavenna, Joanna. *The Ice Museum: In Search of the Lost Land of Thule.* New York: Viking, 2005.

Kershaw, Ian. *Hitler.* London: Longman, 1991.

———. *Hitler: 1889–1936: Hubris.* New York: W. W. Norton, 1999.

———. *Hitler: 1936–1945: Nemesis.* New York: W. W. Norton, 2000.

King, Francis. *The Magical World of Aleister Crowley.* New York: Coward, McCann & Geoghegan, 1978.

Klemperer, Klemens von. *Germany's New Conservatism: Its History and Dilemma in the Twentieth Century.* Princeton, NJ: Princeton University Press, 1968

Koch, Hannsjoachim. *Der deutsche Buergerkrieg.* Munich: Ullstein, 1978.

Koehl, Robert Lewis. *The SS: A History 1919–45.* Stroud, UK: Tempus, 2004.

Kubizek, August. *Young Hitler: The Story of Our Friendship.* Translated by E. V. Anderson. Maidstone, UK: Mann, 1973.

Kuron, Hans Juergen. "Freikorps und Bund Oberland." PhD diss., University of Erlangen, 1960.

Lachman, Gary. *Turn off Your Mind: The Mystic Sixties and the Dark Side of the Age of Aquarius.* New York: Disinformation, 2001.

Landau, Jacob M. *Tekinalp: Turkish Patriot, 1883–1961.* Leiden: Nederlands Historisch-Archaeologisch Instituut te Istandbul, 1984.

Laqueur, Walter. *Young Germany: A History of the German Youth Movement.* New York: Basic Books, 1962.

———. *Russia and Germany: A Century of Conflict.* London: Weidenfeld & Nicolson, 1965.

———. *Weimar: A Cultural History.* New York: Peregrine, 1974.

Large, David Clay. *Where Ghosts Walked: Munich's Road to the Third Reich.* New York: W. W. Norton, 1997.

Larsen, Stein Ugelvik, ed. *Fascism Outside Europe: The European Impulse against Domestic Conditions in the Diffusion of Global Fascism.* Boulder, CO: Social Science Monographs, 2001.

Lee, Martin A. *The Beast Reawakens.* Boston: Little, Brown, 1997.

Lee, Willy. "Pseudoscience in Naziland." *Astounding Science Fiction* 39, no. 3 (1947).

Lennhoff, Eugen, and Oskar Posner. *Internationales Freimauerlexicon.* Zurich: Amalthea-Verlag, 1932.

Lepsius, Johannes. *Der Todesgang der armenischen Volkes.* Potsdam, Germany: Missionshandlung & Verlag, 1919.

Lethaby, W. R. *Architecture, Mysticism, and Myth.* New York: G. Braziller, 1975.

Levy, Richard S. *The Downfall of the Anti-Semitic Political Parties in Imperial Germany.* New Haven, CT: Yale University Press, 1975.

Lewis, Geoffrey. *Turkey.* New York: Praeger, 1960.

Liebenfels, Jörg Lanz von. "Anthropozoon biblicum." *Vierteljahrschrift fur Bibelkunde* 1–2 (1903–1904).

———. "Die heilige Gral." *Stein der Weisen* 20 (1907).

———. *Die Theosophie und die assyrischen "Menschentiere" in ihren Verhaltnis zu den neuesten Resultaten der anthropoligischen Forschung.* Berlin: Gross-Lichterfelde, 1907.

———. "Bismarck und Schonerer." *Alldeutsches Tagblatt,* April 1908.

———. "Rassenmystik, eine Einfuhrung in die ariochristliche Geheimlehre," *Ostara* 78 (1915).

———. *Theozoologie oder die Kunde von den Sodoms-Aefflingen und den Goetterer-Elecktron.* Vienna: Modern Verlag, 1905.

List, Guido von. *Alraunenmaren: Kulturhistorische Novellen und Dichtungen aus germanischer Vorzeit.* Linz: Guido-von-List Gesellschaft, 1903.

———. "Die esoterische Bedeutung religiosen Symbole," *Die Gnosis* I (1903)

———. *Die Geheimnis der Runen* Gross-Lichterfelde, Austria: Guido-von-List Gesellschaft, 1908.

———. *Die Armanenschaft der Ario-Germanen,* vol. 1. Leipzig: E. F. Steinacker, 1908.

———. *Die Rita der Ario-Germanen.* Leipzig: E. F. Steinacker, 1908.

———. *Die Religionen der Ario-Germanen.* Zurich: Guido-von-List Gesellschaft, 1910.

———. *Die Bilderschaft der Ario-Germanen.* Leipzig: E. F. Steinacker, 1910.

———. *Der Ubergang vom Wotanstum zum Christentum.* Zurich: Adolf Burdecke Verlag, 1911.

———. *Die Armanenschaft der Ario-Germanen,* vol. 2. Leipzig: E. F. Steinacker, 1911.

———. *Deutsche-Mythologische Landshaftsbilder.* Leipzig: Adolf Burdecke Verlag, 1913.

———. *Die Ursprache der Ario-Germanen und ihre Mysteriensprache.* Leipzig: Adolf Burdecke Verlag, 1914.

———. *The Secret of the Runes,* trans. Stephen E. Flowers. Rochester, VT: Destiny, 1988.

———. *The Invincible.* Translated by Edred Thorsson. Smithville, TX: Runa-Raven, 1996.

Lohalm, Uwe. *Völkischer Radikalismus: Die Geschichte des Deutschvolkischen Schutz- und Trutz-Bundes, 1919-1923.* Hamburg: Leibniz-Verlag, 1970.

Ludendorff, Erich. *Vom Feldernn zum Weltrevolutionar und Weg bereiter Deutsche*

Volksschöpfung: Meine Lebenserinnerungen von 1919–25. Munich: Ludendorffs Verlag, 1940.

Ludendorff, Erich, and Mathilde Ludendorff. *Ihr Werk und Winken*. Munich: Ludendorffs Verlag, 1937.

Macfie, A. L. *The End of the Ottoman Empire 1908–1923*. London: Longman, 1998.

Machtan, Lothar. *The Hidden Hitler*. Translated by John Brownjohn. New York: Basic Books, 2001.

Magee, Bryan. *The Tristan Chord: Wagner and Philosophy*. New York: Metropolitan Books, 2000.

Mann, Golo. *The History of Germany since 1789*. Translated by Marion Jackson. London: Penguin, 1990.

Mann, Thomas. *Diaries 1918–1939*. Translated by Richard and Clara Winston. New York: H. N. Abrams, 1982.

Maranci, Christina. *Medieval Armenian Architecture: Constructions of Race and Nation*. Leuven, Belgium: Peeters, 2001.

Marby, Friedrich Bernhard. *Sonne und Planeten im Tierkreis: Eine Studie uber Wirken und Bedeutung alter 360 Grade*. Stuttgart: Spieth-Verlag, 1975.

Maser, Werner. *Hitler: Legend, Myth & Reality*. Translated by Peter and Betty Ross. New York: Harper & Row, 1973.

May, Arthur J. *The Hapsburg Monarchy 1867–1914*. Cambridge, MA: Harvard University Press, 1951.

———. *Vienna in the Age of Franz Josef*. Norman: University of Oklahoma Press, 1966.

Mayr, Karl. "I Was Hitler's Boss." *Current History* 2, no. 3 (November 1941).

Meade, Marion. *Madame Blavatsky: The Woman Behind the Myth*. New York: Putnam, 1980.

Miskolczy, Ambrus. *Hitler's Library*. Translated by Redey Szilvia and Michael Webb. Budapest: Central European University Press, 2003.

Mitchell, Allan. *Revolution in Bavaria, 1918–1919: The Eisner Regime and the Soviet Republic*. Princeton, NJ: Princeton University Press, 1965.

Morris, Jr., Warren B. *The Weimar Republic and Nazi Germany*. Chicago: Nelson-Hall, 1982.

Morrow, Jr., John H.. *The Great War: An Imperial History*. New York: Routledge, 2004.

Morton, Frederic. *A Nervous Splendor: Vienna 1888/1889*. London: Weidenfeld & Nicolson, 1980.

Mosse, George L. "The Mystical Origins of National Socialism." *Journal of the History of Ideas* 22 (1961).

———. *The Crisis of German Ideology*. New York: Grosset & Dunlap, 1964.

———. *Nazi Culture: Intellectual, Cultural, and Social Life in the Third Reich*. New York: Grosset & Dunlap, 1966.

———. *Toward the Final Solution: A History of European Racism.* Madison: University of Wisconsin Press, 1985.

Mund, Rudolf. *Jörg Lanz von Liebenfels und der Neue Templer Orden.* Stuttgart Germany: Rudolf Arnold Spieth, 1976.

———. *Der Rasputin Himmlers: Die Wiligut-Saga.* Vienna: Volkstum Verlag, 1982.

Nagl, Johannes Willibald, and Jakob Zeidler. *Deutsch-österreichesche Literaturgeschichte,* vol. 3. Vienna: Carl Fromme, 1937.

Nehru, Jawaharlal. *Toward Freedom: The Autobiography of Jawaharlal Nehru.* Boston: Beacon Press, 1958.

Nettl, J. P. *Rosa Luxemburg,* vol. 1. London: Oxford University Press, 1966.

Noske, Gustav von. *Von Kiel bis Kapp: zur Geschichte der deutschen revolution.* Berlin: Verlag für Politik und Wirtschaft, 1920.

Nova, Fritz. *Alfred Rosenberg: Nazi Theorist of the Holocaust.* New York: Hippocrene, 1986.

Olenhusen, Albrecht Goetz von, ed. *Wege und Abwege: Beitrage zur europaischen Geistesgeschichte der Neuzeit.* Freiburg, Germany: Hochschulverlag, 1990.

Orlow, Dietrich. *The History of the Nazi Party.* Pittsburgh, PA: University of Pittsburgh Press, 1969.

Padfield, Peter. *Himmler: Reichsführer-SS.* New York: Henry Holt, 1990.

Panshin, Alexei, and Cory Panshin. *The World Beyond the Hill: Science Fiction and the Quest for Transcendence.* Los Angeles: J. P. Tarcher, 1989.

Parkinson, Roger. *Tormented Warrior: Ludendorff and the Supreme Command.* New York: Stein & Day, 1978.

Pasi, Marco. "Aleister Crowley: Tra trasgressione e tentazione politica." PhD diss., University of Milan, 1994.

Pauwels, Louis, and Jacques Bergier. *The Morning of the Magicians.* New York: Stein & Day, 1964.

Phelps, Reginald H. "Der Hitler-Bibliothek." *Deutsche Rundschau* 80 (1954).

———. "Anton Drexler: Der Gruender der NSDAP." *Deutsche Rundschau* 87 (1961).

———. "Theodore Fritsch und der Antisemitismus." *Deutsche Rundschau* 87 (1961).

———. "Before Hitler Came: Thule Society and Germanen Orden." *Journal of Modern History* 35 (1963).

———. "Hitler and the Deutsche Arbeiterpartei." *American Historical Review* 68, no. 4 (1963).

———. "Hitlers 'grundlegende' Rede ueber den Antisemitismus." *Vierteljahreschefte fuer Zeitgeschichte* 4 (1968).

Plewnia, Margarete. *Auf dem Weg zu Hitler: Der völkische Publizist Dietrich Éckart.* Bremen, Germany: Schunemann, 1970.

Poliakov, Léon. *The Aryan Myth: A History of Racist and Nationalist Ideas in Europe.* Translated by Edmund Howard. London: Sussex University Press, 1974.

Poulton, Hugh. *Top Hat, Grey Wolf, and Crescent: Turkish Nationalism and the Turkish Republic.* New York: New York University Press, 1997.

Pynsent, Robert B., ed., *Decadence and Innovation: Austro-Hungarian Life and Art at the Turn of the Century.* London: Weidenfeld & Nicolson, 1989.

Rauschning, Hermann. *Hitler Speaks: A Series of Political Conversations with Adolf Hitler on His Real Aims.* London: Thornton Butterworth, 1939.

———. *The Voice of Destruction.* New York: G. P. Putnam's Sons, 1940.

———. *The Conservative Revolution.* New York: G. P. Putnam's Sons, 1941.

Reich, Albert, and O. R. Achenbach. *Vom 9 November, 1918 zum 9 November 1923: Die Entstehung der deutschen Freiheitsbewegung.* Munich: Eher, 1933.

Rittlinger, Herbert. *Geheimdienst mit beschrankter Haftung: Bericht von Bosporus.* Stuttgart: Deutsche Verlags-Anstalt, 1973.

Röhm, Ernst. *Die Geschichte des Hochverraters.* Munich: Franz Eher Verlag, 1934.

Rosenberg, Alfred. Der Mythus des 20. Jahrhunderts. Munich: Hoheneichen-Franz-Eher Verlag, 1925.

———. Gestaltung der Idee: Blut und Ehre, vol. 2. Munich: F. Eher Nachf, 1936.

———, ed. Dietrich Eckart: Ein Vermaechtnis. Munich: Franz Eher Verlag, 1937.

———. *Weltanschauung und Glaubenslehre.* Halle, Germany: Niemeyer, 1939.

———. *Memoirs of Alfred Rosenberg.* Translated by Eric Posselt. Chicago: Ziff-Davis Publishing, 1949.

———. *Letzte Aufzeichnungen.* Edited by Heinrich Haertle. Gottingen, Germany: Plesse Verlag, 1955.

———. *Grossdeutschland: Traum und Tragodie: Rosenbergs Kritik am Hitlerismus.* Edited by Heinrich Haertle. Munich: Haertle, 1970.

———. *Selected Writings.* Edited by Robert Pois. London: J. Cape, 1970.

Ryder, A. J. *The German Revolution of 1918: A Study of German Socialism in War and Revolt.* Cambridge: Cambridge University Press, 1967.

Salomon, Ernst von. *Das Buch vom deutschen Freikorpskaempfer.* Berlin: Wilhelm Lempert-Verlag, 1938.

Schieder, Theodore. *Hermann Rauschnings "Gespräche mit Hitler" als Geschichtsquelle.* Opladen, Germany: Westdeutscher Verlag, 1972.

Schliemann, Heinrich. *Troy and Its Remains: A Narrative of Researches and Discoveries Made on the Site of Ilium, and in the Trojan Plain.* London: J. Murray, 1875.

Schmidt-Paul, Edgar von. *Geschichte der Freikorps 1918–1924.* Stuttgart, Germany: Lutz Nachfolger Scharamm, 1936.

Schwarzenwäller, Wulf. *Rudolf Hess: Der Letzte von Spandau.* Vienna, 1977.

Sebottendorff, Rudolf Freiherr von. *Werbeblatt Germanenorden der Ordensprovinz Bayern*, vol. 1. Bad Aibling, 1918.

———. *Werbeblatt Germanenorden der Ordensprovinz Bayern*, vol. 2. Bad Aibling, 1918.

———. "Erwin Haller, ein deutscher Kaufmann in der Tuerkei." *Münchener Beobachter* 31 (August 1918–May 1919).

———. *Geschichte der Astrologie.* Leipzig: Theosophisches Verlagshaus, 1923.

———. *Die Praxis der altern Tuerkischen Freimaurerei.* Leipzig: H. Bauer, 1924.

———. *Der Talisman der Rosenkreuzers.* Pfullingen, Germany: Johannes Baum Verlag, 1925.

———. *Bevor Hitler kam.* 2nd ed. Munich: Deukula Verlag/Grassinger, 1934.

Sedgwick, Mark. *Against the Modern World: Traditionalism and the Secret Intellectual History of the Twentieth Century.* Oxford: Oxford University Press, 2004.

Serrano, Miguel. *Adolf Hitler: El Último Avatāra.* Santiago, Chile: Ediciones la Nueva Edad, 1984.

Shiel, M. P. *The Purple Cloud.* Boston: Gregg Press, 1977.

Speer, Albert. *Erinnerungen.* Frankfurt am Main: Ullstein, 1969.

———. *Inside the Third Reich.* Translated by Richard and Clara Winston. New York: Crown, 1970.

———. *Spandau: The Secret Diaries.* Translated by Richard and Clara Winston. New York: Macmillan, 1976.

Spielvogel, Jackson, and David Redles. "Hitler's Racial Ideology: Content and Occult Sources." *Simon Wiesenthal Center Annual* 37 (1986).

Stafford, David, ed. *Flight from Reality: Rudolf Hess and His Mission to Scotland, 1941.* London: Pimlico, 2002.

Stauff, Philipp. "Guido von List gestorben." *Münchener Beobachter*, May 24, 1919.

Stocking, George W., ed. *Volksgeist as Method and Ethic: Essays on Boasian Ethnography and the German Anthropological Tradition.* Madison: University of Wisconsin Press, 1996.

Symonds, John. *The Medusa's Head: Or Conversations Between Aleister Crowley and Adolf Hitler.* Thame, Oxfordshire, UK: Mandrake, 1991.

Tiede, Ernst. *Astrologisches Lexikon.* Leipzig: Theosophisches Verlagshaus, 1922.

Till, Wolfgang, ed. *Munchen: "Hauptstadt der Bewegung."* Munich: Münchner Stadtmuseum, 1993.

Toland, John. *Adolf Hitler.* Garden City, NY: Doubleday, 1976.

Toller, Ernst. *I Was a German: The Autobiography of Ernst Toller.* London: Doubleday, 1934.

Toynbee, A. J. *Turkey: A Past and a Future.* London: Hodder & Stoughton, 1917.

Treutzscher, Fritz von. *Armes Volkssturm!* Berlin, 1920.

Trevor-Roper, H. R. *The Last Days of Hitler.* London: Macmillan, 1947.
Trimingham, Spencer. *The Sufi Orders in Islam.* Oxford, UK: Clarendon Press, 1971.
Trotsky, Leon. *The Russian Revolution: The Overthrow of Tzarism and the Triumph of the Soviets.* Garden City, NY: Doubleday, 1959.
Viereck, Peter. *Metapolitics: The Roots of the Nazi Mind.* Rev. ed. New York: Capricorn, 1965.
Wagner, Richard. *Prose Works,* vol. 6. Translated by William Ashton Ellis. London: Kegan Paul, Trench, Trubner, 1897.
———. *Prose Works,* vol. 7. Translated by William Ashton Ellis. London: Kegan Paul, Trench, Trubner, 1898.
Waite, Robert. *Vanguard of Nazism: The Free Corps Movement in Post-War Germany, 1918–1923.* Cambridge, MA: Harvard University Press, 1952.
Walker, Christopher J. *Armenia: The Survival of a Nation.* London: Croom Helm, 1980.
Washington, Peter. *Madame Blavatsky's Baboon: Theosophy and the Emergence of the Western Guru.* London: Secker & Warburg, 1993.
Watt, Richard M. *The Kings Depart: The Tragedy of Germany: Versailles and the German Revolution.* New York: Simon & Schuster, 1968.
Webb, James. *The Flight from Reason.* London: Macdonald, 1971.
———. *The Occult Underground.* LaSalle, IL: Open Court, 1974.
———. *The Occult Establishment.* LaSalle, IL: Open Court. 1976.
Weber, Max. *Economy and Society: An Outline of Interpretive Sociology.* Edited by Guenther Roth and Claus Wittich. Translated by Ephraim Fischoff. Berkeley: University of California Press, 1978.
Weikart, Richard. *From Darwin to Hitler: Evolutionary Ethics, Eugenics, and Racism in Germany.* New York: Palgrave Macmillan, 2004.
Zittel, Bernhard. "Raetemodell Muenchen 1918–1919." *Stimmen der Zeit* 165 (1959).
Zmigrodski, Michael. *Historie du Svastika.* Paris: Ackermann, 1891.
———. *Genealogisches Taschenbuch des adligen Häuser* 12. Brno, 1887.

Published Public Papers

Great Britain. Parliamentary Papers, Miscellaneous no. 31. London, 1916.
Munich. Neue Schriftenreihades Stadtarchivs Munchen, vol. 29. Munich, 1968.
U.S. Government. Nazi Conspiracy and Aggression. Washington, 1946.

Archives

Bavarian Haupstaatsarchiv Munich
Munchen Stadtarchiv Munich
NSDAP Hauptarchiv

Index

Abdulhamid II, 51, 55
Abraham Pasha, 46, 233n14
Adler, Victor, 13, 220n22
Ahnenerbe, 184–85
Akçura, Yusuf, 54
alchemy, 13, 47–48, 49–50, 56, 203, 231n100
Aldebaran, 207–8
Ali Bey, Hüseyinzade, 54–55
Allgemeine Ordens-Nachrichten, 67
Anders, Richard, 184, 231n102, 264n82
Angebert, Jean-Michel, 206
Antébi, Elisabeth, 206
Anthroposophy, 13, 220n22
Antisemiten-Katechismus Fragen (Fritsch), 63, 238n84
anti-Semitism
- Chamberlain, 164
- Eckart, Feder and Rosenberg, 157–59, 256n52
- Fritsch, 62–65, 238n85
- German Workers' Party, 155
- Hess, 167
- Hitler, 150–51, 177–82
- List, 25
- Ludendorff, 88, 242n10
- Nazi Party, 174
- post-WWI, 97–98
- *Protocols of the Elders of Zion*, 160
- Reichshammerbund and Germanenorden, 65–68
- Sebottendorff, 48, 58–60
- Stauff, 67–68
- Thule Society, 122–23
- Vienna, 20, 31
- Wandervögel, 84–85

Arco, Anton von, 113–15, 118, 245n46
Arendt, Hannah, xi, xviii
Ariosophy
- about and roots of, xx, 2–5, 13–14, 215n10, 227n80
- evolution, 8
- German nationalism, 11–12
- Haeckel, 228n82
- Hitler and Nazi Party, 42, 178–82, 186
- Lanz, 37–40
- List, 17–18, 30–32, 49
- post-WWI comfort of, 95
- Rosenberg, 163–65
- Sebottendorff, 60–62, 237n75
- swastika, 188
- Vienna, 20

Armanenschaft, 28–31, 60–61, 227n80, 229n84
Armenian genocide, xx, 55
Aryan race. *See also* Ariosophy; Theosophy
- Fritsch, 63
- Hitler, 177, 180–82
- Lanz, 37–38, 40–41
- List, 28, 30–32, 36
- origins, 4–5, 11–12, 17, 163–64, 207, 215n10
- religion, 164–65
- Sebottendorff, 60–61
- superiority, xv, xx, 2–3, 10, 37, 180, 188
- swastika, 187–88
- Wiligut, 183–84

Association of German National Socialist Jurists, 80
Astrologische Rundschau, 193–94, 228n83
astrology, xxi, 50, 96, 170–71, 193–95

Atatürk, Kemal, 51, 53, 54, 56
Atlantis, 4, 28, 37, 163, 227n79
Audoin-Rouzeau, Stéphane, 87
Auer, Erhard, 79, 80, 104–5, 108–12, 115
Auf gut deutsch, 113, 152, 157–59, 192, 224n59, 255n43
Axelrod, Towia, 132, 146–47, 251n102

Bad Aibling coup attempt on Eisner, 108–10
Baden, Max von, 91
Bakunin, Mikhail, 15
Balzli, Johannes, 18
Barbie, Klaus, 211, 266n24
battle of Munich
  Hoffmann and Thule joint efforts, 125, 128–31
  Luitpold massacre, 138–43
  overview, 94–96
  Palm Sunday Putsch, 125–28
  second Soviet Republic, 131–35
  Thule Society raid, 135–38
  White march, 141–42, 144–47, 168
Bauer, Hermann, 190, 191
Bavaria, revolution in
  background and overview, 99–104
  Eisner's decline and assassination, 113–16
  Eisner's rise, 104–7
  Soviet Republic, 117–20
  Thule Society, 107–13, 116–17
Bavarian People's Party, 114, 255n45
Bavarian Soviet Republic
  battle of Munich (See battle of Munich)
  first, 117–20
  second, 131–35
Beer Hall Putsch, xvii, 32, 73, 115, 158, 197, 242n9
Bekh, Ritter von, 130, 146
Bektashi Sufis, 48, 56
Beobachter. See *Münchener Beobachter*; *Völkischer Beobachter*
Berchtesgaden, 172, 174, 207, 259n126
Berger, Professor, xii, 140
Berger, Rudolf, 32, 224n59
Bergier, Jacques, 203–5
Besant, Annie, 4, 215n10, 219n4
Bevor Hitler kam (Sebottendorff), 71, 149, 197–99, 252n1
Bielefeld, Otto, 193, 263n72
Bierbaumer, Kathe, 76–77, 78, 130, 191–92
Bismarck, Otto von, 10, 85, 86, 96
Black Stone Lodge, 207
Blackwood, Algernon, 7
Blavatsky, Helena Petrovna
  astrology, 194
  doctrine of, 3–4, 12, 163, 181, 214n6, 218n60
  Hartmann, 14, 16–18
  Isis Unveiled, 207
  Lanz, 37, 38
  Levi, 6
  List, 28, 31
  Morning of the Magicians, 204
  The Secret Doctrine, 28, 163, 182, 227n79
  Theosophical Society, 2
Bloodrayne, 210
Blue Star Lodge, 58, 236n59
Bolsheviks. *See also* Communism
  German Revolution, 86, 88–89, 91–93
  Hungary, 117
  Jews and, 122–23, 155, 160, 162
  revolution in Bavaria, 107, 115–16, 126, 133
  Russian Revolution, 91, 158
  Sebottendorff, 60
  Thule Society, 122–23
Bormann, Martin, 162, 167
Botschaft der Sterne, Die (Heindel), 194
Braun, Karl Alfred, 78, 192
Brecht, Bertolt, 102
Brennan, J. H., 206
Brockhusen, Eberhard von, 68, 196, 251n103
Brücke, the, 85
Bruckmann, Hugo and Elsa, 171, 186–87
Bruckner, Anton, 13
Buddhism, 3–4, 188
Bullock, Alan, 203, 213n2
Bulow, Werner von, 195, 225n67
Bulwer-Lytton, Edward, 7, 49, 205, 207, 216n20
Bund der Germanen, 27
Bund Oberland, 252
Bunge, Hans, 197
Burg Werfenstein, 40, 230n96
Bürgerwehr, Munich, 110–11
Burke, Edmund, 143
Buttman, Rudolf, 110–11

Cahun, David Leon, 52
Camus, Albert, 204
capitalism
  Feder, Drexler, and Nazi Party, 151, 152, 154, 158
  Jews, 63, 79, 151, 177
  List, 31

Carnuntum, List's visit to ruins of, 22, 219n9
Carnuntum (List), 25, 219n20
Celaleddin Pasha, Mustafa, 52
Chamberlain, Houston Stewart, xxi, 163–64, 186, 257n85
Chiemgau, Freikorps, 130–31, 146, 248n40, 251n98
Christian Social Union, 114
Citizens Council of the City of Munich, 123, 193
Citizens Union, 159–60
Clarke, John James, 3
Cohen, Moiz, 53–54
Cohn, Norman, 161
Combat League, Thule
 about, 108, 120, 244n15
 battle of Munich, 123–24, 127–30, 134, 144, 146, 159–60, 251n91, n98
 Eisner arrest attempt, 108–10
 infiltration of Schutzwehr and Red Guards, 112
 members of, 73, 78, 111
Coming Race, The (Bulwer-Lytton), 7, 207
Committee of Union and Progress (CUP), 50–53, 54
Communism
 German Revolution. See German Revolution
 Hitler, 175, 177, 253n7
 Hungary, 41
 Turks, 56
Cosmics, the, 187
Crisis of Germany Ideology, The (Mosse), xviii, 203, 219n17, 221n33, 231n100
Cronauer, Franz, 136, 249n63
Crowley, Aleister, 7, 16, 34, 205, 215n17, 218n53, 254n32, 258n113
Czepl, Theodor, 154, 231n102

Dahn, Hans, 73, 112, 190
Daim, Wilfried, 179
Danikin, Erich von, 207
Dannehl, Franz, 73, 112, 197
Darwin, Charles, 6
Darwinism, 4, 6, 7, 10, 53, 227n82
Daumenlang, Anton, xii, 80, 137, 139, 250
Dearborn Independent, 64
Decline of the West, The (Spengler), 102
Deicke, Walter, xii, 74, 137, 138, 191, 251n84
Deutsch-soziale Reformpartei, 64
Deutsche-Mythologische Landschaftsbilder, 25, 186
Deutsche Wehrbuch, Das, 67
Deutsche-Sozialistische Partei, xvi, 64, 157, 239n95, 255n46
"Deutschland Erwache" (Eckart), 156
Deutschlands Erneuerung, 161, 244n16
Deutschnationale Handelsgehilfen Verband, 35, 226n57
Dingfelder, Johannes, 175
Dorenberg, Frieda, 184
Drexler, Anton
 about, 153
 Beobachter, 192
 German Workers' Party, 78, 154–55, 171–72, 259n120
 My Political Awakening, 152
 Political Workers' Circle, 98, 128, 154
 Twenty Five Points, 174–75

Ebert, Friedrich, 93, 106–7, 121–22
Eckart, Dietrich
 about, 155–60, 168, 256n60
 anti-Semitism, 220n22, 256n52
 Beobachter, 192
 German Revolution, 113, 137, 245n43
 German Workers' Party, 152
 Hitler, 172–74, 259n121, n123, n126
 Morning of the Magicians, 204
 Nazi Party, 202
 Swastika Letters, 31–32
 Thule Society, xviii, xx
Eckart, Simon, 192
Eckstein, Friedrich, 13, 17, 58, 217n39
Eco, Umberto, 201, 210
Edda, 28, 60, 74
Edda Society, 35, 88, 184, 195, 221n29, 225n67
Eder, Franz Xaver, 78, 192
Egelhofer, Rudolf, 133–34, 138–41, 143, 146, 250n72–73
Eher, Franz, 76
Ehrhardt, Hermann, 131
Ehrhardt Brigade, 131, 248n43
Eisner, Kurt
 decline and assassination, xvii, 79, 113–16, 117
 rise to power, 79, 91–92, 101, 102–7
 Thule opposition, 108–12
Ellerbeck, Ellegaard, 224n59
Engelman, Ralph, 157
Enver Pasha, 52
Epp, Franz Ritter von, 78, 124, 147, 151, 192
Epp, Freikorps, 124, 126, 131, 142, 144, 146, 247n26
Erzberger, Matthias, 68
Ettl, Ralf, 206, 207

eugenics, 6, 228n82, 244n16
evolution, 5–6, 8, 29, 32, 164–65, 215n10, 222n48
Ewers, Hanns Heinz, 34, 225n66, 245n46

Fahrende Gesellen, 35–36, 112
Feder, Gottfried
  Beobachter, 78, 192
  Eckart, 157, 158
  Hitler, 150, 151, 171, 172
  Nazi Party, 79–80, 174, 253n11
  Schutz-und-Trutzbund, 240n113
  Thule Society, xviii, 31, 79, 113, 151, 154
Fest, Joachim, xiv, xvi–xvii, 1, 168, 196, 203
Fichte, Johann Gottlieb, 9
Fiehler, Karl, 191, 197, 264n87
Ford, Henry, 64, 160
Föster-Peters, Hélène, 24
Foucault's Pendulum (Eco), 201, 209–10
Foundations of the Nineteenth Century, The (Chamberlain), 163
Four Seasons Hotel
  Bavarian revolution, 107–8, 110–13, 116, 124, 128, 135–37, 147
  early Thule Society use, 75, 80
  German Workers' Party, 151
Frank, Hans, xvi, 80, 124, 166, 196–97
Franz Eher Verlag, 76, 78, 179, 192
Frazer, James, 22–23
freemasonry
  blame for WWI, 58, 79, 236n61
  List, 26
  occult underground, 6
  Reuss, 16
  Sebottendorff, 48–49, 56, 195, 198, 209, 234n20
  Young Turks, 51
Freese, G. W., 75
Freikorps
  battle of Munich, 122, 141–42, 144 (*See also* specific Freikorps)
  Chiemgau, 130–31, 146, 248n40, 251n98
  Epp, 124, 126, 131, 142, 144, 146, 247n26
  German Revolution, 93, 95–96, 101, 108, 116 (*See also* specific Freikorps)
  Oberland, See Oberland, Freikorp.
  Regensburg, 137, 142, 144–45
  Schaefer, 109
  Schutzwehr, 108, 112, 125, 127
  Thule Society, xv–xvi, 101, 108, 244n15
  Wurttemberg, 131, 144
Frère, Jean Claude, 206
Freud, Sigmund, 19
Fritsch, Theodor
  anti-Semitism, 62–65, 161
  as editor and publisher, 238n84–85
  Handbuch der Jugenfrage, 35
  Ostara, 228n83
  Protocols of the Elders of Zion, 161
  Schutz-und-Trutzbund, 240n113
  Sebottendorff, 60
  Wandervögel, 84

Galton, Francis, 6
Gaubatz, Georg, 69, 73, 76, 197
George, Stefan, 187
Gerlach, Dankwart, 84, 224n5
German Expressionism, 58, 85
German Labor Front, 170
German People's Party, 73, 112, 178
German Revolution
  about and events of, 91–96, 115–17
  background, 83–89
  Bavaria (*See* battle of Munich; Bavaria, revolution in)
  mobilization, 90–91
German Socialist Party, xvi, 78, 157–58, 174, 191, 255n45
German Workers' Party
  Hitler, xxi, 150–54, 159, 171–72, 201, 260n130
  Thule Society, xvi, xix, 78, 155, 188
  Twenty-Five Points, 175
Germanenorden
  Germanen-Orden-Walvater, 68–69, 71–74, 189, 240n115
  murders of, 68
  Reichshammerbund, 65–66
  roots of, xix, 34–35, 42, 62, 240n112
  Sebottendorff, 60, 62, 68, 71–72, 74–75, 195
  Stauff, 196
  swastika, 188
  Thule Society, 74–75, 135, 189
Germanic League, 27
Gernot, 207
Gerson, Werner, 206
Glauer, Adam Alfred Rudolf. See Sebottendorff, Rudolf von
Gobineau, Joseph Arthur de, 10, 53
Goebbels, Joseph, 166, 167, 170
Goethe, Johann Wolfgang von, 83

Golden Bough, The (Frazer), 22–23
Golden Dawn, 7, 8, 49, 181
Goodrick-Clarke, Nicholas, xvi, 202–3, 208, 214n12, 224n60, 227n82, 230n100, 265n4
Goring, Hugo, 17, 223n57
Gorsleben, Rudolf John, 35, 195, 221n29, 225n67, 263n65
Grand Lodge of British Columbia and Yukon, 209
Grandel, Gottfried, 192
Grange, the, 63
Grassinger, Hans Georg, 78, 157, 191, 197–99, 255n45
Greiner, Josef, 179–80
Grey Wolf, 53, 55, 235n39
Griehl, Arthur, 75, 137
Grimm, Wilhelm and Jacob, 4, 11, 26
Groener, Wilhelm, 93, 95
Guards Cavalry, xii, 96, 131, 139, 141, 144–45
Guido von List Society. See List Society
Gutberlet, Wilhelm, 78

Hagal, 184, 226n67, 240n111
Halgadome, 29, 35, 60–61
Hammer, Der, 64–66, 87, 156, 161, 228n83, 238n91, 257n73
Hammer Gemeinden, 65, 239n95
Hammer Verlag, 63, 161, 238n88, n91
Handbuch der Jugenfrage (Fritsch), 35, 63
Hanfstaengl, Ernst, 34, 162, 257n78, 262n50
Hanioğlu, M. Sükrü, 52
Hapsburg Empire
  crown jewels, 40, 205
  German nationalism, 10, 19–20, 23–24, 105
Harden, Maximilian, 68
Harrer, Karl
  Hitler, 171–72, 258n119, 259n120
  Thule Society and Political Workers' Circle, xviii, xix, 79, 98, 153–55
Hartmann, Franz
astrology, 194
  spiritualism, 243n30
  Theosophy and occultism, 14–18, 218n60, 219n4, 220n22
Hauschofer, Albrecht, 169
Haushofer, Karl, 168–70, 204–5, 207, 258n109
Heidegger, Martin, 149
Heiden, Konrad, 160–61, 174, 202, 259n121
Heimburg, Werner von, 123, 129
Heimerdinger, Erwin von, 68
Heindel, Max, 194
Hellwig, Karl August, 65, 67, 238n59, 238n95
Helsing, Jan van, 208
Herbert, James, 210
Hering, Johannes
  Nazi Party, 80, 185, 262n65, 263n67
  Thule Society and Sebottendorff, 73, 75–76, 80, 185, 190, 197, 236n63, 262n65
Hermetic Order of the Golden Dawn, 7, 8, 49, 181
Herren vom Schwarzen Stein, 207
Hess, Rudolf
  battle of Munich, 124, 129, 147
  Bürgerwehr, 111
    Great Britain, peace mission to, 169–70, 258n113
  Hitler and Nazi Party, 87, 167–71, 186, 195, 202
  Military Tribunal, xvi
  occultism, 204–5
  Thule Society, xvi, 34, 73, 202
Hesse, Hermann, 15, 17, 84, 97, 229n87
Heuss, Theodor, 78
H. G. Grassinger Verlag, 197
Hidden Masters, 3, 14, 16, 205
High Seas Fleet mutiny, 92, 94
Hillmayr, Heinrich, xvii, xix
Himmler, Heinrich
  diet and medical habits, 15
  ideology, 182–85
  List, 30
  occultism, 49, 226n67–68, 231n102
  Rosenberg, 166
  Sebottendorff, 198
  SS, 40, 182, 184
  Thule Society, xvi
Hindenberg, Paul von, 87
Hinduism, 3, 4, 28, 29, 50
Hitler, Adolf
  in army, 106, 150–51, 253n7
  as artist, 101–2
  Beer Hall Putsch, 32, 115, 158, 197
  Christianity, 164–65, 257n92
  diet and health, 15, 217n46
  Eckart, 156
  Feder, 151
  fiction and pseudo-history, 204–5, 209
  Fritsch, 63, 238n86
  German Workers' Party, xix, xxi, 150–53, 254n32, 260n130
  Hess, 167–68, 171
  ideologies, xiii–xiv, xxi, 80, 150–51,

177–82, 186, 213n2
library of, 185–86, 244n16, 261n39
List and Lanz, 36, 37, 42, 186, 260n13
Ludendorff and Kemnitz, 87–88, 242n9–10
Mein Kampf. See *Mein Kampf*
on National Socialism, 1
occultism, 7, 184, 204–5, 215n17
Palm Sunday Putsch, 128, 247n25–26
Pan-Germanism, 24
publishing ownership, 78, 192
rise to power, 32, 171–76, 258n119, 259n125
Rosenberg, 162–63, 165, 257n77
Sebottendorf, 149, 194–95
swastika, 22
Thule Society, 149–51, 171–72, 179, 248n26
Twenty-Five Points, 174–75
Vienna, xv, 13, 20, 24, 36, 179, 213n4
Hitler, Alois, 178
Hochberg, Friedrich Franz von, 41
Hoffmann, Johannes, 117–19, 121–23, 125–26, 131, 135, 140–41
Hofweber, Max, 129, 167
Hoheneichen Verlag, 156, 159, 255n43
Hoher Armanen Orden (HAO), 33, 218n60, 223n58, 225n62
Horniman, Annie, 7
Hotel Vier Jahreszeiten. *See* Four Seasons Hotel
Howe, Ellic, 232n1, 233n6, 236n55–56, 262n65, 264n80
Hummel, Richard, 50, 58, 234n26
Hussein Pasha, 46
Huysmans, J. K., 2

Iffland, Berta Anna, 59, 195, 236n62–63
Illuminati News, 209
Imperial Order of the Knights of Constantine, 195, 263n73
Independent Social Democrats, 90–92, 94, 101–5, 109, 114, 116–18
India, theosophical ties to, 3–5, 214n5, 215n10
International Jew, The (Ford), 64–65
Iskra, 102
Islam, 53, 61–62. See also Sufism

Jackson, Robert H., 167
J. F. Lehmanns Verlag, 72–73, 241n5
Joffe, Adolph, 91
Jones, Nigel H., 131
Josef, Franz, 19, 20
Jostenoode, Harald Graevell van, 40, 223n57, 230n40
juedische Weltpest, Die, 111
Jünger, Ernst, 93
Jugendstil, 101
Jung, Carl, 15, 183, 229n87
Jürgen-Ratthofer, Norbert, 206, 208

Kabbalism, 39, 47–48, 49, 61, 218n60
Kabbalah Unveiled, The (Mathers), 7
Kahr, Gustav Ritter von, 157
kala, 32, 223n56
Kandinsky, Wassily, 101
Kapp Putsch, 131
Kemnitz, Mathilde von, 87–88, 195, 226n67, 243n10
Kershaw, Ian, xvii, 165, 178, 180, 213n2, 227n81, 247n25
Kiel mutiny, 92, 94, 133
Kirchoff, Gunther, 68, 185, 239n111
Kirdorf, Emil, 187
Klages, Ludwig, 187
Knauff, Friedrich, 74, 108, 123, 137, 190
Knights Templar, 40–41, 210
Kraus, Edgar, 112, 124, 146–47, 198, 248n40
Krause, Ernst, 188
Kroenen, Karl Ruprecht, 210
Krohn, Friedrich, 188, 262n50
Kummer, Siegfried Adolf, 35
Kun, Bella, 117, 141
Kunze, Dora, 78, 192, 263n68
Kurz, Heinz, 110, 124, 130

LaForce, Wilhelm, 191, 197
Landauer, Gustav, 118, 122, 145
Landtag, 105, 110, 114–15, 117
Lanz, Adolf Joseph
about and ideologies, 36–40, 227n78–82, 229n84–85
Hammer, 64
Hitler, 42, 179–80, 182, 185
List, 36, 227n77
ONT, 40–42, 184–85, 230n96, n99, 231n102
Ostara, 179–80, 228n83, 229n87
Pan-Germanism, 24
Sebottendorff, 60
swastika, 230n95
Lauterer, Ernst, 31, 222n53–54
Lebensraum, 168, 169, 177
Lebensreform, 15, 33, 62, 64
Lehmann, Julius Friedrich
German Workers' Party, 152

Nazi Party, 172
Pan German League, 72–73
periodicals, 157, 161, 244n16
revolution in Bavaria, 108, 111–12, 146
Rosenberg, 161
Thule Society, xviii, 73, 240n5
Lenin, Vladimir, 15, 88–89, 102, 119, 132–33, 145
Lethaby, W. R., 26
Lèvi, Eliphas, 6–7, 216n20
Levien, Max, 122, 132, 135, 145, 250n73
Levine, Eugen, 120, 132–35, 140, 143, 147, 251n102
Ley, Willy, 206
Liebenfels, Jörg Lanz von. *See* Lanz, Adolf Joseph
Liebknecht, Karl, xii, 89, 90, 91, 93, 95–96, 139
Lindner, Alois, 115
Linnaeus, Carolus, 5
Lipp, Franz, 119, 125
List, Guido von
Ariosophy and Theosophy, 28–33, 49, 173, 219n5, 222n48
associates and influences of, 17–20, 33–36, 225n65, 226n76, 227n77
death, 147, 251n103
Fritsch, 63
List Society, See List Society
paganism and Pan-German movement, 22–27, 210n20, n22, 218n60, 223n58
Sebottendorff, 60–61
youthful years, 20–22, 23, 210n5
List, Karl August, 21, 23
List Society
about and members, 17, 21, 32–36, 224n59–60, 228n83
Hitler and Nazi Party, 36, 186, 205
Reichshammerbund, 65
Stauff, 67–68, 252n103
youth movements, 84
Lodge of the Blue Star, 58, 236n59
Lomer, Georg, 221n33, 233n6
Lotter, Conrad, 111–12
Lotusblüten, 17
Ludendorff, Erich, 87–88, 89, 226n67, 242n9–10
Ludwig III, King, 79, 91, 99, 101, 103, 132–33
Luedecke, Kurt, 163
Lüger, Karl, 33, 223n58
Luitpold massacre
aftermath and retaliation, 146, 190–91, 202, 250n74, 251n84
causes, 96, 133
event details, 137–44, 249n70, 250n74, 251n88
Hitler, 128
Luxemburg, Rosa, xii, 90, 96, 107, 120, 139, 141

Machen, Arthur, 7
Maclellan, Alec, 206
Magick in Theory and Practice (Crowley), 7
Magyarok, Ebredo, 41
Mahler, Gustav, 13
Malthäser Brauhaus, 105, 145
Mann, Golo, 9, 11
Mann, Heinrich, 102
Mann, Thomas, 102, 177, 244n12
Männer, Emil, 134
Marby, Friedrich Bernhard, 35, 226n68
Marx, Karl, 16, 99
Marxism
in Germany, 85, 90, 92, 94, 100, 116, 122
Hitler, 177
Jews, 12
masonry. See freemasonry
Mathers, Samuel Liddell MacGregor, 7, 8, 216n22
Mayr, Karl, 152, 168, 253n7, n13, 255n43
Mayreder, Rosa, 13
Mecklenburg, Johann Albrecht von, 68
Mein Kampf (Hitler)
anti-Semitism, 178, 180
dedication of, 113, 156
Eckart, 172
German Workers' Party, 151–53, 159
German-Britain alliance, 169
Hess, 167
minorities, xiv
as a political program, 213n2
Protocols of the Elders of Zion, 113, 156
publisher of, 76
Stempfle, 199
swastika, 188
Thule Society, 201
Metaphysische Rundschau, 17, 223n57
Meyer, Heinrich, 74
Meyrink, Gustav, 58
Miesbacher Anzeiger, 110
Mignola, Mike, 210
Mikusch, Adelheid von, 130
miscegenation, 30, 38, 40, 69, 72, 180, 182
Mitchell, Allan, xvii, 141
Möhl, Arnold Ritter von, 130, 189

Morning of the Magicians, The (Pauwels and Bergier), 203–6, 210, 265n6, 266n23
Mosse, George L., xviii, xx, 12, 203
Mühsam, Erich, 125
Mueller, Hans Georg, 78, 191
Mueller, Karl Alexander von, 253n7
Mueller, Ludwig, 161
Münchener Beobachter und Sportblatt
German Revolution, 109, 113, 115, 122
Hitler, 150
List, 147
Protocols of the Elders of Zion, 161
Sebottendorff, 76–79
Thule leadership changes, 191
Twenty-Five Points, 174–75
Münchener Post, 189
Münchener Zeitung, 153, 255n43
Münchener-Augsburger Abendzeitung, 154
Mukherji, Asit Krishna, 202
Munchhausen, Karl Friedrich von, 43
Munich
about, 101–3
battle of (See battle of Munich)
Eisner's rise, 104–7
Mysteria Mystica Maxima, 16
Mythus des 20. Jahrhunderts, Der (Rosenberg), 156, 162–65, 217n35, 257n77–78

National Liberal Party, 73, 112, 178
National Socialist German Workers' Party, xvi, 78, 150
National Socialist movement, xvii, 1, 149, 152–53, 221n33
nationalism
folklore and, 22
German in Austria, 24
German metaphysical, 8–12
Ireland and Scotland, 8
Thule Society, xix
Turkish, 51–55, 57–58
Nauhaus, Walter, xii, 73–75, 80, 137–39, 191, 251n84
Nauhaus Lodge, 75
Nazi Party
Aryan racial superiority, xx
Bavarian revolution, 99
Beobachter, 192
Eckart, 156, 172
Feder, 79–80
Fritsch, 63, 65
Hess, 167–68
Lehmann, 73, 244n16
Ludendorff, 87–88, 243n10
opposition to, 187
pseudo-histories of, 203–6, 212
publishing, 76
Röhm, 246
roots of, xiii–xiv, 92, 98, 149, 154
Rosenberg, 113, 165–67
Sebottendorff, 44, 198–99
swastika, 188
Thule Society, 190–91, 196–99, 201–3, 263n67
Twenty-Five Points, 174–75
Young Turks, 53–55
Nehru, Jawaharlal, 4
neo-Nazis, 40, 201, 206–7, 211–12, 229n87, 230n92, n95
neopaganism, xix, xx, 22, 26, 36, 63, 233n6
Neumayer, Josef, 223n58, 225n62
Neurath, Otto, 119
Niekisch, Ernst, 118, 119
Nietzsche, Friedrich, 10, 36, 53, 220n22
Night of the Long Knives, 103, 199, 247n26
Nilus, Segei, 160, 256n64
Nordic mythology, 24, 28–29, 31, 60, 72, 74, 80, 211
Nordland Verlag, 184
Noske, Gustav, 94, 95, 116, 124, 131
Nuremberg Tribunals, xvi, 80, 113, 158, 166, 167, 168, 196–97

Oberland, Freikorps
battle of Munich, 146–47
establishment, 120, 129–30, 189–90
Himmler, 183
Sebottendorff dismissal, 189
Occult Review, 16
Occult Roots of Nazism, The (Goodrick-Clarke), xvi, 203
occult underground
about, 6–8, 17–18, 35
List, 33–35
Ludendorff, 87
Nazi Party, 44
Rosicrucians, 49
Wachler, 221n33
occultism
Hitler and Nazi Party, 44, 181, 185–86, 204–5
revival of, 203–6
roots of, 2, 13–14, 214n2
Thule Society, 76
Order of the Golden Dawn, 7, 8, 49, 181

Ordo Novi Templi (ONT)
- about, 40–42, 230n96, n99, 231n102, 232n106
- Hitler and Nazi Party, 182–85

Ordo Templi Orientis (OTO), 16, 218n53
Origin of Species by Means of Natural Selection, or the Preservation of Favoured Races in the Struggle for Life (Darwin), 6
Orsic, Maria, 207
Ostara, 37, 40, 42, 67, 179–80, 228n83
Österreichischer Alpenverein (Austrian Alpine League), 23
Ott, Johann, 191
Oven, Burghard von, 131, 142

Pacelli, Cardinal, xiii
Pagan Review, 8
paganism, 22, 26, 63, 239n95. *See also* neopaganism
Palm Sunday Putsch, 108, 125–28, 131–32, 133
Palmer, Raymond, 211
Pan-German League, 72–73, 76, 112, 241n5
Pan-Germanism, 19–20, 24–25, 32–33, 54–55, 219n17
Pan-Turanism, 51–56
Pan-Turkism, 51–58
Paulukun, Georg, 119
Pauwels, Louis, 203–5
phrenology, 5–6
Picard, George, 206
Pioda, Alfred, 15
Poehner, Ernst, 158
Pohl, Herman, 65, 66–69, 75, 239n95
Political Workers' Circle, xix, 79, 98, 128, 154–55, 254n32, 258n119
Protocols of the Elders of Zion, The (Rosenberg), xviii, 160–61, 202, 238n92, 256n64

Quisling, Vidkun, 166

race
- Aryan (See Ariosophy; Aryan race)
- evolution and hierarchy, 5–8
- Lanz, 37, 40
- List, 21, 23, 24, 29–31
- racism (See racism)
- theosophy, 4–5, 12

racism. See also anti-Semitism
- Lanz, 40
- of ordinary Germans, xiv, 213n2
- science and, 10, 97–98
- Thule Society, xix–xx
- völkisch ideology, 12
- Young Turks, xx, 54–55

Rasmussen, Knud, 74
rationalism, 1–2, 55
Rauschning, Hermann, 181, 204, 215n17, 261n22
Ravenscroft, Trevor, 205, 208–9, 210
Red Banner, 120
Red Guards
- battle of Munich, 112, 116–17, 123, 128–30, 142, 145–46
- Luitpold massacre, xi–xiii, 138–41
- 2nd Soviet Republic, 132–34

Regensburg, Freikorps, 137, 142, 144–45
Reichshammerbund, 42, 62, 65–67, 73, 112, 189, 238n95, 239n104
Reichstein, Herbert, 226n67, 231n102
Reuss, Theodor, 16, 217n50, 218n53
Riemann, Hans, 76, 197
Riemann-Bucherer, Gertrude, 76
Rilke, Rainer Maria, 102
Ring of the Nibelung, The (Wagner), 11–12
Rite of Memphis, 48, 195, 209
Rittlinger, Herbert, 199–200, 264n100
Röhm, Ernst, xvi, 103, 142, 147, 199, 252
Rohmeder, Wilhelm, 66, 112
Roman Catholic Church
- Eckart, 159
- in Germany, 10, 100, 101
- List and Lanz, 25, 30, 36, 37, 41, 229n85
- Mythus, 165
- in Vienna, 19

Rosenberg, Alfred
Ariosophy, 163–65, 167
- *Beobachter*, 78, 192
- Eckart, 113, 156, 158, 172
- Hitler, 162–63, 257n77
- *Mythus des 20. Jahrhunderts*, 156, 162–65, 257n77–78
- Nazi Party, 165–67, 202, 217n35
- Nuremberg Tribunal, xvi, 197
- *Protocols of the Elders of Zion*, 160–61
- Thule Society, 111, 161–62, 257n73

Rosenkreutz, Christian, 49
Rosicrucianism, 26, 48–49, 56, 199
Rosshalde (Hesse), 97
Rote Hand, 112
runelore
- Lanz, 39
- List, 26, 29, 32, 33–34, 36
- Marby and Kummer, 35

Sebottendorff, 61, 69
Stauff, 67
Thule Society, xxi
Runen, 71, 76
Ruskin, John, 62
Ryder, A. J., 96

Sailor's Putsch, 111–12
Salomon, Ernst von, 202, 249n70
Schaefer, Freikorps, 109
Scheidemann, Philipp, 91, 93, 95
Schlegel, Friedrich, 3, 215n10
Schliemann, Heinrich, 17, 188
Schmidt-Falk, Elsa, 22, 186
Schneppenhorst, Ernst, 121–22, 125, 127, 129, 135
Schuler, Alfred, 187, 224n59
Schultz-Strathaus, Ernst, 170
Schutzstaffel. *See* SS
Schutz-und-Trutzbund, 68, 122, 240n113
Schutzwehr, Freikorps, 108, 112, 125, 127
Schwabing intelligentsia, 102–4, 111
Sebaldt von Werth, Max Ferdinand, 34, 225n66
Sebottendorff, Rudolf von
astrology, 193–95
attacks on and Thule resignation, 189–90, 262n61
background and mystery surrounding, 43–46, 232n1, n5, 233n6
Bavarian revolution, 107–13, 117, 120, 123–30, 144, 147, 245n41
death and last days of, 199–200, 201
early travels to Turkey, 46–50, 234n26, n28
Eisner assassination, 113, 115
fiction and pseudo-history, 207, 209–10
financing of tank, 62, 237n79
Germanen-Orden-Walvater, 68–69, 71–72, 189
Hitler and Nazi Party, xxi, 147, 149, 179, 198–99, 202
Political Workers' Circle, 154, 173
publishing, 76–79
race and anti-Semitism, xx, 4–5, 58–62
swastika, 188–89
third Turkish sojourn, 195
Thule Society beginnings and rings of, xviii, 73–76, 79
Thule Society raid, 135–36
Thule Society size and regrouping, xix, 189–90, 191, 197, 263n67
Turkish citizenship, adoption, and identities, 57, 69, 235n52–54, 236n55–56
Völkischer Beobachter, 191–92
in Volkswehr and Freiburg, 192–93
on WWI, 89, 90
Young Turks and, 51, 52, 53, 55–56, 57–58
Second Soviet Republic, Bavarian
about, 131–35
Luitpold massacre, 138–43
Thule Society raid, 135–38
Secret Doctrine, The (Blavatsky), 28, 227n79
Sedlmeier, Hermann, 109, 117
Seidel, Fritz, 139–40, 143, 250n72–73
Seidlitz, Friedrich Wilhelm von, xii, 76, 137, 140
Seiffertitz, Alfred, 108, 125–27
Sesselman, Max, 158, 191, 197
Shabelsky-Bork, Piotr, 161
shamanism, 46, 52, 56
Sharp, William, 8
Shiel, M. P., 7–8, 216n19
Smith, Jerry E., 206
Social Democratic Party of Austria, 13, 19
Social Democratic Party of Germany
battle of Munich, 121–22, 126
Bavarian Soviet Republic, 120
German Revolution, 95, 97, 116
Hitler, 247
press of, 56
pre-WWI, 65, 81, 85–86
revolution in Bavaria, 101, 104–5, 108–10, 112, 114, 118
World War I, 87, 90–93
Sonnenberg, Max Liebermann von, 64
Spartacist League
battle of Munich, 123, 126, 130, 137, 145, 146
German Revolution, 90, 92, 95, 107
Spear of Destiny (Ravenscroft), 205–6, 208–10
Spear of Longinus, 205, 206, 210
Special Operations 1 (SO1), 169
Speer, Albert, 178, 197
SS (Schutzstaffel)
Aryan racial superiority, xx, 8, 40, 49
List, 30
Night of the Long Knives, 199
ONT, 182–83
phrenology, 5–6, 215n12
pseudo history, 207, 212
Rosenberg, 166–67
Wiligut, 184–85

Statler, Gene A., 210–11
Stauff, Philipp
 Germanenorden, 60, 147, 196, 239n95
 Hitler, 179
 List and List Society, 67–68, 84, 147, 251n103
 Sebottendorff, 60
 Wandervögel, 84
Stauffenberg, Schenken von, 187
Stecher, Karl, 129, 251n91
Steiner, Rudolf, 13, 15, 58, 220n22
Steininger, Babette, 185
Stempfle, Bernhard, 199
Sternecker Beer Hall, 150, 152, 155
Stiegler, Hans, 108
Streicher, Julius, xvi, 158, 169
Strike Force Reichsleiter Rosenberg, 166
Strindberg, August, 49, 230n92, n100
Strzygowski, Josef, 34
Sturm und Drang movement, 9
Stürmer, Der, 158
Sufism, 46, 47–48, 49, 56, 209, 235n46
swastika
 Ariosophy, 55, 67, 164
 Ehrhardt Brigade, 55, 131
 Lanz, 40, 230n95
 List, 22, 28, 36
 origins, 17, 187–89, 262n48, n50
 Reichshammerbund, 67
 Schutz-und-Trutzbund, 68
 Sebottendorff, 61, 72
 Theosophical Society, 5
 Thule Society, xii, xvi, 75–76, 262n50
 Wandervögel, 84

Talisman des Rosenkreuzers, Der (Sebottendorff), 50, 55, 59, 233n6, n10, 234n19, 236n66, 263n71
Tarnhari, 31, 222n53–54
Tekin Alp, 53–54
Termudi, 47–48, 51, 58, 234n19
Teuchert, Franz Carl von, xii, 137
Thaler, Marie, 184
Theosophical Publishing House, 18, 170, 194, 219n4
Theosophical Society
 beginnings and members, 2, 8, 13
 Gobineau, 10
 race, 4–5
 suppression of, 170
 Viennese, 13–14, 17, 33, 224n60
Theosophy
 about, xx, 2–3, 12, 14
 astrology, 194
 Eckart, 255n44
 Hartmann, 16–18
 List, 28–33
 occult underground, 6–8
 race, 4–5, 6
 Sebottendorff, xviii, 60–62
 swastika, 188
Theozoology, 38–39, 227n80
Thule Combat League. *See* Combat League, Thule
Thule Expeditions, 74
Thule Society
 Ariosophy, 4–5, 98
 battle of Munich, 122–27, 129–30, 134–35, 144
 Eisner, 116
 German Revolution, xv–xvi, 92–93, 99–101, 107–13, 117, 120, 244n15
 Hess, 167–68
 Hitler, 149–51, 171–72, 179, 248n26
 international recognition, 202–3
 Internet, 208–9, 210–11
 lack of scholarship on role in shaping Nazism, xvi–xviii, xx–xxi
 Luitpold executions, xii–xiii, 189–90, 191
 members, 66, 240n5
 Nazi Party, xv–xvi, xix, xxi, 174–75, 190–91, 198–99, 201–3
 neo-Nazis, 211–12
 periodicals of, xvi, xviii, 76–79, 221n29
 Political Workers' Circle, 154–55
 post-Sebottendorff leadership, 190–91, 262n65
 Protocols of the Elders of Zion and Rosenberg, 161–62
 pseudo history and fiction, 202–6, 208–10, 212
 raid of, 135–38
 roots, ideologies, and rings, xix–xx, 3, 42, 68–69, 73–76, 79–81
 Sebottendorff, 60–62, 197
 Social Democrats, 86
 swastika, 188–89, 262n50
Thule-Bote, 197
Thule-Seminar, 212
Thurn und Taxis, Gustav Franz Maria von, xi–xii, 136, 138–40, 143, 250n74
Tiede, Ernst, 194, 228n83, 232n102
Timm, Johannes, 108–11
Toland, John, 203
Toller, Ernst, 119–20, 133–34, 136, 140, 147, 246n59
Toynbee, Arnold, 53

Travels and Surprising Adventures of Baron von Munchhausen, The, 43
Treaty of Brest-Litovsk, 89
Treutzschler, Fritz von, 159
Trotsky, Leon, 89, 102, 106
"Turan" (Ali Bey), 54–55
Turkish Hearth, 53
Turkismus und Panturkismus (Alp), 53–54

United Grand Lodge, 234
Unser Vaterland, 157
Ur-Arische Gotteserkenntnis, 194
Utsch, Friedrich, 137

Verein Deutsches Haus, 25, 220n23
Vereinigten Vaterlaendischen Bayerns, 191
Vereinigten Vaterlaendischen Verbaende, 190
Versailles Treaty, 107, 152, 174
Vienna Secession, 14, 32
Vienna Theosophical Society, 13–14, 17, 33, 224n60
Viereck, Peter, 202
Vinberg, Fyodor, 161
völkisch movement. See also specific organizations and people of
    comparison to Pan-Germanism and Pan-Turanism, 53–55
    pre-WWI, 11–12, 15, 18, 23, 25, 65–66, 71–73, 83
    WWI and post-WWI, 83, 84–85, 97, 101, 109, 191–92
Völkischer Beobachter, xvi, 76–78, 109, 163, 170, 191–92, 259n123
Vollrath, Hugo, 18, 194
Voltaire, 3, 43
Vorwarts, 96, 101
Voss, Klara, 50
Vril-Projekt, Das (Jürgen-Ratthofer and Ettl), 206, 207, 208
Vril Society, 206–9

Wachler, Ernst, 64, 221n33, 223n57, 233n6
Wagner, Richard, xxi, 10–13, 101, 121, 259n126
Waiz, Lothar, 207
Waldorf schools, 220
Walküre, Die (Wagner), 121
Walvater, 29, 61, 72, 77
Wandervögel, 21, 35, 84–85, 231n100, 242n3
Wandervögel Fuhrerzeitung, 84
Wannieck, Friedrich, 25, 186, 223n57, 225n62, 243n30
Webb, James, 13
Weber, Arthur, 17, 224n59
Wegener, Paul, 58
Westarp, Heila von, xii, xvii, 61, 136, 143, 249n70, 250n74
Wiegershaus, Friedrich, 35, 223n57
Wieser, Fritz, 158
Wikipedia, 210–11
Wilhelm III, Friedrich, 49
Wiligut, Karl Maria, 183–85, 212, 226n67–68, 239n111
Wilson, Woodrow, 91
Witteck, Anna, 27, 225n62
Wittelsbach dynasty, 61, 96, 100, 101, 107
Witzgall, Karl, 129
Wodan Lodge, 65
Wodanism
    Hitler, 186
    Jung and Wiligut, 183–84
    List, 21, 25–29, 31, 33, 220n23, 226n76, 237n76
    Rosenberg, 165, 260n18
    Sebottendorff, 61
Wohl, Louis de, 195
Wolf, Hugo, 13
Wolf, Karl, 25, 27, 246n13
Wölfl, Johann Walthari, 41, 228n83
Wolzogen, Ernst von, 34, 225n65
Workers' Circle, xix, 79, 98, 128, 154–55, 254n32, 258n119
World War I
    death, destruction, and victims of, 96–98
    German initial support then discontent, 86–90, 242n8
    German Revolution, 91–96
Wurttemberg, Freikorps, 131, 144

Yeats, William Butler, 2, 7, 8
Young Turks, xx, 51–55, 57–59, 237n76

Zanoni (Bulwer-Lytton), 49, 205
Zillman, Paul, 17, 223n57
Zionism, 19–20
Zmigrodski, Michael, 188, 262n48

About the Author

David Luhrssen has taught at the University of Wisconsin–Milwaukee, the Milwaukee Institute of Art and Design, and Milwaukee Area Technical College. Luhrssen is coauthor of several books, including *Changing Times: The Life of Barack Obama*, *Searching for Rock and Roll*, and *A Time of Paradox: America Since 1890*, and has been published in the *Journal of American History*, *Historically Speaking*, and *History Today*, among other journals. Luhrssen received his undergraduate and graduate degrees in history at University of Wisconsin–Milwaukee. He is the arts and entertainment editor at *Shepherd Express*, Milwaukee's weekly newspaper.

CPSIA information can be obtained
at www.ICGtesting.com
Printed in the USA
LVHW030151200321
681975LV00002B/2/J